Data Structures & Algorithms using JavaScript

(ES6 and beyond.)

Second Edition

By Hemant Jain

Data Structures & Algorithms using JavaScript

Hemant Jain

ACKNOWLEDGEMENT

The author is very grateful to GOD ALMIGHTY for his grace and blessing.

My deepest gratitude to my elder brother Dr. Sumant Jain for his help and support. This book would not have been possible without the support and encouragement he provided.

I would like to express profound gratitude to my friends Naveen Kaushik, Love Singhal, Anand Rajashekaran and Harvinder Bholowasia for their invaluable encouragement, supervision and useful suggestion throughout this book writing work. Their support and continuous guidance enable me to complete my work successfully.

Hemant Jain

TABLE OF CONTENTS

TABLE OF CONTENTS

Table of Contents

CHAPTER 0: HOW TO USE THIS BOOK

What this book is about

This book introduces you to the world of data structures and algorithms. Data structures defines the way in which data is arranged in memory for fast and efficient access while algorithms are a set of instruction to solve problems by manipulating these data structures.

Designing an efficient algorithm is a very important skill that all software companies, e.g. Microsoft, Google, Facebook etc. pursues. Most of the interviews for these companies are focused on knowledge of data-structures and algorithms. They look for how candidates use concepts of data structures and algorithms to solve complex problems efficiently. Apart from knowing, a programming language you also need to have good command of these key computer fundamentals to not only qualify the interview but also excel in you jobs as a software engineer.

This book assumes that you are a JavaScript language developer. You are not an expert in JavaScript language, but you are well familiar with concepts of classes, functions, arrays, pointers and recursion. At the start of this book, we will be looking into Complexity Analysis followed by the various data structures and their algorithms. We will be looking into a Linked-List, Stack, Queue, Trees, Heap, Hash-Table and Graphs. We will also be looking into Sorting, Searching techniques.

In last few chapters, we will be looking into various algorithmic techniques. Such as, Brute-Force algorithms, Greedy algorithms, Divide and Conquer algorithms, Dynamic Programming, Reduction and Backtracking.

Preparation Plans

Generally, you have few months time before appearing for a next interview, so it is important to have a solid preparation plan. The preparation plan depends upon the preparation duration and companies that you are planning to target. Below are the three-preparation plan for 1 Month, 3 Month and 5 Month durations.

1 Month Preparation Plans

This preparation plan is for someone who is well familiar with the concepts of data structures and algorithms and just want to revisit these concepts and appear for an interview in a month. Below is the list of topics that we need to study and approximate time to finish them to complete preparation in a month. These are the most important chapters that must be prepared before appearing for an interview.

Time	Chapters	Explanation
Week 1	Chapter 1: Algorithms Analysis Chapter 2: Approach to Solve Algorithm Design Problems Chapter 3: Abstract Data Type	You will get a basic understanding of how to find complexity of a solution. You will come to know how to handle new problems. You will read about a variety of datatypes and their uses.
Week 2	Chapter 4: Sorting Chapter 5: Searching Chapter 13: String Algorithms	Searching, Sorting and String algorithm consists of a major portion of the interviews.

| Week 3 | Chapter 6: Linked List
Chapter 7: Stack
Chapter 8: Queue | Linked list, Stack and Queue are some of the favourites in an interview. |
| Week 4 | Chapter 9: Tree | In this portion, you will read about Trees. Now you are well versed to go for interviews. Best of luck. |

3 Month Preparation Plan

This plan should be used when you have at least three months' time to prepare for an interview. This preparation plan includes nearly everything in this book except algorithm techniques like "dynamic programming", "divide & conquer" etc. Which are asked by specific companies like Google, Facebook, etc. Therefore, until you are planning to face interview with these companies you can withhold these chapters for some time and should focus on the rest of the chapters.

Time	Chapters	Explanation
Week 1	Chapter 1: Algorithms Analysis Chapter 2: Approach to Solve Algorithm Design Problems Chapter 3: Abstract Data Type	You will get a basic understanding of how to find complexity of a solution. You will know how to handle new problems. You will read about a variety of datatypes and their uses.
Week 2 Week 3	Chapter 4: Sorting Chapter 5: Searching Chapter 13: String Algorithms	Searching, sorting and string algorithm consists of a major portion of the interviews.
Week 4 Week 5	Chapter 6: Linked List Chapter 7: Stack Chapter 8: Queue	Linked list, Stack and Queue are some of the favourites in an interview.
Week 6 Week 7	Chapter 9: Tree Chapter 10: Priority Queue / Heap	In this portion, you will read about trees and heap data structures.
Week 8 Week 9	Chapter 11: Hash-Table Chapter 12: Graphs	Hash-Tables are used throughout this book in various places, but now it is time to understand how Hash-Tables are implemented. Graphs are used to propose a solution many real-life problems.
Week 10 Week 11 Week 12	Revision of the chapters listed above.	At this time, you need to revise all the chapters that we have gone through in this book. Whatever remains needs to be completed and the exercise that remain unsolved need to be solved at this time

5 Month Preparation Plan

This plan should be used when we have at least 5 months of time. In this plan, we are going to study the whole book. In addition to this, we need to practice more and more from www.topcoder.com and other resources. If you are targeting for google, Facebook, etc., Then it is highly recommended to join topcoder and make practice as much as possible.

Time	Chapters	Explanation
Week 1 Week 2	Chapter 1: Algorithms Analysis Chapter 2: Approach to Solve Algorithm Design Problems Chapter 3: Abstract Data Type	You will get a basic understanding of how to find complexity of a solution. You will know how to handle unseen problems. You will read about a variety of datatypes and their uses.
Week 3 Week 4 Week 5	Chapter 4: Sorting Chapter 5: Searching Chapter 13: String Algorithms	Searching, sorting and string algorithm consists of a major portion of the interviews.
Week 6 Week 7 Week 8	Chapter 6: Linked List Chapter 7: Stack Chapter 8: Queue	Linked list, Stack and Queue are some of the favourites in an interview.
Week 9 Week 10	Chapter 9: Tree Chapter 10: Heap	This portion you will read about trees and priority queue.
Week 11 Week 12	Chapter 11: Hash-Table Chapter 12: Graphs	Hash-Table is used throughout this book in various places, but now it is time to understand how Hash-Tables are implemented. Graphs are used to propose a solution in many real-life problems.
Week 13 Week 14 Week 15 Week 16	Chapter 14: Algorithm Design Techniques Chapter 15: Brute Force Chapter 16: Greedy Algorithm Chapter 17: Divide-And-Conquer, Decrease-And-Conquer Chapter 18: Dynamic Programming Chapter 19: Backtracking and Branch-And-Bound Chapter 20: Complexity Theory and Np Completeness	These chapters contain various algorithms types and their usage. Once the user is familiar with most of these algorithms. Then the next step is to start solving topcoder problems from topcoder.
Week 17 Week 18 Week 19 Week 20	Revision of the chapters listed above.	At this time, you need to revise all the chapters that we have gone through in this book. Whatever remains needs to be completed and the exercise that may remain needs to be solved at this time

Code downloads

You can download the code of solved Examples in the book from author's GitHub repositories at https://github.com/Hemant-Jain-Author/. At this location the author had solved Examples in various programming languages like Java, GoLang, C#, C++, C, Swift, Python, JavaScript ES5, JavaScript ES6, VB.net, PHP and Ruby.

Summary

These are few preparation plans that can be followed to complete this book while preparing for the interview. It is highly recommended that you should read the problem statement, try to solve the problems by yourself and then only you should investigate the solution to find the approach of this book. Practising more and more problems will increase your thinking power and you will be able to handle unseen problems in an interview. We recommend you to make practising all the problems given in this book, then solve more and more problems from online resources like www.topcoder.com, www.careercup.com etc.

CHAPTER 1: ALGORITHMS ANALYSIS

Introduction

We learn by experience. With experience, it become easy to solve new problems. By looking into various problem-solving algorithms or techniques, we begin to develop a pattern that will help us in solving similar problems.

An **algorithm** is a set of steps to accomplish a task. An algorithm is a computer program is a set of steps that are applied over a set of input to produce a set of output.

Knowledge of algorithm helps us to get desired result faster by applying the appropriate algorithm.

The most important properties of an algorithm are:
1. **Correctness**: The algorithm should be correct. It should be able to process all the given inputs and provide correct output.

2. **Efficiency**: The algorithm should be efficient in solving problems. Efficiency is measured in two parameters. First is Time-Complexity, how quick result is provided by an algorithm. Second is Space-Complexity, how much RAM or memory that an algorithm is going to consume to give desired result.

Time-Complexity is represented by function T(n) - time required versus the input size n.
Space-Complexity is represented by function S(n) - memory used versus the input size n.

Asymptotic analysis

Asymptotic analysis is used to compare the efficiency of algorithm independent of any data set or programming language.

We are generally interested in the order of growth of an algorithm and not interested in the exact time required for running an algorithm. This time is also called Asymptotic-running time.

Big-O Notation

Definition: "f(n) is big-O of g(n)" or f(n) = O(g(n)), if there are two +ve constants c and n0 such that
f(n) ≤ c g(n) for all n ≥ n0,

In other words, c g(n) is an upper bound for f(n) for all n ≥ n0
The function f(n) growth is slower than c g(n)

We can simply say that after a large value of input N the (c.g(n)) will always be greater than f(n).

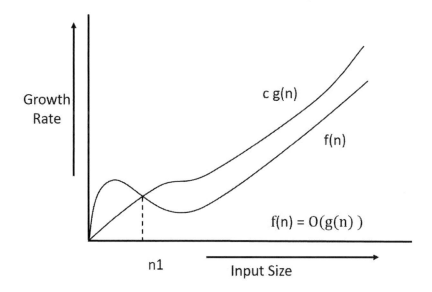

Example : $n^2 + n = O(n^2)$

Omega-Ω Notation

Definition: "f(n) is omega of g(n)." or $f(n) = \Omega(g(n))$ if there are two +ve constants c and n0 such that
c g(n) ≤ f(n) for all n ≥ n0

In other words, c g(n) is lower bound for f(n)
Function f(n) growth is faster than c g(n)

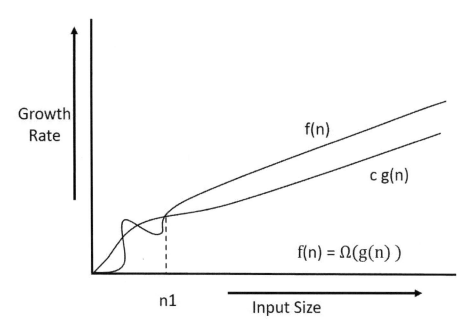

Find relationship of $f(n) = n^c$ and $g(n) = c^n$
$f(n) = \Omega(g(n))$

Theta-Θ Notation

Definition: "f(n) is theta of g(n)." or f(n) = Θ(g(n)) if there are three +ve constants c1, c2 and n0 such that c1 g(n) ≤ f(n) ≤ c2 g(n) for all n ≥ n0

Function g(n) is an asymptotically tight bound on f(n). Function f(n) grows at the same rate as g(n).

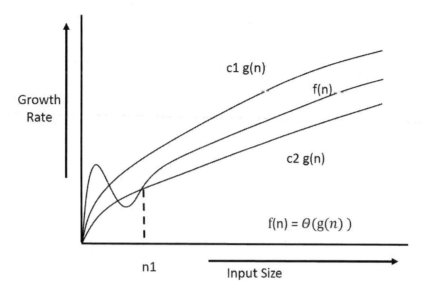

Example : $n^3 + n^2 + n = \Theta(n^3)$

Example : $n^2 + n = \Theta(n^2)$
Find relationship of $f(n) = 2n^2 + n$ and $g(n) = n^2$
f(n) = O(g(n))
f(n) = Θ(g(n))
f(n) = Ω(g(n))

Note:- Asymptotic Analysis is not perfect, but that is the best way available for analysing algorithms.

For Example, say there are two sorting algorithms first take f(n) = 10000*n*log(n) and second $f(n) = n^2$ time. The asymptotic analysis says that the first algorithm is better (as it ignores constants) but, for a small set of data when n is smaller than 10000, the first algorithm will perform better. To consider this drawback of asymptotic analysis case analysis of the algorithm is introduced.

Complexity analysis of algorithms

1. **Worst Case complexity:** It is the complexity of solving the problem for the worst input of size n. It provides the upper bound for the algorithm. This is the most common analysis used.

2. **Average Case complexity**: It is the complexity of solving the problem on an average. We calculate the time for all the possible inputs and then take an average of it.

3. **Best Case complexity**: It is the complexity of solving the problem for the best input of size n.

Time Complexity Order

A list of commonly occurring algorithm Time Complexity in increasing order:

Name	Notation
Constant	$O(1)$
Logarithmic	$O(\log n)$
Linear	$O(n)$
N-LogN	$O(n \log n)$
Quadratic	$O(n^2)$
Polynomial	$O(n^c)$ c is a constant & c>1
Exponential	$O(c^m)$ c is a constant & c>1
Factorial or N-power-N	$O(n!)$ or $O(n^n)$

Below diagram shows growth rate of some of the commonly occurring complexities.

N	Function Growth Rate (Approximate)						
	$O(1)$	$O(\log n)$	$O(n)$	$O(n \log n)$	$O(n^2)$	$O(n^3)$	$O(2^n)$
10	1	3	10	30	10^2	10^3	10^3
10^2	1	6	10^2	6×10^2	10^4	10^6	10^{30}
10^3	1	9	10^3	9×10^3	10^6	10^9	10^{300}
10^4	1	13	10^4	13×10^4	10^8	10^{12}	10^{3000}
10^5	1	16	10^5	16×10^5	10^{10}	10^{15}	10^{30000}
10^6	1	19	10^6	19×10^6	10^{12}	10^{18}	10^{300000}

From the above table the time required for completing some algorithms changes drastically with the growth rate. For same data set, some algorithms will give result in minutes if not seconds, while there are other algorithms that will not be able to complete in days.

Constant Time (1)

An algorithm is said to run in constant time if the output is produced in constant time regardless of the input size.

Examples:
1. Accessing n^{th} element of an Array
2. Push and pop of a stack.
3. Add and remove of a queue.
4. Accessing an element of Hash-Table.

Linear Time O(n)

An algorithm is said to run in linear time if the execution time of the algorithm is directly proportional to the input size.

Examples:
1. Array operations like search element, find min, find max etc.
2. Linked list operations like traversal, find min, find max etc.

Note: when we need to see/ traverse all the nodes of a data-structure for some task then complexity is no less than **O(n)**

Logarithmic Time O(logn)

An algorithm is said to run in logarithmic time if the execution time of the algorithm is proportional to the logarithm of the input size. Each step of an algorithm, a significant portion (eg. half portion) of the input is pruned / rejected out without traversing it.

Example : Binary search algorithm, we will read about this algorithm in this book.

N-LogN Time O(nlog(n))

An algorithm is said to run in nlogn time if execution time of an algorithm is proportional to the product of input size and logarithm of the input size. In these algorithms, each time the input is divided into half (or some proportion) and each portion is processed independently.

Example :
1. Merge-Sort
2. Quick-Sort (Average case)
3. Heap-Sort

Note: Quicksort is a special kind of algorithm to sort an Array of numbers. Its worst-case complexity is $O(n^2)$ and average case complexity is O(n log n).

Quadratic Time,$O(n^2)$

An algorithm is said to run in quadratic time if the execution time of an algorithm is proportional to the square of the input size. In these algorithms each element is compared with all the other elements.

Examples:
1. Bubble-Sort
2. Selection-Sort
3. Insertion-Sort

Exponential Time $O(2^n)$

In these algorithms, all possible subsets of elements of input date are generated.

Factorial Time O(n!)

In these algorithms, all possible permutation of elements of input date are generated.

Deriving the Runtime Function of an Algorithm

Constants

Each statement takes a constant time to run. Time Complexity is O(1)

Loops

The running time of a loop is a product of running time of the statement inside a loop and number of iterations in the loop. Time Complexity is O(n)

Nested Loop

The running time of a nested loop is a product of running time of the statements inside loop multiplied by a product of the size of all the loops. Time Complexity is **O(n^c)**. Where c is the number of loops. For two loops, it will be **O(n^2)**

Consecutive Statements

Just add the running times of all the consecutive statements

If-Else Statement

Consider the running time of the larger of if block or else block and ignore the other block.

Logarithmic statement

If each iteration the input size is decreased by a constant factor. Time Complexity = O(log n).

Time Complexity Examples

Example 1.1
```
function fun1(n) {
    let m = 0;
    for (let i = 0; i < n; i++) {
        m += 1;
    }
    return m;
};

console.log(`Number of instructions O(n):: ${fun1(100)}`);
```

Output:
```
Number of instructions O(n):: 100
```

Analysis:
Time Complexity: O(n), single for loop takes linear time.

Example 1.2
```
function fun2(n) {
    let m = 0;
    for (let i = 0; i < n; i++) {
        for (let j = 0; j < n; j++) {
            m += 1;
```

```
        }
    }
    return m;
};

console.log(`Number of instructions O(n^2):: ${fun2(100)}`);
```

Output:
```
Number of instructions O(n^2):: 10000
```

Analysis:
Time Complexity: $O(n^2)$, two nested for loop takes quadratic time.

Example 1.3
```
function fun3(n) {
    let m = 0;
    for (let i = 0; i < n; i++) {
        for (let j = 0; j < i; j++) {
            m += 1;
        }
    }
    return m;
};

console.log(`Number of instructions O(n^2):: ${fun3(100)}`);
```

Output:
```
Number of instructions O(n^2):: 4950
```

Analysis:
Time Complexity: $O(N+(N-1)+(N-2)+...)$ == $O(N(N+1)/2)$ == $O(n^2)$

Example 1.4
```
function fun4(n) {
    let i = 1;
    let m = 0;
    while (i < n) {
        m += 1;
        i = i * 2;
    };
    return m;
};
console.log(`Number of instructions O(log(n)):: ${fun4(100)}`);
```

Output:
```
Number of instructions O(log(n)):: 7
```

Analysis:
In each iteration, the value of i is doubled. Each iteration problem space is divided into half.
Time Complexity: $O(\log(n))$

Example 1.5

```
function fun5(n) {
    let i = n;
    let m = 0;
    while (i > 0) {
        m += 1;
        i = Math.floor(i / 2);
    };
    return m;
};

console.log(`Number of instructions O(log(n)):: ${fun5(100)}`);
```

Output:
```
Number of instructions O(log(n)):: 7
```

Analysis:
In each iteration, the value of "I" is halved. Same as above each time problem space is divided into half.
Time Complexity: O(log(n))

Example 1.6

```
function fun6(n) {
    let m = 0;
    for (let i = 0; i < n; i++) {
        for (let j = 0; j < n; j++) {
            for (let k = 0; k < n; k++) {
                m += 1;
            }
        }
    }
    return m;
};

console.log(`Number of instructions O(n^3):: ${fun6(100)}`);
```

Output:
```
Number of instructions O(n^3):: 1000000
```

Analysis:
Outer loop will run for n number of iterations. In each iteration of the outer loop, inner loop will run for n iterations of its own. Three nested loops running n number of times.
Time Complexity: (n^3)

Example 1.7

```
function fun7(n) {
    let i;
    let j;
    let k;
    let m = 0;
```

```
    for (i = 0; i < n; i++) {
        for (j = 0; j < n; j++) {
            m += 1;
        }
    }
    for (i = 0; i < n; i++) {
        for (k = 0; k < n; k++) {
            m += 1;
        }
    }
    return m;
};

console.log(`Number of instructions O(n^2):: ${fun7(100)}`);
```

Output:
```
Number of instructions O(n^2):: 20000
```

Analysis:
These two groups of loops are in consecutive so their complexity will add up to form the final complexity of the program. Time Complexity: $O(n^2) + O(n^2) = O(n^2)$

Example 1.8
```
function fun8(n) {
    let m = 0;
    for (let i = 0; i < n; i++) {
        for (let j = 0; j < Math.sqrt(n); j++) {
            m += 1;
        }
    }
    return m;
};

console.log(`Number of instructions O(n^(3/2)):: ${fun8(100)}`);
```

Output:
```
Number of instructions O(n^(3/2)):: 1000
```

Analysis:
Time Complexity: $(n * \sqrt{n}) = O(n^{3/2})$

Example 1.9
```
function fun9(n) {
    let m = 0;
    for (let i = n; i >= 1; i /= 2) {
        for (let j = 0; j < i; j++) {
            m += 1;
        }
    }
    return m;
```

```
};

console.log(`Number of instructions O(n):: ${fun9(100)}`);
```

Output:
```
Number of instructions O(n):: 201
```

Analysis:
For nested loops look for inner loop iterations. Time complexity will be calculated by looking into inner loop. First, it will run for n number of time then n/2 and so on. (n+n/2 +n/4+n/8+n/16 ......)
Time Complexity: O(n)

Example 1.10
```
function fun10(n) {
    let m = 0;
    for (let i = 0; i < n; i++) {
        for (let j = i; j > 0; j--) {
            m += 1;
        }
    }
    return m;
};

console.log(`Number of instructions O(n^2):: ${fun10(100)}`);
```

Output:
```
Number of instructions O(n^2):: 4950
```

Analysis:
O(N+(N-1)+(N-2)+...) = O(N(N+1)/2) // arithmetic progression.
Time Complexity: $O(n^2)$

Example 1.11
```
function fun11(n) {
    let m = 0;
    for (let i = 0; i < n; i++) {
        for (let j = i; j < n; j++) {
            for (let k = j + 1; k < n; k++) {
                m += 1;
            }
        }
    }
    return m;
};

console.log(`Number of instructions O(n^3):: ${fun11(100)}`);
```

Output:
```
Number of instructions O(n^3):: 166650
```

Analysis:
Time Complexity: $O(n^3)$, three loops one inside other.

Example 1.12
```javascript
function fun12(n) {
    let j = 0;
    let m = 0;
    for (let i = 0; i < n; i++) {
        for (; j < n; j++) {
            m += 1;
        }
    }
    return m;
};

console.log(`Number of instructions O(n):: ${fun12(100)}`);
```

Output:
```
Number of instructions O(n):: 100
```

Analysis:
Think carefully once again before finding a solution, j value is not reset at each iteration.
Time Complexity: $O(n)$

Example 1.13
```javascript
function fun13(n) {
    let m = 0;
    for (let i = 1; i <= n; i *= 2) {
        for (let j = 0; j <= i; j++) {
            m += 1;
        }
    }
    return m;
};

console.log(`Number of instructions O(n):: ${fun13(100)}`);
```

Output:
```
Number of instructions O(n):: 134
```

Analysis:
The inner loop will run for 1, 2, 4, 8,… n times in successive iteration of the outer loop.
Time Complexity: $T(n) = O(1 + 2 + 4 + \ldots + n/2 + n) = O(n)$

Master Theorem

The master theorem solves recurrence relations of the form: $T(n) = a\,T(n/b) + f(n)$, Where $a \geq 1$ and $b > 1$. "n" is the size of the problem. "a" is number of sub problem in the recursion/b" is the size of each sub-problem."f(n)" is the cost of the division of the problem into sub problem and merger of results of sub-problems to get the result.

25

It is possible to determine an asymptotic tight bound in these three cases:

- Case 1: when $f(n) = O(n^{\log_b a - \epsilon})$ and constant $\epsilon > 1$, then the final Time complexity is:

  $f(n) = O(n^{\log_b a})$

- Case 2: when $T(n) = \Theta(n^{\log_b a} \cdot \log^k n)$ and constant $k \geq 0$, then the final Time complexity is:

  $T(n) = \Theta(n^{\log_b a} \cdot \log^{k+1} n)$

- Case 3: when $f(n) = \Omega(n^{\log_b a + \epsilon})$ and constant $\epsilon > 1$, Then the final Time complexity is:

  $T(n) = \Theta(f(n))$

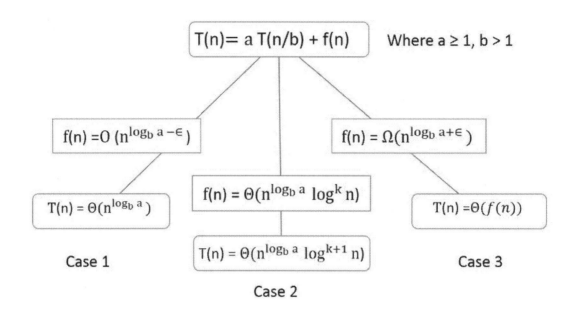

Example 1.14: Take an Example of Merge-Sort, $T(n) = 2\,T(n/2) + n$

Sol:- $\log_b a = \log_2 2 = 1$

$f(n) = n = \Theta(n^{\log_2 2} \log^0 n)$

Case 2 applies and $T(n) = \Theta(n^{\log_2 2} \log^{0+1} n)$

$T(n) = \Theta(n \log(n))$

Example 1.15: Binary Search $T(n) = T(n/2) + O(1)$

Sol:- $\log_b a = \log_2 1 = 0$

$f(n) = 1 = \Theta(n^{\log_2 1} \log^0 n)$

Case 2 applies and $T(n) = \Theta(n^{\log_2 1} \log^{0+1} n)$

$T(n) = \Theta(\log(n))$

Example 1.16: Binary tree traversal $T(n) = 2T(n/2) + O(1)$

Sol:- $\log_b a = \log_2 2 = 1$

$f(n) = 1 = O(n^{\log_2 2 - 1})$

Case 1 applies and $T(n) = \Theta(n^{\log_2 2})$

$T(n) = \Theta(n)$

Example 1.17: $T(n) = 2 T(n/2) + n^2$
Sol:- $\log_b a = \log_2 2 = 1$
$f(n) = n^2 = \Omega(n^{\log_2 2 + 1})$
Case 3 applies and $T(n) = \Theta(f(n))$
$T(n) = \Theta(n^2)$

Example 1.18: $T(n) = 4 T(n/2) + n^2$
Sol:- $\log_b a = \log_2 4 = 2$
$f(n) = n^2 = \Theta(n^{\log_2 4}\log^0 n)$
Case 2 applies and $T(n) = \Theta(n^{\log_2 4}\log^{0+1} n)$
$T(n) = \Theta(n^2 \log n)$

Example 1.19: $T(n) = T(n/2) + 2n$
Sol:- $\log_b a = \log_2 1 = 0$
Case 3
$T(n) = \Theta(n)$

Example 1.20: $T(n) = 16T(n/4) + n$
Sol:- $\log_b a = \log_4 16 = 2$
Case 1
$T(n) = \Theta(n^2)$

Example 1.21: $T(n) = 2T(n/2) + n \log n$
Sol:- $\log_b a = \log_2 2 = 1$
$f(n) = n\log(n) = \Theta(n^{\log_2 2}\log^1 n)$
$T(n) = \Theta(n^{\log_2 2}\log^{0+1} n) = \Theta(n \log(n))$

Example 1.22: $T(n) = 2 T(n/4) + n^{0.5}$
Sol:- $\log_b a = \log_4 2 = 0.5$
Case 2:
$T(n) = \Theta(n^{\log_4 2}\log^{0.5+1} n) = \Theta(n^{0.5} \log^{1.5} n)$

Example 1.23: $T(n) = 2 T(n/4) + n^{0.49}$
Sol:- $\log_b a = \log_4 2 = 0.5$
Case 1:
$T(n) = \Theta(n^{\log_4 2)} = \Theta(n^{0.5})$

Example 1.24: $T(n) = 3T(n/3) + \sqrt{n}$
Sol:- $\log_b a = \log_3 3 = 1$
Case 1
$T(n) = \Theta(n)$

Example 1.25: $T(n) = 3T(n/4) + n \log n$
Sol:-
$f(n) = n \log n = \Omega(n^{\log_4 3}\log^1 n)$
Case 3:
$T(n) = \Theta(n \log(n))$

Example 1.26: T (n) = 3T (n/3) + n/2

Sol:-$\log_b a$ = $\log_3 3$ = 1

Case 2:

T(n) = Θ(n log(n))

Array Based Questions

The following section will discuss the various algorithms that are applicable to Arrays and will follow by list of practice problems with similar approaches.

Sum Array

Problem: Write a method that will return the sum of all the elements of the integer Array, given Array as an input argument.

Example 1.27:

```
function SumArray(arr) {
    const size = arr.length;
    let total = 0;
    for (let index = 0; index < size; index++) {
        total = total + arr[index];
    }
    return total;
};

function test() {
    const numbers = [1, 2, 3, 4, 5, 6, 7, 8, 9, 10];
    const sum = SumArray(numbers);
    console.log(`Sum is :: ${sum}`);
}
```

Output:

```
Sum is :: 55
```

Analysis: All the elements of array are traversed and added. Finally, the result is returned. Time complexity is O(n).

Sequential Search

Problem: Write a method, which will search an Array for some given value.

Example 1.28:

```
function SequentialSearch(arr, value) {
    const size = arr.length;
    for (let i = 0; i < size; i++) {
        if (value === arr[i]) {
            return i;
        }
    }
}
```

```
        return -1;
};

function test() {
    const numbers = [1, 8, 5, 4, 3, 6, 9, 2, 7, 10];
    console.log(SequentialSearch(numbers, 7));
    console.log(SequentialSearch(numbers, 11));
}
```

Output:
```
8
-1
```

Analysis:
- Since we have no idea about the data stored in the array, or if the data is not sorted then we must search the array in sequential manner one by one.
- If we find the value, we are looking for we return its index.
- Else, we return index -1 in the end, as we did not find the value we are looking for.
- The elements of the array are traversed sequentially so the Time complexity is O(n)

Binary Search

If we want to search some value in sorted array, a binary search can be used. We examine the middle position at each step. Depending upon the data that we are searching is greater or smaller than the middle value. We will search either the left or the right portion of the array. At each step, we are eliminating half of the search space, thereby, making this algorithm efficient as compared with the linear search.

Example 1.29: Binary search in a sorted array.
```
function BinarySearch(arr, value) {
    const size = arr.length;
    let mid;
    let low = 0;
    let high = size - 1;
    while (low <= high) {
        mid = Math.floor((low + high) / 2);

        if (arr[mid] === value) {
            return mid;
        } else {
            if (arr[mid] < value) {
                low = mid + 1;
            } else {
                high = mid - 1;
            }
        }
    };
    return -1;
};
```

```
function test() {
    const numbers = [1, 2, 3, 4, 5, 6, 7, 8, 9, 10];
    console.log(BinarySearch(numbers, 7));
    console.log(BinarySearch(numbers, 11));
}
```

Output:
```
6
-1
```

Analysis:
- Since we have data sorted in increasing / decreasing order, we can search efficiently by applying binary search. At each step, we reduce our search space by half.
- At each step, we compare the middle value with the value we are searching. If mid value is equal to the value, we are searching for then we return the middle index.
- If the value is smaller than the middle value, we search the left half of the array.
- If the value is greater than the middle value then we search the right half of the array.
- If we find the value, we are looking for then its index is returned otherwise -1 is returned.
- Time complexity of this algorithm is O(logn).

Rotating an Array by K positions

Problem: Given an Array, you need to rotate its elements K number of times. For Example , an Array [10,20,30,40,50,60] rotate by 2 positions to [30,40,50,60,10,20]

Example 1.30:
```
function rotateArray(a, n, k) {
    reverseArray(a, 0, k - 1);
    reverseArray(a, k, n - 1);
    reverseArray(a, 0, n - 1);
};

function reverseArray(a, start, end) {
    if ((a != null && a instanceof Array) && (typeof start === 'number')
        && (typeof end === 'number')) {
        for (let i = start, j = end; i < j; i++ , j--) {
            const temp = a[i];
            a[i] = a[j];
            a[j] = temp;
        }
    } else
        throw new Error('invalid overload');
};

function test() {
    const numbers = [1, 2, 3, 4, 5, 6, 7, 8, 9, 10];
    rotateArray(numbers, numbers.length, 4)
    console.log(numbers);
}
```

Output:

```
[ 5, 6, 7, 8, 9, 10, 1, 2, 3, 4 ]
```

Analysis:
- Rotating array is done in two parts tricks. In the first part, we first reverse elements of array first half and then second half.

  1,2,3,4,5,6,7,8,9,10   =>   5,6,7,8,9,10,1,2,3,4

  1,2,3,4,5,6,7,8,9,10   =>   4,3,2,1,10,9,8,7,6,5   =>   5,6,7,8,9,10,1,2,3,4
- Then we reverse the whole array there by completing the whole rotation.
- First reversal of the two parts of array is done in O(n) time and the final array reversal is also done in O(n) so the total time complexity of this algorithms is O(n)

Find the largest sum contiguous subarray

Problem: Given an Array of positive and negative integers, find a contiguous subarray whose sum (sum of elements) is maximum.

Example 1.31:

```
function maxSubArraySum(a) {
    const size = a.length;
    let maxSoFar = 0;
    let maxEndingHere = 0;

    for (let i = 0; i < size; i++) {
        maxEndingHere = maxEndingHere + a[i];
        if (maxEndingHere < 0) {
            maxEndingHere = 0;
        }
        if (maxSoFar < maxEndingHere) {
            maxSoFar = maxEndingHere;
        }
    }
    return maxSoFar;
};

function test() {
    const arr = [1, -2, 3, 4, -4, 6, -4, 8, 2];
    console.log(maxSubArraySum(arr));
}
```

Output:

```
15
```

Analysis:
- Maximum subarray in an Array is found in a single scan. We keep track of global maximum sum so far and the maximum sum, which include the current element.
- When we find global maximum value so far is less than the maximum value containing current value, we update the global maximum value.
- Finally return the global maximum value.
- Time complexity is O(n).

Array wave form

Problem: Given an array, arrange its elements in wave form such that odd elements are lesser then its neighbouring even elements.

First Solution: Compare even index values with its neighbour odd index values and swap if odd index is not smaller than even index.

Example 1.32:
```
function WaveArray(arr) {
    const size = arr.length;
    for (let i = 1; i < size; i += 2) {
        if ((i - 1) >= 0 && arr[i] > arr[i - 1]) {
            swap(arr, i, i - 1);
        }
        if ((i + 1) < size && arr[i] > arr[i + 1]) {
            swap(arr, i, i + 1);
        }
    }
};

function test() {
    const arr = [8, 1, 2, 3, 4, 5, 6, 4, 2];
    WaveArray(arr);
    console.log(arr);
};
```

Output:
```
[ 2, 1, 3, 2, 4, 4, 6, 5, 8 ]
```

Time Complexity: O(n)

Second Solution: Sort the array then swap ith and i+1th index value so the array will form a wave.

Example 1.33:
```
function WaveArray(arr) {
    const size = arr.length;
    arr.sort(function cmp(a, b) { return (a - b); })
    for (let i = 0; i < size - 1; i += 2) {
        swap(arr, i, i + 1);
    }
};
```

Time Complexity: O(n)

Index Array

Problem: Given array of size N, containing elements from 0 to N-1. All values from 0 to N-1 are present in array and if they are not there than -1 is there to take its place. Arrange values of array so that value i is stored at arr[i].

Input: [8, -1, 6, 1, 9, 3, 2, 7, 4, -1]
Output: [-1, 1, 2, 3, 4, -1, 6, 7, 8, 9]

First Solution: For each index value pick the element and then put it into its proper place and the element which is in its proper position then pick it and repeat the process again.

Example 1.34:

```
function indexArray(arr, size) {
    for (let i = 0; i < size; i++) {
        let curr = i;
        let value = -1;

        while (arr[curr] !== -1 && arr[curr] !== curr) {
            const temp = arr[curr];
            arr[curr] = value;
            value = curr = temp;
        }

        if (value !== -1) {
            arr[curr] = value;
        }
    }
};

function test() {
    const arr = [8, -1, 6, 1, 9, 3, 2, 7, 4, -1];
    let size = arr.length;
    indexArray2(arr, size);
    console.log(arr);
};
```

Output:
[-1, 1, 2, 3, 4, -1, 6, 7, 8, 9]

Time Complexity: O(n), it looks like quadratic time complexity but the inner loop traverse elements only one. Once inner loop elements are processed then the elements at that position will be either that index value or it will contain -1.

Second Solution: For each index, we will pick the value at an index and put that value at its proper position.

Example 1.35:

```
function indexArray2(arr, size) {
    let temp;
```

```
        for (let i = 0; i < size; i++) {
            while (arr[i] !== -1 && arr[i] !== i) {
                temp = arr[i];
                arr[i] = arr[temp];
                arr[temp] = temp;
            }
        }
};
```

Time Complexity: O(n), it looks like quadratic time complexity but the inner loop swaps elements once no matter how many times the outer loop run. Once inner loop elements are processed then the elements at that position will be either that index value or it will contain -1.

Sort 1toN

Problem: Given an array of length N. It contains unique elements from 1 to N. Sort the elements of the array.

First Solution: For each index value pick the element and then put it into its proper place and the element which is in its proper position then pick it and repeat the process again.

Example 1.36:
```
function Sort1toN(arr, size) {
    let curr;
    let value;
    let next;
    for (let i = 0; i < size; i++) {
        curr = i;
        value = -1;

        while (curr >= 0 && curr < size && arr[curr] !== curr + 1) {
            next = arr[curr];
            arr[curr] = value;
            value = next;
            curr = next - 1;
        }
    }
};
function test() {
    const arr = [8, 5, 6, 1, 9, 3, 2, 7, 4, 10];
    let size = arr.length;
    Sort1toN(arr, size);
    console.log(arr);
};
```

Output:
```
[ 1, 2, 3, 4, 5, 6, 7, 8, 9, 10 ]
```

Time Complexity: O(n), it looks like quadratic time complexity but the inner loop traverse elements only one. Once inner loop elements are processed then the elements at that position will be either that index value or it will contain -1.

Second Solution: For each index, we will pick the value at that index and put that value at its proper position.

Example 1.37: Swapping the elements

```
function Sort1toN2(arr, size) {
    let temp;
    for (let i = 0; i < size; i++) {
        while (arr[i] !== i + 1 && arr[i] > 1) {
            temp = arr[i];
            arr[i] = arr[temp - 1];
            arr[temp - 1] = temp;
        }
    }
};
```

Time Complexity: O(n), it looks like quadratic time complexity but the inner loop swaps elements once no matter how many times the outer loop run. Once inner loop elements are processed then the elements at that position will be either that index value or it will contain -1.

Smallest Positive Missing Number

Problem: Given an unsorted array, find smallest positive number missing in the array.

First Solution: Brute force approach, for each number in range we find if the number is present in the array.

Example 1.38:

```
function SmallestPositiveMissingNumber(arr, size) {
    let found;
    for (let i = 1; i < size + 1; i++) {
        found = 0;
        for (let j = 0; j < size; j++) {
            if (arr[j] === i) {
                found = 1;
                break;
            }
        }
        if (found === 0) {
            return i;
        }
    }
    return -1;
};
function test() {
    const arr = [8, 5, 6, 1, 9, 11, 2, 7, 4, 10];
    const size = arr.length;
    console.info(`Smallest Positive Missing Number :$
{SmallestPositiveMissingNumber(arr, size)}`);
```

```
};
```

Output:
```
Smallest Positive Missing Number :3
```

Time Complexity: $O(n^2)$

Second Solution: Using hash table to keep track of elements.

Example 1.39:
```
function SmallestPositiveMissingNumber2(arr, size) {
    const hs = new Set();
    for (var i = 0; i < size; i++) {
        hs.add(arr[i]);
    }

    for (var i = 1; i < size + 1; i++) {
        if (hs.has(i) === false)
            return i;
    }
    return -1;
};
```

Time Complexity: $O(n)$, Space Complexity: $O(n)$ for hash table.

Third Solution: Using an auxiliary array to sore values. We know the range so we had created an auxiliary array then traverse the input array. Mark the values that are found in array.

Example 1.40:
```
function SmallestPositiveMissingNumber3(arr, size) {
    const aux = new Array(size).fill(-1);

    for (var i = 0; i < size; i++) {
        if (arr[i] > 0 && arr[i] <= size) {
            aux[arr[i] - 1] = arr[i];
        }
    }

    for (var i = 0; i < size; i++) {
        if (aux[i] !== i + 1) {
            return i + 1;
        }
    }
    return -1;
};
```

Time Complexity: $O(n)$, Space Complexity: $O(n)$ for auxiliary array.

Forth Solution: Rearranging the elements in the given array. By rearranging the elements, we can find the missing element with constant space complexity in linear time.

Example 1.41:
```
function SmallestPositiveMissingNumber4(arr, size) {
    let temp;
    for (var i = 0; i < size; i++) {
        while (arr[i] !== i + 1 && arr[i] > 0 && arr[i] <= size) {
            temp = arr[i];
            arr[i] = arr[temp - 1];
            arr[temp - 1] = temp;
        }
    }

    for (var i = 0; i < size; i++) {
        if (arr[i] !== i + 1) {
            return i + 1;
        }
    }
    return -1;
};
```

Time Complexity: O(n), Space Complexity: O(1).

Maximum Minimum Array

Problem: Given a sorted array, rearrange it in maximum-minimum form.
Input: [1, 2, 3, 4, 5, 6, 7]
Output: [7, 1, 6, 2, 5, 3, 4]

First Solution: Using auxiliary array, create a copy of the input array. Traverse from start and end of array, and put these values in input array in alternatively.

Example 1.42:
```
function MaxMinArr(arr, size) {
    const aux = arr.slice(0, size);
    let start = 0;
    let stop = size - 1;
    for (let i = 0; i < size; i++) {
        if (i % 2 === 0) {
            arr[i] = aux[stop];
            stop -= 1;
        }
        else {
            arr[i] = aux[start];
            start += 1;
        }
    }
};
```

```
/* Testing code */
function test() {
    const arr = [1, 2, 3, 4, 5, 6, 7];
    const size = arr.length;
    MaxMinArr(arr, size);
    console.log(arr);
};
```

Output:
```
[ 7, 1, 6, 2, 5, 3, 4 ]
```

Time Complexity: O(n), Space Complexity: O(n).

Second Solution: Without using any auxiliary array. Use reverse array operation on the array and change the array as follows:

1, 2, 3, 4, 5, 6, 7
7, 6, 5, 4, 3, 2, 1
7, 1, 2, 3, 4, 5, 6
7, 1, 6, 5, 4, 3, 2
7, 1, 6, 2, 3, 4, 5
7, 1, 6, 2, 5, 4, 3
7, 1, 6, 2, 5, 3, 4

Example 1.43:
```
function MaxMinArr2(arr, size) {
    for (let i = 0; i < (size - 1); i++) {
        ReverseArr(arr, i, size - 1);
    }
};

function ReverseArr(arr, start, stop) {
    while (start < stop) {
        swap(arr, start, stop);
        start += 1;
        stop -= 1;
    }
};
```

Time Complexity: $O(n^2)$, Space Complexity: O(1).

Max Circular Sum

Problem: Given an array you need to find maximum sum of arr[i]* (i+1) for all element such that you can rotate the array.

Example 1.44:
```
function maxCircularSum(arr, size) {
    let sumAll = 0;
    let currVal = 0;
```

```
    let maxVal;
    for (var i = 0; i < size; i++) {
        sumAll += arr[i];
        currVal += (i * arr[i]);
    }

    maxVal = currVal;
    for (var i = 1; i < size; i++) {
        currVal = (currVal + sumAll) - (size * arr[size - i]);
        if (currVal > maxVal) {
            maxVal = currVal;
        }
    }
    return maxVal;
};

function test() {
    const arr = [10, 9, 8, 7, 6, 5, 4, 3, 2, 1];
    console.info(`Max Circulr Sum: ${maxCircularSum(arr, arr.length)}`);
};
```

Output:

```
Max Circulr Sum: 290
```

Time Complexity: O(n), Space Complexity: O(1).

Array Index Max Diff

Problem: Given an array arr[], find maximum distance of index j and i, such that arr[j] > arr[i]

First Solution: Brute force, for each index call it i find index j such that arr[j] > arr[i]. We will need two loops one to select index i and another to traverse index i+1 to size of array.

Example 1.45:

```
function ArrayIndexMaxDiff(arr, size) {
    let maxDiff = -1;
    let j;
    for (let i = 0; i < size; i++) {
        j = size - 1;
        while (j > i) {
            if (arr[j] > arr[i]) {
                maxDiff = Math.max(maxDiff, j - i);
                break;
            }
            j -= 1;
        }
    }
    return maxDiff;
};
```

```
function test() {
    const arr = [33, 9, 10, 3, 2, 60, 30, 33, 1];
    console.info(`ArrayIndexMaxDiff : ${ArrayIndexMaxDiff(arr,
arr.length)}`);
};
```

Output:
```
ArrayIndexMaxDiff : 6
```

Time Complexity: $O(n^2)$, Space Complexity: $O(1)$.

Second Solution: Pre-processing and creating two auxiliary arrays. Always keep decreasing minimum values in decreasing order.

Example 1.46:
```
function ArrayIndexMaxDiff2(arr, size) {
    const leftMin = new Array(size);
    const rightMax = new Array(size);
    leftMin[0] = arr[0];
    let i;
    let j;
    let maxDiff;

    for (i = 1; i < size; i++) {
        if (leftMin[i - 1] < arr[i]) {
            leftMin[i] = leftMin[i - 1];
        }
        else {
            leftMin[i] = arr[i];
        }
    }

    rightMax[size - 1] = arr[size - 1];
    for (i = size - 2; i >= 0; i--) {
        if (rightMax[i + 1] > arr[i]) {
            rightMax[i] = rightMax[i + 1];
        }
        else {
            rightMax[i] = arr[i];
        }
    }
    i = 0;
    j = 0;
    maxDiff = -1;
    while (j < size && i < size) {
        if (leftMin[i] < rightMax[j]) {
            maxDiff = Math.max(maxDiff, j - i);
            j = j + 1;
        }
        else {
```

```
            i = i + 1;
        }
    }
    return maxDiff;
};
```

Time Complexity: O(n), Space Complexity: O(n).

Max Path Sum

Problem: Given two arrays in increasing order you need to find maximum sum by choosing few consecutive elements from one array then few elements form other array. The elements switching can happened at transition points only when elements value is same in both the array.

arr1 = [12, 13, **18**, 20, 22, **26**, 70]
arr2 = [11, 15, **18**, 19, 20, **26**, 30, 31]

Max Sum elements: 11, 15, 18, 19, 20, 22, 26, 70
Max Sum: 201

Example 1.47:
```
function maxPathSum(arr1, size1, arr2, size2) {
    let i = 0;
    let j = 0;
    let result = 0;
    let sum1 = 0;
    let sum2 = 0;
    while (i < size1 && j < size2) {
        if (arr1[i] < arr2[j]) {
            sum1 += arr1[i];
            i += 1;
        }
        else if (arr1[i] > arr2[j]) {
            sum2 += arr2[j];
            j += 1;
        }
        else {
            result += Math.max(sum1, sum2);
            result = result + arr1[i];
            sum1 = 0;
            sum2 = 0;
            i += 1;
            j += 1;
        }
    }
    while (i < size1) {
        sum1 += arr1[i];
        i += 1;
    }
```

```
    while (j < size2) {
        sum2 += arr2[j];
        j += 1;
    }
    result += Math.max(sum1, sum2);
    return result;
};

/* Testing code */
function test() {
    const arr1 = [12, 13, 18, 20, 22, 26, 70];
    const arr2 = [11, 15, 18, 19, 20, 26, 30, 31];
    console.info(`Max Path Sum :: ${maxPathSum(arr1, arr1.length, arr2,
arr2.length)}`);
};
```

Output:
```
Max Path Sum :: 201
```

Time Complexity: O(n), Space Complexity: O(n).

Recursive Function

A recursive function is a function that calls itself, directly or indirectly.

A recursive method consists of two parts: Termination Condition and Body (which includes recursive expansion).
1. **Termination Condition:** A recursive method always contains one or more terminating condition. A condition in which recursive method processes a simple case and does not call itself.
2. **Body** (including recursive expansion): The main logic of the recursive method is contained in the body of the method. It also contains the recursion expansion statement that, in turn, calls the method itself.

Three important properties of recursive algorithm are:
1) A recursive algorithm must have a termination condition.
2) A recursive algorithm must change its state, and move towards the termination condition.
3) A recursive algorithm must call itself.

Note: The speed of a recursive program is slower because of stack overheads. If the same task can be done using an iterative solution (using loops), then we should prefer an iterative solution in place of recursion to avoid stack overhead.

Note: Without termination condition, the recursive method may run forever and will finally consume all the stack memory.

Factorial

Problem: Given a value N find N! , N! = N* (N-1).... 2*1.

Example 1. 48: Factorial Calculation.

```
function factorial(i) {
    if (i <= 1) {
        return 1;
    }
    return i * factorial(i - 1);
};
console.info("factorial 5 is ::", factorial(5))
```

Output:

```
factorial 5 is :: 120
```

Analysis: Each time method fn is calling fn-1. Time Complexity is **O(N)**

Print Base 16 Integers

Problem: Given an integer in decimal form print its hexadecimal form.

Example 1.49: Generic print to some specific base method.

```
function printHaxIntUtil(number, base, arr) {
    const conversion = "0123456789ABCDEF";
    const digit = (number % base);
    number = Math.floor(number / base);
    if (number !== 0) {
        printHaxIntUtil(number, base, arr);
    }
    arr.push(conversion[digit]);
};

function test() {
    console.log(printHaxInt(100, 16));
}
```

Output:

```
64
```

Analysis:
- Base value is provided along with the number in the function parameter.
- Remainder of the number is calculated and stored in digit.
- If the number is greater than base then, number divided by base is passed as an argument to the printInt() method recursively.
- Number will be printed with higher order first then the lower order digits.

Time Complexity is **O(N)**

Tower of Hanoi

Problem: The **Tower of Hanoi**, we are given three rods and N number of disks, initially all the disks are added to first rod (the leftmost one) is in decreasing size order. The objective is to transfer the entire stack of disks from first tower to third tower (the rightmost one), moving only one disk at a time and never a larger one onto a smaller.

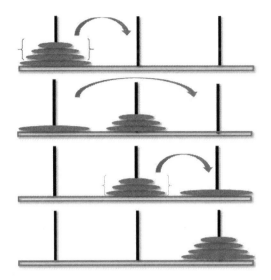

Example 1.50:

```javascript
function towerOfHanoi(num, src, dst, temp) {
    if (num < 1) {
        return;
    }
    towerOfHanoi(num - 1, src, temp, dst);
    console.log(`Move ${num} disk  from peg ${src} to peg ${dst}`);
    towerOfHanoi(num - 1, temp, dst, src);
};

function test() {
    const num = 3;
    console.info("The sequence of moves are :");
    towerOfHanoi(num, 'A', 'C', 'B');
    return 0;
};
```

Output:

```
The sequence of moves are :
Move 1 disk  from peg A to peg C
Move 2 disk  from peg A to peg B
Move 1 disk  from peg C to peg B
Move 3 disk  from peg A to peg C
Move 1 disk  from peg B to peg A
Move 2 disk  from peg B to peg C
Move 1 disk  from peg A to peg C
```

Analysis: If we want to move N disks from source to destination, then we first move N-1 disks from source to temp, and then move the lowest Nth disk from source to destination. Then it will move N-1 disks from temp to destination.

Greatest common divisor (GCD)

Problem: Find the greatest common divisor.

Example 1.51:
```
function GCD(m, n) {
    if (m < n) {
        return (GCD(n, m));
    }
    if (m % n === 0) {
        return (n);
    }
    return (GCD(n, m % n));
};

function test() {
    console.log(GCD(15, 7));
};
```

Output:
```
1
```

Analysis: Euclid's algorithm is used to find gcd. GCD(n, m) == GCD(m, n mod m).

Fibonacci number

Problem: Given N, find the Nth number in the Fibonacci series.

Example 1.52:
```
function fibonacci(n) {
    if (n <= 1) {
        return n;
    }
    return fibonacci(n - 1) + fibonacci(n - 2);
};

function test() {
    console.log(fibonacci(8));
}
```

Output:
```
21
```

Analysis: Fibonacci numbers are calculated by adding sum of the previous two numbers.

Note:- There is an inefficiency in the solution we will look better solution in coming chapters.

All permutations of an integer list

Problem: Generate all permutations of an integer array.

Example 1.53:
```
function permutation(arr, i, length) {
    if (length === i) {
        console.log(arr);
        return;
    }

    let j = i;
    for (j = i; j < length; j++) {
        swap(arr, i, j);
        permutation(arr, i + 1, length);
        swap(arr, i, j);
    }
};

function test() {
    const arr = [1, 2, 3]
    permutation(arr, 0, 3);
};
```

Output:
```
[ 1, 2, 3 ]
[ 1, 3, 2 ]
[ 2, 1, 3 ]
[ 2, 3, 1 ]
[ 3, 2, 1 ]
[ 3, 1, 2 ]
```

Analysis: In permutation method at each recursive call number at index, "i" is swapped with all the numbers that are right of it. Since the number is swapped with all the numbers in its right one by one it will produce all the permutation possible.

Binary search using recursion

Problem: Given an array of integers in increasing order, you need to find if some value is present in array using recursion.

Example 1.54: Search a value in an increasing order sorted list of integers.
```
function BinarySearchRecursive(arr, value) {
    return BinarySearchRecursiveUtil(arr, 0, arr.length - 1, value);
}

function BinarySearchRecursiveUtil(arr, low, high, value) {
    if (low > high)
        return -1;
```

```
    const mid = Math.floor((low + high) / 2);
    if (arr[mid] === value) {
        return mid;
    }

    if (arr[mid] < value) {
        return BinarySearchRecursiveUtil(arr, mid + 1, high, value);
    } else {
        return BinarySearchRecursiveUtil(arr, low, mid - 1, value);
    }
};

function test() {
    const numbers = [1, 2, 3, 4, 5, 6, 7, 8, 9, 10];
    console.log(BinarySearchRecursive(numbers, 7));
    console.log(BinarySearchRecursive(numbers, 11));
}
```

Output:

```
6
-1
```

Analysis: Similar iterative solution we have already seen. Now let us look into the recursive solution of the same problem. In this solution, we are diving the search space into half and discarding the rest. This solution is very efficient as at each step we are rejecting half the search space / array.

Exercise

1. True or false
    a. $5n + 10n^2 = O(n^2)$
    b. $n \log n + 4n = O(n)$
    c. $\log(n^2) + 4 \log(\log n) = O(\log n)$
    d. $12n^{1/2} + 3 = O(n^2)$
    e. $3^n + 11n^2 + n^{20} = O(2^n)$
2. What is the best-case runtime complexity of searching an Array?
3. What is the average-case runtime complexity of searching an Array?
4. Given array of positive numbers, you need to find the maximum sum under constraint that no two elements should be adjacent.

CHAPTER 2: APPROACH TO SOLVE ALGORITHM DESIGN PROBLEMS

Introduction

Theoretical knowledge of the algorithm is essential, yet it is not enough. When an interviewer asks to develop a program in an interview, then interviewee should follow our five-step approach to solve it. Master this approach and you will perform better than most of the candidates in interviews.

Five steps for solving algorithm design questions are:
1. Constraints
2. Ideas Generation
3. Complexities
4. Coding
5. Testing

Constraints

Solving a technical question is not just about knowing the algorithms and designing a good software system. The interviewer wants to know you approach towards any given problem. Many people make mistakes, as they do not ask clarifying questions about a given problem. They assume many things simultaneously and begin working with that. There is lot of data that is missing that you need to collect from your interviewer before beginning to solve a problem.

In this step, you will capture all the constraints about the problem. We should never try to solve a problem that is not completely defined. Interview questions are not like exam paper where all the details about a problem are well defined. In the interview, the interviewer expects you to ask questions and clarify the problem.

For Example , when the problem statement says that write an algorithm to sort numbers.
1. The first information you need to capture is what kind of data is provided. Let us assume interviewer respond with the answer Integer.
2. The second information that you need to know what is the size of data. Your algorithm differs if the input data size if 100 integers or 1billion integers.

Basic guideline for the Constraints for an array of numbers:
1. How many numbers of elements are therein an array?
2. What is the range of value in each element? What is the min and max value?
3. What is the kind of data in each element? Is it an integer or a floating point?
4. Does the array contain unique data or not?

Basic guideline for the Constraints for an array of string:
1. How many numbers of elements are there in the array?
2. What is the length of each string? What is the min and max length?
3. Does the array contain unique data or not?

Basic guideline for the Constraints for a Graph
1. How many nodes are there in the graph?
2. How many edges are there in the graph?
3. Is it a weighted graph? What is the range of weights?
4. Is the graph directed or undirected?
5. Is there is a loop in the graph?
6. Is there negative sum loop in the graph?
7. Does the graph have self-loops?

We will see this in graph chapter that depending upon the constraints the algorithm applied changes and so is the complexity of the solution.

Idea Generation

We will cover a lot of theoretical knowledge in this book. It is impossible to cover all the questions as new ones are created every day. Therefore, you should know how to handle new problems. Even if you know the solution of a problem asked by the interviewer then also you need to have a discussion with the interviewer and try to reach to the solution. You need to analyse the problem also because the interviewer may modify a question a little bit so the approach to solve it will vary.

How to solve an unseen problem? The solution to this problem is that you need to do a lot of practice and the more you will practise the more you will be able to solve any unseen question, which come before you. When you have solved enough problems, you will be able to see a pattern in the questions and will be able to solve unseen problems easily.

Following is the strategy that you need to follow to solve an unknown problem:
1. Try to simplify the task in hand.
2. Try a few Examples
3. Think of a suitable data-structure.
4. Think about similar problems that you have already solved.

Try to simplify the task in hand

Let us investigate the following problem: Husbands and their wives are standing in random in a line. They have been numbered, for husbands H1, H2, H3 and so on. Their corresponding wives have been numbered, W1, W2, W3 and so on. You need to arrange them so that H1 will stand first, followed by W1, then H2 followed by W2 and so on.

At the first look, it looks difficult, but it is a simple problem. Try to find a relation of the final position.
$P(Hi) = i*2 - 1, P(Wi) = i*2$

For rest of the algorithm we are leaving you to do something like Insertion-Sort and you are done.

Try a few Examples

In the above problem if you have tried it with some Example for 3 husband-wife pair then you will reach to the same formula that we have shown in the previous section. Sometime applying some more Examples will help you to solve the problem.

Think of a suitable data-structure

For some problems, it is straightforward to choose which data structure will be most suitable. For Example , if we have a problem finding min/max of some given value, then probably heap is the data structure we are looking for. We have seen several data structure throughout this book. We must figure out which data-structure will suite our need.

Let us investigate a problem: We are given a stream of data, at any time we can be asked to tell the median value of the data and maybe we can be asked to pop median data.

We can think about some sort of tree, may be balanced tree where the root is the median. Wait! It is not so easy to make sure the tree root to be a median.

A heap can give us minimum or maximum so we cannot get the desired result from it too. However, what if we use two heap a max heap and a min heap. The smaller values will go to max heap and the bigger values will go to min heap. In addition, we can keep the count of how many elements are there in the heap. The rest of the algorithm you can think yourself.

For every unseen problem think about the data structures, you know and may be one of them or some combination of them will solve your problem.

Think about similar problems you have already solved. Let us suppose you are given; two linked list head pointer and they meet at some point and need to find the point of intersection. However, in place of the end of both the linked list to be a null pointer, there is a loop.

You know how to find intersection point of two intersecting linked-list, you know how to find if a linked list has a loop (three-pointer solution). Therefore, you can apply both solutions to find the solution of the problem in hand.

Complexities

Solving a problem is not just finding a correct solution. The solution should be fast and should have reasonable memory requirement. You have already read about Big-O notation in the previous chapters. You should be able to do Big-O analysis. In case you think the solution, you have provided is not optimal and maybe there is a better solution, then try to figure it out.

Most interviewers expect that you should be able to find the time and Space Complexity of the algorithms. You should be able to compute the time and Space Complexity instantly. Whenever you are solving any problem, you should find the complexity associated with it from this you would be able to choose the best solutions. In some problems there is some trade-offs between Space and Time Complexity, so you should know these trade-offs. Sometime taking some bit more space saves a lot of time and make your algorithm much faster.

Coding

At this point, you have already captured all the constraints of the problem, proposed few solutions, evaluated the complexities of the various solutions and picked the solution to do final coding. Never ever, jump into coding before discussing constraints, Idea generation and complexity with the interviewer.

We are accustomed to coding in an IDE like visual studio. So many people struggle when asked to write code on a whiteboard or some blank sheet. Therefore, we should have a little practice to the coding on a sheet of paper. You should think before coding because there is no back button in sheet of paper. Always try to write modular code. Small functions need to be created so that the code is clean and managed. If there is a swap function so just use this function and tell the interviewer that you will write it later. Everybody knows that you can write swap code.

Testing

Once the code is written, you are not yet done. It is most important that you test your code with several small test cases. It shows that you understand the importance of testing. It also gives confidence to your interviewer that you are not going to write a buggy code. Once you are done with coding, you go through your code line-by-line with some small test cases. This is just to make sure that your code is working as it is supposed to work.

You should test few test cases.
Normal test cases: These are the positive test cases, which contain the most common scenario, and focus is on the working of the base logic of the code. For Example , if we are solving some problems for linked list, then this test may contain, what will happen when a linked list with 3 or 4 nodes is given as input. These test cases you should always contemplate before stating that the code is done.

Edge cases: These are the test cases, which are designed to test the boundaries of the code. For the same linked list algorithm, edge cases may be created to test how the code behaves when an empty list is passed or just one node is passed. Edge cases may help to make your code more robust. Just few checks need to be added to the code to take care of these conditions.

Load testing: In this kind of test, your code will be tested with a huge data. This will allow us to test if your code is slow or too much memory intensive.

Always follow these five steps never jump to coding before doing constraint analysis, idea generation, and Complexity Analysis: At least, never miss the testing phase.

Example

Let us suppose the interviewer ask you to give a best sorting algorithm.
Some interviewee will directly jump to Quick-Sort **O(nlogn)**. Oops, mistake! You need to ask many questions before beginning to solve this problem.

Questions 1: What is the kind of data? Are they integers?
Answer: Yes, they are integers.

Questions 2: How much data are we going to sort?
Answer: May be thousands.

Questions 3: What exactly is this data about?
Answer: They store a person's age

Questions 4: What kind of data-structure is used to hold this data?
Answer: Data are given in the form of some list

Questions 5: Can we modify the given data-structure? In addition, many, many more…?
Answer: No, you cannot modify the data structure provided

OK, from the first answer, we will deduce that the data is integer. The data is not very big it just contains a few thousand entries. The third answer is interesting; from this, we deduce that the range of data is 1-150. Data is provided in a list. From fifths answer we deduce that we must create our own data structure and we cannot modify the array provided. So finally, we conclude, we can just use bucket sort to sort the data. The range is just 1-150 so we need just 151-capacity integral list. Data is under thousands so we do not have to worry about data overflow and we get the solution in linear time **O(N)**.

Note: We will read sorting in the coming chapters.

Summary

At this point, you know the process of handling unseen problems very well. In the coming chapter we will be looking into a lot of various data structures and the problems they solve. It may be possible that the user is not able to understand some portion of this chapter as knowledge of rest of the book is needed, so they can read this chapter again after they have read the rest of the data structures portion. A huge number of problems are solved in this book. However, it is recommended that first try to solve them by yourself, and then look for the solution. Always think about the complexity of the problem. In the interview interaction is the key to get problem described completely and discuss your approach with the interviewer.

CHAPTER 3: ABSTRACT DATA TYPE& JAVASCRIPT COLLECTIONS

Abstract data type (ADT)

An abstract data type (ADT) is a logical description of the data and the operations that are allowed on it. ADT is defined as a user point of view of a data. ADT concerns about the possible values of the data and the interface exposed by it. ADT does not concern about the actual implementation of the data structure.

For Example , a user wants to store some integers and find their mean value. ADT for this data structure will support two function one for adding integers and other to get mean value. ADT for this data structure does not talk about how exactly it will be implemented.

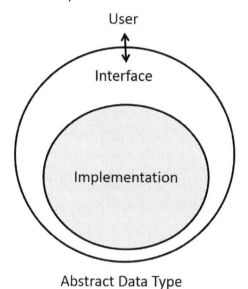

Abstract Data Type

Data-Structure

Data structures are concrete representations of data and is defined as a programmer point of view of data. Data-structure represents how data will be stored in memory. All data-structures have their own pros and cons. Depending upon the type of problem we choose a data-structure that is best suited for it.

For Example , we can store data in an array, a linked-list, stack, queue, tree, etc.

Note:- In this chapter, we will be studying various data structures and their API. So that the user can use them without knowing their internal implementation.

Javascript Collection Framework

Javascript programming language provides a Javascript Collection Framework, which is a set of high quality, high performance & reusable data-structures and algorithms.

The following are the advantages of using a Javascript collection framework:

1. Programmers do not have to implement basic data structures and algorithms repeatedly. Thereby it prevents the reinvention the wheel. Thus, the programmer can devote more effort in business logic.
2. The Javascript Collection Framework code is well-tested, high quality and high-performance code there by enhance the quality of the programs.
3. Development cost is reduced as basic data structures and algorithms are implemented in Collections framework.
4. Easy for the reviewing and understanding other developer's programs as other developer's also uses the Collection framework. In addition, the collection framework is well documented.

Stack

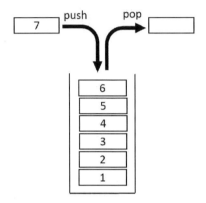

Stack is a special kind of data structure that follows Last-In-First-Out (LIFO) strategy. This means that the element that is added last will be the first to be removed.

The various applications of stack are:
1. Recursion: recursive calls are implemented using system stack.
2. Postfix evaluation of expression.
3. Backtracking implemented using stack.
4. Depth-first search of trees and graphs.
5. Converting a decimal number into a binary number etc.

Stack ADT Operations

Push(k): Adds value k to the top of the stack

Pop(): Remove element from the top of the stack and return its value.

Top(): Returns the value of the element at the top of the stack

Size(): Returns the number of elements in the stack

IsEmpty(): determines whether the stack is empty. It returns true if the stack is empty otherwise return false.

Note: All the above stack operations are implemented in **O(1)**Time Complexity.

Stack implementation using JavaScript List

Stack is implemented using List collection. List behave as stack if we add data using append() and remove using pop() function.

Example 3.1:
```
function test() {
    const stack = ([]);
    stack.push(1);
    stack.push(2);
    stack.push(3);
    console.info(`Stack : ${stack}`);
    console.info(`Stack size : ${stack.length}`);
    console.info(`Stack pop : ${stack.pop()}`);
    console.info(`Stack top : ${stack[stack.length - 1]}`);
    console.info(`Stack isEmpty : ${stack.length == 0}`);
};
```

Output:
```
Stack : 1,2,3
Stack size : 3
Stack pop : 3
Stack top : 2
Stack isEmpty : false
```

Queue

A queue is a First-In-First-Out (FIFO) kind of data structure. The element that is added to the queue first will be the first to be removed and so on.

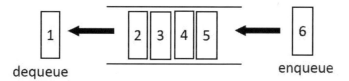

dequeue   enqueue

Queue has the following application uses:
1. Access to shared resources (e.g., printer)
2. Multiprogramming
3. Message queue
4. BFS, breadth first traversal of graph or tree are implemented using queue.

Queue ADT Operations:

Add(K): Adds a new element k to the back of the queue.
Remove(): Removes an element from the front of the queue and return its value.
Front(): Returns the value of the element at the front of the queue.
Size(): Returns the number of elements inside the queue.
IsEmpty(): Returns 1 if the queue is empty otherwise returns 0

Note: All the above queue operations are implemented in **O(1)** Time Complexity.

Queue implementation in Javascript Collection

Deque is the class implementation of doubly ended queue. If we use append(), popleft() it will behave as a queue.

Example 3.2:

```
class Queue {
    constructor() {
        this.stk1 = [];
        this.stk2 = [];
    }

    add(value) {
        this.stk1.push(value);
    }

    remove() {
        let value;
        if (this.stk2.length > 0) {
            return this.stk2.pop();
        }
        while (this.stk1.length > 0) {
            value = this.stk1.pop();
            this.stk2.push(value);
        };
        return this.stk2.pop();
    }

    front() {
        let value;
        if (this.stk2.length < 1) {
            while (this.stk1.length > 0) {
                value = this.stk1.pop();
                this.stk2.push(value);
            };
        }
        return this.stk2[this.stk2.length - 1];
    }

    isEmpty() {
        return (this.stk1.length + this.stk2.length) === 0
    }

    size() {
        return (this.stk1.length + this.stk2.length)
    }
}
```

```
function test() {
    const que = new Queue();
    que.add(1);
    que.add(2);
    que.add(3);
    console.info(que);
    console.info(`Queue size : ${que.size()}`);
    console.info(`Queue fornt : ${que.front()}`);
    console.info(`Queue remove : ${que.remove()}`);
    console.info(`Queue size : ${que.size()}`);
    console.info(`Queue isEmpty : ${que.isEmpty()}`);
};
```

Output
```
Queue { stk1: [ 1, 2, 3 ], stk2: [] }
Queue size : 3
Queue fornt : 1
Queue remove : 1
Queue size : 2
Queue isEmpty : false
```

Tree

Tree is a hierarchical data structure. The top element of a tree is called the root of the tree. Except the root element, every element in a tree has a parent element, and zero or more child elements. The tree is the most useful data structure when you have hierarchical information to store.

There are many types of trees, for Example , binary-tree, Red-black tree, AVL tree, etc.

Binary Tree

A binary tree is a type of tree in which each node has at most two children (0, 1 or 2) which are referred as left child and right child.

Binary Search Trees (BST)

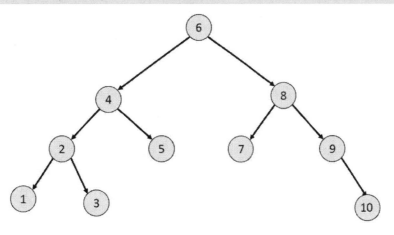

A binary search tree (BST) is a binary tree on which nodes are ordered in the following way:
1. The key in the left subtree is less than or equal to the key in its parent node.
2. The key in the right subtree is greater than the key in its parent node.

Binary Search Tree ADT Operations

Insert(k): Inserts an element k into the tree.
Delete(k): Deletes an element k from the tree.
Search(k): Searches a value k into the tree if it is present or not.
FindMax(): Finds the maximum value stored in the tree.
FindMin(): Finds the minimum value stored in the tree.

The Average time complexity of all the above operations on a binary search tree is O(logn), the case when the tree is balanced. The worst-case time complexity is O(**n**) when the tree is not balanced.

There are two types of skewed tree.
1. Right Skewed binary tree: A binary tree in which each node is having either a right child or no child.
2. Left Skewed binary tree: A binary tree in which each node is having either a left child or no child.

Binary Tree implementation

For implementation of Binary trees , please refer Tree chapter.

Priority Queue / Heap

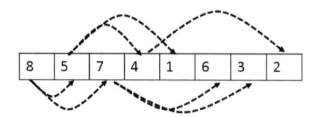

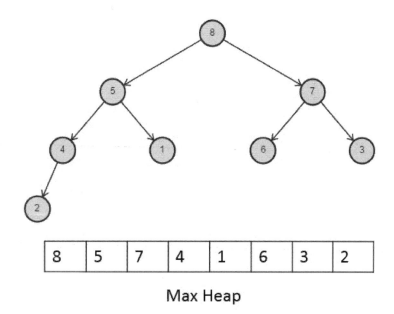

| 8 | 5 | 7 | 4 | 1 | 6 | 3 | 2 |

Max Heap

Priority queue is implemented using a binary heap data structure. In a heap, the records are stored in an array. Each node in the heap follows the same rule that the parent value is greater (or smaller) than its children.

There are two types of the heap data structure:
1. Max heap: Value of each node should be greater than or equal to the values of each of its children.
2. Min heap: Value of each node should be smaller than or equal to the values of each of its children.

A heap is a useful data structure when you want to get max/min value one by one from data. Heap-Sort uses heap to sort data in increasing or decreasing order.

Heap ADT Operations

Insert() - Adds a new element to the heap. The Time Complexity of this operation is O(log(n))
Remove() - Extracts max for max heap case (or min for min heap case). The Time Complexity of this operation is O(log(n))
Heapify() – Converts a list of numbers in a list into a heap. This operation has a Time Complexity **O(n)**

Priority Queue implementation

For implementation of priority queue, please refer Priority queue chapter.

Hash-Table

Hash Function

Object --------------------------------> Index

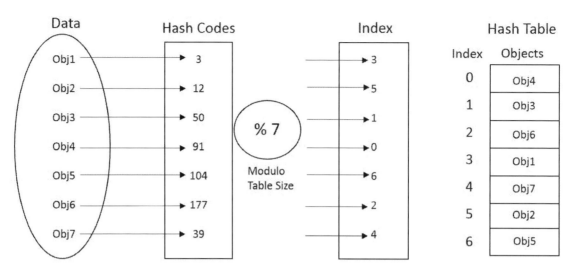

A Hash-Table is a data structure that maps keys to values. Each position of the Hash-Table is called a slot. The Hash-Table uses a hash function to calculate an index of data in an array. We use the Hash-Table when the number of key-value pair stored are small relatively to the number of possible keys.

The process of storing data using a hash function is as follows:
1. Create an array of size M to store data, this array is called Hash-Table.
2. Find a hash code of a key by passing it through a hash function.
3. Take module of hash code by the size of Hash-Table to get the index where data will be stored.
4. Finally store this data in the designated index.

The process of searching data in Hash-Table using a hash function is as follows:
1. Find a hash code of the key which we are searching, by passing it through a hash function.
2. Take module of hash code by the size of Hash-Table to get the index of the table where data is stored.
3. Finally, retrieve the value from the designated index.

Hash-Table Abstract Data Type (ADT)

ADT of Hash-Table contains the following functions:
Insert(x): Add x to the data set.
Delete(x): Delete x from the data set.
Search(x): Searches x in data set.

The Hash-Table is a useful data structure for implementing dictionary. The average time to search for an element in a Hash-Table is **O(1)**.

Dictionary implementation in JavaScript Collection

A Dictionary is a data structure that maps keys to values. A Dictionary uses a hash table so the key value pairs are not stored in sorted order. Dictionary does not allow duplicate keys but values can be duplicate.

Example 3.3: Map implementation in JavaScript.

```javascript
const hm = {};
hm["Apple"] = 150;
hm["Mango"] = 70;
hm["Banana"] = 40;

const keys = Object.keys(hm);
const count = keys.length;
console.info(`Fruits count :: ${count}`);

for (let index = 0; index < count; index++) {
    key = keys[index]
    console.info(`${key} price :${hm[key]}`);
}
console.info(`Apple price available ::${hm.hasOwnProperty("Apple")}`);
console.info(`Grapes price available :: ${hm.hasOwnProperty("Grapes")}`);

delete hm["Apple"]
console.info(`Apple price available ::${hm.hasOwnProperty("Apple")}`);
```

Output

```
Fruits count :: 3
Apple price :150
Mango price :70
Banana price :40
Apple price available ::true
Grapes price available :: false
Apple price available ::false
```

Set implementation of Javascript Collections

Set is a class, which is used to store only unique elements. Set is implemented using a hash table. Since Set is implemented using a hash table its elements are not stored in sequential order.

Sets
- Sets are like dictionaries in JavaScript, except that they consist of only keys with no associated values.
- Essentially, they are a collection of data with no duplicates.
- They are very useful when it comes to remove duplicate data from data collections.

Example 3.4: Set implementation in JavaScript collections.

```javascript
const hs = new Set();
hs.add("India")
hs.add("USA")
hs.add("Brazil")

console.info(hs);
```

```
for (const value of hs.values()) {
    console.info(value);
}

console.info(`Hash Table contains USA : ${hs.has("USA")}`);
console.info(`Hash Table contains UK : ${hs.has("UK")}`);

hs.delete("USA")

console.info(hs);
console.info(`Hash Table contains USA : ${hs.has("USA")}`);
```

Output
```
Set { 'India', 'USA', 'Brazil' }
India
USA
Brazil
Hash Table contains USA : true
Hash Table contains UK : false
Set { 'India', 'Brazil' }
Hash Table contains USA : false
```

Counter implementation

Counters are used to count the number of occurrence of values in a List.

Example 3.5
```
class CountMap {
    constructor() {
        this.hm = new Map();
    }

    insert(key) {
        if (this.hm.has(key)) {
            const cnt = this.hm.get(key);
            this.hm.set(key, cnt + 1);
        } else {
            this.hm.set(key, 1);
        }
    }

    remove(key) {
        if (this.hm.has(key)) {
            if (this.hm.get(key) === 1)
                this.hm.delete(key);
            else {
                const cnt = this.hm.get(key);
```

```
                this.hm.set(key, cnt - 1);
            }
        }
    }

    get(key) {
        if (this.hm.has(key))
            return this.hm.get(key);
        return 0;
    }

    find(key) {
        return this.hm.has(key);
    }
}

/* Testing Code */
const cm = new CountMap();
cm.insert(2);
cm.insert(2);
cm.remove(2);
console.log(`count of 2 is : ${cm.get(2)}`);
cm.remove(2);
console.log(`count of 2 is : ${cm.get(2)}`);
console.log(`count of 3 is : ${cm.get(3)}`);
```

Output
```
tcount of 2 is : 1
count of 2 is : 0
count of 3 is : 0
```

Dictionary / Symbol Table

A symbol table is a mapping between a string (key) and a value, which can be of any datatype. A value can be an integer such as occurrence count, dictionary meaning of a word and so on.

Binary Search Tree (BST) for Strings

Binary Search Tree (BST) is the simplest way to implement symbol table. Simple string compare function can be used to compare two strings. If all the keys are random, and the tree is balanced. Then on an average key lookup can be done in logarithmic time.

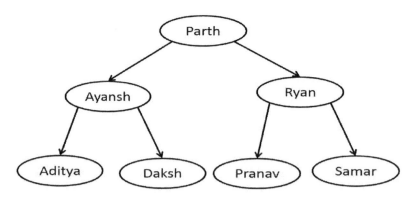

Binary Search Tree as Dictionary

Hash-Table

The Hash-Table is another data structure, which can be used for symbol table implementation. Below is the Hash-Table diagram, we can see that the name of a person is taken as key, and their meaning is the value of the search. The first key is converted into a hash code by passing it to appropriate hash function. Inside hash function, the size of Hash-Table is also passed, which is used to find the actual index where values will be stored. Finally, the value that is meaning of name is stored in the Hash-Table.

Hash-Table has an excellent lookup of constant time.

Graphs

A graph is a data structure that represents a network. It contains a collection of nodes called vertices, and their connections called edges. An edge is a path between two nodes. These edges can be either directed or undirected. If a path is directed then you can move only in one direction, while in an undirected path you can move in both the directions. There can be a cost associated with the edges.

Graph Algorithms

Depth-First Search (DFS)

In the DFS algorithm, we start from starting point and go into depth of graph until we reach a dead end and then move up to parent node (Backtrack). In DFS, we use stack to get the next vertex to start a search. Alternatively, we can use recursion (which uses system stack) to do the same.

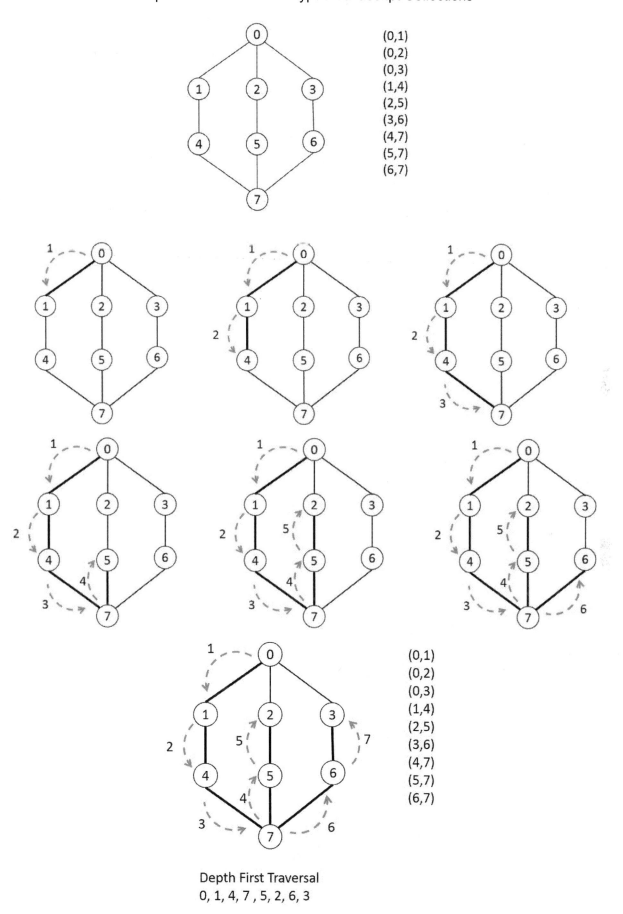

(0,1)
(0,2)
(0,3)
(1,4)
(2,5)
(3,6)
(4,7)
(5,7)
(6,7)

(0,1)
(0,2)
(0,3)
(1,4)
(2,5)
(3,6)
(4,7)
(5,7)
(6,7)

Depth First Traversal
0, 1, 4, 7 , 5, 2, 6, 3

Breadth-First Search (BFS)

In BFS algorithm, a graph is traversed in layer-by-layer fashion. The graph is traversed closer to the starting point. The queue is used to implement BFS.

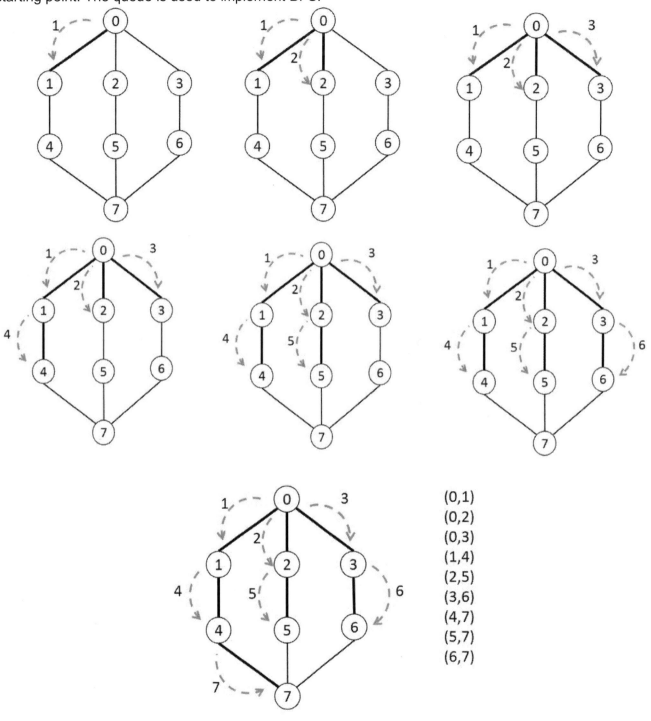

(0,1)
(0,2)
(0,3)
(1,4)
(2,5)
(3,6)
(4,7)
(5,7)
(6,7)

Breadth First Traversal
0, 1, 2, 3, 4, 5, 6, 7

Sorting Algorithms

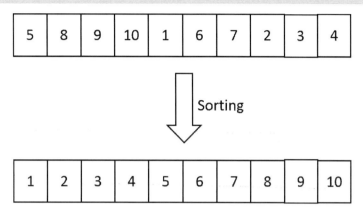

Sorting is the process of placing elements from a collection into ascending or descending order. Sorting arranges data elements in order so that searching become easier.

There are good sorting functions available which does sorting in **O(nlogn)** time, so in this book when we need sorting we will use sort() function and will assume that the sorting is done in **O(nlogn)** time.

Counting Sort

Counting sort is the simplest and most efficient type of sorting. Counting sort has a strict requirement of a predefined range of data.

Sort how many people are there in which age group. We know that the age of people can vary between 1 and 130. We can directly store counts in an array of size 130.

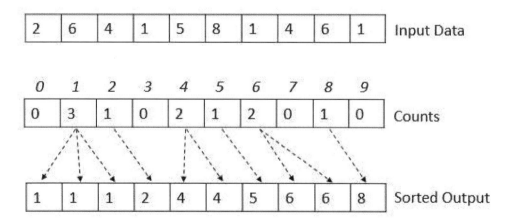

If we know the range of input, then sorting can be done using counting in O(n+k). Where n is the number of elements and k is the possible range, in above Example it is 130.

End note

This chapter has provided a brief introduction of the various data structures, algorithms and their complexities. In the next chapters, we will study all these data structure in details. If you know interface of a data structure, you can use it to solve other problems without knowing its internal implementation.

CHAPTER 4: SORTING

Introduction

Sorting is the process of arranging elements in ascending or descending order. For Example , when we play cards, we sort cards according to their value so that we can find the required card easily.

When we go to some library, the books are arranged according to streams (Algorithm, Operating systems, Networking etc.). Sorting arranges data elements in order so that searching become easier. When books are arranged in proper indexing order, then it is easy to find a book we are looking for.

This chapter discusses algorithms for sorting an array of items. Understanding sorting algorithms are the first step towards understanding algorithm analysis. Many sorting algorithms are developed and analysed.

Sorting algorithms like Bubble-Sort, Insertion-Sort and Selection-Sort are easy to implement and are suitable for the small input set. However, for large dataset they are slow. Sorting algorithms like Merge-Sort, Quick-Sort and Heap-Sort are some of the algorithms that are suitable for sorting large dataset. However, they are overkill if we want to sort a small dataset.

Some other algorithms are there to sort a huge data set that cannot be stored in memory completely, for which external sorting technique is developed.

Before we start a discussion of the various algorithms one by one. First, we should look at comparison function that is used to compare two values.

Less function will return true if value1 is less than value2 otherwise it will return false.
```
less = (value1, value2) => value1 < value2;
```

More function will return true if value1 is greater than value2 otherwise it will return false.
```
more = (value1, value2) => value1 > value2;
```

The value in various sorting algorithms is compared using one of the above functions and it will be swapped depending upon the return value of these functions. If more() comparison function is used, then sorted output will be increasing in order and if less() is used then resulting output will be in descending order.

Type of Sorting

Internal Sorting: All the elements can be read into memory at the same time and sorting is performed in memory.
1. Selection-Sort
2. Insertion-Sort
3. Bubble-Sort
4. Quick-Sort
5. Merge-Sort

External Sorting: In this type of sorting, the dataset is so big that it is impossible to load the whole dataset into memory so sorting is done in chunks.
  1. Merge-Sort

Bubble-Sort

Bubble-Sort is the slowest algorithm for sorting. It is easy to implement and used when data is small.

In Bubble-Sort, we compare each pair of adjacent values. We want to sort values in increasing order so if the second value is less than the first value then we swap these two values. Otherwise, we will go to the next pair. Thus, largest values bubble to the end of the array.

After the first pass, the largest value will be in the rightmost position. We will have N number of passes to get the array completely sorted.

First Pass

5	1	2	4	3	7	6	Swap
1	5	2	4	3	7	6	Swap
1	2	5	4	3	7	6	Swap
1	2	4	5	3	7	6	Swap
1	2	4	3	5	7	6	No Swap
1	2	4	3	5	7	6	Swap
1	2	4	3	5	6	7	

Example 4.1:
```
function bubbleSort(arr, compare) {
    const size = arr.length;
    let temp;
    for (let i = 0; i < (size - 1); i++) {
        for (let j = 0; j < size - i - 1; j++) {
            if (compare(arr[j], arr[j + 1])) {
                temp = arr[j];
                arr[j] = arr[j + 1];
                arr[j + 1] = temp;
            }
        }
    }
};

/* Testing Code */
more = (value1, value2) => value1 > value2;
const array = [9, 1, 8, 2, 7, 3, 6, 4, 5];
bubbleSort(array, more);
console.log(array);
```

Output:
[1, 2, 3, 4, 5, 6, 7, 8, 9]

Analysis:
- The outer loop represents the number of swaps that are done for comparison of data.
- The inner loop is used to do the comparison of data. At the end of each inner loop iteration, the largest value is moved to the end of the array. In the first iteration the largest value, in the second iteration the second largest and so on.
- more() function is used for comparison which means when the value of the first argument is greater than the value of the second argument then perform a swap. By this we are sorting in increasing order if we have, the less() function in place of more() then array will be sorted in decreasing order.

Complexity Analysis:
Each time the inner loop execute for (n-1), (n-2), (n-3)...(n-1) + (n-2) + (n-3) + ... + 3 + 2 + 1 = n(n-1)/2

Worst case performance	$O(n^2)$
Average case performance	$O(n^2)$
Space Complexity	O(1) as we need only one temp variable
Stable Sorting	Yes

Modified (improved) Bubble-Sort

When there is, no more swap in one pass of the outer loop the array is already sorted. At this point, we should stop sorting. This sorting improvement in Bubble-Sort is extremely useful when we know that, except few elements rest of the array is already sorted.

Example 4.2:
```
function bubbleSort2(arr, compare) {
    const size = arr.length;
    let temp;
    let swapped = 1;
    for (let i = 0; i < (size - 1) && swapped === 1; i++) {
        swapped = 0;
        for (let j = 0; j < size - i - 1; j++) {
            if (compare(arr[j], arr[j + 1])) {
                temp = arr[j];
                arr[j] = arr[j + 1];
                arr[j + 1] = temp;
                swapped = 1;
            }
        }
    }
};
```

By applying this improvement, best-case performance of this algorithm is improved when an array is nearly sorted. In this case, we just need one single pass and the best-case complexity is **O(n)**

Complexity Analysis:

Worst case performance	$O(n^2)$
Average case performance	$O(n^2)$
Space Complexity	$O(1)$
Adaptive: When array is nearly sorted	$O(n)$
Stable Sorting	Yes

Insertion-Sort

Insertion-Sort Time Complexity is **$O(n^2)$** which is same as Bubble-Sort but perform a bit better than it. It is the way we arrange our playing cards. We keep a sorted subarray. Each value is inserted into its proper position in the sorted sub-array in the left of it.

5	6	2	4	7	3	1	Insert 5
5	6	2	4	7	3	1	Insert 6
2	5	6	4	7	3	1	Insert 2
2	4	5	6	7	3	1	Insert 4
2	4	5	6	7	3	1	Insert 7
2	3	4	5	6	7	1	Insert 3
1	2	3	4	5	6	7	Insert 1

Example 4.3:

```
function insertionSort(arr, compare) {
    const size = arr.length;
    let temp;
    for (let i = 1; i < size; i++) {
        temp = arr[i];
        for (var j = i; j > 0 && compare(arr[j - 1], temp); j--) {
            arr[j] = arr[j - 1];
```

```
        }
    arr[j] = temp;
  }
};
```

Analysis:
- The outer loop is used to pick the value we want to insert into the sorted array in left.
- The value we want to insert we have picked and saved in a temp variable.
- The inner loop is doing the comparison using the more() function. The values are shifted to the right until we find the proper position of the temp value for which we are doing this iteration.
- Finally, the value is placed into the proper position. In each iteration of the outer loop, the length of the sorted array increases by one. When we exit the outer loop, the whole array is sorted.

Complexity Analysis:

Worst case time complexity	$O(n^2)$
Best case time complexity	$O(n)$
Average case time complexity	$O(n^2)$
Space Complexity	$O(1)$
Stable sorting	Yes

Selection-Sort

Selection-Sort traverse the unsorted array and put the largest value at the end of it. This process is repeated (n-1) number to times. This algorithm also has quadratic time complexity. but performs better than both bubble and Insertion-Sort as a smaller number of swaps are required. The sorted array is created backward in Selection-Sort.

5	6	2	4	7	3	1	Swap
5	6	2	4	1	3	7	Swap
5	3	2	4	1	6	7	Swap
1	3	2	4	5	6	7	No Swap
1	3	2	4	5	6	7	Swap
1	2	3	4	5	6	7	No Swap
1	2	3	4	5	6	7	

Example 4.4:
```
function selectionSort(arr, compare) {
    const size = arr.length;
    let max;
    let temp;
    for (let i = 0; i < size - 1; i++) {
        max = 0;
        for (let j = 1; j < size - i; j++) {
            if (compare(arr[j], arr[max])) {
                max = j;
```

```
            }
        }
        temp = arr[size - 1 - i];
        arr[size - 1 - i] = arr[max];
        arr[max] = temp;
    }
};
```

Analysis:

- The outer loop decides the number of times the inner loop will iterate. For an input of N elements, the inner loop will iterate N number of times.
- In each iteration of the inner loop, the largest value is calculated and is placed at the end of the array.
- This is the final replacement of the maximum value to the proper location. The sorted array is created backward.

Complexity Analysis:

Worst Case time complexity	$O(n^2)$
Best Case time complexity	$O(n^2)$
Average case time complexity	$O(n^2)$
Space Complexity	$O(1)$
Stable Sorting	No

The same algorithm can be implemented by creating the sorted array in the front of the array.

Example 4.5:

```
function selectionSort2(arr, compare) {
    const size = arr.length;
    let min;
    let temp;
    for (let i = 0; i < size - 1; i++) {
        min = i;
        for (let j = i + 1; j < size; j++) {
            if (compare(arr[min], arr[j])) {
                min = j;
            }
        }
        temp = arr[i];
        arr[i] = arr[min];
        arr[min] = temp;
    }
};
```

Merge-Sort

Merge sort divide the input into two halves recursively. In each step, the data is divided into two half. The two parts are sorted separately and finally combine the result into final sorted output.

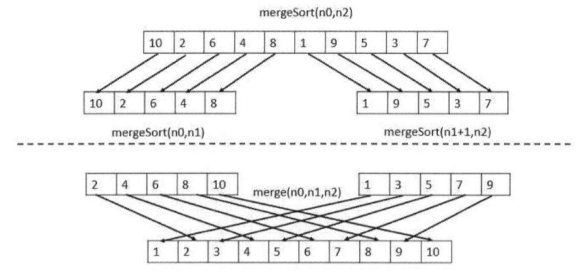

Example 4.6:

```
function merge(arr, tempArray, lowerIndex, middleIndex, upperIndex, compare)
{
    let lowerStart = lowerIndex;
    const lowerStop = middleIndex;
    let upperStart = middleIndex + 1;
    const upperStop = upperIndex;
    let count = lowerIndex;
    while (lowerStart <= lowerStop && upperStart <= upperStop) {
        if (compare(arr[lowerStart], arr[upperStart])) {
            tempArray[count++] = arr[lowerStart++];
        }
        else {
            tempArray[count++] = arr[upperStart++];
        }
    };
    while (lowerStart <= lowerStop) {
        tempArray[count++] = arr[lowerStart++];
    };
    while (upperStart <= upperStop) {
        tempArray[count++] = arr[upperStart++];
    };
    for (let i = lowerIndex; i <= upperIndex; i++) {
        arr[i] = tempArray[i];
    }
};

function mergeSortUtil(arr, tempArray, lowerIndex, upperIndex, compare) {
    if (lowerIndex >= upperIndex) {
        return;
    }
```

```
    const middleIndex = Math.floor((lowerIndex + upperIndex) / 2);
    mergeSortUtil(arr, tempArray, lowerIndex, middleIndex, compare);
    mergeSortUtil(arr, tempArray, middleIndex + 1, upperIndex, compare);
    merge(arr, tempArray, lowerIndex, middleIndex, upperIndex, compare);
};

function mergeSort(arr, compare) {
    const size = arr.length;
    const tempArray = new Array(size);
    mergeSortUtil(arr, tempArray, 0, size - 1, compare);
};
```

Analysis:
- Time Complexity of Merge-Sort is **O(nlogn)** in all 3 cases (best, average and worst) as Merge-Sort always divides the array into two halves and takes linear time to merge two halves.
- It requires the equal amount of additional space as the unsorted array. Hence, it is not at all recommended for searching large unsorted arrays.
- It is the best Sorting technique for sorting Linked Lists.

Complexity Analysis:

Worst Case time complexity	O(nlogn)
Best Case time complexity	O(nlogn)
Average case time complexity	O(nlogn)
Space Complexity	O(n)
Stable Sorting	Yes

Quick-Sort

Quick sort algorithm:
- Quick sort is recursive algorithm. In each step, we select a pivot (let us say first element of array).
- Partition the array into two parts, such that all the elements of the array which are smaller than the pivot should be moved to the left side of array and all the elements that are greater than pivot are at moved the right side of the array.
    - o Select pivot as first element in the array.
    - o Use two index variables lower and upper.
    - o Set lower index as second element in the array and upper index as last element of the array.
    - o Increase lower index till value at lower index is less than pivot.
    - o Then decrement upper index till the value at upper index is greater than pivot.
    - o Then swap the value at lower and upper index.
    - o Repeat the above 3 steps till upper index is greater than lower index.
    - o In the end, swap value at pivot and upper index.
- Then we sort the left and right sub-array separately.
- When the algorithm returns the whole array is sorted.

Below diagram demonstrating the partition step in quick sort.

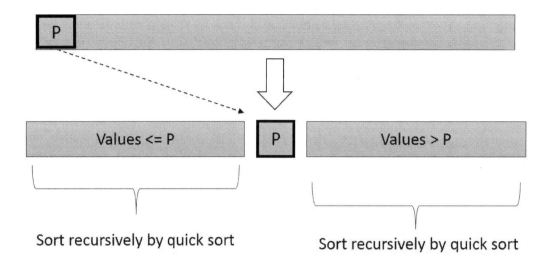

Below diagram demonstrating partition step of quicksort.

6	4ᴸ	5	1	8	2	9	7	3	ᵁ 10	Pivot value is 6
6	4	5ᴸ	1	8	2	9	7	3	ᵁ 10	Move lower index as 4 < 6
6	4	5	1ᴸ	8	2	9	7	3	ᵁ 10	Move lower index as 5 < 6
6	4	5	1	8ᴸ	2	9	7	3	ᵁ 10	Move lower index as 1 < 6
6	4	5	1	8ᴸ	2	9	7	ᵁ 3	10	Move upper index as 10 > 6
6	4	5	1	3ᴸ	2	9	7	ᵁ 8	10	Swap lower & upper index values
6	4	5	1	3	2ᴸ	9	7	ᵁ 8	10	Move lower index as 3 < 6
6	4	5	1	3	2	9ᴸ	7	ᵁ 8	10	Move lower index as 2 < 6
6	4	5	1	3	2	9ᴸ	ᵁ 7	8	10	Move upper index as 8 > 6
6	4	5	1	3	2	ᵁ 9ᴸ	7	8	10	Move upper index as 7 > 6
6	4	5	1	3	ᵁ 2	9ᴸ	7	8	10	Move upper index as 9 > 6
2	4	5	1	3	6	9	7	8	10	Swap pivot & upper index values

Quick sort demonstrated using diagram.

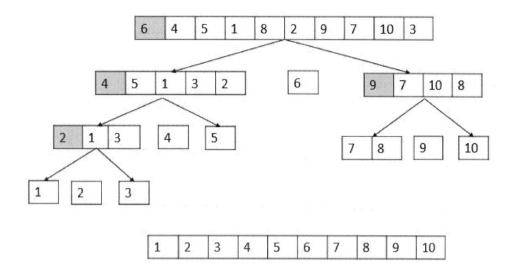

Example 4.7:

```
less = (value1, value2) => value1 < value2;

more = (value1, value2) => value1 > value2;

swap = (arr, first, second) => {
    const temp = arr[first];
    arr[first] = arr[second];
    arr[second] = temp;
};

function quickSortUtil(arr, lower, upper) {
    if (upper <= lower)
        return;

    const pivot = arr[lower];
    const start = lower;
    const stop = upper;
    while (lower < upper) {
        while (arr[lower] <= pivot && lower < upper) {
            lower++;
        };
        while (arr[upper] > pivot && lower <= upper) {
            upper--;
        };
        if (lower < upper) {
            swap(arr, upper, lower);
        }
    };
    swap(arr, upper, start);
    quickSortUtil(arr, start, upper - 1);
    quickSortUtil(arr, upper + 1, stop);
```

```
};

function quickSort(arr) {
    const size = arr.length;
    quickSortUtil(arr, 0, size - 1);
};

/* Testing Code */
const array = [3, 4, 2, 1, 6, 5, 7, 8, 1, 1];
quickSort(array);
console.log(array);
```

Output:
```
[ 1, 1, 1, 2, 3, 4, 5, 6, 7, 8 ]
```

- The space required by Quick-Sort is very less, only O(nlogn) additional space is required.
- Quicksort is not a stable sorting technique. It can reorder elements with identical keys.

Complexity Analysis:

Worst Case time complexity	$O(n^2)$
Best Case time complexity	O(nlogn)
Average case time complexity	O(nlogn)
Space Complexity	O(nlogn)
Stable Sorting	No

Quick Select

Quick select algorithm is used to find the element, which will be at the Kth position when the array will be sorted without sorting the whole array. Quick select is very similar to Quick-Sort in place of sorting the whole array we just ignore the one-half of the array at each step of Quick-Sort and just focus on the region of array on which the kth element lies.

Example 4.8:

```
function quickSelectUtil(arr, lower, upper, k) {
    if (upper <= lower)
        return;

    const pivot = arr[lower];
    const start = lower;
    const stop = upper;
    while (lower < upper) {
        while (arr[lower] <= pivot && lower < upper) {
            lower++;
        };
        while (arr[upper] > pivot && lower <= upper) {
            upper--;
        };
        if (lower < upper) {
```

```
            swap(arr, upper, lower);
        }
    };
    swap(arr, upper, start);
    if (k < upper)
        quickSelectUtil(arr, start, upper - 1, k);
    if (k > upper)
        quickSelectUtil(arr, upper + 1, stop, k);
};

function quickSelect(arr, k) {
    quickSelectUtil(arr, 0, arr.length - 1, k);
};


/* Testing Code */
const array = [3, 4, 2, 1, 6, 5, 7, 8, 10, 9];
quickSelect(array, 5);
console.log(`Fifth value is : ${array[4]}`);
```

Output:
```
Fifth value is : 5
```

Complexity Analysis:

Worst Case time complexity	$O(n^2)$
Best Case time complexity	$O(\log n)$
Average case time complexity	$O(\log n)$
Space Complexity	$O(n\log n)$

Bucket Sort

Bucket sort is the simplest and most efficient type of sorting. Bucket sort has a strict requirement of a predefined range of data.

Like, sort how many people are in which age group. We know that the age of people can vary between 0 and 130.We can directly store counts in an array of size 130.
If we know the range of input, then sorting can be done using counting in O(n+k). Where n is the number of elements and k is the possible range, in above Example it is 130.

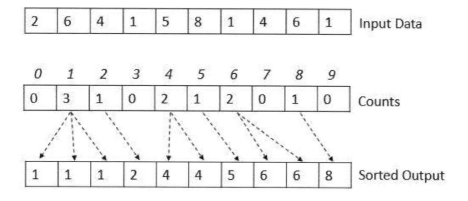

79

Example 4.9:

```
function bucketSort(arr, lowerRange, upperRange) {
    const range = upperRange - lowerRange;
    const size = arr.length;
    const count = new Array(range).fill(0);

    let i;
    for (i = 0; i < size; i++) {
        count[arr[i] - lowerRange]++;
    }

    j = 0;
    for (i = 0; i < range; i++) {
        for (; count[i] > 0; count[i]--) {
            arr[j++] = i + lowerRange;
        }
    }
};

/* Testing Code */
const arr = [23, 24, 22, 21, 26, 25, 27, 28, 21, 21];
bucketSort(arr, 20, 30);
console.log(arr);
```

Output:

[21, 21, 21, 22, 23, 24, 25, 26, 27, 28]

Analysis:
- We have created a count array to store counts.
- Count array elements are initialized to zero.
- Index corresponding to input array is incremented.
- Finally, the information stored in count array is saved in the array.

Complexity Analysis:

Data structure	Array
Worst case performance	O(n+k)
Average case performance	O(n+k)
Worst case Space Complexity	O(k)

k - Number of distinct elements.
n - Total number of elements in array.

Generalized Bucket Sort

There are cases when the element falling into a bucket are not unique but are in the same range. When we want to sort an index of a name, we can use the pointer bucket to store names.

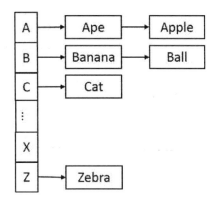

The buckets are already sorted and the elements inside each bucket can be kept sorted by using an Insertion-Sort algorithm. We are leaving this generalized bucket sort implementation to the reader of this book. The similar data structure will be defined in the coming chapter of Hash-Table using separate chaining.

Heap-Sort

Heap-Sort we will study in the Heap chapter.

Complexity Analysis:

Data structure	Array
Worst case performance	O(nlogn)
Average case performance	O(nlogn)
Worst case Space Complexity	O(1)

Tree Sorting

In-order traversal of the binary search tree can also be a sorting algorithm. We will see this in binary search tree section of tree chapter.

Complexity Analysis:

Worst Case time complexity	$O(n^2)$
Best Case time complexity	O(nlogn)
Average case time complexity	O(nlogn)
Space Complexity	O(n)
Stable Sorting	Yes

External Sort (External Merge-Sort)

When data needs to be sorted is huge and it is not possible to load it completely in memory (RAM), for such a dataset we use external sorting. Such data is sorted using external Merge-Sort algorithm. First data is picked in chunks and it is sorted in memory. Then this sorted data is written back to disk. Whole data are sorted in chunks using Merge-Sort. Now we need to combine these sorted chunks into final sorted data.

Then we create queues for the data, which will read from the sorted chunks. Each chunk will have its own queue. We will pop from this queue and these queues are responsible for reading from the sorted chunks. Let us suppose we have K different chunks of sorted data each of length M.

The third step is using a Min-Heap, which will take input data from each of this queue. It will take one element from each queue. The minimum value is taken from the Heap and added to the final output. Then queue from which this minimum value element is added to the heap will again be popped and one more element from this queue is added to the Heap. Finally, when the data is exhausted from some queue that queue is removed from the input list. Finally, we will get a sorted data coming out from the heap.

We can optimize this process further by adding an output buffer, which will store data coming out of Heap and will do a limited number of the write operation in the final Disk space.

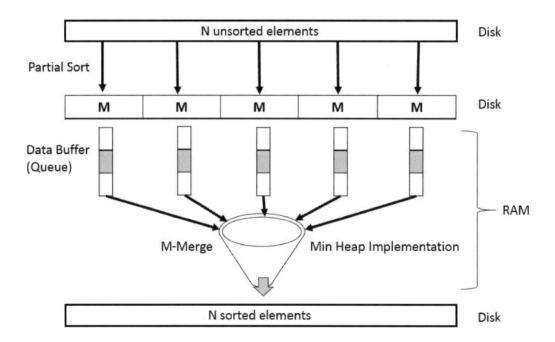

Note: No one will be asking to implement external sorting in an interview, but it is good to know about it.

Stable Sorting

A sorting algorithm is said to be stable if two elements with equal key value appear in same order in sorted output as they are in unsorted input. Stable sorting algorithms guarantees not to reorder elements with identical keys.

Comparisons of the various sorting algorithms.

Below is comparison of various sorting algorithms:

Sort	Average Time	Best Time	Worst Time	Space	Stable
Bubble Sort	$O(n^2)$	$O(n^2)$	$O(n^2)$	$O(1)$	Yes
Modified Bubble Sort	$O(n^2)$	$O(n)$	$O(n^2)$	$O(1)$	Yes
Selection Sort	$O(n^2)$	$O(n^2)$	$O(n^2)$	$O(1)$	No
Insertion Sort	$O(n^2)$	$O(n)$	$O(n^2)$	$O(1)$	Yes
Heap Sort	$O(n * log(n))$	$O(n * log(n))$	$O(n * log(n))$	$O(1)$	No
Merge Sort	$O(n * log(n))$	$O(n * log(n))$	$O(n * log(n))$	$O(n)$	Yes
Quick Sort	$O(n * log(n))$	$O(n * log(n))$	$O(n^2)$	$O(n)$ worst case $O(log(n))$ average case	No
Bucket Sort	$O(n\ k)$	$O(n\ k)$	$O(n\ k)$	$O(n\ k)$	Yes

Selection of Best Sorting Algorithm

No sorting algorithm is perfect. Each of them has their own pros and cons. Let us read one by one:

Quick-Sort: When you do not need a stable sort and average case performance matters more than worst-case performance. When data is random, we prefer the Quick-Sort. Average case time complexity of Quick-Sort is **O(nlogn)** and worst-case time complexity is **O(n²)**. Space Complexity of Quick-Sort is **O(logn)** auxiliary storage, which is stack space used in recursion.

Merge-Sort: When you need a stable sort and Time Complexity of **O(nlogn)**, Merge-Sort is used. In general, Merge-Sort is slower than Quick-Sort because of lot of copy happens in the merge phase. There are two uses of Merge-Sort when we want to merge two sorted linked lists and Merge-Sort is used in external sorting.

Heap-Sort: When you do not need a stable sort and you care more about worst-case performance than average case performance. It has guaranteed to be **O(nlogn)**, and uses **O(1)** auxiliary space, means you will not unpredictably run out of memory on very large inputs.

Insertion-Sort: When we need a stable sort, When N is guaranteed to be small, including as the base case of a Quick-Sort or Merge-Sort. Worst-case time complexity is **O(n²)**. It has a very small constant factor multiplied to calculate actual time taken. Therefore, for smaller input size it performs better than Merge-Sort or Quick-Sort. It is also useful when the data is already pre-sorted. In this case, its running time is **O(N)**.

Bubble-Sort: Where we know the data is nearly sorted. Say only two elements are out of place. Then in one pass, Bubble Sort will make the data sorted and in the second pass, it will see everything is sorted and then exit. Only takes 2 passes of the array.

Selection-Sort: Best, Worst & Average Case running time all are **O(n²)**. It is only useful when you want to do something quick. They can be used when you are just doing some prototyping.

Counting-Sort: When you are sorting data within a limited range.

Radix-Sort: When log(N) is significantly larger than K, where K is the number of radix digits.

Bucket-Sort: When your input is uniformly distributed.

Problems based on sorting

Partition 0 and 1

Problem: Given an array containing 0s and 1s. Write an algorithm to sort array so that 0s come first followed by 1s. Also find the minimum number of swaps required to sort the array.

First Solution: Start from both ends, left will store start index and right will store end index. Traverse left forward till we have 0s value in the array. Then traverse right backward till we have 1s in the end. Then swap the two and follow the same process till left is less than right.

Example 4.10:
```
function Partition01(arr, size) {
    let left = 0;
    let right = size - 1;
    let count = 0;
    while (left < right) {
        while (arr[left] === 0) {
            left += 1;
        }

        while (arr[right] === 1) {
            right -= 1;
        }
        if (left < right) {
            swap(arr, left, right);
            count += 1;
        }
    }
    return count;
};

function test() {
    const arr = [0, 1, 1, 0, 1, 0, 1, 1, 0, 0, 0, 1];
    Partition01(arr, arr.length);
    console.log(arr);
```

84

```
}
```

Output:
```
[ 0, 0, 0, 0, 0, 0, 1, 1, 1, 1, 1, 1 ]
```

Time complexity looks like quadratic (loop inside loop) but it is linear or O(n). As at each iteration of inner loop, either left is increasing or right is decreasing. Once left is equal or greater than right the loops stop. Therefore, in total the inner loops combined runs for N number of times.

Partition 0, 1 and 2

Problem: Given an array containing 0s, 1s and 2s. Write an algorithm to sort array so that 0s come first followed by 1s and then 2s in the end.

First Solution: You can use a counter for 0s, 1s and 2s. Then replace the values in the array. This will take two passes. What if we want to do this in single pass?

Second Solution: The basic approach is to use three indices. First left, second right and third to traverse the array. Index left starts form 0, Index right starts from N-1. We traverse the array whenever we find a 0 we swap it with the value at start and increment start. And whenever we find a 2 we swaps this value with right and decrement right. When traversal is complete and we reach the right then the array is sorted.

Example 4.11:
```
function Partition012(arr, size) {
    let left = 0;
    let right = size - 1;
    let i = 0;
    while (i <= right) {
        if (arr[i] === 0) {
            swap(arr, i, left);
            i += 1;
            left += 1;
        }
        else if (arr[i] === 2) {
            swap(arr, i, right);
            right -= 1;
        }
        else {
            i += 1;
        }
    }
};

function test() {
    const arr2 = [0, 1, 1, 0, 1, 2, 1, 2, 0, 0, 0, 1];
    Partition012(arr2, arr2.length);
    console.log(arr2);
};
```

Output:
```
[ 0, 0, 0, 0, 0, 1, 1, 1, 1, 1, 2, 2 ]
```

Time complexity is linear or O(n).

Range Partition

Problem: Given an array of integer and a range. Write an algorithm to partition array so that values smaller than range come to left, then values under the range followed with values greater than the range.

First Solution: The basic approach is to use three indices. First left, second right and third to traverse the array. Index left starts form 0, Index right starts from N-1. We traverse the array whenever we find a value lower than range, we swap it with the value at start and increment start. And whenever we find a value greater than range, we swap this value with right and decrement right. When traversal is complete, we have the array partitioned about range.

Example 4.12:
```
function RangePartition(arr, size, lower, higher) {
    let start = 0;
    let end = size - 1;
    let i = 0;
    while (i <= end) {
        if (arr[i] < lower) {
            swap(arr, i, start);
            i += 1;
            start += 1;
        }
        else if (arr[i] > higher) {
            swap(arr, i, end);
            end -= 1;
        }
        else {
            i += 1;
        }
    }
};

function test() {
    const arr = [1, 21, 2, 20, 3, 19, 4, 18, 5, 17, 6, 16, 7, 15, 8, 14, 9,
13, 10, 12, 11];
    RangePartition(arr, arr.length, 9, 12);
    console.log(arr);
};
```

Output:
```
[ 1, 2, 3, 4, 5, 8, 6, 7, 11, 10, 12, 9, 15, 16, 14, 17, 13, 18, 19, 20,
21 ]
```

Time complexity is linear or O(n).

Minimum swaps

Problem: Minimum swaps required to bring all elements less than given value together at the start of array.

First Solution: Use quick sort kind of technique by taking two index one from start and another from end and try to use the given value as key. Count the number of swaps that is answer.

Example 4.13:

```
function minSwaps(arr, size, val) {
    let swapCount = 0;
    let first = 0;
    let second = size - 1;
    let temp;
    while (first < second) {
        if (arr[first] < val)
            first += 1;
        else if (arr[second] >= val)
            second -= 1;
        else {
            temp = arr[first];
            arr[first] = arr[second];
            arr[second] = temp;
            swapCount += 1;
        }
    }
    return swapCount;
};

function test(){
    let arr = [2,7,5,6,1,3,4,9,10,8]
    let val = 5
    console.log(minSwaps(arr, 10, val))
}
```

Output:
3

Time complexity is linear or O(n).

Absolute Sort

Problem: Sort array according to the absolute difference from the given value.

Solution: Any sorting algorithms can be used to solve this problem we are using BubbleSort. The only change is comparing function more. Which will take another field ref.

Example 4.14:
```
function AbsMore(value1, value2, ref) {
    return (Math.abs(value1 - ref) > Math.abs(value2 - ref));
};

function AbsBubbleSort(arr, size, ref) {
    for (let i = 0; i < (size - 1); i++) {
        for (let j = 0; j < (size - i - 1); j++) {
            if (AbsMore(arr[j], arr[j + 1], ref)) {
                swap(arr, j, j + 1);
            }
        }
    }
};

function test() {
    const array = [9, 1, 8, 2, 7, 3, 6, 4, 5];
    const ref = 5;
    AbsBubbleSort(array, array.length, ref);
    console.log(array);
};
```

Output:
```
[ 5 6 4 7 3 8 2 9 1 ]
```

Time complexity is linear or O(n).

Equation Sort

Problem: Sort array according to the equation $A.X^2$.

Solution: Any sorting algorithms can be used to solve this problem also. The only change is comparing function more. Which will take another field A.

Example 4.15:
```
function EqMore(value1, value2, A) {
    value1 = A * value1 * value1;
    value2 = A * value2 * value2;
    return value1 > value2;
};
```

Sort by Order

Problem: Given two array, sort first array according to the order defined in second array.

Solution: First the input array is traversed and frequency of values is calculated using HashTable. The order array is traversed and those values which are in original array / hashtable are displayed and removed from hashtable. Then the rest of the values of hashtable is printed to screen.

Example 4.16:

```javascript
function SortByOrder(arr, size, arr2, size2) {
    const ht = new Map();
    const ret = new Array(size);
    let retIndex = 0;

    let value;
    for (var i = 0; i < size; i++) {
        if (ht.has(arr[i])) {
            value = ht.get(arr[i]);
            ht.set(arr[i], value + 1);
        } else {
            ht.set(arr[i], 1);
        }
    }
    for (let j = 0; j < size2; j++) {
        if (ht.has(arr2[j])) {
            value = ht.get(arr2[j]);
            for (var k = 0; k < value; k++) {
                ret[retIndex++] = arr2[j];
            }
            ht.delete(arr2[j]);
        }
    }

    for (var i = 0; i < size; i++) {
        if (ht.has(arr[i])) {
            value = ht.get(arr[i]);
            for (var k = 0; k < value; k++) {
                ret[retIndex++] = arr[i];
            }
            ht.delete(arr[i]);
        }
    }
    for (var i = 0; i < size; i++) {
        arr[i] = ret[i];
    }
};

function test() {
    const arr = [2, 1, 2, 5, 7, 1, 9, 3, 6, 8, 8];
    const arr2 = [2, 1, 8, 3];
    SortByOrder(arr, arr.length, arr2, arr2.length);
    console.log("SortByOrder", arr)
};
```

Output:
```
SortByOrder [ 2, 2, 1, 1, 8, 8, 3, 5, 7, 9, 6 ]
```

Time complexity is O(n).

Separate even and odd numbers in List

Problem: Given an array of even and odd numbers, write a program to separate even numbers from the odd numbers.

First Solution: allocate a separate list, then scan through the given list, and fill even numbers from the start and odd numbers from the end.

Second Solution: Algorithm is as follows.
1. Initialize the two variables left and right. Variable left=0 and right= size-1.
2. Keep increasing the left index until the element at that index is even.
3. Keep decreasing the right index until the element at that index is odd.
4. Swap the number at left and right index.
5. Repeat steps 2 to 4 until left is less than right.

Example 4.17:
```
function seperateEvenAndOdd(data, size) {
    let left = 0;
    let right = size - 1;
    while (left < right) {
        if (data[left] % 2 === 0)
            left++;
        else if (data[right] % 2 === 1)
            right--;
        else {
            swap(data, left, right);
            left++;
            right--;
        }
    }
};

function test(){
    let arr = [2,7,5,6,1,3,4,9,10,8]
    seperateEvenAndOdd(arr, 10)
    console.log(arr)
}
```

Output:
```
[ 2, 8, 10, 6, 4, 3, 1, 9, 5, 7 ]
```

Time complexity is linear or O(n).

Array Reduction

Problem: Element left after reductions. Given an array of positive elements. You need to perform reduction operation. In each reduction operation smallest positive element value is picked and all the elements are subtracted by that value. You need to print the number of elements left after each reduction process.

Input: [5, 1, 1, 1, 2, 3, 5]

Output:
4 corresponds to [4, 1, 2, 4]
3 corresponds to [3, 1, 3]
2 corresponds to [2, 2]
0 corresponds to [0]

Example 4.18:
```
function ArrayReduction(arr, size) {
    arr.sort(function cmp(a, b) { return (a - b); });
    let count = 1;
    let reduction = arr[0];
    for (let i = 0; i < size; i++) {
        if (arr[i] - reduction > 0) {
            reduction = arr[i];
            count += 1;
        }
    }
    console.info(`Total number of reductions ${count}`);
    return count
};

function test() {
    const arr = [5, 1, 1, 1, 2, 3, 5];
    ArrayReduction(arr, arr.length);
};
```

Output:
```
Total number of reductions 4
```

Time complexity: O(nlogn). O(nlogn) required for sorting.

Problem: If it is asked to find the total number of reduction operations that are needed. Then this can be done in linear time.

Hint: The total number of reductions is equal to the total number of distinct elements.

Merge Array

Problem: Given two sorted arrays. Sort the elements of these arrays so that first half of sorted elements will lie in first array and second half lies in second array. Extra space allowed is O(1).

Solution: The first array will contain smaller part of the sorted output. We traverse the first array. Always compare the value of first array with the first element of the second array. If first array value is small than first element of second array we iterate further. If the first array value is greater than first element of second array. Then copy value of first element of second array into first array. And insert value of first array into second array in sorted order. Second array is always kept sorted so we need to compare only its first element.

Time complexity will O(M*N) where M is length of first array and N is length of second array.

Example 4.19:

```
function merge(arr1, size1, arr2, size2) {
    let index = 0;
    let temp;
    while (index < size1) {
        if (arr1[index] <= arr2[0]) {
            index += 1;
        }
        else {
            temp = arr1[index]
            arr1[index] = arr2[0];
            arr2[0] = temp;

            index += 1;
            for (let i = 0; i < (size2 - 1); i++) {
                if (arr2[i] < arr2[i + 1])
                    break;

                temp = arr2[i]
                arr2[i] = arr2[i + 1];
                arr2[i + 1] = temp;
            }
        }
    }
};

function test() {
    const arr1 = [1, 5, 9, 10, 15, 20];
    const arr2 = [2, 3, 8, 13];
    merge(arr1, arr1.length, arr2, arr2.length);
    console.log(arr1);
    console.log(arr2);
};
```

Output:
```
[ 1, 2, 3, 5, 8, 9 ]
[ 10, 13, 15, 20 ]
```

Check Reverse

Problem: Given an array of integers, find if reversing a sub-array makes the array sorted.

Solution: In this algorithm start and stop are the boundary of reversed sub-array whose reversal makes the whole array sorted.

Example 4.20:

```
function checkReverse(arr, size) {
    let start = -1;
    let stop = -1;
    for (var i = 0; i < (size - 1); i++) {
        if (arr[i] > arr[i + 1]) {
            start = i;
            break;
        }
    }
    if (start === -1)
        return true;

    for (var i = start; i < (size - 1); i++) {
        if (arr[i] < arr[i + 1]) {
            stop = i;
            break;
        }
    }
    if (stop === -1)
        return true;
    if (arr[start - 1] > arr[stop] || arr[stop + 1] < arr[start])
        return false;

    for (var i = stop + 1; i < size - 1; i++) {
        if (arr[i] > arr[i + 1]) {
            return false;
        }
    }
    return true;
};

function test() {
    const arr = [1, 3, 8, 5, 4, 3, 10, 11, 12, 18, 28];
    console.log("checkReverse : ", checkReverse(arr, arr.length))
};
```

Output:
```
checkReverse :   true
```

Time complexity is linear or O(n).

Union Intersection Sorted

Problem: Given two unsorted arrays, find union and intersection of these two arrays.

Solution: Sort both the arrays. Then traverse both the array, when we have common elements, we add it to intersection list and union list, when we have uncommon elements then we add it only union list.

Example 4.21:
```
function UnionIntersectionSorted(arr1, size1, arr2, size2) {
    let first = 0;
    let second = 0;
    const unionArr = new Array();
    const interArr = new Array();
    let uIndex = 0;
    let iIndex = 0;

    while (first < size1 && second < size2) {
        if (arr1[first] === arr2[second]) {
            unionArr[uIndex++] = arr1[first];
            interArr[iIndex++] = arr1[first];
            first += 1;
            second += 1;
        }
        else if (arr1[first] < arr2[second]) {
            unionArr[uIndex++] = arr1[first];
            first += 1;
        }
        else {
            unionArr[uIndex++] = arr2[second];
            second += 1;
        }
    }
    while (first < size1) {
        unionArr[uIndex++] = arr1[first];
        first += 1;
    }
    while (second < size2) {
        unionArr[uIndex++] = arr2[second];
        second += 1;
    }
    console.log("Union : ", unionArr);
    console.log("Intersection : ", interArr);
};

function UnionIntersectionUnsorted(arr1, size1, arr2, size2) {
    arr1.sort(function cmp(a, b) { return (a - b); });
    arr2.sort(function cmp(a, b) { return (a - b); });
    UnionIntersectionSorted(arr1, size1, arr2, size2);
};

function test() {
    const arr1 = [1, 11, 2, 3, 14, 5, 6, 8, 9];
    const arr2 = [2, 4, 5, 12, 7, 8, 13, 10];
    UnionIntersectionUnsorted(arr1, arr1.length, arr2, arr2.length);
```

```
};
```

Output:
```
Union :  [ 1, 2, 3, 4, 5, 6, 7, 8, 9, 10, 11, 12, 13, 14 ]
Intersection :  [ 2, 5, 8 ]
```

Time complexity is O(nlogn). O(nlogn) required for sorting.

Exercise

1. In given text file, print the words with their frequency. Now print the kth word in term of frequency.

   Hint:-
   a) First solution maybe you can use the sorting and return the kth element.
   b) Second Solution: You can use the kth element quick select algorithm.
   c) Third Solution: You can use Hashtable or Trie to keep track of the frequency. Use Heap to get the Kth element.

2. In given K input streams of number in sorted order. You need to make a single output stream, which contains all the elements of the K streams in sorted order. The input streams support ReadNumber() operation and output stream support WriteNumber() operation.

   Hint:-
   a) Read the first number from all the K input streams and add them to a Priority Queue. (Nodes should keep track of the input stream; data added to the PQ is value & stream id.)
   b) Dequeue one element at a time from PQ, put this element value to the output stream, Read the input stream number and from the same input stream add another element to PQ.
   c) If the stream is empty, just continue
   d) Repeat until PQ is empty.

3. In given K sorted Lists of fixed length M. Also, given a final output list of length M*K. Give an efficient algorithm to merge all the arrays into the final list, without using any extra space.

   Hint: you can use the end of the final list to make PQ.

4. How will you sort 1 PB numbers? 1 PB = 1000 TB.

5. What will be the complexity of the above solution?

6. Any other improvement can be done on question 3 solution if the number of CPU cores is eight.

7. In given integer list that support three functions findMin, findMax, findMedian. Sort the array.

8. In given pile of patient files of High, mid and low priority. Sort these files such that higher priority comes first, then mid and last low priority.

   Hint: Bucket sort.

9. Write pros and cons of Heap-Sort, Merge-Sort and Quick-Sort.

10. In given rotated-sorted list of N integers. (The array was sorted then it was rotated some arbitrary number of times.) If all the elements in the array were unique, find the index of some value.

    Hint: Modified binary search

11. In the problem 9, what if there are repetitions allowed and you need to find the index of the first occurrence of the element in the rotated-sorted list.

12. Merge two sorted Lists into a single sorted list.

    Hint: Use merge method of Merge-Sort.

13. Given an array contain 0's and 1's, sort the array such that all the 0's come before 1's.

14. Given an array of English characters, sort the array in linear time.

15. Write a method to sort an array of strings so that all the anagrams are next to each other.

    Hint:-
    a) Loop through the array.
    b) For each word, sort the characters and add it to the hash map with keys as sorted word and value as the original word. At the end of the loop, you will get all anagrams as the value to a key (which is sorted by its constituent chars).
    c) Iterate over the hashmap, print all values of a key together and then move to the next key.
    Space Complexity: O(n), Time Complexity: O(n)

16. Given an array, sort elements in the order of their frequency.
    Hint: First, the frequency of various elements of array is calculated by adding it to HashTable. Then sorting of the new data structures with value and key is done. The sorting function first give preference to frequency then value.

CHAPTER 5: SEARCHING

Introduction

Searching is the process of finding an item in a collection of items. The item may be a keyword in a file, a record in a database, a node in a tree or a value in an array etc.

Why Searching?

Imagine you are in a library with millions of books. You want to get a specific book with specific title. How will you find it? You will search the book in the section of library, which contains the books whose name starts with the initial letter of the desired book. Then you continue matching with a whole book title until you find your book. (By doing this small heuristic method you have reduced the search space by a factor of 26, consider we have an equal number of books whose title begin with particular char.)

Similarly, computer stores lots of information and to retrieve this information efficiently, we need very efficient searching algorithms. To make searching efficient, we keep the data in some proper order. If you keep the data organized in proper order, it is easy to search required value or key. For Example , keeping the data in sorted order is one of the ways to organize data.

Different Searching Algorithms

- Linear Search – Unsorted Input
- Linear Search – Sorted Input
- Binary Search (Sorted Input)
- String Search: Tries, Suffix Trees, Ternary Search.
- Hashing and Symbol Tables

Linear Search – Unsorted Input

When elements of an array are not ordered or sorted and we want to search for a value, we need to scan the full list until we find the desired value. This kind of algorithm is known as unordered linear search. The major problem with this algorithm is less performance or high Time Complexity in worst case.

Example 5.1
```
function linearSearchUnsorted(arr, value) {
    const size = arr.length;
    for (let i = 0; i < size; i++) {
        if (value === arr[i]) {
            return true;
        }
    }
    return false;
};
```

```
function test() {
    const first = [1, 3, 5, 7, 6, 4, 2];
    console.log(linearSearchUnsorted(first, 7));
    console.log(linearSearchUnsorted(first, 9));
}
```

Output:
```
true
false
```

Time Complexity: O(n). As we need to traverse the complete list in worst case. Worst case is when your desired element is at the last position of the array. Here, 'n' is the size of the array.

Space Complexity: O(1). No extra memory is used to allocate the array.

Linear Search – Sorted

If elements of the array are sorted either in increasing order or in decreasing order, searching for a desired element will be much more efficient than unordered linear search. In many cases, we do not need to traverse the complete list. If the array is sorted in increasing order. We can traverse it from beginning and when we encounter a value greater than the key, we stop searching further and declare that the key is not present in the array. This is how this algorithm saves the time and improves the performance.

Example 5.2
```
function linearSearchSorted(arr, value) {
    const size = arr.length;
    for (let i = 0; i < size; i++) {
        if (value === arr[i]) {
            return true;
        }
        else if (value < arr[i]) {
            return false;
        }
    }
    return false;
};

function test() {
    const second = [2, 4, 6, 8, 10, 12, 14, 16, 21, 23, 24];
    console.log(linearSearchSorted(second, 8));
    console.log(linearSearchSorted(second, 9));
};
```

Output:
```
true
false
```

Time Complexity: O(n). As we need to traverse the complete list in worst case. Worst case is when your desired element is at the last position of the sorted list. However, in the average case this algorithm is more efficient even though the growth rate is same as unsorted.

Space Complexity: O(1). No extra memory is used to allocate the array.

Binary Search

How do we search a word in a dictionary? In general, we go to some approximate page (mostly middle) and start searching from that word. If we see the word that we are searching is in the same page then we are done with the search. Else, if we see that alphabetically the word, we are searching is in the first half then we reject the second half and wise versa. We apply the same procedure repeatedly until we find the desired keyword.

Binary Search also works in the same way. When we want to search some key value in a sorted list. We go to the middle point from the sorted list and start comparing with the desired value. If the desired value is equal to the middle value then we are done. If the value is greater than the middle value then we reject the first half. If the value is less than the middle value then we reject the second half. At each comparison, we are reducing our search space by half.

Note: Binary search requires the array to be sorted otherwise binary search cannot be applied.

Example 5.3
```
function Binarysearch(arr, value) {
    let low = 0;
    let high = arr.length - 1;
    let mid;
    while (low <= high) {
        mid = Math.floor((low + high) / 2);
        if (arr[mid] === value) {
            return true;
        }
        else if (arr[mid] < value) {
            low = mid + 1;
        }
        else {
            high = mid - 1;
        }
    };
    return false;
};

function test() {
    const second = [2, 4, 6, 8, 10, 12, 14, 16, 21, 23, 24];
    console.log(Binarysearch(second, 10));
};
```

Output:
```
true
```

Time Complexity: O(logn). We always take half input and throw out the other half. So, the recurrence relation for binary search is T(n) = T(n/2) + c. Using master theorem (divide and conquer), we get T(n) = O(logn), Space Complexity: O(1)

Example 5.4: Binary search implementation using recursion.

```
function BinarySearchRecursive(arr, value) {
    return BinarySearchRecursiveUtil(arr, 0, arr.length - 1, value);
}

function BinarySearchRecursiveUtil(arr, low, high, value) {
    if (low > high) {
        return false;
    }
    const mid = Math.floor((low + high) / 2);
    if (arr[mid] === value) {
        return true;
    }
    else if (arr[mid] < value) {
        return BinarySearchRecursiveUtil(arr, mid + 1, high, value);
    }
    else {
        return BinarySearchRecursiveUtil(arr, low, mid - 1, value);
    }
};

function test() {
    const second = [2, 4, 6, 8, 10, 12, 14, 16, 21, 23, 24];
    console.log(BinarySearchRecursive(second, 10));
};
```

Output:
```
true
```

Time Complexity: O(logn). Space Complexity: O(logn) for system stack in recursion

String Searching Algorithms

Refer String chapter.

Hashing and Symbol Tables

Refer Hash-Table chapter.

How sorting is useful in Selection Algorithm?

Selection problems can be converted into sorting problems. Once the array is sorted, it is easy to find the minimum / maximum (or desired element) from the sorted list. The method 'Sorting and then Selecting' is inefficient for selecting a single element, but it is efficient when many selections need to be made from the array. It is because only one initial expensive sort is needed, followed by many cheap selection operations.

For Example , if we want to get the maximum element from an array. After sorting the array, we can simply return the last element from the array. What if we want to get second maximum? Now, we do not have to sort the array again and we can return the second last element from the sorted list. Similarly, we can return the kth maximum element by just one scan of the sorted list.

So, with the above discussion, sorting is used to improve the performance. In general, this method requires **O(nlogn)** (for sorting) time.

Problems in Searching

First Repeated element in the array

Problem: Given an unsorted list of n elements, find the first element, which is repeated.

First Solution: Exhaustive search or Brute force; for each element in list find if there is some other element with the same value. This is done using two loops, first loop to select the element and second loop to find its duplicate entry.

Time Complexity is $O(n^2)$ and Space Complexity is $O(1)$

Example 5.5
```
function FirstRepeated(arr) {
    const size = arr.length;
    for (let i = 0; i < size; i++) {
        for (let j = i + 1; j < size; j++) {
            if (arr[i] === arr[j]) {
                return arr[i];
            }
        }
    }
    return 0;
};

function test() {
    first = [7, 9, 3, 11, 3, 5, 7]
    console.log(`FirstRepeated :: ${FirstRepeated(first)}`);
}
```

Output:
```
FirstRepeated :: 7
```

Second Solution: Hash-Table; using Hash-Table, we can keep track number of times an element came in the array. First scan just populates the Hashtable. In the second, scan just look the occurrence of the elements in the Hashtable. If occurrence is more for some element, then we have our solution and the first repeated element.

Hash-Table insertion and finding take constant time O(1) so the total time complexity of the algorithm is O(n) time. Space Complexity is also O(n) for maintaining hash.

Print Duplicates in List

Problem: Given an array of n numbers, print the duplicate elements in the array.

First Solution: Exhaustive search or Brute force; for each element in list, find if there is some other element with the same value. This is done using two loop, first loop to select the element and second loop to find its duplicate entry.

Example 5.6

```
function printRepeating(arr) {
    const size = arr.length;
    let output = "Repeating elements are :";
    for (let i = 0; i < size; i++) {
        for (let j = i + 1; j < size; j++) {
            if (arr[i] === arr[j]) {
                output += " " + arr[i];
                break
            }
        }
    }
    console.log(output)
};

function test() {
    const first = [1, 3, 5, 3, 1, 4, 2, 2, 3];
    printRepeating(first);
};
```

Output:
```
Repeating elements are : 1 3 3 2
```

Time Complexity is $O(n^2)$ and Space Complexity is $O(1)$

Second Solution: Sorting; Sort all the elements in the array and after this in a single scan, we can find the duplicates.

Example 5.7

```
function printRepeating2(arr) {
    const size = arr.length;
    arr.sort(function cmp(a, b) { return (a - b); })
    let output = "Repeating elements are :";
    for (let i = 1; i < size; i++) {
        if (arr[i] === arr[i - 1]) {
            output += " " + arr[i];
        }
    }
    console.log(output)
};
```

Sorting algorithms take O(n log n) time and single scan take O(n) time.
Time Complexity is O(n log n) and Space Complexity is O(1)

Third Solution: Hash-Table, using Hash-Table, we can keep track of the elements we have already seen and we can find the duplicates in just one scan.

Example 5.8

```javascript
function printRepeating3(arr) {
    const hs = {};
    const size = arr.length;
    let output = "Repeating elements are :";
    for (let i = 0; i < size; i++) {
        if (arr[i] in hs) {
            output += " " + arr[i];
        }
        else {
            hs[arr[i]] = 1;
        }
    }
    console.log(output)
};
```

Hash-Table insert and find take constant time O(1) so the total time complexity of the algorithm is O(n) time. Space Complexity is also O(n)

Forth Solution: Counting, this solution is only possible if we know the range of the input. If we know that, the elements in the array are in the range 0 to n-1. We can reserve an array of length n call it counter and when we see an element, we can increase its corresponding count. In just one single scan, we know the duplicates. If we know the range of the elements, then this is the fastest way to find the duplicates.

Example 5.9

```javascript
function printRepeating4(arr) {
    const size = arr.length;
    const count = new Array(size).fill(0);
    let output = "Repeating elements are :";
    for (let i = 0; i < size; i++) {
        if (count[arr[i]] > 0) {
            output += " " + arr[i];
        }
        else {
            count[arr[i]]++;
        }
    }
    console.log(output)
};
```

Counting solution just uses an array so inserting and finding take constant time O(1) so the total time complexity of the algorithm is O(n) time. Space Complexity for creating count list is also O(n)

Remove duplicates in an integer list

Problem: Remove duplicate in an integer list.

First Solution: Sorting, Steps are as follows:
1. Sort the array.
2. Take two references. A subarray will be created with all unique elements starting from 0 to the first reference (The first reference points to the last index of the subarray). The second reference iterates through the array from 1 to the end. Unique numbers will be copied from the second reference location to first reference location and the same elements are ignored.

Time Complexity calculation:
Time to sort the array = **O(nlogn)**. Time to remove duplicates = **O(n)**.
Overall Time Complexity = **O(nlogn)**.
No additional space is required so Space Complexity is **O(1)**.

Example 5.10
```
function removeDuplicates(array) {
    let j = 0;
    const size = array.length;
    if (size === 0) {
        return [];
    }
    array.sort(function cmp(a, b) { return (a - b); });
    for (let i = 1; i < size; i++) {
        if (array[i] !== array[j]) {
            j++;
            array[j] = array[i];
        }
    }
    return array.slice(0, j + 1);
};

function test() {
    first = [1, 2, 3, 1, 2, 3, 5, 6, 7, 7, 8, 9, 3, 4, 5]
    console.log(removeDuplicates(first));
}
```

Output:
```
[ 1, 2, 3, 4, 5, 6, 7, 8, 9 ]
```

Second Solution: Use a Hash Table to keep track the elements already visited. Create a output array and add only unique elements to it and also add that value to hash table.
Overall Time Complexity is **O(n)**.

Space Complexity is **O(n)** for hash table.
Other solutions of the previous problems can also be used to solve this problem.

Find the missing number in an array

Problem: In given list of n-1 elements, which are in the range of 1 to n. There are no duplicates in the array. One of the integers is missing. Find the missing element.

First Solution: Exhaustive search or Brute force, for each value in the range 1 to n, find if there is some element in list which have the same value. This is done using two loops, first loop to select value in the range 1 to n and the second loop to find if this element is in the array or not.

Time Complexity is $O(n^2)$ and Space Complexity is $O(1)$.

Example 5.11
```javascript
function findMissingNumber(arr) {
    const size = arr.length;
    let found;
    for (let i = 1; i <= size; i++) {
        found = false;
        for (let j = 0; j < size; j++) {
            if (arr[j] === i) {
                found = true;
                break;
            }
        }
        if (found === false) {
            return i;
        }
    }
    return MAX_VALUE;
};

function test() {
    const first = [1, 3, 5, 7, 2, 4, 8, 9, 10];
    const i = 0;
    console.log(findMissingNumber(first));
};
```

Output:
6

Second Solution: Sorting; Sort all the elements in the array and after this in a single scan, we can find the duplicates.

Sorting algorithms takes O(n.logn) time and single scan takes O(n) time.
Time Complexity of an algorithm is O(n.logn) and Space Complexity is O(1)

Third Solution: Hash-Table, using Hash-Table; we can keep track of the elements we have already seen and we can find the missing element in just one scan.

Hash-Table insertion and finding take constant time O(1) so the total time complexity of the algorithm is O(n) time. Space Complexity is also O(n)

Forth Solution: Counting, we know the range of the input so counting will work. As we know that, the elements in the array are in the range 0 to n. We can reserve an array of length n and when we see an element, we can increase its count. In just one single scan, we know the missing element.

Counting solution just uses an array so insertion and finding take constant time O(1) so the total time complexity of the algorithm is O(n) time. Space Complexity for creating count list is also O(n)

Fifth Solution: You can modify the given input list. Modify the given input list in such a way that in the next scan you can find the missing element.

When you scan through the array. When at index "index", the value stored in the array will be arr[index] so add the number "n + 1" to arr[arr[index]]. Always read the value from the array using a reminder operator "%". When you scan the array for the first time and modify all the values, then in one single scan you can see if there is some value in the array which is smaller than "n+1" that index is the missing number.
In this solution, the array is scanned two times, Time Complexity of this algorithm is O(n). Space Complexity is O(1)

Sixth Solution: Summation formula to find the sum of n numbers from 1 to n. Subtract the values stored in the array and you will have your missing number.
Time Complexity of this algorithm is O(n). Space Complexity is O(1)

Seventh Solution: XOR approach to find the sum of n numbers from 1 to n. XOR the values stored in the array and you will have your missing number.
Time Complexity of this algorithm is O(n). Space Complexity is O(1)

Example 5.12:
```
function findMissingNumber2(arr, range) {
    if ((arr != null && arr instanceof Array) && (typeof range ===
'number')) {
        let i;
        const size = arr.length;
        let xorSum = 0;
        for (i = 1; i <= range; i++) {
            xorSum ^= i;
        }
        for (i = 0; i < size; i++) {
            xorSum ^= arr[i];
        }
        return xorSum;
    }
    else
        throw new Error('invalid overload');
};
```

Eighth Solution: Using set, first all the values in list to set then look for value from 1 to upperRange in the set if we do not find some value then return that value.

Example 5.13:

```
function findMissingNumber3(arr, upperRange) {
    const size = arr.length;
    const st = new Set();
    let i = 0;
    while (i <= size) {
        st.add(arr[i])
        i += 1;
    }
    i = 1;
    while (i <= upperRange) {
        if (st.has(i) === false)
            return i;
        i += 1;
    }
    console.info("NoNumberMissing");
    return -1;
};
```

Note: Same problem can be asked in many forms (sometime you mustperform xor of the range):
1. There are numbers in the range of 1-n out of which all appears single time but there is one that appear two times.
2. All the elements in the range 1-n are appearing 16 times and one element appears 17 times. Find the element that appears 17 times.

Missing Values

Problem: Given an array, find the maximum and minimum value in the array and also find the values in range minimum and maximum that are absent in the array.

First Solution: Brute force approach, traverse the array find minimum and maximum value. Then find values from minimum to maximum in the array. Time complexity of this solution will be $O(n^2)$

Second Solution: Sorting approach, we can sort the given array. Then traverse the whole array and print the missing values. Time complexity of this solution will be O(nlogn) for sorting and traversal will take O(n) so the overall Time complexity is O(nlogn).

Third Solution: Hashtable approach, we can traverse the array and insert its elements in a hashtable. Also, in this single traversal we can find smallest and largest value in the array. Now find if the values between minimum and maximum are present in hashtable. If such values are not present then print those values.

Time complexity of this algorithm is O(n). Space complexity is O(n) for hashtable.

Odd Count Element

Problem: Given an array in which all the elements appear even number of times except one, which appear odd number of times. Find the element which appear odd number of times.

First Solution: XOR approach, XOR all the elements of the array the elements which appear even number of times will cancel themselves. Finally, we will get the number we are searching.
Time Complexity of this algorithm is O(n). Space Complexity is O(1)

Second Solution: Use Hashtable to keep track of frequency. Then traverse the Hashtable to find the odd number of times appearing element.
Time Complexity of this algorithm is O(n). Space Complexity is O(n)

Example 5.14

```
function OddCount(arr, size) {
    const ctr = ({});
    let count = 0;
    let i;
    for (i = 0; i < size; i++) {
        if (ctr.has(arr[i]))
            ctr.set(arr[i], ctr.get(arr[i]) + 1);
        else
            ctr.set(arr[i], 1);
    }
    for (i = 0; i < size; i++) {
        if (ctr.has(arr[i]) && (ctr.get(arr[i]) % 2 == 1)) {
            console.info(arr[i]);
            count++;
        }
    }
    console.info(`Odd count is :: ${count}`);
};

function test() {
    const first = [1, 3, 2, 7, 2, 4, 3, 8, 9, 9, 4, 7, 1, 12];
    const size = first.length
    OddCount(first, size);
}
```

Output:
```
Odd count is :: 2
```

Odd Elements

Problem: Given an array in which all the elements appear even number of times except two, which appear odd number of times. Find the elements which appear odd number of times in O(n) time complexity and O(1) space complexity.

Solution:
- Since space complexity required is O(1) so we cannot use Hashtable.
- We know that when we xor all the elements of array then the even number of appearing elements will cancel themselves. So, we have sum of the two values we are searching for.
- If we can divide the array elements in two groups such that these two values go in different groups and then xor the values in these groups then we can get these values separately.
- As shown in the algorithm below right most set bit is used to separate these two elements.

Example 5.15:

```
function OddNumbers(arr, size) {
    let xorSum = 0;
    let first = 0;
    let second = 0;
    let setBit;
    for (var i = 0; i < size; i++) {
        xorSum = xorSum ^ arr[i];
    }
    setBit = xorSum & ~(xorSum - 1);
    for (var i = 0; i < size; i++) {
        if ((arr[i] & setBit) !== 0)
            first ^= arr[i];
        else
            second ^= arr[i];
    }
    console.info(first + second);
};

function test() {
    const first = [1, 3, 2, 7, 2, 4, 3, 8, 9, 9, 4, 7, 1, 12];
    const size = first.length
    OddNumbers(first, size);
}
```

Output:

```
12 8
```

Sum Distinct

Problem: Given an array of size N, the elements in the array may be repeated. You need to find sum of distinct elements of the array. If there is some value repeated then they should be added once.

Example 5.16:

```
function SumDistinct(arr, size) {
    let sum = 0;
    arr.sort(function cmp(a, b) { return (a - b); });
    for (let i = 0; i < (size - 1); i++) {
        if (arr[i] !== arr[i + 1])
            sum += arr[i];
    }
    sum += arr[size - 1];
    console.info(sum);
};

function test() {
    const first = [1, 3, 2, 7, 2, 4, 3, 8, 9, 9, 4, 7, 1, 12];
    const size = first.length
    SumDistinct(first, size)
}
```

Output:
46

Analysis: Sort the input array. Duplicate values will come adjacent. Create a sum variable and add only those values to it which are not equal to its next value.

Time Complexity of this algorithm is O(n). Space Complexity is O(1)

Two elements whose sum is closest to zero

Problem: In given List of integers, both +ve and -ve. You need to find the two elements such that their sum is closest to zero.

First Solution: Exhaustive search or Brute force; for each element in the array find the other element whose value when added will give minimum absolute value. This is done using two loops, first loop to select the element and second loop to find the element that should be added to it so that the absolute of the sum will be minimum or close to zero.

Time Complexity is $O(n^2)$ and Space Complexity is O(1)

Example 5.17:

```
function minabsSumPair(arr) {
    const size = arr.length;
    if (size < 2) {
        console.log("Invalid Input");
        return;
    }
    let minFirst = 0;
    let minSecond = 1;
    let sum;
    let minSum = Math.abs(arr[0] + arr[1]);
    for (let l = 0; l < size - 1; l++) {
        for (let r = l + 1; r < size; r++) {
            sum = Math.abs(arr[l] + arr[r]);
            if (sum < minSum) {
                minSum = sum;
                minFirst = l;
                minSecond = r;
            }
        }
    }
    console.log(`Elements with minimum sum are : ${arr[minFirst]} , $
{arr[minSecond]}`);
};

function test() {
    const first = [1, 3, 5, 7, 2, 4, -12, 8, -9, 9, 10];
    minabsSumPair(first);
}
```

Output:
```
Elements with minimum sum are : -9 , 9
```

Second Solution: Sorting
Steps are as follows:
1. Sort all the elements in the array.
2. Take two variable firstIndex = 0 and secondIndex = size -1
3. Compute sum = arr[firstIndex]+arr[secondIndex]
4. If the sum is equal to 0 then we have the solution
5. If the sum is less than 0 then we will increase first
6. If the sum is greater than 0 then we will decrease the second
7. We repeat the above process 3 to 6, until we get the desired pair or we get first >= second

Example 5.18:
```javascript
function minabsSumPair2(arr) {
    const size = arr.length;
    if (size < 2) {
        console.log("Invalid Input");
        return;
    }
    arr.sort(function cmp(a, b) { return (a - b); });
    let minFirst = 0;
    let minSecond = size - 1;
    let minSum = Math.abs(arr[minFirst] + arr[minSecond]);
    let sum;
    for (let l = 0, r = size - 1; l < r;) {
        sum = (arr[l] + arr[r]);
        if (Math.abs(sum) < minSum) {
            minSum = Math.abs(sum);
            minFirst = l;
            minSecond = r;
        }
        if (sum < 0) {
            l++;
        }
        else if (sum > 0) {
            r--;
        }
        else {
            break;
        }
    }
    console.log(` The two elements with minimum sum are : ${arr[minFirst]} ,
${arr[minSecond]}`);
};
```

Time Complexity is O(nlogn) and Space Complexity is O(1)

Find Pair in an array

Problem: Given an array of n numbers, find two elements such that their sum is equal to "value"

First Solution: Exhaustive search or Brute force, for each element in list find if there is some other element, which sums up to the desired value. This is done using two loops, first loop is to select the element and second loop is to find another element.

Time Complexity is $O(n^2)$ and Space Complexity is $O(1)$

Example 5.19

```
function FindPair(arr, value) {
    const size = arr.length;
    for (let i = 0; i < size; i++) {
        for (let j = i + 1; j < size; j++) {
            if ((arr[i] + arr[j]) === value) {
                console.log(`The pair is : ${arr[i]},${arr[j]}`);
                return 1;
            }
        }
    }
    return 0;
};

function test() {
    const first = [1, 3, 5, 7, 3, 14, 8, 9, 10];
    console.log(FindPair(first, 9));
}
```

Output:
```
The pair is : 1,8
true
```

Second Solution: Sorting, Steps are as follows:
1. Sort all the elements in the array.
2. Take two variables first and second. Variable first= 0 and second = size -1
3. Compute sum = arr[first]+arr[second]
4. If the sum is equal to the desired value, then we have the solution
5. If the sum is less than the desired value, then we will increase the first
6. If the sum is greater than the desired value, then we will decrease the second
7. We repeat the above process until we get the desired pair or we get first >= second

Sorting algorithms takes $O(n.logn)$ time and single scan takes $O(n)$ time.
Time Complexity is $O(n.logn)$ and Space Complexity is $O(1)$

Example 5.20:
```
function FindPair2(arr, value) {
    let first = 0;
    const size = arr.length;
    let second = size - 1;
```

```
    let curr;
    arr.sort(function cmp(a, b) { return (a - b); });
    while (first < second) {
        curr = arr[first] + arr[second];
        if (curr === value) {
            console.log(`The pair is ${arr[first]},${arr[second]}`);
            return 1;
        }
        else if (curr < value) {
            first++;
        }
        else {
            second--;
        }
    };
    return 0;
};
```

Third Solution: Hash-Table, using Hash-Table; we can keep track of the elements we have already seen and we can find the pair in just one scan.

1. For each element, insert the value in Hashtable. Let's say current value is arr[index]
2. If value - arr[index] is in the Hashtable then we have the desired pair.
3. Else, proceed to the next entry in the array.

Hash-Table insertion and finding take constant time O(1) so the total time complexity of the algorithm is O(n) time. Space Complexity is also O(n)

Example 5.21:
```
function FindPair3(arr, value) {
    const hs = {};
    const size = arr.length;
    for (let i = 0; i < size; i++) {
        if ((value - arr[i]) in hs) {
            console.log(`The pair is : ${arr[i]} , ${value - arr[i]}`);
            return 1;
        }
        hs[arr[i]] = 1;
    }
    return 0;
};
```

Forth Solution: Counting approach, this approach is only possible if we know the range of the input. If we know that, the elements in the array are in the range 0 to n. We can reserve an array of length n and when we see an element, we can increase its count. In place of the Hashtable in the above approach, we will use this list and will find out the pair.

Counting approach just uses an array so insertion and finding take constant time O(1) so the total time complexity of the algorithm is O(n) time. Space Complexity for creating count list is also O(n)

Find the Pair in two Lists

Problem: Given two list X and Y. Find a pair of elements (x_i, y_i) such that $x_i \in X$ and $y_i \in Y$ where $x_i + y_i =$ value.

First Solution: Exhaustive search or Brute force; loop through element x_i of X and see if you can find (value – x_i) in Y. This is done using two loops, first loop is to select an element from X and second loop is to find its corresponding value in Y.

Time Complexity is $O(n^2)$ and Space Complexity is $O(1)$

Second Solution: Sorting; Sort all the elements in the second list Y. For each element of X you can see if that element is there in Y by using binary search.

Sorting algorithms take $O(m.logm)$ and searching will take $O(n.logm)$ time.
Time Complexity is $O(n.logm)$ or $O(m.logm)$ and Space Complexity is $O(1)$

Third Solution: Sorting, Steps are as follows:
1. Sort the elements of both X and Y in increasing order.
2. Take the sum of the smallest element of X and the largest element of Y.
3. If the sum is equal to the value, we got our pair.
4. If the sum is smaller than value, take next element of X
5. If the sum is greater than value, take the previous element of Y

Sorting algorithms take $O(n.logn) + O(m.logm)$ for sorting and searching will take $O(n+m)$ time.
Time Complexity is $O(n.logn)$ and Space Complexity is $O(1)$

Forth Solution: Hash-Table, Steps are as follows:
1. Scan through all the elements in the array Y and insert them into Hashtable.
2. Now scan through all the elements of list X, let us suppose the current element is x_i see if you can find (value - x_i) in the Hashtable.
3. If you find the value, you got your pair.
4. If not, then go to the next value in the array X.

Hash-Table insertion and finding take constant time $O(1)$ so the total time complexity of the algorithm is $O(n)$ time. Space Complexity is also $O(n)$

Fifth Solution: Counting; this approach is only possible if we know the range of the input. Same as Hashtable implementation just use a simple list in place of Hashtable and you are done.
Counting approach just uses an array so insertion and finding take constant time $O(1)$ so the total time complexity of the algorithm is $O(n)$ time. Space Complexity for creating count list is also $O(n)$

Find Difference Pair

Problem: In an array of positive integers, find a pair whose absolute value of difference is equal to a given value.

First Solution: Brute force, find all the possible pair and find if absolute value of their difference is equal to the given value. Time complexity will $O(n^2)$

Example 5.22:
```
function FindDifference(arr, size, value) {
    for (let i = 0; i < size; i++) {
        for (let j = i + 1; j < size; j++) {
            if (Math.abs(arr[i] - arr[j]) === value) {
                console.info(`The pair is:: ${arr[i]} & ${arr[j]}`);
                return true;
            }
        }
    }
    return false;
};

function test() {
    const first = [1, 5, 4, 3, 2, 7, 8, 9, 6];
    console.info(FindDifference(first, first.length, 6));
};
```

Output:
```
The pair is:: 1 & 7
true
```

Second Solution: Using sorting, the performance can be improved by sorting the array. We take two indices from start of the array at index 0, call them first and second. When difference of values is less than the desired value then we increase the second index or if the value if difference is grater then the desired value, we increase the first index. Time complexity is O(nlogn)which is for sorting operation.

Example 5.23:
```
function FindDifference2(arr, size, value) {
    let first = 0;
    let second = 0;
    let diff;
    arr.sort(function cmp(a, b) { return (a - b); });
    while (first < size && second < size) {
        diff = Math.abs(arr[first] - arr[second]);
        if (diff === value) {
            console.info(`The pair is::${arr[first]} & ${arr[second]}`);
            return true;
        }
        else if (diff > value)
            first += 1;
        else
            second += 1;
    }
    return false;
};
```

Find Min Diff

Problem: Given an array of integers, find the element pair with minimum difference.

First Solution: you can always pick two elements, find difference between them, and find the elements with minimum difference using two loops and comparing each pair. Time complexity is O(n²)

Second Solution: This performance can be improved by sorting the array. Since we need minimum sum so the pair which we are searching is adjacent to each other. Time complexity is O(nlogn)

Example 5.24

```
function findMinDiff(arr, size) {
    arr.sort(function cmp(a, b) { return (a - b); });
    let diff = 9999999;
    for (let i = 0; i < (size - 1); i++) {
        if ((arr[i + 1] - arr[i]) < diff)
            diff = arr[i + 1] - arr[i];
    }
    return diff;
};

function test() {
    const first = [1, 5, 4, 3, 2, 7, 8, 9, 6];
    console.info(findMinDiff(first, first.length));
};
```

Output:

```
1
```

Minimum Difference Pair

Problem: Given two arrays, find minimum difference pair such that it should take one element from each array.

First Solution: Brute force solution, you can always pick two elements, one form the first array and another from second array. Then find their difference to find minimum difference. Time complexity is O(nm)

Second Solution: This performance can be improved by sorting the arrays. Since we need minimum difference pair. We will pick one element form first array and find its difference from one element form second array. If the difference is negative then we will increase index of first array and if the difference id positive then we will increase index of second array.

Time Complexity is O(nlogn + mlogm) for sorting and O(n+m) for comparison.
Total time complexity: O(nlogn + mlogm)

Example 5.25

```
function MinDiffPair(arr1, size1, arr2, size2) {
    let minDiff = 9999999;
    let first = 0;
    let second = 0;
    let out1 = 0;
    let out2 = 0;
```

```
    let diff;
    arr1.sort(function cmp(a, b) { return (a - b); });
    arr2.sort(function cmp(a, b) { return (a - b); });
    while (first < size1 && second < size2) {
        diff = Math.abs(arr1[first] - arr2[second]);
        if (minDiff > diff) {
            minDiff = diff;
            out1 = arr1[first];
            out2 = arr2[second];
        }
        if (arr1[first] < arr2[second])
            first += 1;
        else
            second += 1;
    }
    console.info(`The pair is :: ${out1}, ${out2}`);
    console.info(`Minimum difference is :: ${minDiff}`);
    return minDiff;
};

function test() {
    const first = [1, 5, 4, 3, 2, 7, 8, 9, 6];
    const second = [3, 2, 7, 8, 9, 6];
    console.info(MinDiffPair(first, first.length, second, second.length));
};
```

Output:
```
The pair is :: 2,2
Minimum difference is :: 0
0
```

Closest Pair

Problem: Given an array of positive integers and a number. You need to find a pair in array whose sum is closest to given number.

First Solution: Brute force, for each pair find their sum and get its absolute difference from the given value. This can be done using two loops. Time complexity is $O(n^2)$

Example 5.26
```
function ClosestPair(arr, size, value) {
    let diff = 999999;
    let first = -1;
    let second = -1;
    let curr;
    for (let i = 0; i < size; i++) {
        for (let j = i + 1; j < size; j++) {
            curr = Math.abs(value - (arr[i] + arr[j]));
            if (curr < diff) {
                diff = curr;
```

```
                first = arr[i];
                second = arr[j];
            }
        }
    }
    console.info(`closest pair is ::${first}${second}`);
};

function test() {
    const first = [1, 5, 4, 3, 2, 7, 8, 9, 6];
    ClosestPair(first, first.length, 6);
};
```

Output:
```
closest pair is :: 1, 5
```

Second Solution: Sorting, performance of above solution can be improved by sorting the array. Since we need a pair whose sum is closest to the given value. We start two index one from start and other from end. Add these two index values call it current. If the current sum is grater then than the given value then decreases the end index and if the current sum is smaller than the value then we increase the start index.

Time complexity is O(nlogn) for sorting and O(n) for searching pair. So overall Time complexity is O(nlogn)

Example 5.27:
```
function ClosestPair2(arr, size, value) {
    let first = 0;
    let second = 0;
    let start = 0;
    let stop = size - 1;
    let diff;
    let curr;
    arr.sort(function cmp(a, b) { return (a - b); })
    diff = 9999999;
    while (start < stop) {
        curr = (value - (arr[start] + arr[stop]));
        if (Math.abs(curr) < diff) {
            diff = Math.abs(curr);
            first = arr[start];
            second = arr[stop];
        }
        if (curr === 0) {
            break;
        }
        else if (curr > 0) {
            start += 1;
        }
        else {
            stop -= 1;
```

```
        }
    }
    console.info(`closest pair is :: ${first}, ${second}`);
};
```

Sum of Pair Equal to Rest Array

Problem: Given an array find if there is a pair whose sum is equal to the sum of rest of the elements of the array.

Solution: Sort the array. Sum all the elements of the array call this value total. Find a pair in the sorted array whose sum is total/2. Total time complexity is O(nlogn).

Example 5.28
```
function SumPairRestArray(arr, size) {
    var total;
    let curr;
    arr.sort(function cmp(a, b) { return (a - b); });
    var total = 0;
    for (let i = 0; i < size; i++) {
        total += arr[i];
    }
    value = Math.floor(total / 2);
    let low = 0;
    let high = size - 1;
    while (low < high) {
        curr = arr[low] + arr[high];
        if (curr === value) {
            console.info(`Pair is :: ${arr[low]}${arr[high]}`);
            return true;
        }
        else if (curr < value)
            low += 1;
        else
            high -= 1;
    }
    return false;
};

function test() {
    const first = [1, 2, 4, 3, 7, 3];
    SumPairRestArray(first, first.length);
};
```

Output:
```
Pair is :: 3, 7
```

Zero Sum Triplets

Problem: Given an array of integers, you need to find a triplet whose sum 0.

First Solution: Brute force, for each triplet find their sum. This can be done using three loops. Time complexity is $O(n^3)$

Example 5.29:

```
function ZeroSumTriplets(arr, size) {
    for (let i = 0; i < (size - 2); i++) {
        for (let j = i + 1; j < (size - 1); j++) {
            for (let k = j + 1; k < size; k++) {
                if (arr[i] + arr[j] + arr[k] === 0)
                    console.info(`Triplet :: ${arr[i]}${arr[j]}${arr[k]}`);
            }
        }
    }
};

function test() {
    const first = [1, 2, -4, 3, 7, -3];
    ZeroSumTriplets(first, first.length);
    console.info()
    ZeroSumTriplets2(first, first.length);
};
```

Output:

```
Triplet :: 1, 2, -3
Triplet :: 1, -4, 3
Triplet :: -4, 7, -3
```

Second Solution: We can increase performance by sorting. Sort the given array. Select element from the array in a loop and then find other two values such that their sum is negative of the first value. Time complexity is $O(n^2)$

Example 5.30:

```
function ZeroSumTriplets2(arr, size) {
    let start;
    let stop;
    arr.sort(function cmp(a, b) { return (a - b); });
    for (let i = 0; i < (size - 2); i++) {
        start = i + 1;
        stop = size - 1;
        while (start < stop) {
            if (arr[i] + arr[start] + arr[stop] === 0) {
                console.info(`Triplet :: ${arr[i]}${arr[start]}$
{arr[stop]}`);
                start += 1;
                stop -= 1;
            }
```

```
                else if (arr[i] + arr[start] + arr[stop] > 0)
                    stop -= 1;
                else
                    start += 1;
        }
    }
};
```

Find Triplet

Problem: Given an array of integers, you need to find a triplet whose sum equal to given value.

First Solution: Brute force, for each triplet find their sum. This can be done using three loops. Time complexity is $O(n^3)$

Example 5.31:
```
function findTriplet(arr, size, value) {
    for (let i = 0; i < (size - 2); i++) {
        for (let j = i + 1; j < (size - 1); j++) {
            for (let k = j + 1; k < size; k++) {
                {
                    if ((arr[i] + arr[j] + arr[k]) === value)
                        console.info(`Triplet :: ${arr[i]}${arr[j]}$
{arr[k]}`);
                };
            };
        };
    }
};

function test() {
    const first = [1, 2, -4, 3, 7, -3];
    findTriplet(first, first.length, 6);
    findTriplet2(first, first.length, 6);
};
```

Output:
```
Triplet :: 1, 2, 3
Triplet :: 2, 7, -3
Triplet :: -4, 3, 7
```

Second Solution: We can increase performance by sorting. Sort the given array. Select first element from the array in a loop and then find other two values such that sum of all three is equal to the given value. Time complexity is $O(n^2)$

Example 5.32:
```
function findTriplet2(arr, size, value) {
    let start;
    let stop;
    arr.sort(function cmp(a, b) { return (a - b); });
```

```
    for (let i = 0; i < size - 2; i++) {
        start = i + 1;
        stop = size - 1;
        while (start < stop) {
            if (arr[i] + arr[start] + arr[stop] === value) {
                console.info(`Triplet ::${arr[i]}${arr[start]}$
{arr[stop]}`);
                start += 1;
                stop -= 1;
            }
            else if (arr[i] + arr[start] + arr[stop] > value)
                stop -= 1;
            else
                start += 1;
        }
    }
};
```

A+B = C Triplet

Problem: Given an array of integers, you need to find a triplet such that sum of two elements of triplet is equal to the third value. We need to find triplet (A, B, C) such that A+B = C.

First Solution: Brute force, for each triplet find if constraint A+B=C satisfies. This can be done using three loops. Time complexity is O(n^3)

Second Solution: We can increase performance by sorting. Sort the given array in decreasing order. Select first element from the array in a loop and then find other two values such that sum of these two is equal to the first value.
Time complexity is O(n^2)

Example 5.33:
```
function ABCTriplet(arr, size) {
    let start;
    let stop;
    arr.sort(function cmp(a, b) { return (a - b); });
    for (let i = 0; i < (size - 1); i++) {
        start = 0;
        stop = size - 1;
        while (start < stop) {
            if (arr[i] === arr[start] + arr[stop]) {
                console.info(`Triplet :: ${arr[i]}, ${arr[start]}, $
{arr[stop]}`);
                start += 1;
                stop -= 1;
            }
            else if (arr[i] < arr[start] + arr[stop])
                stop -= 1;
            else
                start += 1;
```

```
        }
    }
};

function test() {
    const first = [1, 2, -4, 3, 8, -3];
    ABCTriplet(first, first.length);
};
```

Output:
```
Triplet :: 3, 1, 2
```

Smaller than triplets Count

Problem: Given an array of integers, you need to find a triplet such that sum of elements of triplet is less than the value. We need to find triplets (A, B, C) such that A+B+C < value.

First Solution: Brute force, for each triplet find if constraint A+B+C < value satisfies. This can be done using three loops. Time complexity is $O(n^3)$

Second Solution: We can increase performance by sorting. Sort the given array. Select first element from the array in a loop and then find other two values such that sum of all three is less than the given value. Time complexity is $O(n^2)$

Example 5.34:
```
function SmallerThenTripletCount(arr, size, value) {
    let start;
    let stop;
    let count = 0;
    arr.sort(function cmp(a, b) { return (a - b); });
    for (let i = 0; i < (size - 2); i++) {
        start = i + 1;
        stop = size - 1;
        while (start < stop) {
            if (arr[i] + arr[start] + arr[stop] >= value)
                stop -= 1;
            else {
                count += stop - start;
                start += 1;
            }
        }
    }
    console.info(count);
};

function test() {
    const first = [1, 2, -4, 3, 7, -3];
    SmallerThenTripletCount(first, first.length, 6);
};
```

Output:
```
13
```

Arithmetic progression triplet

Problem: Given a sorted array find all Arithmetic progression triplet possible.

Example 5.35:
```
function APTriplets(arr, size) {
    let j;
    let k;
    for (let i = 1; i < size - 1; i++) {
        j = i - 1;
        k = i + 1;
        while (j >= 0 && k < size) {
            if (arr[j] + arr[k] === 2 * arr[i]) {
                console.info(`Triplet ::${arr[j]}${arr[i]}${arr[k]}`);
                k += 1;
                j -= 1;
            }
            else if (arr[j] + arr[k] < 2 * arr[i])
                k += 1;
            else
                j -= 1;
        }
    }
};

function test() {
    const first = [1, 2, 3, 4, 9, 17, 23];
    APTriplets(first, first.length);
};
```

Output:
```
AP Triplet ::1, 2, 3
AP Triplet ::2, 3, 4
AP Triplet ::1, 9, 17
```

Geometric Progression Triplet

Problem: Given a sorted array find all geometric progression triplet possible.

Example 5.36:
```
function GPTriplets(arr, size) {
    let j;
    let k;
    for (let i = 1; i < size - 1; i++) {
        j = i - 1;
        k = i + 1;
```

```
        while (j >= 0 && k < size) {
            if (arr[j] * arr[k] === arr[i] * arr[i]) {
                console.info(`Triplet is :: ${arr[j]}${arr[i]}${arr[k]}`);
                k += 1;
                j -= 1;
            }
            else if (arr[j] + arr[k] < 2 * arr[i])
                k += 1;
            else
                j -= 1;
        }
    }
};

function test() {
    const first = [1, 2, 3, 4, 9, 17, 23];
    GPTriplets(first, first.length);
};
```

Output:
```
GP Triplet is :: 1, 2, 4
GP Triplet is :: 1, 3, 9
```

Number of Triangles

Problem: Given an array of positive integers representing edges of triangles. Find the number of triangles that can be formed from these elements representing sides of triangles. For a triangle sum of two edges is always greater than third edge.
Input: [1, 2, 3, 4, 5]
Output: 3,   Corresponds to (2, 3, 4) (2, 4, 5) (3, 4, 5)

First Solution: Brute force solution, by picking all the triplets and then checking if the triangle property holds. Time Complexity is $O(n^3)$

Example 5.37:
```
function numberOfTriangles(arr, size) {
    let count = 0;
    for (let i = 0; i <= (size - 3); i++) {
        for (let j = i + 1; j <= (size - 2); j++) {
            for (let k = j + 1; k <= size-1; k++) {
                if ((arr[i] + arr[j] > arr[k]) && (arr[k] + arr[j] > arr[i])
&& (arr[i] + arr[k] > arr[j])){
                    count += 1;
                }
            }
        }
    }
    return count;
};
```

```
function test() {
    const first = [1, 2, 5, 4, 3, 6];
    console.log(numberOfTriangles(first, first.length));
};
```

Output:

```
7
```

Second Solution: This solution takes advantage of one simple property. In a sorted array, If sum of arr[i] & arr[j] is greater arr[k] then sum of arr[i] & arr[j+1] is also greater than arr[k]. This improvement makes time complexity of this algorithm as $O(n^2)$

Example 5.38:

```
function numberOfTriangles2(arr, size) {
    let k;
    let count = 0;
    arr.sort(function cmp(a, b) { return (a - b); });
    for (let i = 0; i < (size - 2); i++) {
        k = i + 2;
        for (let j = i + 1; j < (size - 1); j++) {
            while (k < size && arr[i] + arr[j] > arr[k]) {
                k += 1;
            };
            count += k - j - 1;
        }
    }
    return count;
};
```

Find max appearing element in an array

Problem: In given list of n numbers, find the element, which appears maximum number of times.

First Solution: Exhaustive search or Brute force; for each element in array, find how many times this value appears in array. Keep track of the maxCount and when some element count is greater than maxCount then update the maxCount. This is done using two loops, first loop to select the element and second loop to count the occurrence of that element.
Time Complexity is $O(n^2)$ and Space Complexity is $O(1)$

Example 5.39:

```
function getMax(arr) {
    let max = arr[0];
    const size = arr.length;
    let count = 1;
    let maxCount = 1;
    for (let i = 0; i < size; i++) {
        count = 1;
        for (let j = i + 1; j < size; j++) {
            if (arr[i] === arr[j]) {
                count++;
```

```
            }
        }
        if (count > maxCount) {
            max = arr[i];
            maxCount = count;
        }
    }
    return max;
};

function test() {
    const first = [1, 3, 5, 3, 1, 2, 4, 2, 2];
    console.log(getMax(first));
};
```

Output:

```
2
```

Second Solution: Sorting; Sort all the elements in the array. In a single scan, we can find the counts. Sorting algorithms takes O(n.logn) time and single scan takes O(n) time.

Time Complexity is O(n.logn) and Space Complexity is O(1)

Example 5.40:

```
function getMax2(arr) {
    let max = arr[0];
    const size = arr.length;
    let maxCount = 1;
    let curr = arr[0];
    let currCount = 1;
    arr.sort(function cmp(a, b) { return (a - b); });
    for (let i = 1; i < size; i++) {
        if (arr[i] === arr[i - 1]) {
            currCount++;
        }
        else {
            currCount = 1;
            curr = arr[i];
        }
        if (currCount > maxCount) {
            maxCount = currCount;
            max = curr;
        }
    }
    return max;
};
```

Third Solution: Counting, this approach is possible only if we know the range of the input. If we know that, the elements in the array are in the range 0 to n-1. We can traverse an array of length n and when we see an element, we can increase its count. In just one single scan, we know the duplicates. If we know the range of the elements, then this is the fastest way to find the max count.

Counting approach just uses list so to increase count take constant time O(1) so the total time complexity of the algorithm is O(n) time. Space Complexity for creating count list is also O(n)

Example 5.41:

```
function getMax3(arr, range) {
    let max = arr[0];
    const size = arr.length;
    let maxCount = 1;
    const count = new Array(range).fill(0);
    for (let i = 0; i < size; i++) {
        count[arr[i]]++;
        if (count[arr[i]] > maxCount) {
            maxCount = count[arr[i]];
            max = arr[i];
        }
    }
    return max;
};
```

Majority element in an array

Problem: In given an array of n elements. Find the majority element, which appears more than n/2 times. Return 0 in case there is no majority element.

First Solution: Exhaustive search or Brute force, for each element in array find how many times its value appears in array. Keep track of the maxCount and when some element count is greater than maxCount then update the maxCount. This is done using two loops, first loop to select the element and second loop to count the occurrence of that element. If the final maxCount is greater than n/2 we have a majority otherwise we do not have any majority.

Time Complexity is $O(n^2) + O(1) = O(n^2)$ and Space Complexity is O(1)

Example 5.42:

```
function getMajority(arr) {
    const size = arr.length;
    let max = 0;
    let count = 0;
    let maxCount = 0;
    for (let i = 0; i < size; i++) {
        count = 1;
        for (let j = i + 1; j < size; j++) {
            if (arr[i] === arr[j]) {
                count++;
            }
        }
```

```
        if (count > maxCount) {
            max = arr[i];
            maxCount = count;
        }
    }
    if (maxCount > Math.floor(size / 2)) {
        return max;
    }
    else {
        return 0;
    }
};

function test() {
    const first = [1, 3, 5, 3, 1, 2, 4, 2, 2, 2, 2, 2, 2];
    console.log(getMajority(first));
}
```

Output:

2

Second Solution: Sorting, Sort all the elements in the array. If there is a majority then the middle element at the index n/2 must be the majority number. So, just single scan can be used to find its count and see if the majority is there or not.

Sorting algorithms take O(n.logn) time and single scan take O(n) time.
Time Complexity is O(n.logn) and Space Complexity is O(1)

Example 5.43:

```
function getMajority2(arr) {
    const size = arr.length;
    const majIndex = Math.floor(size / 2);
    let count = 0;
    let i;
    let candidate;
    arr.sort(function cmp(a, b) { return (a - b); });
    candidate = arr[majIndex];
    for (i = 0; i < size; i++) {
        if (arr[i] === candidate) {
            count++;
        }
    }
    if (count > Math.floor(size / 2)) {
        return arr[majIndex];
    }
    else {
        return 0;
    }
};
```

Third Solution: This is a cancellation approach (Moore's Voting Algorithm), if all the elements stand against the majority and each element is cancelled with one element of majority, if there is majority then majority prevails.

- Set the first element of the array as majority candidate and initialize the count to be 1.
- Start scanning the array.
  - o If we get some element whose value is same as a majority candidate, then we increase the count.
  - o If we get an element whose value is different from the majority candidate, then we decrement the count.
  - o If count become 0, that means we have a new majority candidate. Make the current candidate as majority candidate and reset count to 1.
  - o At the end, we will have the only probable majority candidate.
- Now scan through the array once again to see if that candidate we found above have appeared more than n/2 times.

Counting approach just scans throw list two times. Time Complexity is O(n) time. Space Complexity for creating count list is also O(1)

Example 5.44:

```
function getMajority3(arr) {
    const size = arr.length;
    let majIndex = 0;
    let count = 1;
    let i;
    let candidate;

    for (i = 1; i < size; i++) {
        if (arr[majIndex] === arr[i]) {
            count++;
        }
        else {
            count--;
        }
        if (count === 0) {
            majIndex = i;
            count = 1;
        }
    }

    candidate = arr[majIndex];
    count = 0;
    for (i = 0; i < size; i++) {
        if (arr[i] === candidate) {
            count++;
        }
    }

    if (count > Math.floor(size / 2)) {
        return arr[majIndex];
    }
```

```
        else {
            return 0;
        }
};
```

Is Majority

Problem: Given a sorted array find if there is a majority and find the majority element.

First Solution: Using brute force traversal of the array we can find the number of occurrences of the middle element in the array. If number of occurrences is not greater than or equal to ceil of count/2 then there is no majority.

Time complexity is O(N)

Second Solution: Since the array is sorted our first thought should be binary search. We can find the probable majority candidate at size/2 location. Then we need to find its first occurrence in the sorted array say it index i. Then once we have index i then if majority exists then element at index i+n/2 also last value same as majority candidate.

Time complexity is O(logN)

Example 5.45:
```
function isMajority(arr, size) {
    const majority = arr[Math.floor(size / 2)];
    const i = FirstIndex(arr, size, 0, size - 1, majority);
    if (((i + size / 2) <= (size - 1)) && arr[i + Math.floor(size / 2)] ===
majority)
        return true;
    else
        return false;
};

function test() {
    const first = [1, 3, 5, 3, 1, 2, 4, 2, 2, 2, 2, 2, 2];
    console.log(isMajority(first, first.length))
}
```

Output:
```
true
```

Find 2nd largest number in an array with minimum comparisons

Problem: Suppose you are given an unsorted list of n distinct element. How will you identify the second largest element with minimum number of comparisons?

First Solution: Find the largest element in the array. Then replace the last element with the largest element. Then search the second largest element in the remaining n-1 elements.

The total number of comparisons is: (n-1) + (n-2)

Second Solution: Sort the array and then give the (n-1) element. This approach is still more inefficient.

Third Solution: Using priority queue / Heap; in this approach, we will study heap chapter. Use buildHeap() function to build heap from the array. This is done in n comparisons. Arr[0] is the largest number, and the greater among arr[1] and arr[2] is the second largest.
The total number of comparisons are: (n-1) + 1 = n

Find a median of an array

Problem: In an unsorted list of numbers of size n, if all the elements of the array are sorted then find the element, which lie at the index n/2.

First Solution: Sort the array and return the element in the middle.
Sorting algorithms takes O(n.logn).
Time Complexity is O(n.logn) and Space Complexity is O(1)

Example 5.46:
```
function getMedian(arr) {
    const size = arr.length;
    arr.sort(function cmp(a, b) { return (a - b); });
    const mid = Math.floor(size / 2);
    return arr[mid];
};

function test() {
    const first = [10, 10, 5, 7, 9, 11, 12, 8, 5, 3, 10];
    console.log(`median value is :: ${getMedian(first)}`);
}
```

Output:
```
median value is :: 9
```

Second Solution: Use QuickSelect algorithm. This algorithm we will look in the next chapter.

The Average case time complexity of this algorithm will be O(n)

Find maxima in a bitonic list

Problem: A bitonic list comprises of an increasing sequence of integers immediately followed by a decreasing sequence of integers.

First Solution: Sequential search, traverse through the array and find a point at which the next value is less than the current value. This is the maxima and return this value.

Second Solution: Binary search method, since the elements are sorted in some order, we should go for algorithm like binary search.

The steps are as follows:
1. Take two variables for storing start and end index. Variable start=0 and end=size-1
2. Find the middle element of the array.
3. See if the middle element is the maxima. If yes, return the middle element.
4. Alternatively, if the middle element is in increasing part, then we need to look for in mid+1 and end.
5. Alternatively, if the middle element is in the decreasing part, then we need to look in the start and mid-1.
6. Repeat step 2 to 5 until we get the maxima.

Example 5.47:

```
function FindMaxBitonicArray(arr) {
    const size = arr.length;
    let start = 0;
    let end = size - 1;
    let mid;
    if (size < 3) {
        console.log("error");
        return -1;
    }
    while (start <= end) {
        mid = Math.floor((start + end) / 2);
        if (arr[mid - 1] < arr[mid] && arr[mid + 1] < arr[mid]) {
            return mid;
        }
        else if (arr[mid - 1] < arr[mid] && arr[mid] < arr[mid + 1]) {
            start = mid + 1;
        }
        else if (arr[mid - 1] > arr[mid] && arr[mid] > arr[mid + 1]) {
            end = mid - 1;
        }
        else {
            break;
        }
    };
    console.log("NoMaximaFound");
    return -1;
};

function test() {
    const first = [1, 3, 5, 7, 9, 11, 12, 8, 5, 3, 1];
    console.log(FindMaxBitonicArray(first));
}
```

Output:
6

Note:- This algorithm works with strictly increasing then decreasing bitonic array. If there are repetitive values then this algorithm will fail.

Search element in a bitonic list

Problem: A bitonic list comprises of an increasing sequence of integers immediately followed by a decreasing sequence of integers. Find an element in a bitonic list.

Solution: To search an element in a bitonic list:
1. Find the index or maximum element in the array. By finding the end of increasing part of the array, using binary search.
2. Once we have the maximum element, search the given value in increasing part of the array using binary search.
3. If the value is not found in increasing part, search the same value in decreasing part of the array using binary search.

Example 5.48:
```
function SearchBitonicArray(arr, key) {
    const size = arr.length;
    const max = FindMaxBitonicArray(arr);
    let k = BinarySearch(arr, 0, max, key, true);
    if (k !== -1) {
        return true;
    }
    k = BinarySearch(arr, max + 1, size - 1, key, false);
    if (k !== -1) {
        return true;
    }
    return false;
};

function test() {
    const first = [1, 3, 5, 7, 9, 11, 12, 8, 5, 3, 1];
    console.log(SearchBitonicArray(first, 8));
}
```

Output:
```
true
```

Occurrence counts in sorted List

Problem: Given a sorted list arr[] find the number of occurrences of a number.

First Solution: Brute force, Traverse the array and in linear time we will get the occurrence count of the number. This is done using one loop.

Time Complexity is O(n) and Space Complexity is O(1)

Example 5.49:
```
function findKeyCount(arr, key) {
    const size = arr.length;
    let count = 0;
    for (let i = 0; i < size; i++) {
```

```
            if (arr[i] === key) {
                count++;
            }
        }
    return count;
};

function test() {
    const first = [1, 3, 5, 6, 6, 6, 6, 7, 9];
    console.info(findKeyCount(first, 6));
};
```

Output:

```
4
```

Second Solution: Since we have sorted list, we should think about some binary search.
1. First, we should find the first occurrence of the key.
2. Then we should find the last occurrence of the key.
3. Take the difference of these two values and you will have the solution.

Example 5.50:

```
function findKeyCount2(arr, key) {
    const size = arr.length;
    const firstIndex = findFirstIndex(arr, 0, size - 1, key);
    const lastIndex = findLastIndex(arr, 0, size - 1, key);
    return (lastIndex - firstIndex + 1);
};

function findFirstIndex(arr, start, end, key) {
    if (end < start) {
        return -1;
    }
    const mid = Math.floor((start + end) / 2);
    if (key === arr[mid] && (mid === start || arr[mid - 1] !== key)) {
        return mid;
    }
    if (key <= arr[mid]) {
        return findFirstIndex(arr, start, mid - 1, key);
    }
    else {
        return findFirstIndex(arr, mid + 1, end, key);
    }
};

function findLastIndex(arr, start, end, key) {
    if (end < start) {
        return -1;
    }

    const mid = Math.floor((start + end) / 2);
```

```
    if (key === arr[mid] && (mid === end || arr[mid + 1] !== key)) {
        return mid;
    }
    if (key < arr[mid]) {
        return findLastIndex(arr, start, mid - 1, key);
    }
    else {
        return findLastIndex(arr, mid + 1, end, key);
    }
};
```

Stock purchase-sell

Problem: In given list, in which nth element is the price of the stock on nth day. You are asked to buy once and sell once, on what date you will be buying and at what date you will be selling to get maximum profit.

Or

In given list of numbers, you need to maximize the difference between two numbers, such that you can subtract the number, which appears before form the number that appear after it.

First Solution: Brute force; for each element in the array, find other element whose difference is maximum or for which profit is maximum. This is done using two loops, first loop to select buy date index and the second loop to find its selling date entry.
Time Complexity is $O(n^2)$ and Space Complexity is $O(1)$

Second Solution: Another clever solution is to keep track of the smallest value seen so far from the start. At each point, we can find the difference and keep track of the maximum profit. This is a linear solution.

Time Complexity is $O(n)$ time. Space Complexity for creating count list is also $O(1)$

Example 5.51:
```
function maxProfit(stocks) {
    const size = stocks.length;
    let buy = 0;
    let sell = 0;
    let curMin = 0;
    let currProfit = 0;
    let maxProfit = 0;

    for (let i = 0; i < size; i++) {
        if (stocks[i] < stocks[curMin]) {
            curMin = i;
        }
        currProfit = stocks[i] - stocks[curMin];
        if (currProfit > maxProfit) {
            buy = curMin;
            sell = i;
            maxProfit = currProfit;
        }
```

```
    }
    console.log(`Purchase day is- ${buy} at price ${stocks[buy]}`);
    console.log(`Sell day is- ${sell} at price ${stocks[sell]}`);
};

function test() {
    const first = [10, 10, 5, 7, 9, 11, 12, 8, 5, 3, 10];
    maxProfit(first);
}
```

Output:
```
Purchase day is- 2 at price 5
Sell day is- 6 at price 12
```

Find median of two sorted Lists.

Problem: Given two sorted lists. Find the median of the arrays if they are combined to form a bigger list.

First Solution: We need to Keep track of the index of both the array, say the index are i and j. keep increasing the index of the array which ever have a smaller value. Use a counter to keep track of the elements that we have already traced. Once count is equal to the half of the combined length of two lists, we have our median.

Time Complexity is O(n) and Space Complexity is O(1)

Example 5.52:
```
function findMedian(arrFirst, arrSecond) {
    const sizeFirst = arrFirst.length;
    const sizeSecond = arrSecond.length;
    const medianIndex = Math.ceil((sizeFirst + sizeSecond) / 2);
    let i = 0;
    let j = 0;
    let count = 0;

    while (count < medianIndex - 1) {
        if (i < sizeFirst - 1 && arrFirst[i] < arrSecond[j]) {
            i++;
        }
        else {
            j++;
        }
        count++;
    };
    if (arrFirst[i] < arrSecond[j]) {
        return arrFirst[i];
    }
    else {
        return arrSecond[j];
    }
};
```

```
function test() {
    const first = [10, 10, 5, 7, 9, 11];
    const second = [12, 8, 5, 3, 10];
    first.sort(function cmp(a, b) { return (a - b); });
    second.sort(function cmp(a, b) { return (a - b); });
    console.log(`median value is :: ${findMedian(first, second)}`);
}
```

Output:
```
median value is :: 7
```

Search 01 List

Problem: In given list of 0's and 1's in which all the 0's come before 1's. Write an algorithm to find the index of the first 1.

Or

You are given an array which contains either 0 or 1, and they are in sorted order Ex. a [] = {0, 0, 0, 1, 1, 1, 1}, How will you count no of 1's and 0's?

First Solution: Linear Search, we can always find the index of first 1 in the array using traversal.
Time Complexity is O(n) and Space Complexity is O(1)

Second Solution: Binary Search, since the array is sorted using binary search to find the desired index.

Time Complexity is O(logn) and Space Complexity is O(1)

Example 5.53:
```
function BinarySearch01(arr) {
    const size = arr.length;
    if (size === 0) {
        return 0;
    }
    return BinarySearch01Util(arr, 0, size - 1);
};

function BinarySearch01Util(arr, start, end) {
    if (end < start) {
        return -1;
    }
    const mid = Math.floor((start + end) / 2);
    if ("1" === arr[mid] && "0" === arr[mid - 1]) {
        return mid;
    }
    if ("0" === arr[mid]) {
        return BinarySearch01Util(arr, mid + 1, end);
    }
    else {
        return BinarySearch01Util(arr, start, mid - 1);
    }
```

```
};

function test() {
    const first = "00000000111";
    console.log(`BinarySearch01 index is :: ${BinarySearch01(first)}`);
}
```

Output:
```
BinarySearch01 index is :: 8
```

Find Value In Rotated array

Problem: Given a sorted list S of N integer. S is rotated an unknown number of times. Find given value in the array.

First Solution: Linear Search, we can always find the index of first 1 in the array using traversal.
Time Complexity is O(n) and Space Complexity is O(1)

Second Solution: Since the array is sorted, we can use modified binary search to find the element.
Time Complexity is O(logn) and Space Complexity is O(1)

Example 5.54:
```
function BinarySearchRotateArray(arr, key) {
    const size = arr.length;
    return BinarySearchRotateArrayUtil(arr, 0, size - 1, key);
};

function BinarySearchRotateArrayUtil(arr, start, end, key) {
    if (end < start) {
        return -1;
    }
    const mid = Math.floor((start + end) / 2);
    if (key === arr[mid]) {
        return mid;
    }
    if (arr[mid] > arr[start]) {
        if (arr[start] <= key && key < arr[mid]) {
            return BinarySearchRotateArrayUtil(arr, start, mid - 1, key);
        }
        else {
            return BinarySearchRotateArrayUtil(arr, mid + 1, end, key);
        }
    }
    else {
        if (arr[mid] < key && key <= arr[end]) {
            return BinarySearchRotateArrayUtil(arr, mid + 1, end, key);
        }
        else {
            return BinarySearchRotateArrayUtil(arr, start, mid - 1, key);
        }
    }
```

```
    }
};

function test() {
    first = [8, 9, 10, 11, 3, 5, 7]
    console.log(`BinarySearchRotateArray index is :: $
{BinarySearchRotateArray(first, 7)}`);
    console.log(`BinarySearchRotateArray index is :: $
{BinarySearchRotateArray(first, 6)}`);
}
```

Output:
```
BinarySearchRotateArray index is :: 6
BinarySearchRotateArray index is :: -1
```

Find max value in a Sorted and Rotated array

Problem: Given a sorted list S of N integer. S is rotated an unknown number of times. Find largest element in the array.

First Solution: Linear Search, we can always find the index of first 1 in the array using traversal. Time Complexity is O(n) and Space Complexity is O(1)

Second Solution: Since the array is sorted, we can use modified binary search to find the element. Time Complexity is O(logn) and Space Complexity is O(1)

Example 5.55:
```
function RotationMaxUtil(arr, start, end) {
    if (end <= start) {
        return arr[start];
    }
    const mid = Math.floor((start + end) / 2);
    if (arr[mid] > arr[mid + 1])
        return arr[mid];
    if (arr[start] <= arr[mid])
        return RotationMaxUtil(arr, mid + 1, end);
    else
        return RotationMaxUtil(arr, start, mid - 1);
};

function RotationMax(arr, size) {
    return RotationMaxUtil(arr, 0, size - 1);
}

function test() {
    first = [8, 9, 10, 11, 3, 5, 7]
    console.log(`RotationMax is :: ${RotationMax(first, first.length)}`);
}
```

Output:
```
RotationMax is :: 11
```

Count Rotation

Problem: Given a rotated array find the count of rotation.

Example 5.56:
```
function CountRotation(arr, size) {
    const maxIndex = RotationMaxIndexUtil(arr, 0, size - 1);
    return (maxIndex + 1) % size;
};

function RotationMaxIndexUtil(arr, start, end) {
    if (end <= start)
        return start;
    const mid = Math.floor((start + end) / 2);
    if (arr[mid] > arr[mid + 1])
        return mid;
    if (arr[start] <= arr[mid])
        return RotationMaxIndexUtil(arr, mid + 1, end);
    else
        return RotationMaxIndexUtil(arr, start, mid - 1);
};

function test() {
    first = [8, 9, 10, 11, 3, 5, 7]
    console.log(`CountRotation is :: ${CountRotation(first,
first.length)}`);
}
```

Output:
```
CountRotation is :: 4
```

Minimum Absolute Difference Adjacent Circular Array

Problem: Given an array of integers, find minimum absolute difference of adjacent element consider circular array.

Example 5.57:
```
function minAbsDiffAdjCircular(arr, size) {
    if (size < 2)
        return -1;
    let diff = 9999999;
    for (let i = 0; i < size; i++) {
        diff = Math.min(diff, Math.abs(arr[i] - arr[(i + 1) % size]));
    }
    return diff;
};
```

```
function test() {
    const arr = [5, 29, 18, 51, 11];
    console.info(minAbsDiffAdjCircular(arr, arr.length));
};
```

Output:
6

Transform List

Problem: How would you swap elements of an array like [a1 a2 a3 a4 b1 b2 b3 b4] to convert it into [a1 b1 a2 b2 a3 b3 a4 b4]?

Approach:
- First swap elements in the middle pair
- Next swap elements in the middle two pairs
- Next swap elements in the middle three pairs
- Iterate n-1 steps.

Example 5.58:
```
function transformArrayAB(str) {
    arr = str.split("");
    const size = str.length;
    const N = Math.floor(size / 2);
    for (let i = 1; i < N; i++) {
        for (let j = 0; j < i; j++) {
            swap(arr, N - i + 2 * j, N - i + 2 * j + 1);
        }
    }
    return arr.join("");
};

function test() {
    first = "aaaabbbb"
    console.log(transformArrayAB(first));
}
```

Output:
abababab

Check if two Lists are permutation of each other

Problem: In given two integer Lists; You must check whether they are permutation of each other.

First Solution: Sorting; Sort all the elements of both the arrays and Compare each element of both the arrays from beginning to end. If there is no mismatch, return true. Otherwise, false.
Sorting algorithms takes O(n.logn) time and comparison takes O(n) time.
Time Complexity is O(n.logn) and Space Complexity is O(1)

Example 5.59:

```
function checkPermutation(array1, array2) {
    const size1 = array1.length;
    const size2 = array2.length;
    if (size1 !== size2) {
        return false;
    }
    console.log(array1)
    array1.sort(function cmp(a, b) { return (a - b); });
    array2.sort(function cmp(a, b) { return (a - b); });
    console.log(array1)
    for (let i = 0; i < size1; i++) {
        if (array1[i] !== array2[i]) {
            return false;
        }
    }
    return true;
};

function test() {
    const first = [1, 2, 3, 1, 2, 3, 5, 6, 7, 7, 8, 9, 3, 4, 5];
    const second = [1, 2, 4, 5, 3, 1, 2, 3, 5, 6, 7, 7, 8, 9, 3];

    console.log(`checkPermutation ${checkPermutation(first, second)}`)
};
```

Output:
```
checkPermutation true
```

Second Solution: Hash-Table (Assumption: No duplicates).
1. Create a Hash-Table for all the elements of the first list.
2. Traverse the other list from beginning to the end and search for each element in the Hash-Table.
3. If all the elements are found in, the Hash-Table return true, otherwise return false.

Hash-Table insert and find take constant time O(1) so the total time complexity of the algorithm is O(n) time. Space Complexity is also O(n)

Time Complexity = O(n) (For creation of Hash-Table and look-up),
Space Complexity = O(n) (For creation of Hash-Table).

Searching for an element in a 2-d sorted list

Problem: In given 2-dimensional list. Each row and column are sorted in ascending order. How would you find an element in it?

Solution: The algorithm works as:
1. Start with element at last column and first row
2. If the element is the value we are looking for, return true.
3. If the element is greater than the value we are looking for, go to the element at previous column but same row.

4. If the element is less than the value we are looking for, go to the element at next row but same column.
5. Return false, if the element is not found after reaching the element of the last row of the first column. Condition (row < r && column >= 0) is false.

Example 5.60:

```
function FindElementIn2DArray(arr, r, c, value) {
    let row = 0;
    let column = c - 1;
    while (row < r && column >= 0) {
        if (arr[row][column] === value) {
            return true;
        }
        else if (arr[row][column] > value) {
            column--;
        }
        else {
            row++;
        }
    };
    return false;
};

function test() {
    const f = new Array(10);
    let count = 0;
    for (let i = 0; i < 10; i++) {
        f[i] = new Array(10);
        for (let j = 0; j < 10; j++) {
            f[i][j] = count++;
        }
    }
    console.log(FindElementIn2DArray(f, 10, 10, 21));
    console.log(FindElementIn2DArray(f, 10, 10, 121));
}
```

Output:
```
true
false
```

Running time = **O(N)**.

Arithmetic progression

Problem: Given an array of N integers, you need to find if array elements can form an Arithmetic progression.

First Solution: Arithmetic relation can be found only by sorting the elements. Then traversing that AP exists. Time complexity will O(nlogn) for sorting

144

Example 5.61:

```
function isAP(arr, size) {
    if (size <= 1)
        return true;
    arr.sort(function cmp(a, b) { return (a - b); });
    const diff = arr[1] - arr[0];
    for (let i = 2; i < size; i++) {
        if (arr[i] - arr[i - 1] !== diff)
            return false;
    }
    return true;
};

function test() {
    const first = [3, 6, 9, 12, 15];
    const size = first.length;

    console.log(`isAP ${isAP(first, size)}`)
};
```

Output:

```
isAP true
```

Second Solution: We can find the first and second lowest elements of the array in single traversal. By this, we can find first value of AP and increment value of AP. We traverse values in input array and add them to hashtable. Finally, we have first element of AP and difference so we can test that all the elements are in HashTable.

Time complexity is O(n) and space complexity is O(n) for hashtable.

Example 5.62:

```
function isAP2(arr, size) {
    let first = 9999999;
    let second = 9999999;
    let value;
    let diff;
    const hs = new Set();
    for (var i = 0; i < size; i++) {
        if (arr[i] < first) {
            second = first;
            first = arr[i];
        } else if (arr[i] < second)
            second = arr[i];
    }
    diff = second - first;

    for (var i = 0; i < size; i++) {
        if (hs.has(arr[i]))
            return false;
        hs.add(arr[i]);
```

```
        }

    for (var i = 0; i < size; i++) {
        value = first + i * diff;
        if (!hs.has(value))
            return false;
    }
    return true;
};
```

Third Solution: We can solve this problem in O(n) time and O(1) space. We find the first and second lowest elements of the array in single traversal. Now we will traverse the array again and will put each element into its proper position by swapping. Index of each element will be **(value – first) / diff**. We will keep the count also so that we can find duplicate values too.

Example 5.63:
```
function isAP3(arr, size) {
    let first = 9999999;
    let second = 9999999;
    const count = new Array(size).fill(0);
    let index = -1;
    for (var i = 0; i < size; i++) {
        if (arr[i] < first) {
            second = first;
            first = arr[i];
        }
        else if (arr[i] < second)
            second = arr[i];
    }
    const diff = second - first;
    for (var i = 0; i < size; i++) {
        index = (arr[i] - first) / diff ;
        if (index > size - 1 || count[index] !== 0)
            return false;
        count[index] = 1;
    }
    for (var i = 0; i < size; i++) {
        if (count[i] !== 1)
            return false;
    }
    return true;
};
```

Balance Point

Problem: Given an array, you need to find balance point or balance index. An index is balanced index if the element in the left of it and elements in the right of it have same sum.

Solution: Create two set first and second. Sum all the element from index 1 to size-1 in second. One by one add elements to first set and remove them from second set.

Time complexity is O(n)

Example 5.64:

```
function findBalancedPoint(arr, size) {
    let first = 0;
    let second = 0;
    for (var i = 1; i < size; i++) {
        second += arr[i];
    }
    for (var i = 0; i < size; i++) {
        if (first === second) {
            return i;
        }
        if (i < size - 1)
            first += arr[i];
        second -= arr[i + 1];
    }
    return -1;
};

function test() {
    const arr = [-7, 1, 5, 2, -4, 3, 0];
    console.info("BalancedPoint : " , findBalancedPoint(arr, arr.length));
};
```

Output:
```
BalancedPoint :   3
```

Find Floor and Ceil

Problem: Given a sorted array you need to find ceil or floor of an input value. A ceil is the value in array which is just greater than the given input value. A floor is a value in array which is just smaller than the given input value.

Solution: Since the array is sorted the floor and ceil can be found by binary search like algorithm. Time complexity will O(logn)

Example 5.65:

```
function findFloor(arr, size, value) {
    let start = 0;
    let stop = size - 1;
    let mid;
    while (start <= stop) {
        mid = Math.floor((start + stop) / 2);
        if (arr[mid] === value || (arr[mid] < value && (mid === size - 1 ||
arr[mid + 1] > value)))
            return arr[mid];
        else if (arr[mid] < value)
            start = mid + 1;
```

147

```
        else
            stop = mid - 1;
    }
    console.log("Floor value not found.")
    return -9999;
};

function test() {
    const arr = [-7, 1, 2, 3, 6, 8, 10];
    console.info("findFloor : " , findFloor(arr, arr.length, 4));
};
```

Output:
```
findFloor :  3
```

Example 5.66:
```
function findCeil(arr, size, value) {
    let start = 0;
    let stop = size - 1;
    let mid;
    while (start <= stop) {
        mid = Math.floor((start + stop) / 2);
        if (arr[mid] === value || (arr[mid] > value && (mid === 0 || arr[mid
- 1] < value)))
            return arr[mid];
        else if (arr[mid] < value)
            start = mid + 1;
        else
            stop = mid - 1;
    }
    console.log("Ceil value not found.")
    return 9999;
};

function test() {
    const arr = [-7, 1, 2, 3, 6, 8, 10];
    console.info("findCeil : " , findCeil(arr, arr.length, 4));
};
```

Output:
```
findCeil :  6
```

Closest Number

Problem: Given a sorted array and a number. You need to find the element in array which is closest to the given number.

Solution: Since the array is sorted, we can perform binary search.

Example 5.67:

```
function ClosestNumber(arr, size, num) {
    let start = 0;
    let stop = size - 1;
    let output = -1;
    let minDist = 9999;
    let mid;
    while (start <= stop) {
        mid = Math.floor((start + stop) / 2);
        if (minDist > Math.abs(arr[mid] - num)) {
            minDist = Math.abs(arr[mid] - num);
            output = arr[mid];
        }
        if (arr[mid] === num)
            break;
        else if (arr[mid] > num)
            stop = mid - 1;
        else
            start = mid + 1;
    }
    return output;
};

function test() {
    const arr = [-7, 1, 2, 3, 6, 8, 10];
    console.info("ClosestNumber : " , ClosestNumber(arr, arr.length, 4));
};
```

Output:
```
ClosestNumber :  3
```

Duplicate K Distance

Problem: Given an array of integers, you need to find if duplicate values exist in the range of K units.

In array [1, 2, 3, 1, 4, 5] and range 3 the answer will be true. As 1 repeat in the range 3.
However, in the same array if the range is 2 then the answer is false.

Solution: We keep mapping of values and their index in a Hashtable. We traverse the array for each element we first look if this value is already present in the Hashtable. If it is not present then we add element as key and its index as value in the hashtable. If the element is present in the hashtable then we can find if the repeated value is in the range by subtracting current index with the index of the previous repetition. We keep on updating the index corresponds to the value.

Time complexity is O(n) and space complexity is O(n)

Example 5.68:

```
function DuplicateKDistance(arr, size, k) {
    const hm = new Map();
```

```
    for (let i = 0; i < size; i++) {
        if (hm.has(arr[i]) && i - hm.get(arr[i]) <= k) {
            console.log(`Value:${arr[i]} Index: ${hm.get(arr[i])} & ${i}`);
            return true;
        } else
            hm.set(arr[i], i);
    }
    return false;
};

function test() {
    const arr = [2, 3, 1, 4, 2, 1];
    DuplicateKDistance(arr, arr.length, 3);
};
```

Output:
```
Value:1 Index: 2 & 5
```

Frequency Counts

Problem: Given an array of size N, which contain integers from 1 to N. Elements can appear any number of times. Print frequency of all elements in the array also print the missing elements frequency as 0

Input: [1, 2, 2, 2, 1]
Output:
1: 2
2: 3
3: 0
4: 0
5: 0

First Solution: Use Hashtable to keep track of value and its frequency. Traverse in the range and keep on printing the values.

Second Solution: Using sorting we can sort the array first, then we can traverse the array and print the element and its frequency.

Third Solution: Using auxiliary array, now since we have data in the range 1 to N so an extra auxiliary array can be used to keep track of frequency. While traversing the input array, we found a value V then its corresponding index in the auxiliary array will be (V-1), since array indexing starts form 0.

Fourth Solution: Now solve this problem in linear time, without using any extra space. We have to look carefully that this problem provides us with extra information regarding the range of values from 1 to N.

We traverse the input array, we found a value V then its corresponding index values in the array is (V - 1) if there is some valid value in the range (1 to N) in that index then we copy that value to our traversal index and then mark the value at index (V-1) as -1. If the value at index (V-1) is not in range then we decrease it by 1. Now we can print absolute value to the output.

Example 5.69:

```
function frequencyCounts(arr, size) {
    let index;
    for (var i = 0; i < size; i++) {
        while (arr[i] > 0) {
            index = arr[i] - 1;
            if (arr[index] > 0) {
                arr[i] = arr[index];
                arr[index] = -1;
            }
            else {
                arr[index] -= 1;
                arr[i] = 0;
            }
        }
    }
    for (var i = 0; i < size; i++) {
        console.info((i + 1) , Math.abs(arr[i]));
    }
};

function test() {
    const arr = [1, 2, 2, 2, 1];
    frequencyCounts(arr, arr.length);
};
```

Output:
```
1 2
2 3
3 0
4 0
5 0
```

K Largest Elements

Problem: Given an array of integers of size N, you need to print k largest elements in the array in order in which they appear in the array.

First Solution: Another solution is to sort the array and again find the kth largest element. Scan the array and print all the elements which have value greater than or equal to the kth largest element.

Example 5.70:

```
function KLargestElements(arrIn, size, k) {
    const arr = new Array(size);
    for (var i = 0; i < size; i++) {
        arr[i] = arrIn[i];
    }
    arr.sort(function cmp(a, b) { return (a - b); });
    for (var i = 0; i < size; i++) {
```

```
            if (arrIn[i] > arr[size - k]) {
                console.info(arrIn[i]);
            }
        }
};

function test() {
    const arr = [1, 3, 4, 2, 2, 1, 5, 9, 3];
    KLargestElements(arr, arr.length, 4);
};
```

Output:
```
4
5
9
```

Second Solution:
First copy the array into another array. Then using quick select find the N-Kth elements in the array. Then scan the original array and print all the elements which have value Greater than or equal to k. O(N) for k and O(N) for scan.

Example 5.71:
```
function KLargestElements2(arrIn, size, k) {
    const arr = new Array(size);
    for (var i = 0; i < size; i++) {
        arr[i] = arrIn[i];
    }
    QuickSelectUtil(arr, 0, size - 1, size - k);
    for (var i = 0; i < size; i++) {
        if (arrIn[i] > arr[size - k]) {
            console.info(arrIn[i]);
        }
    }
};

function QuickSelectUtil(arr, lower, upper, k) {
    if (upper <= lower)
        return;
    const pivot = arr[lower];
    const start = lower;
    const stop = upper;
    while (lower < upper) {
        while (arr[lower] <= pivot) {
            lower++;
        }
        while (arr[upper] > pivot) {
            upper--;
        }
        if (lower < upper) {
            swap(arr, upper, lower);
```

```
        }
    }
    swap(arr, upper, start);
    if (k < upper)
        QuickSelectUtil(arr, start, upper - 1, k);
    if (k > upper)
        QuickSelectUtil(arr, upper + 1, stop, k);
};
```

Note: Quick Select algorithms, closely related to quick sort can be studied in shorting chapter.

Note: There is a catch in the above solutions It may happen that the number of values printed may me more than K so make sure they are exactly k.

Fix Point

Problem: Given a sorted array of distinct integers, you need to find the fix point. Fix point is an index of array in which index and value is same.

First Solution: Brute force approach, traverse the array to find fix point. Time complexity is O(n)

Example 5.72:
```
function FixPoint(arr, size) {
    for (let i = 0; i < size; i++) {
        if (arr[i] === i)
            return i;
    }
    return -1;
};

function test() {
    const arr = [-1, 0, 2, 3, 6, 7, 9, 10, 18];
    console.log(FixPoint(arr, arr.length));
};
```

Output:
2

Second Solution: Since the array is sorted, we should think about binary sort algorithm.

Example 5.73:
```
function FixPoint2(arr, size) {
    let low = 0;
    let high = size - 1;
    let mid;
    while (low <= high) {
        mid = Math.floor((low + high) / 2);
        if (arr[mid] === mid)
            return mid;
        else if (arr[mid] < mid)
```

```
            low = mid + 1;
        else
            high = mid - 1;
    }
    return -1;
};
```

Sub Array Sums

Problem: Given an array of positive integers, you need to find if there is some range in array such that if we add all the elements in that range then it became equal to given value.

Example 5.74:
```
function subArraySums(arr, size, value) {
    let first = 0;
    let second = 0;
    let sum = arr[first];
    while (second < size && first < size) {
        if (sum === value){
            console.info("values between index : ", first ,"&", second);
            return true;
        }
        if (sum < value) {
            second += 1;
            if (second < size)
                sum += arr[second];
        }
        else {
            sum -= arr[first];
            first += 1;
        }
    }
    return false;
};

function test() {
    const arr = [1, 3, 4, 4, 6, 7, 7, 8, 8];
    console.log(subArraySums(arr, arr.length, 17));
};
```

Output:
```
values between index : 1 & 4
true
```

Time complexity: O(n)

Maximum contiguous subarray sum

Problem: Given an array of positive and negative integers, find maximum contiguous subarray in A.

154

Example 5.75: <u>Kadane's Algorithm</u> to find maximum contiguous subarray sum.

```
function MaxConSub(arr, size) {
    let currMax = 0;
    let maximum = 0;
    for (let i = 0; i < size; i++) {
        currMax = Math.max(arr[i], currMax + arr[i]);
        if (currMax < 0)
            currMax = 0;
        if (maximum < currMax)
            maximum = currMax;
    }
    return maximum;
};

function test() {
    const arr = [1, -2, 3, 4, -4, 6, -4, 8, 2];
    console.log(MaxConSub(arr, arr.length));
};
```

Output:
```
15
```

Maximum contiguous subarray sum (A-B)

Problem: Given an array A of integers and array B of integers, find maximum contiguous subarray in A Such that it does not contains elements in B.

First Solution: Kadane's Algorithm is modified by using a HashTable to solve this problem.

Example 5.76:
```
function MaxConSubArr(A, sizeA, B, sizeB) {
    let currMax = 0;
    let maximum = 0;
    const hs = new Set();
    for (var i = 0; i < sizeB; i++)
        hs.add(B[i]);
    for (var i = 0; i < sizeA; i++){
        if (hs.has(A[i]))
            currMax = 0;
        else
            currMax = Math.max(A[i], currMax + A[i]);

        if (currMax < 0)
            currMax = 0;

        if (maximum < currMax)
            maximum = currMax;
    }
```

```
        console.info(maximum);
        return maximum;
};

function test() {
    const arr = [1, 2, 3, 4, 4, 6, 4, 8, 2];
    const arr2 = [2,4, 8, 18, 10];
    console.log(MaxConSubArr(arr, arr.length, arr2, arr2.length));
};
```

Output:

6

Second Solution: Sort array B. In place of binary search is used to find if some element is present in B.

Time complexity: O(MlogM + NlogM) For sorting and then for search each element.

Example 5.77:

```
function MaxConSubArr2(A, sizeA, B, sizeB) {
    B.sort(function cmp(a, b) { return (a - b); });
    let currMax = 0;
    let maximum = 0;
    for (let i = 0; i < sizeA; i++) {
        if (Binarysearch(B, A[i]))
            currMax = 0;
        else {
            currMax = Math.max(A[i], currMax + A[i]);
            if (currMax < 0)
                currMax = 0;
            if (maximum < currMax)
                maximum = currMax;
        }
    }
    console.info(maximum);
    return maximum;
};
```

Rain Water

Problem: Given an array of N non-negative integers. Each element of array represents a bar of histogram. Considering that each bar is one unit wide. You need to find how much water can be accommodate in the structure.

For Example : [4, 0, 1, 5] will contain 7 units of water.

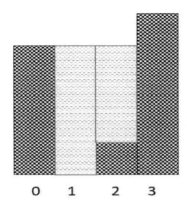

Solution: This problem can be solved very easily if we are able to find how much water a particular bar of unit width can contain.

Water contained at i^{th} index = minimum (maximum length in left, maximum length in right) − length i^{th} bar.

Example 5.78:

```
function RainWater(arr, size) {
    const leftHigh = new Array(size);
    const rightHigh = new Array(size);
    let max = arr[0];
    leftHigh[0] = arr[0];

    for (var i = 1; i < size; i++) {
        if (max < arr[i])
            max = arr[i];
        leftHigh[i] = max;
    }
    max = arr[size - 1];
    rightHigh[size - 1] = arr[size - 1];
    for (var i = (size - 2); i >= 0; i--) {
        if (max < arr[i])
            max = arr[i];
        rightHigh[i] = max;
    }
    let water = 0;
    for (var i = 0; i < size; i++) {
        water += Math.min(leftHigh[i], rightHigh[i]) - arr[i];
    }
    console.info(`Water : ${water}`);
    return water;
};

function test() {
    const arr = [4, 0, 1, 5];
    RainWater(arr, arr.length);
};
```

Output:
```
Water : 7
```

Time complexity: O(N)

Further optimization on the above problem in a single iteration the water is calculated along with leftMax and rightMax calculation.

Example 5.79:

```
function RainWater2(arr, size) {
    let water = 0;
    let leftMax = 0;
    let rightMax = 0;
    let left = 0;
    let right = size - 1;
    while (left <= right) {
        if (arr[left] < arr[right]) {
            if (arr[left] > leftMax)
                leftMax = arr[left];
            else
                water += leftMax - arr[left];
            left += 1;
        }
        else {
            if (arr[right] > rightMax)
                rightMax = arr[right];
            else
                water += rightMax - arr[right];
            right -= 1;
        }
    }
    console.info(`Water : ${water}`);
    return water;
};
```

Exercise

1. In given list of n elements, we need to find the first repeated element. Which of the following methods will work for us? If a method works, then implement it.
   - Brute force exhaustive search.
   - Use Hash-Table to keep an index of the elements and use the second scan to find the element.
   - Sorting the elements.
   - If we know the range of the element then we can use counting technique.

   Hint: When order in which elements appear in input is important, we cannot use sorting.

2. In given list of n elements, write an algorithm to find three elements in an array whose sum is a given value.

   Hint: Try to do this problem using a brute force approach. Then try to apply the sorting approach along with a brute force approach. Time Complexity is O(n^2)

3. In given list of −ve and +ve numbers, write a program to separate −ve numbers from the +ve numbers.

4. In given list of 1's and 0's, write a program to separate 0's from 1's.
   Hint: QuickSelect, counting

5. In given list of 0's, 1's and 2's, write a program to separate 0's, 1's and 2's.

6. In given list whose elements is monotonically increasing with both negative and positive numbers. Write an algorithm to find the point at which list becomes positive.

7. In a sorted list, find a number. If found then return the index if not found then insert into the array.

8. Find max in sorted rotated list.

9. Find min in the sorted rotated list.

10. Find kth Smallest Element in the Union of Two Sorted Lists

CHAPTER 6: LINKED LIST

Introduction

Let us suppose we have an array that contains following five elements 1, 2, 4, 5, 6. We want to insert a new element with value "3" in between "2" and "4". In the array, we cannot do it so easily. We need to create another array that is long enough to store the current values and one more space for "3". Then we need to copy these elements in the new space. This copy operation is inefficient. To remove this inefficiency in addition of new data linked list is used.

Linked List

The linked list is a list of items, called nodes. Nodes have two parts, value part and link part. Value part is used to stores the data. The value part of the node can be a basic data-type like an integer or it can be some other data-type like a structure. The link part is a pointer, which is used to store addresses of the next element in the list.

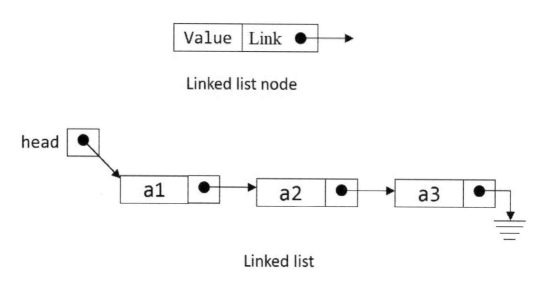

Linked list node

Linked list

The various parts of linked list:
1. **Head**: Head is a pointer that holds the address of the first node in the linked list.
2. **Nodes**: Items in the linked list are called nodes.
3. **Value**: The data that is stored in each node of the linked list.
4. **Link**: Link part of the node is used to store the reference of another node.
   a. We will use "next" and "prev" to store address of next or previous nodes.

Types of Linked list

There are different types of linked lists. The main difference among them is how their nodes connected to each other. We will discuss singly linked list, doubly linked list, circular linked list and doubly circular linked list.

Singly Linked List

Each node (Except the last node) has a reference to the next node in the linked list. The link portion of node contains the address of the next node. The link portion of the last node contains the value null.

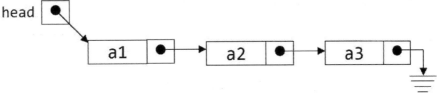

Let us look at the Node. The Value part of node is of type integer, but it can be some other data-type. The link part of node is named as Pointer in the below diagram.

Example 6.1: Singly Linked List node structure

```
class LinkedListNode {
    constructor(v, n) {
        this.value = v;
        this.next = n;
    }
}

class LinkedList {
    constructor() {
        this.length = 0;
    }
}
```

For a singly linked, we should always test these three test cases:
- Zero element / Empty linked list.
- One element / Single node case.
- General case.

One node and zero node case are used to test boundary cases. It is always mandatory to take care of these cases before submitting code.

The various basic operations that we can perform on linked lists, many of these operations require list traversal:
- Insert an element in the list, this operation is used to create a linked list.
- Print various elements of the list.
- Search an element in the list.
- Delete an element from the list.
- Reverse a linked list.

Insert element in linked list

An element can be inserted into a linked list in various orders. Some of the Example cases are mentioned below:

1. Insertion of an element at the start of linked list
2. Insertion of an element at the end of linked list
3. Insertion of an element at the Nth position in linked list
4. Insert element in sorted order in linked list

Insert element at the Head

Problem: Insert an element at the start of linked list.

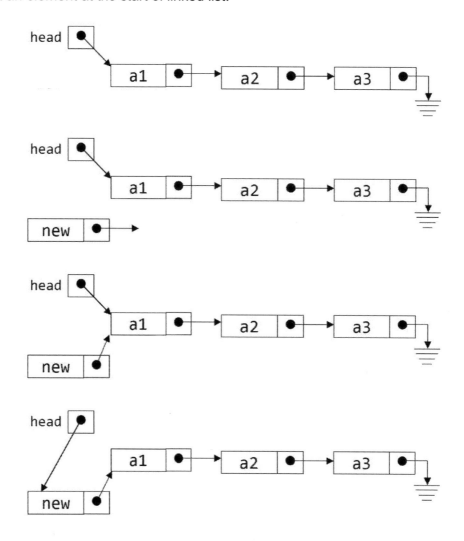

Example 6.2:

```
addHead(value) {
    this.head = new LinkedListNode(value, this.head);
    this.length++;
}
```

Analysis:
- We need to create a new node with the value passed to the function as argument.
- The next pointer of the new node will point to the head of the linked list or null in case when list is empty.
- The newly created node will become head of the linked list.

Time Complexity: O(1).

Insertion of an element at the end

Problem: Insertion of an element at the end of linked list

Example 6.3:
```
addTail(value) {
    const newNode = new LinkedListNode(value, null);
    let curr = this.head;
    if (this.head == null) {
        this.head = newNode;
    }
    while (curr.next != null) {
        curr = curr.next;
    };
    curr.next = newNode;
}
```

Analysis:
- New node is created and the value is stored inside it and store null value to its next pointer.
- If the list is empty then this new node will become head of linked list.
- If list is not empty then we must traverse to the end of the list.
- Finally, new node is added to the end of the list.

Time Complexity: O(n).

Note: This operation is inefficient as each time you want to insert an element you have to traverse to the end of the list. Therefore, the complexity of creation of the list is $O(n^2)$. So how to make it efficient we must keep track of the last element by keeping a tail pointer. Therefore, if it is required to insert element at the end of linked list, then we will keep track of the tail reference also.

Traversing Linked List

Problem: Print various elements of a linked list

Example 6.4:
```
print() {
    let temp = this.head;
    while (temp != null) {
        process.stdout.write(`${temp.value} `);
        temp = temp.next;
    };
    process.stdout.write("\n");
}
```

Analysis:
- We will traverse the list and print the value stored in nodes. List is traversed by making head pointing to its next.

Time Complexity: O(n).

Complete code for list creation and printing the list.

Example 6.5: Test code for linked list creation, adding value at head and printing elements.
```
const ll = new LinkedList();
ll.addHead(1);
ll.addHead(2);
ll.addHead(3);
ll.print();
```

Output:
```
3 2 1
```

Analysis:
- New instance of linked list is created. Various elements are added to list by calling InsertNode() method.
- Finally all the content of list is printed to screen by calling PrintList() method.

Sorted Insert

Problem: Insert an element in sorted order in linked list given head pointer

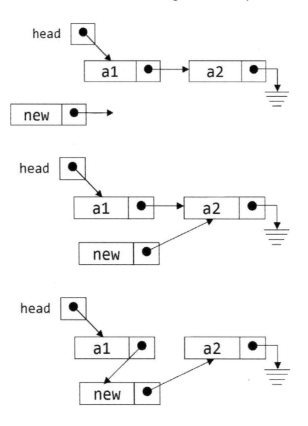

Example 6.6:
```
sortedInsert(value) {
    const newNode = new LinkedListNode(value, null);
    let curr = this.head;
    if (curr == null || curr.value > value) {
        newNode.next = this.head;
        this.head = newNode;
        return;
    }
    while (curr.next != null && curr.next.value < value) {
        curr = curr.next;
    };
    newNode.next = curr.next;
    curr.next = newNode;
}
```

Analysis:
- A new empty node of the linked list is created. And initialized by storing an argument value into its value. Next of the node will point to null.
- If the list is empty or if the value stored in the first node is greater than the new created node value. Then this new created node will be added to the start of the list. And head need to be modified.
- In all other cases, we iterate through the list to find the proper position where the node can be inserted to keep the list sorted.
- Finally, the node will be added to the list.

Time Complexity: O(n).

Search Element in a Linked-List

Problem: Search element in linked list. Given a head pointer and value. Returns 1 if value found in list else returns 0.

Example 6.7:
```
isPresent(data) {
    let temp = this.head;
    while (temp != null) {
        if (temp.value === data)
            return true;
        temp = temp.next;
    };
    return false;
}
```

Analysis:
- Using a loop, we will iterate through the list.
- Value of each element of list is compared with the given value. If value is found, then the function will return true.
- If the value is not found, then false will be returned from the function in the end.

Time Complexity: O(n).

Note: Search in a single linked list can only be done in one direction. Since all elements in the list have reference to the next item in the list. Therefore, traversal of linked list is linear in nature.

Delete First element in a linked list.

Problem: Delete element at the head of the linked list.

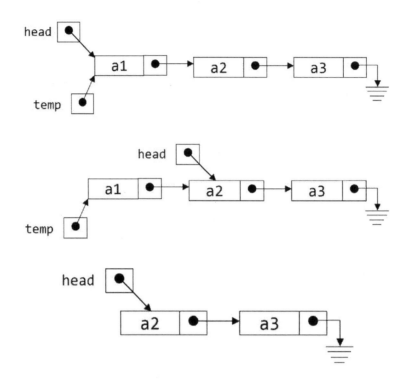

Example 6.8:
```
removeHead() {
    if (this.isEmpty())
        throw new Error("EmptyListError");

    const value = this.head.value;
    this.head = this.head.next;
    this.length--;
    return value;
}
```

Analysis:
- First, we need to check if the list is already empty. If empty then return.
- If list is not empty then the head of the list will store the reference of next node of the current head.

Time Complexity: O(1).

Delete node from the linked list given its value.

Problem: Delete the first node whose value is equal to the given value.

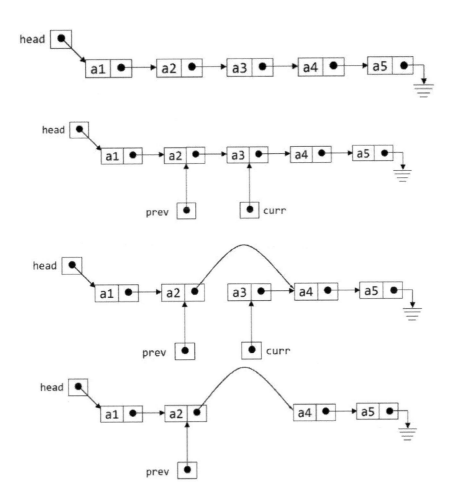

Example 6.9:

```
deleteNode(delValue) {
    let temp = this.head;
    if (this.isEmpty())
        return false;

    if (delValue === this.head.value) {
        this.head = this.head.next;
        this.length--;
        return true;
    }

    while (temp.next != null) {
        if (temp.next.value === delValue) {
            temp.next = temp.next.next;
            this.length--;
            return true;
        }
        temp = temp.next;
    };
    return false;
}
```

Analysis:
- There are two cases, first case when the node that need to be deleted is first node and second case when the node that need to be deleted is not the first node in the list. When the node that need to be deleted is first node then head of the linked list will be modified. In other cases, it will not modify.
- First, we check if the first node is the node with the value, we are searching for then the head of the list will point to the next reference of the current head.
- In other case, we will traverse the link list using a while loop and try to find the node that need to be deleted. If the node is found then, we will point its previous node next point to the node next to the node we want to remove.

Time Complexity: O(n).

Delete all the occurrence of particular value in linked list.

Problem: Delete all the nodes whose value is equal to the given value.

Example 6.10:

```
deleteNodes(delValue) {
    let currNode = this.head;
    let nextNode;
    while (currNode != null && currNode.value === delValue) {
        this.head = currNode.next;
        currNode = this.head;
    };

    while (currNode != null) {
        nextNode = currNode.next;
        if (nextNode != null && nextNode.value === delValue) {
            currNode.next = nextNode.next;
        }
        else {
            currNode = nextNode;
        }
    };
}
```

Analysis:
- In the first while loop we will remove all the nodes that are at the front of the list, which have valued equal to the value we want to delete. In this, we need to update head of the list.
- In the second while loop, we will remove all the nodes that are not at the beginning of the list and have value equal to the value we want to delete. Remember that we are not returning we traverse till the end of the list.

Time Complexity: O(n).

Delete a single linked list

Problem: Given a pointer of head of linked list, delete all the elements of a list.

Example 6.11:

```
freeList() {
    this.head = null;
    this.length = 0;
}
```

Analysis: Mark head of list as null.

Time Complexity: O(n).

Reverse a linked list.

Problem: Reverse a singly linked List iteratively using three Pointers

Example 6.12:

```
reverse() {
    let curr = this.head;
    let prev = null;
    let next = null;
    while (curr != null) {
        next = curr.next;
        curr.next = prev;
        prev = curr;
        curr = next;
    };
    this.head = prev;
}
```

Analysis: The list is iterated. Make next variable point to the next of current node. Make nextof current node point to previous node. Make prev as current node and curr as next node.

Time Complexity: O(n).

Recursively Reverse a singly linked List

Problem: Reverse a singly linked list using Recursion.

Example 6.13:

```
reverseRecurseUtil(currentNode, nextNode) {
    if (currentNode == null)
        return null;

    if (currentNode.next == null) {
        currentNode.next = nextNode;
        return currentNode;
    }
    const ret = this.reverseRecurseUtil(currentNode.next, currentNode);
    currentNode.next = nextNode;
    return ret;
```

```
}

reverseRecurse() {
    this.head = this.reverseRecurseUtil(this.head, null);
}
```

Analysis:
- ReverseRecurse() function will call a reverseRecurseUtil() function to reverse the list and the pointer returned by the reverseRecurseUtil will be the head of the reversed list.
- The current node will point to the nextNode that is previous node of the old list.

Time Complexity: O(n).

Note: A linked list can be reversed using two solutions the First solution is by using three pointers. The Second solution is using recursion both are linear solution, but three-pointer solution is more efficient.

Remove duplicates from the linked list

Problem: Remove duplicate values from the linked list. The linked list is sorted and it contains some duplicate values, you need to remove those duplicate values. (You can create the required linked list using SortedInsert() function)

Example 6.14:
```
removeDuplicate() {
    let curr = this.head;
    while (curr != null) {
        if (curr.next != null && curr.value === curr.next.value) {
            curr.next = curr.next.next;
        }
        else {
            curr = curr.next;
        }
    };
}
```

Analysis: Traverse the list, if there is a node whose value is equal to its next node's value than current node next will point to the next of next node. Whole list is processed and the repeated values are removed from the list.

Time Complexity: O(n).

Copy List Reversed

Problem: Copy the content of linked list in another linked list in reverse order. If the original linked list contains elements in order 1,2,3,4, the new list should contain the elements in order 4,3,2,1.

Example 6.15:
```
CopyListReversed() {
    let tempNode = null;
```

```
    let tempNode2 = null;
    let curr = this.head;
    while (curr != null) {
        tempNode2 = new LinkedListNode(curr.value, tempNode);
        curr = curr.next;
        tempNode = tempNode2;
    };
    const ll2 = new LinkedList();
    ll2.head = tempNode;
    return ll2;
}
```

Analysis: Traverse the list and add the node value to the head of new list. Since the list is traversed in the forward direction and each node is added to the head of the new list the new list is formed is reverse of the original list.

Time Complexity: O(n).

Copy the content of given linked list into another linked list

Problem: Copy the content of given linked list into another linked list. If the original linked list contains elements in order 1,2,3,4, the new list should contain the elements in order 1,2,3,4.

Example 6.16:
```
copyList() {
    let headNode = null;
    let tailNode = null;
    let tempNode = null;
    let curr = this.head;
    if (curr == null)
        return null;
    headNode = new LinkedListNode(curr.value, null);
    tailNode = headNode;
    curr = curr.next;
    while (curr != null) {
        tempNode = new LinkedListNode(curr.value, null);
        tailNode.next = tempNode;
        tailNode = tempNode;
        curr = curr.next;
    };
    const ll2 = new LinkedList();
    ll2.head = headNode;
    return ll2;
}
```

Analysis: Traverse the list and add the node's value to new list, but this time always at the end of the list. Another pointer tailNode is used to keep track of the end of the list. Since the list is traversed in the forward direction and each node's value is added to the end of new list. Therefore, the formed list is same as the given list.

Time Complexity: O(n).

Compare List

Problem: Compare the values of two linked lists given their head pointers.

Example 6.17: Recursive Solution

```
compareList(head) {
    return this.compareListUtil(this.head, head);
}

compareListUtil(head1, head2) {
    if (head1 == null && head2 == null)
        return true;
    else if ((head1 == null) || (head2 == null) || (head1.value !==
head2.value))
        return false;
    else
        return this.compareListUtil(head1.next, head2.next);

}
```

Analysis:
- List is compared recursively. Moreover, if we reach the end of the list and both the lists are null. Then both the lists are equal and so return true.
- List is compared recursively. If either one of the list is empty or the value of corresponding nodes is unequal, then the lists are not equal and compareList()function will return false.
- Recursively calls compare list function for the next node of the current nodes.

Example 6.18: Iterative Solution

```
compareList2(head) {
    let head1 = this.head;
    let head2 = head;
    while (head1 == null &&
        head2 == null) {
        if (head1.value !== head2.value)
            return false;
        head1 = head1.next;
        head2 = head2.next;
    }
    if (head1 == null && head2 == null)
        return true;
    return false;
}
```

Analysis:
- Traverse both the list in a loop and if any point if the values of both the nodes of the list is not equal then return false that they are not equal lists.
- If at the end if both the lists are completely traversed then return true else return false if any one of them have some untraversed elements.

Time Complexity: Both solutions have same O(n) time complexity.

Find Length

Problem: Find the length of given linked list.

Example 6.19:
```
findLength() {
    let curr = this.head;
    let count = 0;
    while (curr != null) {
        count++;
        curr = curr.next;
    };
    return count;
}
```

Analysis: Length of linked list is found by traversing the list until we reach the end of list.

Time Complexity: O(n).

Nth Node from Beginning

Problem: Find Nth node from beginning

Example 6.20:
```
nthNodeFromBegining(index) {
    if (index > this.size() || index < 1)
        throw new Error('invalid arguments');;
    let count = 0;
    let curr = this.head;
    while (curr != null && count < index - 1) {
        count++;
        curr = curr.next;
    };
    return curr.value;
}
```

Analysis: Nth node can be found by traversing the list N-1 number of time and then return the node.If list does not have N elements then the method return null.

Time Complexity: O(K) if we are searching kth node from start.

Nth Node from End

Problem: Find Nth node from end

Example 6.21:

```
nthNodeFromEnd(index) {
    const size = this.size();
    let startIndex;
    if (size !== 0 && size < index) {
        throw new Error('invalid arguments');
    }
    startIndex = size - index + 1;
    return this.nthNodeFromBegining(startIndex);
}
```

Analysis: First, find the length of list, then nth node from end will be (length – nth +1) node from the beginning.

Time Complexity: O(n).

Example 6.22:

```
nthNodeFromEnd2(index) {
    let count = 1;
    let forward = this.head;
    let curr = this.head;
    while (forward != null && count <= index) {
        count++;
        forward = forward.next;
    };
    if (forward == null)
        throw new Error('invalid arguments');

    while (forward != null) {
        forward = forward.next;
        curr = curr.next;
    };
    return curr.value;
}
```

Analysis: Second solution is to use two pointers one is N steps / nodes ahead of the other when forward pointer reach the end of the list then the backward pointer will point to the desired node.

Time Complexity: O(n).

Loop Detect

Problem: Find if there is a loop in a linked list. If there is a loop, then return true and if there is no loop found then return false.

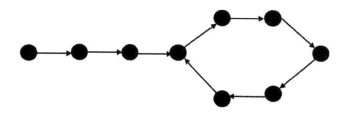

There are many ways to find if there is a loop in a linked list:

First Solution: User some map or hash-table
  a) Traverse through the list.
  b) If the current node is, not there in the Hash-Table then insert it into the Hash-Table.
  c) If the current node is already in the Hashtable then we have a loop.

Second Solution: Slow pointer and fast pointer approach (SPFP), we will use two pointers, one will move 2 steps at a time and another will move 1 step at time. If there is, a loop then both will meet at a point.

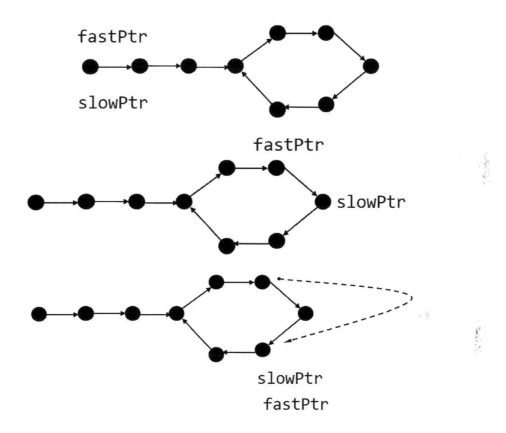

Example 6.23:
```
loopDetect() {
    let slowPtr;
    let fastPtr;
    slowPtr = fastPtr = this.head;
    while (fastPtr.next != null && fastPtr.next.next != null) {
        slowPtr = slowPtr.next;
        fastPtr = fastPtr.next.next;
        if (slowPtr === fastPtr) {
            console.log("loop found");
            return true;
        }
    };
    console.log("loop not found");
    return false;
}
```

Analysis:
- The list is traversed with two pointers, one is slow pointer and another is fast pointer. Slow pointer always moves one-step. Fast pointer always moves two steps. If there is no loop, then control will come out of while loop. So, return false.
- If there is a loop, then there comes a point in a loop where the fast pointer will come and try to pass slow pointer and they will meet at a point. When this point arrives, we come to know that there is a loop in the list. So, return true.

Time Complexity: O(n).

Third Solution: Reverse list loop detect approach, if there is a loop in a linked list, then reverse list function will give head of the original list as the head of the new list.

Example 6.24: Find if there is a loop in a linked list. Use reverse list approach.

```
reverseListLoopDetect() {
    const tempHead = this.head;
    this.reverse();
    if (tempHead === this.head) {
        this.reverse();
        console.log("loop found");
        return true;
    }
    else {
        this.reverse();
        console.log("loop not found");
        return false;
    }
}
```

Analysis:
- Store pointer of the head of list in a temp variable.
- Reverse the list
- Compare the reversed list head pointer to the current list head pointer.
- If the head of reversed list and the original list are same then reverse the list back and return true.
- If the head of the reversed list and the original list are not same, then reverse the list back and return false. Which means there is no loop.

Time Complexity: O(n).

Note: Both SPFP and Reverse List approaches are linear in nature, but still in SPFP approach, we do not require to modify the linked list so it is preferred.

Loop Type Detect

Problem: Find if there is a loop in a linked list. If there is no loop, then return 0, if there is loop return 1, if the list is circular then 2. Use slow pointer fast pointer approach.

Example 6.25:
```
loopTypeDetect() {
    let slowPtr = this.head;
    let fastPtr = this.head;
    while (fastPtr.next != null && fastPtr.next.next != null) {
        if (this.head === fastPtr.next || this.head === fastPtr.next.next) {
            console.log("circular list loop found");
            return 2;
        }
        slowPtr = slowPtr.next;
        fastPtr = fastPtr.next.next;
        if (slowPtr === fastPtr) {
            console.log("loop found");
            return 1;
        }
    };
    console.log("loop not found");
    return 0;
}
```

Analysis: This program is same as the loop detect program only if it is a circular list than the fast pointer reaches the slow pointer at the head of the list this means that there is a loop at the beginning of the list.

Time Complexity: O(n).

Remove Loop

Problem: Given there is a loop in linked list remove the loop.

Example 6.26:
```
removeLoop() {
    const loopPoint = this.loopPointDetect();
    if (loopPoint == null)
        return;
    let firstPtr = this.head;
    if (loopPoint === this.head) {
        while (firstPtr.next !== this.head)
            firstPtr = firstPtr.next;
        firstPtr.next = null;
        return;
    }
    let secondPtr = loopPoint;
    while (firstPtr.next !== secondPtr.next) {
        firstPtr = firstPtr.next;
        secondPtr = secondPtr.next;
    };
    secondPtr.next = null;
}
```

```
loopPointDetect() {
    let slowPtr = this.head;
    let fastPtr = this.head;
    while (fastPtr.next != null && fastPtr.next.next != null) {
        slowPtr = slowPtr.next;
        fastPtr = fastPtr.next.next;
        if (slowPtr === fastPtr) {
            return slowPtr;
        }
    };
    return null;
}
```

Analysis:
- Loop through the list by two pointer, one fast pointer and one slow pointer. Fast pointer jumps two nodes at a time and slow pointer jump one node at a time. The point where these two pointers intersect is a point in the loop.
- If that intersection point is head of the list, this is a circular list case and you need to again traverse through the list and make the node before head point to null.
- In the other case, you need to use two pointer variables one starts from head and another starts form the intersection-point. They both will meet at the point of loop. (You can mathematically prove it ;))

Time Complexity: O(n), all operations are linear in nature.

Find Intersection

Problem: In given two-linked list that meet at some point, find that intersection point.

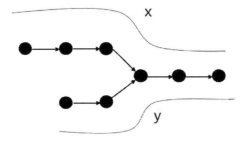

Example 6.27:
```
findIntersection(head, head2) {
    let l1 = 0;
    let l2 = 0;
    let tempHead = head;
    let tempHead2 = head2;
    while (tempHead != null) {
        l1++;
        tempHead = tempHead.next;
    };

    while (tempHead2 != null) {
        l2++;
        tempHead2 = tempHead2.next;
```

```
    };
    let diff;
    if (l1 < l2) {
        const temp = head;
        head = head2;
        head2 = temp;
        diff = l2 - l1;
    }
    else {
        diff = l1 - l2;
    }
    for (; diff > 0; diff--) {
        head = head.next;
    }
    while (head !== head2) {
        head = head.next;
        head2 = head2.next;
    };
    return head;
}
```

Analysis: Find length of both the lists. Find the difference of length of both the lists. Increment the longer list by diff steps, and then increment both the lists and get the intersection point.

Time Complexity: O(n).

Doubly Linked List

In a Doubly Linked list, there are two pointers in each node. These pointers are called prev and next. The prev pointer of the node will point to the node before it and the next pointer will point to the node next to the given node.

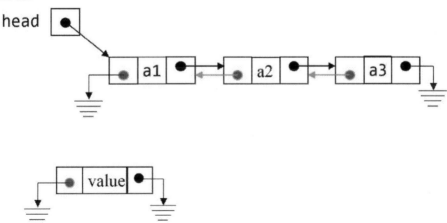

Let us look at the Node. The value part of the node is of type integer, but it can be of some other datatype. The two link pointers are prev and next.

Example 6.28: Doubly Linked List node class.
```
class DLLNode {
    constructor(v, nxt, prv) {
```

179

```
        this.value = v;
        this.next = nxt;
        this.prev = prv;
    }
}

class DoublyLinkedList {
    constructor() {
        this.head = null;
        this.tail = null;
        this.length = 0;
    }
}
```

Basic operations of Linked List

Basic operation of a linked list requires traversing a linked list. The various operations that we can perform on linked lists, many of these operations require list traversal:

1. Insert an element in the list, this operation is used to create a linked list.
2. Print various elements of the list.
3. Search an element in the list.
4. Delete an element from the list.
5. Reverse a linked list.

Search in a doubly linked list can only be done in one direction. Since all elements in the list has reference to the next item in the list. Therefore, traversal of linked list is linear in nature.

In doubly linked list linked list below are few cases that we need to keep in mind while coding:
- Zero element case (head will be modified)
- One element case (head can be modified)
- First element (head can be modified)
- General case

Note: Any program that is likely to change head pointer is to be passed as a double reference, which is pointing to head pointer.

Insert at Head

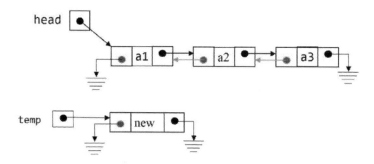

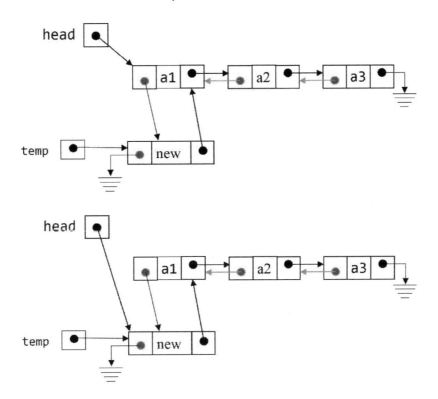

Problem: Insert node at the start of the linked list.

Example 6.29:
```
addHead(value) {
    const newNode = new DLLNode(value, null, null);
    if (this.length === 0) {
        this.tail = this.head = newNode;
    }
    else {
        this.head.prev = newNode;
        newNode.next = this.head;
        this.head = newNode;
    }
    this.length++;
}
```

Analysis: Insert in double linked list is similar as insert in a singly linked list.
- Create a node assign null to prev pointer of the node.
- If the list is empty then tail and head will point to the new node.
- If the list is not empty then prev of head will point to newNode and next of newNode will point to head. Then head will be modified to point to newNode.

Time Complexity: O(1).

Sorted Insert

Problem: Insert elements in linked list in sorted order.

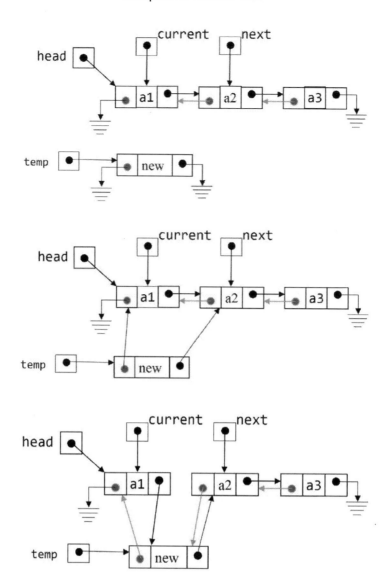

Example 6.30:
```
sortedInsert(value) {
    const temp = new DLLNode(value, null, null);
    let curr = this.head;
    if (curr == null) {
        this.head = temp;
        this.tail = temp;
    }
    if (this.head.value <= value) {
        temp.next = this.head;
        this.head.prev = temp;
        this.head = temp;
    }
    while (curr.next != null && curr.next.value > value) {
        curr = curr.next;
    };
    if (curr.next == null) {
        this.tail = temp;
```

```
        temp.prev = curr;
        curr.next = temp;
    }
    else {
        temp.next = curr.next;
        temp.prev = curr;
        curr.next = temp;
        temp.next.prev = temp;
    }
}
```

Analysis:
- We need to consider only element case first. In this case, both head and tail will modify.
- Then we need to consider the case when head will be modified when new node is added to the beginning of the list.
- Then we need to consider general cases
- Finally, we need to consider the case when tail will be modified.

Time Complexity: O(n).

Remove Head

Problem: Remove head node of the linked list.

Example 6.31:

```
removeHead() {
    if (this.isEmpty())
        throw new Error("EmptyListError");
    const value = this.head.value;
    this.head = this.head.next;
    if (this.head == null)
        this.tail = null;
    else
        this.head.prev = null;
    this.length--;
    return value;
}
```

Analysis:
- If the list is empty then we do not do anything.
- Head will point to next of head. If now head is not null then its prev will point to null.
- Update the list so that its head will point to second node.

Time Complexity: O(1).

Delete a node

Problem: Delete node with given value in a linked list

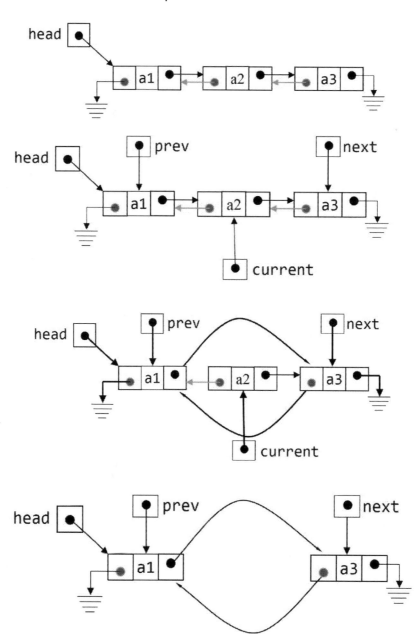

Example 6.32:

```
removeNode(key) {
    let curr = this.head;
    if (curr == null)
        return false;

    if (curr.value === key) {
        this.head = this.head.next;
        this.length--;
        if (this.head != null)
            this.head.prev = null;
        else
            this.tail = null;
        return true;
    }
```

```
    while (curr.next != null) {
        if (curr.next.value === key) {
            curr.next = curr.next.next;
            if (curr.next == null)
                this.tail = curr;
            else
                curr.next = curr;
            this.length--;
            return true;
        }
        curr = curr.next;
    };
    return false;
}
```

Analysis: Traverse the list find the node that needs to be removed. Then remove it and adjust next pointer of the node before it and prev pointer of the node next to it.

Time Complexity: O(n).

Remove Duplicate

Problem: Consider the list as sorted remove the repeated value nodes of the list.

Example 6.33:
```
removeDuplicate() {
    let curr = this.head;
    let deleteMe;
    while (curr != null) {
        if ((curr.next != null) && curr.value === curr.next.value) {
            deleteMe = curr.next;
            curr.next = deleteMe.next;
            curr.next.prev = curr;
            if (deleteMe === this.tail) {
                this.tail = curr;
            }
        }
        else {
            curr = curr.next;
        }
    };
}
```

Analysis:
- Head can never modify.
- Find the node that have value same as the previous node. Remove this node by pointer adjustment for it.

Time Complexity: O(n).

Reverse a doubly linked List iteratively

Problem: Reverse elements of doubly linked list iteratively.

Example 6.34:
```
reverseList() {
    let curr = this.head;
    let tempNode;
    while (curr != null) {
        tempNode = curr.next;
        curr.next = curr.prev;
        curr.prev = tempNode;
        if (curr.prev == null) {
            this.tail = this.head;
            this.head = curr;
            return;
        }
        curr = curr.prev;
    };
}
```

Analysis: Traverse the list. Swap the next and prev. then traverse to the direction curr. Prev, which is next before swap. If you reach the end of the list then set head and tail.

Time Complexity: O(n).

Copy List Reversed

Problem: Copy the content of the list into another list in reverse order.

Example 6.35:
```
copyListReversed() {
    const dll = new DoublyLinkedList();
    let curr = this.head;
    while (curr != null) {
        dll.addHead(curr.value);
        curr = curr.next;
    };
    return dll;
}
```

Analysis:
- Traverse through the list and copy the value of the nodes into another list by calling addHead() method.
- Since the new nodes are added to the head of the list, the new list formed have nodes order reverse there by making reverse list.

Time Complexity: O(n).

Copy List

Problem: Copy the content of the list into another in same order.

Example 6.36:
```
copyList() {
    const dll = new DoublyLinkedList();
    let curr = this.head;
    while (curr != null) {
        dll.addTail(curr.value);
        curr = curr.next;
    };
    return dll;
}
```

Analysis:
- Traverse through the list and copy the value of the nodes into another list by calling addTail() method.
- Since the new nodes are added to the tail of the list, the new list formed have nodes order same as the original list.

Time Complexity: O(n).

Search list

Problem: Search a value in a linked list.

Solution: Traverse the list same as done in singly linked list.

Free List

Problem: Free all elements of linked list

Solution: Traverse the list and remove nodes is the same way as done in singly linked list.

Print list

Problem: Print all the elements of linked list.

Solution: Traverse the list and print the value of each node in doubly linked list is same as done in singly linked list.

Find Length

Problem: Find number of elements in linked list.

Solution: Traverse the list and find its length in doubly linked list is same as done in singly linked list.

Compare Lists

Problem: Compare two linked lists.

Solution: Traverse both the lists and compare in doubly linked list is same as done in singly linked list.

Circular Linked List

This type is like the singly linked list except that the last element points to the first node of the list. The link portion of the last node contains the address of the first node.

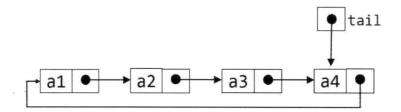

Note: In circular linked list, we can insert at the end and remove nodes at the head in constant time. These two operations efficiencies make it appropriate for use as a queue.

Example 6.37: Circular Linked List node.

```
class CLNode {
    constructor(v, n) {
        this.value = v;
        this.next = n;
    }
}

class CircularLinkedList {
    constructor() {
        this.length = 0;
        this.tail = null;
    }
}
```

Analysis: In the circular linked list, node is just like normal singly linked list. The last element node next always points to first node of the list.

Insert element in front

Problem: Add element to the head of circular linked list.

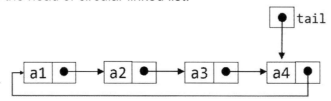

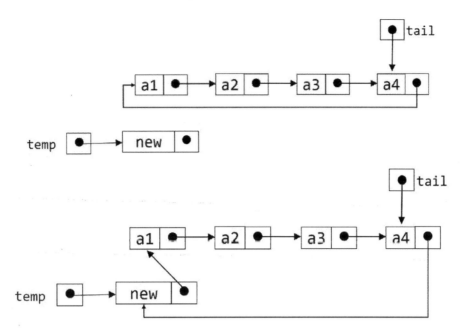

Example 6.38:

```
addHead(value) {
    const temp = new CLNode(value, null);
    if (this.isEmpty()) {
        this.tail = temp;
        temp.next = temp;
    }
    else {
        temp.next = this.tail.next;
        this.tail.next = temp;
    }
    this.length++;
}
```

Analysis:
- First, we create node with given value and its next pointing to null.
- If the list is empty then tail of the list will point to it. In addition, the next of node will point to itself
- If the list is not empty then the next of the new node will be next of the tail. In addition, tail next will start pointing to the new node.
- Thus, the new node is added to the head of the list.
- The demo program creates an instance of CircularLinkedList. Then add some value to it and finally print the content of the list.

Time Complexity: O(1).

Insert element at the end

Problem: Insert element at the end of circular linked list.

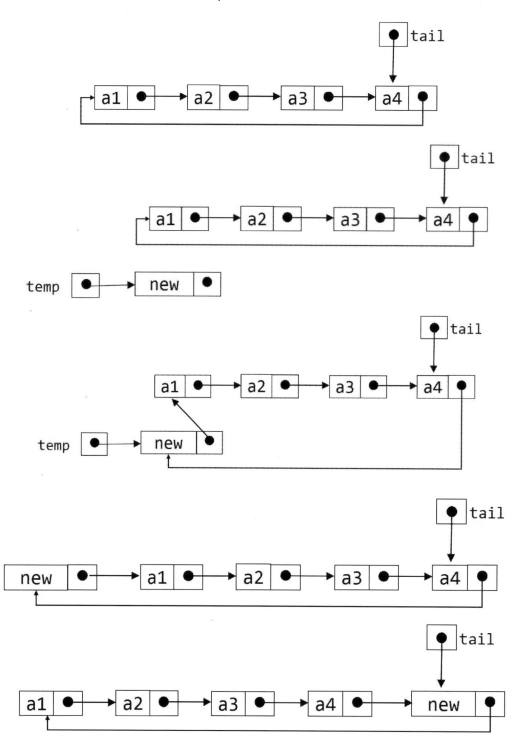

Example 6.39:

```
addTail(value) {
    const temp = new CLNode(value, null);
    if (this.isEmpty()) {
        this.tail = temp;
        temp.next = temp;
    }
    else {
        temp.next = this.tail.next;
        this.tail.next = temp;
        this.tail = temp;
```

```
    }
    this.length++;
}
```

Analysis: Adding node at the end is same as adding at the beginning. We just need to modify tail pointer in place of the head pointer.

Time Complexity: O(1).

Search element in the list

Problem: Search value in a circular linked list.

Example 6.40:
```
find(data) {
    let temp = this.tail;
    for (let i = 0; i < this.length; i++) {
        if (temp.value === data)
            return true;
        temp = temp.next;
    }
    return false;
}
```

Analysis: Iterate through the list to find if value is there or not.

Time Complexity: O(n).

Print the content of list

Problem: Print all the elements of a circular linked list.

Example 6.41:
```
print() {
    if (this.isEmpty()) {
        return;
    }
    let temp = this.tail.next;
    while (temp !== this.tail) {
        process.stdout.write(`${temp.value} `);
        temp = temp.next;
    };
    process.stdout.write(`${temp.value}\n`);
}
```

Analysis: In circular list, end of list is not there so we cannot check with null. In place of null, tail is used to check end of the list.

Time Complexity: O(n).

Remove element in the front

Problem: Remove first element of the linked list.

Example 6.42:

```
removeHead() {
    if (this.isEmpty()) {
        throw new Error("EmptyListException");
    }

    const value = this.tail.next.value;
    if (this.tail === this.tail.next)
        this.tail = null;
    else
        this.tail.next = this.tail.next.next;
    this.length--;
    return value;
}
```

Analysis:
- If the list is empty then return.
- If next node of tail is same as tail then it is a single node case. Mark tail as null.
- If it is not a single node case then point tail node next to second node from the head.

Time Complexity: O(1).

Remove a node given its value

Problem: Delete a node with given value in a circular linked list

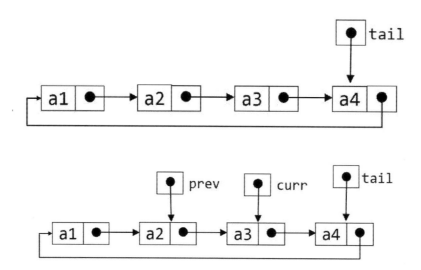

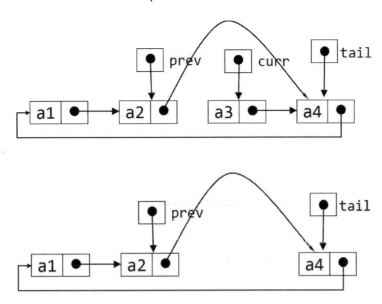

Example 6.43:
```
removeNode(key) {
    if (this.isEmpty()) {
        return false;
    }

    let prev = this.tail;
    let curr = this.tail.next;
    const head = this.tail.next;
    if (curr.value === key) {
        if (curr === curr.next)
            this.tail = null;
        else
            this.tail.next = this.tail.next.next;
        return true;
    }
    prev = curr;
    curr = curr.next;
    while (curr !== head) {
        if (curr.value === key) {
            if (curr === this.tail)
                this.tail = prev;
            prev.next = curr.next;
            return true;
        }
        prev = curr;
        curr = curr.next;
    };
    return false;
}
```

Analysis: Find the node that needs to be removed. Only difference is that while traversing the list end of list is tracked by the tail pointer in place of null. If the node that need to be removed is other than tail node then tail node pointer is not modified. If the node that need to be removed is tail node then tail node pointer of the list will be modified.

Time Complexity: O(n).

Delete List

Problem: Delete a circular linked list.

Example 6.44:
```
freeList() {
    this.tail = null;
    this.length = 0;
}
```

Analysis: Tail node will point to null. The whole list memory is collected by garbage collection.

Time Complexity: O(1).

Copy circular linked-list reversed

Problem: Copy a circular linked list in reversed order.

Example 6.45:
```
copyListReversed() {
    const cl = new CircularLinkedList();
    let curr = this.tail.next;
    const head = curr;

    if (curr != null) {
        cl.addHead(curr.value);
        curr = curr.next;
    }
    while (curr !== head) {
        cl.addHead(curr.value);
        curr = curr.next;
    };
    return cl;
}
```

Time Complexity: O(n).

Copy circular linked list

Problem: Copy a circular linked list.

Example 6.46:
```
copyList() {
    const cl = new CircularLinkedList();
```

```
    let curr = this.tail.next;
    const head = curr;

    if (curr != null) {
        cl.addTail(curr.value);
        curr = curr.next;
    }
    while (curr !== head) {
        cl.addTail(curr.value);
        curr = curr.next;
    };
    return cl;
}
```

Time Complexity: O(n).

Doubly Circular list

In a Doubly Circular Linked list, there are two pointers in each node. These pointers are called prev and next. The prev pointer of the node will point to the node before it and the next pointer will point to the node next to the given node. The previous node of first element points to the last node of the list and the next pointer of last node points to the first node of the list.

In doubly linked list, we have following cases:
1. Zero element case.
2. Only element.
3. General case
4. Avoid using recursion solutions it makes life harder

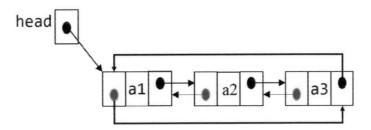

Example 6.47: Node of Doubly Circular Linked List.
```
class DCLLNode {
    constructor(v, nxt, prv) {
        this.value = v;
        this.next = nxt;
        this.prev = prv;
    }
}

class DoublyCircularLinkedList {
    constructor() {
        this.head = null;
        this.tail = null;
```

```
            this.length = 0;
        }
}
```

Analysis: The node of doubly circular linked list is same as node of doubly linked list. Only difference is that the previous pointer of first node points to last node of list and next pointer of last node points to first node of the list.

Insert Node at head

Problem: Insert value at the front of the list.

Example 6.48:
```
addHead(value) {
    const newNode = new DCLLNode(value, null, null);
    if (this.length === 0) {
        this.tail = this.head = newNode;
        newNode.next = newNode;
        newNode.prev = newNode;
    }
    else {
        newNode.next = this.head;
        newNode.prev = this.head.prev;
        this.head.prev = newNode;
        newNode.prev.next = newNode;
        this.head = newNode;
    }
    this.length++;
}
```

Analysis:
- A new node is created and if the list is empty then head and tail will point to it. The newly created newNode's next and prev also point to newNode.
- If the list is not empty then the pointers are adjusted and a new node is added to the front of the list. Only head needs to be changed in this case.
- Size of the list is increased by one.

Time Complexity: O(1).

Insert Node at tail

Problem: Insert value at the end of a linked list.

Example 6.49:
```
addTail(value) {
    const newNode = new DCLLNode(value, null, null);
    if (this.length === 0) {
        this.head = this.tail = newNode;
        newNode.next = newNode;
```

```
        newNode.prev = newNode;
    }
    else {
        newNode.next = this.tail.next;
        newNode.prev = this.tail;
        this.tail.next = newNode;
        newNode.next.prev = newNode;
        this.tail = newNode;
    }
    this.length++;
}
```

Analysis:
- A new node is created and if the list is empty then head and tail will point to it. The newly created newNode's next and prev also point to newNode.
- If the list is not empty then the pointers are adjusted and a new node is added to the end of the list. Only tail needs to be changed in this case.
- Size of the list is increased by one.

Time Complexity: O(1).

Remove head node

Problem: Remove node at the head of a doubly circular linked list

Example 6.50:
```
removeHead() {
    if (this.length === 0)
        throw new Error("EmptyListError");
    const value = this.head.value;
    this.length--;
    if (this.length === 0) {
        this.head = null;
        this.tail = null;
        return value;
    }
    const next = this.head.next;
    next.prev = this.tail;
    this.tail.next = next;
    this.head = next;
    return value;
}
```

Analysis: Remove node in a doubly circular linked list is just same as remove node in a circular linked list. Just few extra pointers need to be adjusted.

Time Complexity: O(1).

Remove tail node

Problem: Remove tail node of a linked list.

Example 6.51:
```
removeTail() {
    if (this.length === 0)
        throw new Error("EmptyListError");
    const value = this.tail.value;
    this.length--;
    if (this.length === 0) {
        this.head = null;
        this.tail = null;
        return value;
    }
    const prev = this.tail.prev;
    prev.next = this.head;
    this.head.prev = prev;
    this.tail = prev;
    return value;
}
```

Analysis: In case of empty list return. In case of single node case head and tail will store null. In other cases, next of second last node will point to head, previous of head will point to second last node.

Time Complexity: O(1).

Delete list

Problem: Free a linked list.

Solution: Delete complete list is same as given in circular linked list.

Search value

Problem: Search a value in doubly circular linked list.

Solution: Algorithm for searching a value in doubly circular linked list is same as circular linked list.

Print List

Problem: Print all the elements of linked list.

Solution: Algorithm to print content of doubly circular list is same as given in circular linked list.

Exercise

1. Insert an element at kth position from the start of linked list. Return true if success and if list is not long enough, then return -1.
    Hint: Take a pointer of head and then advance it by K steps forward, and inserts the node.

2. Insert an element at kth position from the end of linked list. Return true if success and if list is not long enough, then return -1.

    Hint: Take a pointer of head and then advance it by K steps forward, then take another pointer and then advance both simultaneously, so that when the first pointer reaches the end of a linked list then second pointer is at the point where you need to Insert the node.

3. Consider there is a loop in a linked list, write a program to remove loop if there is a loop in this linked list.

4. In the above SearchList program return, the count of how many instances of same value are found else if value not found then return 0. For Example , if the value passed is "4". The elements in the list are 1,2,4,3 & 4. The program should return 2.

    Hint: In place of return true in the above program increment a counter and then return its value.

5. Given two linked list head-pointer and they meet at some point and need to find the point of intersection. However, in place of the end of both the linked list to be a null pointer there is a loop.

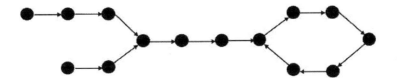

6. If linked list having a loop is given. Count the number of nodes in the linked list

7. We were supposed to write the complete code for the addition of polynomials using Linked Lists. This takes time if you do not have it by heart, so revise it well.

8. In given two linked lists. We must find whether the data in one is reverse that of data in another. No extra space should be used and traverse the linked lists only once.

9. Find the middle element in a singly linked list. Tell the complexity of your solution.

    Hint:- First Solution: Find the length of linked list. Then find the middle element and return it.
    Second Solution: Use two pointer one will move fast and another will move slow, make sure you handle border case properly. (Even length and odd length linked list cases.)

10. Print list in reverse order.

    Hint: Use recursion.

11. In a huge linked list, you are given a pointer to some middle node. Write a program to remove this node.

Hint: Copy the values of next node to current node. Then remove next node.

12. Given a special list, whose node have extra pointer random which point to some other node in linked list. Create another list that is copy of the given list. Also, make sure that random pointer is also allocated to respective node in new list.

Hint: Traverse the list and go on adding nodes to the list, which have same value but have random pointer points to null. Now traverse the modified list again. Let us call the node, which was already present in the list as old node and the node, which is added as new node. Find the random pointer node pointed of old node and assign its next node to the random pointer of new node. Follow this procedure for all the nodes. Finally separate the old and new nodes. The list formed by new nodes is the desired list.

CHAPTER 7: STACK

Introduction

A stack is a basic data structure that organizes items in last-in-first-out (LIFO) manner. Last element inserted in a stack will be the first to be removed from it.

The real-life analogy of the stack is "stack of plates". Imagine a stack of plates in a dining area everybody takes a plate at the top of the stack, thereby uncovering the next plate for the next person.

Stack allow to only access the top element. The elements that are at the bottom of the stack are the one that is going to stay in the stack for the longest time.

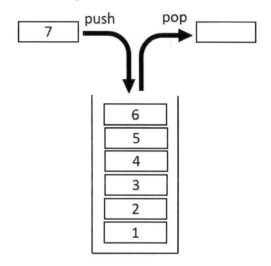

Computer science also has the common Example of a stack. Function call stack is a good Example of a stack. Function test() calls function foo() and then foo() calls bar(). These function calls are implemented using stack. First, bar() exists, then foo() and then finally test().

As we navigate from web page to web page, the URL of web pages are kept in a stack, with the current page URL at the top. If we click back button, then each URL entry is popped one by one.

The Stack Abstract Data Type

Stack abstract data type is defined a class, which follows LIFO or last-in-first-out for the elements, added to it.
The stack should support the following operations:
1. Push(): Which adds a single element at the top of the stack
2. Pop(): Which removes a single element from the top of a stack.
3. Top(): Reads the value of the top element of the stack (does not remove it)
4. isEmpty(): Returns 1 if stack is empty
5. Size(): Returns the number of elements in a stack.

Push : Add value to the top of a stack

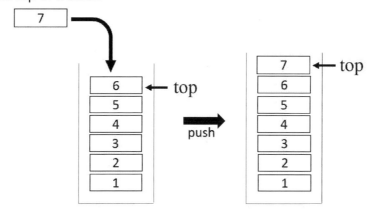

Pop : Remove the top element of the stack and return it to the caller function.

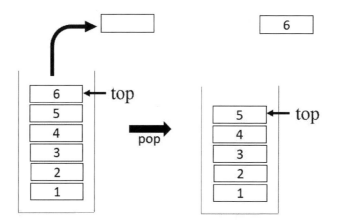

The stack can be implemented using an array or a linked list.
1. When stack is implemented using arrays, its capacity is fixed.
2. In case of a linked list, there is no such limit on the number of elements it can contain.

When a stack is implemented, using an array top of the stack is managed using an index variable called top.

When a stack is implemented using a linked list, push() and pop() is implemented using insert at the head of the linked list and remove from the head of the linked list.

Stack using array

Problem: Implement a stack using a fixed length array.

Example 7.1: Stack implementation using array

```
class Stack {
    constructor(capacity) {
        if (capacity === undefined) { capacity = 1000; }
        this.top = -1;
        this.data = new Array(capacity);
    }
}
```

```
    /* other methods */
}
```

isEmpty() function returns true if stack is empty or false in all other cases.

```
isEmpty() {
    return (this.top === -1);
}
```

length() function returns the number of elements in the stack.

```
size() {
    return (this.top + 1);
}
```

The print function will print the elements of the array.

```
print() {
    for (let i = this.top; i >= 0; i--) {
        console.log(this.data[i]);
    }
}
```

push() function append value to the data.

```
push(value) {
    this.top++;
    this.data[this.top] = value;
}
```

In the **pop**() function, first it will check that the stack is not empty. Then it will pop the value from data array and return it.

```
pop() {
    if (this.isEmpty()) {
        throw new Error("StackEmptyException");
    }
    const topVal = this.data[this.top];
    this.top--;
    return topVal;
}
```

top() function returns the value of stored in the top element of stack (does not remove it)

```
top() {
    if (this.isEmpty()) {
        throw new Error("StackEmptyException");
    }
    return this.data[this.top];
}
```

Test code for stack.

```
const s = new Stack();
s.push(1);
s.push(2);
s.push(3);
```

```
console.info(s.pop());
console.info(s.pop());
console.info(s.pop());
```

Output:
```
3
2
1
```

Analysis:
- Stack object is declared and initialized.
- push() and pop() functions to are used to add and remove values to the stack.

Stack using linked list

Problem: Stack can be implemented using a linked list. Add elements at the head of list and remove form the head of the list.

Example 7.2: Implement stack using a linked list.
```
class StackNode {
    constructor(v, n) {
        this.value = v;
        this.next = n;
    }
};

class Stack {
    constructor() {
        this.head = null;
        this.length = 0;
    }

    size() {
        return this.length;
    }

    isEmpty() {
        return this.length === 0;
    }

    peek() {
        if (this.isEmpty()) {
            throw new Error("StackEmptyError");
        }
        return this.head.value;
    }

    push(value) {
        this.head = new StackNode(value, this.head);
```

```
            this.length++;
    }

    pop() {
        if (this.isEmpty()) {
            throw new Error("StackEmptyError");
        }
        const value = this.head.value;
        this.head = this.head.next;
        this.length--;
        return value;
    }

    insertAtBottom(value) {
        if (this.isEmpty()) {
            this.push(value);
        }
        else {
            const temp = this.pop();
            this.insertAtBottom(value);
            this.push(temp);
        }
    }

    print() {
        let temp = this.head;
        while (temp != null) {
            console.log(temp.value);
            temp = temp.next;
        };
    }
}

const s = new Stack();
s.push(1);
s.push(2);
s.push(3);
console.info(s.pop());
console.info(s.pop());
console.info(s.pop());
```

Output:
```
3
2
1
```

Analysis:
- Stack implemented using a linked list is simply insertion and deletion at the head of a singly linked list.

- In StackPush() function, memory is created for one node. Then the value is stored into that node. Finally, the node is inserted at the beginning of the list.
- In StackPop() function, the head of the linked list starts pointing to the second node. And the value of first node is returned.

System stack and Method Calls

Methods calls are implemented using stack called system stack. When a method is called, the current execution is stopped and the control goes to the called method. After the called method exits / returns, the execution resumes from the point at which the execution was stopped.

To get the exact point at which execution should be resumed, the address of the next instruction is stored in the system stack. When the method call completes, the address at the top of the stack is taken out.

Example 7.3: Function call flow

```
function function2() {
    console.log("fun2 line 1");
};
function function1() {
    console.log("fun1 line 1");
    function2();
    console.log("fun1 line 2");
};
function test() {
    console.log("test line 1");
    function1();
    console.log("test line 2");
};

test();
```

Output:
```
test line 1
fun1 line 1
fun2 line 1
fun1 line 2
test line 2
```

Analysis:
- This program starts with call of test() method.
- The first statement of test() will be executed. This will print "test line 1" as output.
- Then statement function1() is called. Before control goes to function1() then next instruction that is address of next line is stored in the system stack.
- Control goes to function1() method.
- The first statement inside function1() is executed, this will print "fun1 line 1" to output.
- function2() is called from function1(). Before control goes to function2() address of the next instruction that is address of next line is added to the system stack.
- Control goes to function2() method.

206

- "fun2 line 1" is printed to screen.
- When function2() exits, control come back to function1(). Then the program reads the next instruction from the stack, and the next line is executed and print "fun1 line 2" to screen.
- When fun1 exits, control comes back to the test method. Then program reads the next instruction from the stack and executes it and finally "test line 2" is printed to screen.

Points to remember:
1. Methods are implemented using a stack.
2. When a method is called the address of the next instruction is pushed into the stack.
3. When a method is finished the address of the execution is taken out of the stack.

Problems in Stack

Sorted Insert

Problem: Given a stack whose elements are sorted, write a function which will insert elements in sorted order. With highest at the top and lowest at the bottom.

Solution: Pop elements from stack till the top of stack is grater then the current value. Then add current value and then add the popped elements to the stack again. Time complexity O(n)

Example 7.4:
```
function sortedInsert(stk, element) {
    let temp;
    if (stk.length <= 0 || element > stk[stk.length - 1])
        stk.push(element);
    else {
        temp = stk.pop();
        sortedInsert(stk, element);
        stk.push(temp);
    }
}

function test() {
    const stk = ([]);
    stk.push(1);
    stk.push(2);
    stk.push(4);
    stk.push(5);
    sortedInsert(stk, 3)
    console.info(stk);
};
```

Output:
```
[ 1, 2, 3, 4, 5 ]
```

Sort Stack

Problem: Given a stack, sort elements such that largest value is at the top.

First Solution: Recursively call sort stack function. Then call sorted insert function inside recursion to make the stack sorted. Time complexity is $O(n^2)$

Example 7.5:
```
function sortStack(stk) {
    let temp;
    console.log(stk)
    console.log(stk.length)
    if (stk.length > 0) {
        temp = stk.pop();
        sortStack(stk);
        sortedInsert(stk, temp);
    }
}

function test() {
    const stk = ([]);
    stk.push(1);
    stk.push(5);
    stk.push(3);
    stk.push(2);
    stk.push(4);
    sortStack(stk)
    console.info(stk);
};
```

Output:
```
[ 1, 2, 3, 4, 5 ]
```

Second Solution: Same problem can be solved iteratively by using another stack stk2. We use a stack stk2 which will store elements always in sorted order. Each time new element is popped form the original input stack and get added to the new stack. Time Complexity is $O(n^2)$

Example 7.6:
```
function sortStack2(stk) {
    let temp;
    const stk2 = ([]);
    while (stk.length > 0) {
        temp = stk.pop();
        while (stk2.length > 0 && stk2[stk2.length - 1] < temp) {
            stk.push(stk2.pop());
        };
        stk2.push(temp);
    }
    while (stk2.length > 0) {
        stk.push(stk2.pop());
```

```
        }
}
```

Bottom Insert

Problem: Given stack write a function to insert element at the bottom of the stack.

Solution: Pop elements from stack recursively till it is empty. Once empty then insert the input value in the stack. Then again put the popped values back to the stack. Time complexity is O(n)

Example 7.7:
```
function bottomInsert(stk, element) {
    let temp;
    if (stk.length == 0)
        stk.push(element);
    else {
        temp = stk.pop();
        bottomInsert(stk, element);
        stk.push(temp);
    }
};

function test() {
    const stk = ([]);
    stk.push(1);
    stk.push(2);
    stk.push(3);
    bottomInsert(stk, 4)
    console.info(stk);
};
```

Output:
```
[ 4, 1, 2, 3 ]
```

Reverse Stack

Problem: Given a stack, reverse its elements.

First Solution: Using recursion, in a recursion pop element from stack and use bottomInsert function to add them at the bottom. Finally, the whole stack will be reversed. Time complexity is O(n²)

Example 7.8:
```
function reverseStack(stk) {
    if (stk.length == 0) {
        return;
    } else {
        const value = stk.pop();
        reverseStack(stk);
        bottomInsert(stk, value);
```

```
        }
}

function test() {
    const stk = ([]);
    stk.push(1);
    stk.push(2);
    stk.push(3);
    console.info("Stack before reversal", stk);
    reverseStack3(stk)
    console.info("Stack after reversal", stk);
};
```

Output:
```
Stack before reversal [ 1, 2, 3 ]
Stack after reversal [ 3, 2, 1 ]
```

Second Solution: Using queue, pop all the elements of the stack insert them into queue then remove elements from queue and insert them into stack and stack elements will be reversed. Time complexity is O(n)

Example 7.9:
```
function reverseStack2(stk) {
    const que = new Deque();
    while (stk.length > 0) {
        que.add(stk.pop());
    };

    while (que.isEmpty() === false) {
        stk.push(que.remove());
    };
};
```

Reverse K Element in a Stack

Problem: Reverse k elements at the top of the stack.

Solution: Create a queue, pop k elements from stack and add them to queue. Then remove form queue and push them back to the stack. Top k elements will be reversed. Time complexity is O(n)

Example 7.10:
```
function reverseKElementInStack(stk, k) {
    const que = new Deque();
    let i = 0;
    while (stk.length > 0 && i < k) {
        que.add(stk.pop());
        i++;
    };
    while (que.isEmpty() === false) {
        stk.push(que.remove());
```

```
    };
};

function test() {
    const stk = ([]);
    stk.push(1);
    stk.push(2);
    stk.push(3);
    stk.push(4);
    reverseKElementInStack(stk, 2)
    console.info(stk);
};
```

Output:
```
[ 1, 2, 4, 3 ]
```

Reverse Queue

Problem: Reverse elements of a queue.

Solution: Remove all the elements of the queue and push them to the stack till queue is empty. Then pop elements from stack and add them to the queue. Finally, all the elements of queue are reversed. Time complexity is O(n)

Example 7.11:
```
function reverseQueue(que) {
    const stk = ([]);
    while (que.isEmpty() === false) {
        stk.push(que.remove());
    };
    while (stk.length > 0) {
        que.add(stk.pop());
    };
};

function test() {
    const que = new Deque()
    que.add(1);
    que.add(2);
    que.add(3);
    console.log(que)
    reverseQueue(que)
    console.info(que);
};
```

Output:
```
Deque { data: [ 1, 2, 3 ] }
Deque { data: [ 3, 2, 1 ] }
```

Reverse K Element in a Queue

Problem: Reverse first K elements in a queue.

Solution: Use a stack, remove first K elements of queue and push them into stack. Then pop the element from stack and add them to the queue. The K elements are reversed but they are added to the end of queue. So, we need to bring those elements at the start of queue by removing the elements at the front and adding them at the back of queue. Time complexity is O(n)

Example 7.12:
```
function reverseKElementInQueue(que, k) {
    const stk = ([]);
    let i = 0;
    let diff;
    let temp;
    while (que.isEmpty() === false && i < k) {
        stk.push(que.remove())
        i++;
    }
    while (stk.length > 0) {
        que.add(stk.pop());
    }
    diff = que.size() - k;
    while (diff > 0) {
        temp = que.remove();
        que.add(temp);
        diff -= 1;
    }
};

function test() {
    const que = new Deque()
    que.add(1);
    que.add(2);
    que.add(3);
    que.add(4);
    console.log(que)
    reverseKElementInQueue(que, 2)
    console.info(que);
};
```

Output:
```
Deque { data: [ 1, 2, 3, 4 ] }
Deque { data: [ 2, 1, 3, 4 ] }
```

Min stack

Problem: Design a stack in which we can get minimum value in stack should also work in **O(1)** Time Complexity.

Hint: Keep two stack one will be general stack, which will just keep the elements. The second will keep the min value.

1. Push: Push an element to the top of stack1. Compare the new value with the value at the top of the stack2. If the new value is smaller, then push the new value into stack2. Or push the value at the top of the stack2 to itself once more.
2. Pop: Pop an element from top of stack1 and return. Pop an element from top of stack2 too.
3. Min: Reads from the top of the stack2 this value will be the min.

Stack using a queue

Problem: How to implement a stack using a queue. Analyze the running time of the stack operations.

See queue chapter for its solution.

Balanced Parenthesis

Problem: Write a program to check balanced symbols (such as {}, (), []). The closing symbol should be matched with the most recently seen opening symbol.
e.g. {()} is legal, {() ({})} is legal, but {(() and {()} are not legal

Example 7.13:
```
function isBalancedParenthesis(expn) {
    const stk = [];
    for (let index = 0; index < expn.length; index++) {
        const ch = expn[index];
        switch (ch) {
            case '{':
            case '[':
            case '(':
                stk.push(ch);
                break;
            case '}':
                if (stk.pop() !== '{') {
                    return false;
                }
                break;
            case ']':
                if (stk.pop() !== '[') {
                    return false;
                }
                break;
            case ')':
                if (stk.pop() !== '(') {
                    return false;
                }
                break;
        }
    }
    return (stk.length == 0);
```

```
}

function test() {
    const expn = "{()}[]";
    const value = isBalancedParenthesis(expn);
    console.log(`Given Expn:${expn}`);
    console.log(`Is Balanced Parenthesis : ${value}`);
}
```

Output:
```
Given Expn:{()}[]
Is Balanced Parenthesis : true
```

Analysis:
- Traverse the input string when we get an opening parenthesis, we push it into stack. Moreover, when we get a closing parenthesis then we pop a parenthesis from the stack and compare if it is the corresponding closing parenthesis.
- We return false if there is a mismatch of parenthesis.
- If at the end of the whole staring traversal, we reach to the end of the string and the stack is empty then we have balanced parenthesis.

Max Depth Parenthesis

Problem: Given a balanced parenthesis expression you need to find maximum depth of parenthesis. For Example "()" maximum depth is 1 and for "((()))()" maximum depth is 3.

First Solution: Create a stack, when we get opening parenthesis then we insert it to the stack and increase depth counter. When we get a closing parenthesis then we pop opening parenthesis from stack and decrease the depth counter. We keep track of depth to find maximum depth.

Example 7.14:
```
function maxDepthParenthesis(expn, size) {
    const stk = ([]);
    let maxDepth = 0;
    let depth = 0;
    let ch;
    for (let i = 0; i < size; i++) {
        ch = expn[i];
        if (ch == '(') {
            stk.push(ch);
            depth += 1;
        }
        else if (ch == ')') {
            stk.pop();
            depth -= 1;
        }
        if (depth > maxDepth)
            maxDepth = depth;
    }
    return maxDepth;
```

```
}

function test() {
    const expn = "((((A)))((((BBB()))))()()()())";
    const size = expn.length;
    const value = maxDepthParenthesis(expn, size);
    console.info(`Given expn ${expn}`);
    console.info(`Max depth parenthesis is ${value}`);
};
```

Output:
```
Given expn ((((A)))((((BBB()))))()()()())
Max depth parenthesis is 6
```

Second Solution: We do not need to find if the expression is balanced or not. It is given that it is balanced to we don't need a stack as shown in previous solution.

Example 7.15:
```
function maxDepthParenthesis2(expn, size) {
    let maxDepth = 0;
    let depth = 0;
    let ch;
    for (let i = 0; i < size; i++) {
        ch = expn[i];
        if (ch == '(')
            depth += 1;
        else if (ch == ')')
            depth -= 1;
        if (depth > maxDepth)
            maxDepth = depth;
    }
    return maxDepth;
}
```

Longest Continuous Balanced Parenthesis

Problem: Given a string of opening and closing parenthesis, you need to find a sub-string which have balanced parenthesis.

Example 7.16:
```
function longestContBalParen(string, size) {
    const stk = ([]);
    stk.push(-1);
    let length = 0;
    for (let i = 0; i < size; i++) {
        if (string[i] == '(')
            stk.push(i);
        else {
            stk.pop();
            if (stk.length != 0)
```

```
                length = Math.max(length, i - stk[stk.length - 1]);
            else
                stk.push(i);
        }
    }
    return length;
}

function test() {
    const expn = "())((()))(())()(()";
    const size = expn.length;
    const value = longestContBalParen(expn, size);
    console.info(`longestContBalParen : ${value}`);
};
```

Output:
```
longestContBalParen : 12
```

Reverse Parenthesis

Problem: How many reversals will be needed to make an unbalanced expression to balanced expression.
Input: ")(())(((("
Output: 3

Input: ")(((("
Output: 3

Solution:
- First the parenthesis which are already balanced don't need to be flipped so they are first removed. What all the parenthesis which are balanced is removed then we will have the parenthesis of the form "...))((((...".
- So let's call the total number of open parenthesis is OpenCount and total number of closed parenthesis is CloseCount.
- When OpenCount is even CloseCount is also even and their half element reversal will make the expression balanced.
- When OpenCount is odd and also CloseCount, then once you had reversed
- OpenCount/2 and CloseCount/2. You will be left with ")(" which need 2 more reversal, so the formula is derived from this.
    Total number of reversal = math.ceil (OpenCount / 2) + math.ceil(CloseCount / 2)

Example 7.17:
```
function reverseParenthesis(expn, size) {
    const stk = ([]);
    let openCount = 0;
    let closeCount = 0;
    let ch;
    if (size % 2 === 1) {
        console.info(`Invalid odd length ${size}`);
        return -1;
```

```
    }
    for (let i = 0; i < size; i++) {
        ch = expn[i];
        if (ch == '(')
            stk.push(ch);
        else if (ch == ')')
            if (stk.length !== 0 && stk[stk.length - 1] == '(')
                stk.pop();
            else
                stk.push(')');
    }
    while (stk.length !== 0) {
        if (stk.pop() == '(')
            openCount += 1;
        else
            closeCount += 1;
    }
    const reversal = Math.ceil(openCount / 2.0) + Math.ceil(closeCount /
2.0);
    return reversal;
}

function test() {
    const expn  = ")(())(((";
    const size = expn.length;
    const value = reverseParenthesis(expn, size);
    console.info(`reverse Parenthesis is : ${value}`);
};
```

Output:
```
reverse Parenthesis is : 3
```

Find Duplicate Parenthesis

Problem: Given an expression, you need to find duplicate or redundant parenthesis in it. Redundant parenthesis are those parenthesis pair which does not change the outcome of expression.

Solution: A parenthesis pair is redundant if it contains 0 or 1 element between them. The algorithm works by adding all the element except ')' to the stack. When we get a ')' at that point we find its corresponding pair and count all the elements between this pair. If the number of elements is 0 or 1 then we have a redundant parenthesis.

Example 7.18:
```
function findDuplicateParenthesis(expn, size) {
    const stk = ([]);
    let ch;
    let count;
    for (let i = 0; i < size; i++) {
        ch = expn[i];
        if (ch == ')') {
```

```
                count = 0;
                while (stk.length !== 0 && stk[stk.length - 1] != '(') {
                    stk.pop();
                    count += 1;
                }
                if (count <= 1)
                    return true;
            }
            else
                stk.push(ch);
        }
    return false;
};

function test() {
    const expn = "(((a+b))+c)";
    const size = expn.length;
    const value = findDuplicateParenthesis(expn, size);
    console.info(`Duplicate Found : ${value}`);
};
```

Output:
```
Duplicate Found : true
```

Print Parenthesis Number

Problem: Given an expression, Number each parenthesis pair such that for each pair the opening and closing parenthesis have same number.
Example :
Input: '(((a+(b))+(c+d)))'
Output: [1, 2, 3, 4, 4, 3, 5, 5, 2, 1]

Example 7.19:
```
function printParenthesisNumber(expn, size) {
    let ch;
    const stk = ([]);
    let output = "";
    let count = 1;
    for (let i = 0; i < size; i++) {
        ch = expn[i];
        if (ch == '(') {
            stk.push(count);
            output += count;
            count += 1;
        }
        else if (ch == ')')
            output += stk.pop();
    }
    console.info("Parenthesis Count : ", output);
}
```

```
function test() {
    const expn1 = "(((a+(b))+(c+d)))";
    const expn2 = "(((a+b))+c)(((";
    let size = expn1.length;
    console.info(`Given expn ${expn1}`);
    printParenthesisNumber(expn1, size);
    size = expn2.length;
    console.info(`Given expn ${expn2}`);
    printParenthesisNumber(expn2, size);
};
```

Output:
```
Given expn (((a+(b))+(c+d)))
Parenthesis Count :  1234435521
Given expn (((a+b))+c)(((
Parenthesis Count :  123321456
```

Infix, Prefix and Postfix Expressions

When we have an algebraic expression like A + B then we know that the variable A is being added to variable B. This type of expression is called infix expression because the operator "+" is there between operands A and operand B.

Now consider another infix expression A + B * C. In the expression there is a problem that in which order + and * work. Are A and B are added first and then the result is multiplied. Alternatively, B and C are multiplied first and then the result is added to A. This makes the expression ambiguous. To deal with this ambiguity we define the precedence rule or use parentheses to remove ambiguity.

So, if we want to multiply B and C first and then add the result to A. Then the same expression can be written unambiguously using parentheses as A + (B * C). On the other hand, if we want to add A and B first and then the sum will be multiplied by C we will write it as (A + B) * C. Therefore, in the infix expression to make the expression unambiguous, we need parenthesis.

Infix expression: In this notation, we place operator in the middle of the operands.
<Operand><Operator >< Operand >

Prefix expressions: In this notation, we place operator at the beginning of the operands.
<Operator>< Operand >< Operand >

Postfix expression: In this notation, we place operator at the end of the operands.
<Operand><Operand ><Operator >

Infix Expression	Prefix Expression	Postfix Expression
A + B	+ AB	AB +
A + (B * C)	+ A * BC	ABC * +

Infix Expression	Prefix Expression	Postfix Expression
(A + B) * C	* + ABC	A B + C *

Now comes the most obvious question why we need so unnatural Prefix or Postfix expressions when we already have infix expressions which words just fine for us. The answer to this is that infix expressions are ambiguous and they need parenthesis to make them unambiguous. While postfix and prefix notations do not need any parenthesis.

Infix-to-Postfix Conversion

Problem: Function to convert infix expression to postfix expression.

Example 7.20:
```
function precedence(x) {
    if (x === '(') {
        return (0);
    }
    if (x === '+' || x === '-') {
        return (1);
    }
    if (x === '*' || x === '/' || x === '%')
        return (2);
    if (x === '^') {
        return (3);
    }
    return (4);
}

function infixToPostfix(expn) {
    const stk = [];
    let output = "";
    let out;
    for (let index = 0; index < expn.length; index++) {
        const ch = expn[index];
        if (ch <= '9' && ch >= '0') {
            output = output + ch;
        } else {
            switch (ch) {
                case '+':
                case '-':
                case '*':
                case '/':
                case '%':
                case '^':
                    while (stk.length != 0
                        && precedence(ch) <= precedence(stk[stk.length -
1])) {
                        out = stk.pop();
```

```
                            output = `${output} ${out}`;
                        };
                        stk.push(ch);
                        output = `${output} `;
                        break;
                    case '(':
                        stk.push(ch);
                        break;
                    case ')':
                        while (stk.length != 0 && (out = stk.pop()) !== '(') {
                            output = `${output} ${out} `;
                        };
                        break;
                }
            }


        }
        while (stk.length != 0) {
            out = stk.pop();
            output = `${output} ${out}`;
        };
        return output;
}

function test() {
    const expn = "10+((3))*5/(16-4)";
    const value = infixToPostfix(expn);
    console.log(`Infix Expn: ${expn}`);
    console.log(`Postfix Expn: ${value}`);
}
```

Output:

```
Infix Expn: 10+((3))*5/(16-4)
Postfix Expn: 10 3 5 * 16 4 -  / +
```

Analysis:

- Print operands in the same order as they arrive.
- If the stack is empty or contains a left parenthesis "(" on top, we should push the incoming operator in the stack.
- If the incoming symbol is a left parenthesis "(", push left parenthesis in the stack.
- If the incoming symbol is a right parenthesis ")", pop from the stack and print the operators until you see a left parenthesis ")". Discard the pair of parentheses.
- If the precedence of incoming symbol is higher than the precedence of operator at the top of the stack, then push it to the stack.
- If the incoming symbol has, an equal precedence compared to the top of the stack, use association. If the association is left to right, then pop and print the symbol at the top of the stack and then push the incoming operator. If the association is right to left, then push the incoming operator.
- If the precedence of incoming symbol is lower than the precedence of operator on the top of the stack, then pop and print the top operator. Then compare the incoming operator against the new operator at the top of the stack.

- At the end of the expression, pop and print all operators on the stack.

Infix-to-Prefix Conversion

Problem: Function to convert infix expression to postfix expression.

Example 7.21:

```
function infixToPrefix(expn) {
    expn = reverseString(expn);
    expn = replaceParanthesis(expn);
    expn = infixToPostfix(expn);
    expn = reverseString(expn);
    return expn;
}

function reverseString(expn) {
    let reverse = "";
    let upper = expn.length - 1;

    while (upper >= 0) {
        reverse += expn[upper];
        upper--;
    };
    return reverse;
}

function replaceParanthesis(expn) {
    let retval = "";
    const size = expn.length;
    let index = 0;
    while (index < size) {
        if (expn[index] === '(') {
            retval += ')';
        } else if (expn[index] === ')') {
            retval += '(';
        } else {
            retval += expn[index];
        }
        index++;
    };

    return retval;
}

function test() {
    const expn = "10+((3))*5/(16-4)";
    const value = infixToPrefix(expn);
    console.log(`Infix Expn: ${expn}`);
    console.log(`Prefix Expn: ${value}`);
}
```

Output:
```
Infix Expn: 10+((3))*5/(16-4)
Prefix Expn: + 10 * 3 / 5  - 16 4
```

Analysis:

1. Reverse the given infix expression.
2. Replace '(' with ')' and ')' with '(' in the reversed expression.
3. Now, apply infix to postfix subroutine already discussed.
4. Reverse the generated postfix expression and this will give required prefix expression.

Postfix Evaluate

Problem: Write a function to evaluate a postfix expression. Such as: expression "1 2 + 3 4 + *" gives output 21

Example 7.22:
```javascript
function postfixEvaluate(expn) {
    const stk = [];
    let temp;
    const tokens = expn.split(" ");
    for (const tok in tokens) {
        temp = parseInt(tokens[tok]);
        if (isNaN(temp) === false) {
            stk.push(temp);
        }
        else {
            num1 = stk.pop();
            num2 = stk.pop();
            op = tokens[tok];
            switch (op) {
                case '+':
                    stk.push(num1 + num2);
                    break;
                case '-':
                    stk.push(num1 - num2);
                    break;
                case '*':
                    stk.push(num1 * num2);
                    break;
                case '/':
                    stk.push(num1 / num2);
                    break;
            }
        }
    }
    return stk.pop();
}
```

```
function test() {
    expn = "6 5 2 3 + 8 * + 3 + *";
    value = postfixEvaluate(expn);
    console.log(`Given Postfix Expn: ${expn}`);
    console.log(`Result after Evaluation: ${value}`);
}
```

Output:
```
Result after Evaluation: 288
```

Analysis:
1) Create a stack to store values or operands.
2) Scan through the given expression and do following for each element:
    a) If the element is a number, then push it into the stack.
    b) If the element is an operator, then pop values from the stack. Evaluate the operator over the values and push the result into the stack.
4) When the expression is scanned completely, the number in the stack is the result.

Stack Based Rejection Method

Stack Based Rejection technique is used when processing data follow specific property of rejection. That value at some index can be used to reject some other values that are processed before it. The values that are rejected are those values, which are unimportant for the rest of the processing. Below Examples of "Stock Span Problem", "Get Max Rectangular Area in a Histogram" "Stock Analyst Problem" etc. are few of its Example .

Stock Span Problem

Problem: In given list of daily stock price in an array A[i]. Find the span of the stocks for each day. A span of stock is the maximum number of days for which the price of stock was lower than that day.

Or

Given a histogram, find the number of consecutive bars in the left side of the current bar that have values less than the current bar.

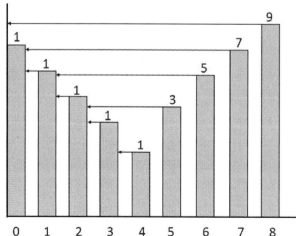

First Solution: Brute force, two loops are used. Outer loop to select the bar / elements in histogram. Inner loop is used to find count of consecutive bars smaller to current bar.

Example 7.23:
```
function StockSpanRange(arr) {
    const SR = new Array(arr.length);
    SR[0] = 1;
    for (let i = 1; i < arr.length; i++) {
        SR[i] = 1;
        for (let j = i - 1; (j >= 0) && (arr[i] >= arr[j]); j--) {
            SR[i]++;
        }
    }
    return SR;
}

function test() {
    let arr = [6, 5, 4, 3, 2, 4, 5, 7, 9];
    let value = StockSpanRange(arr);
    console.info("StockSpanRange : ", value);
}
```

Output:
```
StockSpanRange :   [ 1, 1, 1, 1, 1, 4, 6, 8, 9 ]
```

Time complexity: $O(n^2)$, length of each bar is compared with the bars before it.

Second Solution: The above algorithms for each bar we are comparing length of bars before it. If somehow, we can get the index of the bar that is before current bar and is having length greater than the current bar. Let us suppose the index of this hypothetical bar is M and index of current bar is N then the stock span range will be (N − M). By using a stack such index can be obtained by doing some bookkeeping.

Let us call stock input array as "arr". Create a stack to store index value and add value 0 to it. Then traverse the values in stock input array. Let call current index we are analysing as "curr", the index at the top of stack is "top". For each value of the stock input arr[curr] is compared with arr[top]. If value arr[curr] is less than or equal to arr[top] then add curr to the stack. If value of arr[curr] is greater than arr[top] then start popping values from stack till arr[curr] > arr[top]. Then add curr to the stack. Store stock range to SR[curr] = curr − top. Repeat this process for all the index of input array and SR array will be populated.

Example 7.24:
```
function StockSpanRange2(arr) {
    const stk = ([]);
    const SR = new Array(arr.length);
    stk.push(0);
    SR[0] = 1;
    for (let i = 1; i < arr.length; i++) {
        while ( stk.length > 0 && arr[stk[stk.length - 1]] <= arr[i]) {
            stk.pop();
        };
        SR[i] = (stk.length == 0) ? (i + 1) : (i - stk[stk.length - 1]);
        stk.push(i);
    }
```

```
      return SR;
}
```

For each value in input array, index is added to stack only once and that index can be taken out of stack only once. Each comparison operation leads to either adding a value to stack or taking a value out of stack. Therefore, if there are n elements in array then at most there will be 2n comparison so this algorithm is linear.

Time complexity is O(n), space complexity will also be O(n) for stack.

Get Max Rectangular Area in a Histogram

Problem: In given histogram of rectangle bars of each one unit wide. Find the maximum area rectangle in the histogram.

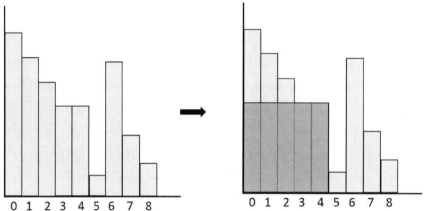

First Solution: Brute force approach. We use two loops to find the desired greatest area. First loop to find the right boundary of a rectangle and then another inner loop to find the left boundary of the rectangle. This approach has time complexity of $O(n^2)$

Example 7.25:
```
function GetMaxArea(arr) {
    const size = arr.length;
    let maxArea = -1;
    let currArea;
    let minHeight = 0;
    for (let i = 1; i < size; i++) {
        minHeight = arr[i];
        for (let j = i - 1; j >= 0; j--) {
            if (minHeight > arr[j]) {
                minHeight = arr[j];
            }
            currArea = minHeight * (i - j + 1);
            if (maxArea < currArea) {
                maxArea = currArea;
            }
        }
    }
    return maxArea;
```

```
}
function test() {
    const arr = [7, 6, 5, 4, 4, 1, 6, 3, 1];
    const size = arr.length;
    let value = GetMaxArea(arr);
    console.info(`GetMaxArea :: ${value}`);

    value = GetMaxArea2(arr);
    console.info(`GetMaxArea :: ${value}`);
}
```

Output:
```
GetMaxArea :: 20
```

Second Solution: Using Stack
- Create a stack that contain index in increasing order.
- When a current index value is smaller than the values at the top of the stack, current index is added to the stack.
- When a current index value is smaller than the values at the top of the stack, stack is popped till the top value is less than the current index value.
- The value that is popped out from stack will contribute to create rectangle. The height of rectangle is arr[top] and width will be "i" if stack is empty and is (I – stk[-1] - 1)

Time complexity is O(n)

Example 7.26:
```
function GetMaxArea2(arr) {
    const size = arr.length;
    const stk = [];
    let maxArea = 0;
    let top;
    let topArea;
    let i = 0;
    while (i < size) {
        while ((i < size) && (stk.length == 0 || arr[stk[stk.length - 1]] <=
arr[i])) {
            stk.push(i);
            i++;
        }
        while ((stk.length > 0) && (i === size || arr[stk[stk.length - 1]] >
arr[i])) {
            top = stk[stk.length - 1];
            stk.pop();
            topArea = arr[top] * ((stk.length == 0)? i : i - stk[stk.length
- 1] - 1);
            if (maxArea < topArea) {
                maxArea = topArea;
            }
        }
    }
```

```
    }
    return maxArea;
}
```

Stock Analyst Problem

Problem: A stock analyst had approached you to write a program to find stock hike points in some stocks. A stock hike point is the values of stock that is greater than all its previous values. You are provided stock price in an infinite stream with most recent value first (in term of time the data is provided in reverse order.).

For Example , in stock values are [20, 19, 10, 21, 40, 35, 39, 50, 45, 42], stock hike points values are 20, 21, 40 and 50 but the data is provided in reverse order.

Analysis:
- Data is provided in order of old value first then new values. Then this can be done in linear time just by using a single variable to store maximum value so far. However, in our problem data is provided in reverse order.
- When we are processing some value at that time we do not know if it will become a hike point.
- We will use a stack to store the data. We read input from stream; if value at top of stack is smaller than input value then we pop value from stack until the value at the top of stack is smaller than the input value. Then we add the input value to stack.
- If the value at the top of stack is greater than the input value then we add the input value to the stack. At the end, the content of stack is stock hike points.
- Time complexity of this solution is O(n)

Next Larger Element

Problem: Function to print next larger element of each element of array.

First Solution: Brute force approach, for each index we can traverse the array indexes right to it to find a larger value. Time complexity is O(n²)

Example 7.27:
```
function nextLargerElement(arr, size) {
    const output = new Array(size);
    let outIndex = 0;
    let next;
    for (let i = 0; i < size; i++) {
        next = -1;
        for (let j = i + 1; j < size; j++) {
            if (arr[i] < arr[j]) {
                next = arr[j];
                break;
            }
        }
        output[outIndex++] = next;
    }
    console.log(output)
```

```
};

function test() {
    const arr = [13, 21, 3, 6, 20, 3];
    const size = arr.length;
    nextLargerElement(arr, size);
};
```

Output:
```
[ 21, -1, 6, 20, -1, -1 ]
```

Second Solution: let us suppose we are processing elements of array. The elements which are less than ith element is does not have largest element on the right of ith index. So, we can say the elements which are left of ith element and which are less the ith element are independent of the elements at the index higher than ith. So, stack-based reduction method applies.

- Create an empty stack. This stack will contain index of elements, which have value in decreasing order.
- We will traverse through input array.
- If the top of stack is smaller than the current element, then pop from the stack and mark its next larger element as current index. We will pop from stack and repeat this process until the value of index at the top of the stack is grater then the current value.
- When we processed the input array then for those indexes for which we have a next largest element is populated.
- The indexes which are present in the stack do not have any next largest element to we should mark those indexes in the output array as -1.

Example 7.28:
```
function nextLargerElement2(arr, size) {
    const stk = ([]);
    const output = new Array(size);
    let index = 0;
    let curr;
    for (let i = 0; i < size; i++) {
        curr = arr[i];
        while (stk.length > 0 && arr[stk[stk.length - 1]] <= curr) {
            index = stk.pop();
            output[index] = curr;
        }
        stk.push(i);
    }

    while (stk.length > 0) {
        index = stk.pop();
        output[index] = -1;
    }
    console.log(output)
}
```

Next Smaller Element

Problem: Function to print next smallest element of each element of array.

First Solution: Brute force approach, for each index we can traverse the array indexes right to it to find a smaller value. Time complexity is $O(n^2)$

Second Solution: let us suppose we are processing elements of array. The elements that are greater than ith element does not have smaller element on the right of ith index. Therefore, we can say the elements which are left of ith element and which are grater the ith element are independent of the elements at the index higher than ith. So, stack-based reduction method applies.

Example 7.29:
```
function nextSmallerElement(arr, size) {
    const stk = ([]);
    const output = new Array(size);
    let curr;
    let index;
    for (let i = 0; i < size; i++) {
        curr = arr[i];
        while (stk.length > 0 && arr[stk[stk.length - 1]] > curr) {
            index = stk.pop();
            output[index] = curr;
        }
        stk.push(i);
    }

    while (stk.length > 0) {
        index = stk.pop();
        output[index] = -1;
    }

    console.log(output)
}

function test() {
    const arr = [13, 21, 3, 6, 20, 3];
    const size = arr.length;
    nextSmallerElement(arr, size);
};
```

Output:
```
[ 3, 3, -1, 3, 3, -1 ]
```

Next Larger Element Circular

Problem: Function to print next larger element of each element of circular array.
Input: [6, 3, 9, 8, 10, 2, 1, 15, 7]
Output: [9, 9, 10, 10, 15, 15, 15, -1, 9]

First Solution: Brute force approach, let us suppose the number of elements in array is n. For each index, we will traverse (n-1) number of nodes (in circular manner) to find a larger value. Time complexity is $O(n^2)$

Second Solution: The solution of this problem is same as Next Largest Element problem. The only difference is that (2n – 1) nodes are traversed. As for each node, the farthest node that have its effect is at max (n-1) distance apart. Therefore, total (n + n -1) nodes are traversed. Time Complexity of stack-based reduction process is O(n)

Example 7.30:

```
function nextLargerElementCircular(arr, size) {
    const stk = ([]);
    let curr;
    let index;
    const output = new Array(size);
    for (let i = 0; i < (2 * size - 1); i++) {
        curr = arr[i % size];
        while (stk.length > 0 && arr[stk[stk.length - 1]] <= curr) {
            index = stk.pop();
            output[index] = curr;
        }
        stk.push(i % size);
    }

    while (stk.length > 0) {
        index = stk.pop();
        output[index] = -1;
    }
    console.log(output)
}

function test() {
    const arr = [6, 3, 9, 8, 10, 2, 1, 15, 7];
    const size = arr.length;
    nextLargerElementCircular(arr, size);
};
```

Output:
```
[ 9, 9, 10, 10, 15, 15, 15, -1, 9 ]
```

Depth-First Search with a Stack

In a depth-first search, we traverse down a path until we get a dead end; then we backtrack by popping a stack to get an alternative path.
- Create a stack
- Create a start point
- Push the start point onto the stack
- While (value searching is not found and the stack is not empty)
    - Pop the stack

- o Find all possible points after the one which we just tried
- o Push these points onto the stack

Grid Based Problems (Using Recursion.)

In grid-based problems, we are given some condition using which we need to traversal a 2D array. For Example , in a chessboard find minimum number of steps required to move a knight from source position to destination position. Or Given fruits arranged in grid that is represented by 2D array some fruits are rotten and we need to find how many days are needed for all the fruits rot if each day a rotten fruit rots it neighbours.

In these problems, we can use BFS or DFS traversal to move from one state to another. We create a 2D array which is used to find if some particular state is already processed or not. At each step while processing a particular state, we find all the possible states that can be reached from it. We move from one state to another by using DFS or BFS traversal. Few Examples of grid-based problems that are solved below are Rotten Fruit, Steps of knight, Distance nearest Fill, Largest Island, Number of Islands.

Rotten Fruit

Problem: Given that, fruits are arranged in a 2-dimensional grid. Among which few fruits are rotten. In one day, a rotten fruit rot adjacent fruits that comes to its contact. You need to find the maximum number of days in which the fruits of whole grid will rot.

First Solution: Using DFS / Recursion, each fruit can rot at max 4 other fruits that are adjacent to it.

Example 7.31:
```
function RottenFruitUtil(arr, maxCol, maxRow, currCol, currRow, traversed,
day) {
    if (currCol < 0 || currCol >= maxCol || currRow < 0 || currRow >= maxRow
||
        traversed[currCol][currRow] <= day || arr[currCol][currRow] === 0)
        return;
    traversed[currCol][currRow] = day;
    RottenFruitUtil(arr, maxCol, maxRow, currCol - 1, currRow, traversed,
day + 1);
    RottenFruitUtil(arr, maxCol, maxRow, currCol + 1, currRow, traversed,
day + 1);
    RottenFruitUtil(arr, maxCol, maxRow, currCol, currRow + 1, traversed,
day + 1);
    RottenFruitUtil(arr, maxCol, maxRow, currCol, currRow - 1, traversed,
day + 1);
}

const Max_Int = 2147483647

function RottenFruit(arr, maxCol, maxRow) {
    const traversed = Array(maxRow);
    for (var i = 0; i < maxRow; i++) {
        traversed[i] = Array(maxCol).fill(Max_Int)
```

```
        }

    for (var i = 0; i < maxCol - 1; i++) {
        for (var j = 0; j < maxRow - 1; j++) {
            if (arr[i][j] === 2)
                RottenFruitUtil(arr, maxCol, maxRow, i, j, traversed, 0);
        }
    }

    let maxDay = 0;
    for (var i = 0; i < maxCol - 1; i++) {
        for (var j = 0; j < maxRow - 1; j++) {
            if (arr[i][j] === 1) {
                if (traversed[i][j] === Max_Int)
                    return -1;
                if (maxDay < traversed[i][j])
                    maxDay = traversed[i][j];
            }
        }
    }
    return maxDay;
}

function test() {
    const arr = [[1, 0, 1, 1, 0],
    [2, 1, 0, 1, 0],
    [0, 0, 0, 2, 1],
    [0, 2, 0, 0, 1],
    [1, 1, 0, 0, 1]];

    console.info(RottenFruit(arr, 5, 5));
};
```

Output:
3

Analysis: We create a traversed array to keep track of nodes which are already processed.

Steps of Knight

Problem: Given a chessboard and a knight start position. You need to find minimum number of steps required to move a knight from start position to final position.

Solution: Each knight can go to 8 other positions. Find if the positions are not already visited and do the DFS traversal of the chess board.

Example 7.32:
```
function StepsOfKnightUtil(size, currCol, currRow, traversed, dist) {
    if (currCol < 0 || currCol >= size || currRow < 0 || currRow >= size )
        return;
```

```
    if (traversed[currCol][currRow] <= dist)
        return;

    traversed[currCol][currRow] = dist;
    StepsOfKnightUtil(size, currCol - 2, currRow - 1, traversed, dist + 1);
    StepsOfKnightUtil(size, currCol - 2, currRow + 1, traversed, dist + 1);
    StepsOfKnightUtil(size, currCol + 2, currRow - 1, traversed, dist + 1);
    StepsOfKnightUtil(size, currCol + 2, currRow + 1, traversed, dist + 1);
    StepsOfKnightUtil(size, currCol - 1, currRow - 2, traversed, dist + 1);
    StepsOfKnightUtil(size, currCol + 1, currRow - 2, traversed, dist + 1);
    StepsOfKnightUtil(size, currCol - 1, currRow + 2, traversed, dist + 1);
    StepsOfKnightUtil(size, currCol + 1, currRow + 2, traversed, dist + 1);
}

function StepsOfKnight(size, srcX, srcY, dstX, dstY) {
    const traversed = Array(size);
    for (let i = 0; i < size; i++) {
        traversed[i] = Array(size).fill(Max_Int)
    }

    StepsOfKnightUtil(size, srcX - 1, srcY - 1, traversed, 0);
    const retval = traversed[dstX - 1][dstY - 1];
    return retval;
}

function test() {
    console.info(StepsOfKnight(20, 10, 10, 20, 20));
};
```

Output:
8

Distance nearest Fill

Problem: Given a matrix 2D array, with some cells filled by 1 and other 0. You need to create a 2D array that will contain the minimum distance of each 0 element to any one of the cells with value 1.

Solution: Grid based traversal using DFS is performed to find the nearest fill. We create a 2-dimensional traversed array to keep track of distance.

Example 7.33:
```
function DistNearestFillUtil(arr, maxCol, maxRow, currCol, currRow,
traversed, dist) {
    if (currCol < 0 || currCol >= maxCol || currRow < 0 || currRow >=
maxRow)
        return;
    if (traversed[currCol][currRow] <= dist)
        return;
    traversed[currCol][currRow] = dist;
```

```
    DistNearestFillUtil(arr, maxCol, maxRow, currCol - 1, currRow,
traversed, dist + 1);
    DistNearestFillUtil(arr, maxCol, maxRow, currCol + 1, currRow,
traversed, dist + 1);
    DistNearestFillUtil(arr, maxCol, maxRow, currCol, currRow + 1,
traversed, dist + 1);
    DistNearestFillUtil(arr, maxCol, maxRow, currCol, currRow - 1,
traversed, dist + 1);
}

function DistNearestFill(arr, maxCol, maxRow) {
    const traversed = Array(maxRow);
    for (var i = 0; i < maxRow; i++) {
        traversed[i] = Array(maxCol).fill(Max_Int)
    }

    for (var i = 0; i < maxCol; i++) {
        for (let j = 0; j < maxRow; j++) {
            if (arr[i][j] === 1)
                DistNearestFillUtil(arr, maxCol, maxRow, i, j, traversed,
0);
        }
    }

    for (var i = 0; i < maxCol; i++) {
        console.info(traversed[i]);
    }
}

function test() {
    const arr = [[1, 0, 1, 1, 0],
    [1, 1, 0, 1, 0],
    [0, 0, 0, 0, 1],
    [0, 0, 0, 0, 1],
    [0, 0, 0, 0, 1]];

    DistNearestFill(arr, 5, 5);
};
```

Output:
```
[ 0, 1, 0, 0, 1 ]
[ 0, 0, 1, 0, 1 ]
[ 1, 1, 2, 1, 0 ]
[ 2, 2, 2, 1, 0 ]
[ 3, 3, 2, 1, 0 ]
```

Largest island

Problem: Given a map represented by 2D array. 1s are land and 0s are water. You need to find largest land mass. Largest landmass has largest number of 1s.

235

Or

Given a map represented by 2D array in which 1s are land and 0s are water. You need to find the largest path that contain largest number of 1s.

Solution: Largest island is found by doing DFS traversal of neighboring nodes of a current node. Largest island of current node is sum of largest island of all the neighboring nodes + 1 (for current node).

Example 7.34:

```
function findLargestIslandUtil(arr, maxCol, maxRow, currCol, currRow, value,
traversed) {
    if (currCol < 0 || currCol >= maxCol || currRow < 0 || currRow >=
maxRow)
        return 0;
    if (traversed[currCol][currRow] === 1 || arr[currCol][currRow] !==
value)
        return 0;
    traversed[currCol][currRow] = 1;
    return 1 +
findLargestIslandUtil(arr, maxCol, maxRow, currCol - 1, currRow - 1, value,
traversed) +
findLargestIslandUtil(arr, maxCol, maxRow, currCol - 1, currRow, value,
traversed) +
findLargestIslandUtil(arr, maxCol, maxRow, currCol - 1, currRow + 1, value,
traversed) +
findLargestIslandUtil(arr, maxCol, maxRow, currCol, currRow - 1, value,
traversed) +
findLargestIslandUtil(arr, maxCol, maxRow, currCol, currRow + 1, value,
traversed) +
findLargestIslandUtil(arr, maxCol, maxRow, currCol + 1, currRow - 1, value,
traversed) +
findLargestIslandUtil(arr, maxCol, maxRow, currCol + 1, currRow, value,
traversed) +
findLargestIslandUtil(arr, maxCol, maxRow, currCol + 1, currRow + 1, value,
traversed);
}

function findLargestIsland(arr, maxCol, maxRow) {
    let maxVal = 0;
    let currVal = 0;
    const traversed = Array(maxRow);

    for (var i = 0; i < maxRow; i++) {
        traversed[i] = Array(maxCol).fill(Max_Int)
    }

    for (var i = 0; i < maxCol; i++) {
        for (let j = 0; j < maxRow; j++) {
            currVal = findLargestIslandUtil(arr, maxCol, maxRow, i, j,
arr[i][j], traversed);
            if (currVal > maxVal)
```

```
            maxVal = currVal;
        }
    }
    return maxVal;
}

function test() {
    const arr = [[1, 0, 1, 1, 0],
    [1, 0, 0, 1, 0],
    [0, 1, 1, 1, 1],
    [0, 1, 0, 0, 0],
    [1, 1, 0, 0, 1]];

    console.info(`Largest Island : ${findLargestIsland(arr, 5, 5)}`);
};
```

Output:
```
Largest Island : 12
```

Number of islands

Problem: Given a map represented by 2D array. 1s are land and 0s are water. You need to find number of islands. An island is a land mass formed by group of connected 1s.

Hint: Solve this problem in same way you had solved the above largest island problem.

Snake and Ladder Problem

Problem: Given a snake and ladder board, which starts with 1 and end at 100. You need to find the minimum number of dice throws required to reach 100th cell from 1st cell. There is list of snakes' coordinates provided and list of ladder coordinate provided as pair.

Hint: create a dice count array of length 100. Process each cell start from 1st to 100th. Each cell has 6 outcomes. Which changes with the presence of snakes and leader. Use BFS or DFS and reach destination.

Palindrome string

Problem: Find if given string is a palindrome or not using a stack.
Definition of palindrome: A palindrome is a sequence of characters that is same backward or forward.
E.g. "AAABBBCCCBBBAAA", "ABA" & "ABBA"

Hint: Push characters to the stack until the half-length of the string. Then pop these characters and then compare. Make sure you take care of the odd length and even length.

Find Celebrity Problem

Problem: In a party, there is possibility that a celebrity had visited it. A celebrity is a person who does not know anyone in the party and everyone in the party knows celebrity. You want to find celebrity in the party. You can ask only one question DoYouKnow (X, Y), which means to X you can ask only one question that do you know Y. X will answer the question as yes or no.

First Solution: brute force approach, you can traverse the guest one by one and ask them if they know the other guest one by one. If you find a guest who do not know anyone then you have a probable candidate. If the guest is known to all other guest than he is a celebrity.
This is an inefficient solution with complexity of $O(N^2)$

Second Solution: Use stack,
- We add the entire guest list index from 1 to N in a stack. We take two index values out of stack and store them in two variables first and second.
- If the guest at index first knows guest at index second, then first is not celebrity so copy second to first. Else if the guest at index first does not know guest second, then second is not celebrity.
- In both the cases pop another element from stack and mark it second.
- At each comparison, one value is rejected.
- At last first will contain the probable celebrity.
- Then we need to check that the celebrity candidate is known by all the other guests.

Example 7.35:

```
function findCelebrity(relation, count) {
    const stk = ([]);
    let first = 0;
    let second = 0;
    for (var i = 0; i < count; i++) {
        stk.push(i);
    }
    first = stk.pop();

    while (stk.length !== 0) {
        second = stk.pop();
        if (isKnown(relation, first, second))
            first = second;
    }

    for (var i = 0; i < count; i++) {
        if (first !== i && isKnown(relation, first, i))
            return -1;
        if (first !== i && isKnown(relation, i, first) === false)
            return -1;
    }
    return first;
}

function test() {
    const arr = [[1, 0, 1, 1, 0],
    [1, 0, 0, 1, 0],
    [0, 0, 1, 1, 1],
    [0, 0, 0, 0, 0],
    [1, 1, 0, 1, 1]];
```

```
    console.info(`Celebrity : ${findCelebrity(arr, 5)}`);
    console.info(`Celebrity : ${findCelebrity2(arr, 5)}`);
};
```

Output:
```
Celebrity : 3
```

Third Solution: let us suppose we have guest list as [g1, g2, g3, g4 …]. We take two index counters namely first and second. First is assigned 0 value and second is assigned 1 value.

We will ask guest at index first if he know guest at index second. If answer is yes then we make first = second and second = second + 1 (guest at first index is not a celebrity.)
If the answer is no then we make second = second + 1 (guest at index second is not a celebrity.)
In the end, we will have probable celebrity at the first index.
Then check that the guest at the first index is known by all the other guests.

Example 7.36:
```
function findCelebrity2(relation, count) {
    let first = 0;
    let second = 1;

    for (var i = 0; i < (count - 1); i++) {
        if (isKnown(relation, first, second))
            first = second;
        second = second + 1;
    }

    for (var i = 0; i < count; i++) {
        if (first !== i && isKnown(relation, first, i))
            return -1;
        if (first !== i && isKnown(relation, i, first) === false)
            return -1;
    }
    return first;
};
```

Problem: In the above question, the party can also contain stranger who is not known by anyone and who don't know anyone. Find celebrity function should return 0 in this case. Do the needful modifications in the solution of above problem.

Uses of Stack

- Recursion can also be done using stack. (In place of the system stack)
- The function call is implemented using stack.
- When we want to reverse a sequence, we just push everything in stack and pop from it.
- Grammar checking, balance parenthesis, infix to postfix conversion, postfix evaluation of expression etc.

Exercise

1. Converting Decimal Numbers to Binary Numbers using stack data structure.
   Hint: store reminders into the stack and then print the stack.

2. Convert an infix expression to prefix expression.
   Hint: Reverse given expression, apply infix to postfix, and then reverse the expression again.
   Step 1. Reverse the infix expression.
       5^E+D*) C^B+A (
   Step 2. Make Every '(' as ')' and every ')' as '('
       5^E+D*(C^B+A)
   Step 3. Convert an expression to postfix form.
   Step 4. Reverse the expression.
       +*+A^BCD^E5

3. Write an HTML opening tag and closing tag-matching program.
   Hint: parenthesis matching.

4. Write a function that will transform Postfix to Infix Conversion

5. Write a function that will transform Prefix to Infix Conversion

6. Write a palindrome matching function, which ignores characters other than English alphabet and digits. String "Madam, I'm Adam." should return true.

CHAPTER 8: QUEUE

Introduction

A queue is a basic data structure that organizes items in first-in-first-out (FIFO) manner. First element, inserted into a queue, will be the first to be removed. It is also known as "first-come-first-served".

The real-life analogy of queue is typical lines in which we all participate time to time.
- We wait in a line of railway reservation counter.
- We wait in the cafeteria line.
- We wail in a queue when we call to some customer-care.

The elements, which are at the front of the queue, are the one that stayed in the queue for the longest time.

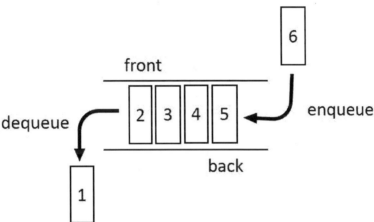

Computer science also has many common Examples of queues. We issue a print command from our office to a single printer per floor. The print tasks are lined up in a printer queue. The print command that is issued first will be printed before the next commands in line.

In addition to printing queues, operating system is also using different queues to control process scheduling. Processes are added to processing queue, which is used by an operating system for various scheduling algorithms.

Soon we will study about graphs and will come to know about breadth-first traversal of graph also uses queue.

The Queue Abstract Data Type

Queue abstract data type is defined as a class whose instance follows FIFO or first-in-first-out for the elements, added to it.

Queue should support the following operations:
1. add(): Which adds a single element at the back of a queue
2. remove(): Which removes a single element from the front of a queue.
3. isEmpty(): Returns 1 if the queue is empty
4. size(): Returns the number of elements in a queue.

Queue Using Deque

Example 8.1:

```
class Queue {
    constructor() {
        this.Capacity = 1000;
        this.front = 0;
        this.back = 0;
        this.size = 0;
        this.data = new Array(this.Capacity);
    }

    add(value) {
        if (this.size >= this.Capacity) {
            console.log("Queue is full.");
            return false;
        }
        else {
            this.size++;
            this.data[this.back] = value;
            this.back = (++this.back) % (this.Capacity - 1);
        }
        return true;
    }

    remove() {
        let value;
        if (this.size <= 0) {
            console.log("Queue is empty.");
            return 0;
        }
        else {
            this.size--;
            value = this.data[this.front];
            this.front = (++this.front) % (this.Capacity - 1);
        }
        return value;
    }

    isEmpty() {
        return this.size === 0;
    }

    length() {
        return this.size;
    }
}
```

```
/* Testing Code */
const que = new Queue();
que.add(1);
que.add(2);
que.add(3);
while (que.isEmpty() === false) {
    console.log(que.remove());
}
```

Output:
```
1
2
3
```

Analysis:
- Hear queue is created from a list.
- Add() to insert one element at the back of the queue.
- Remove()to delete one element from the front of the queue.

Queue Using linked list

Queue is implemented using a circular linked list. The advantage of using circular linked list is that we can get head and tail node in constant time. When we want to insert, we add at tail. When we need to delete, we delete form the head of list.

Example 8.2:
```
class QueueNode {
    constructor(v, n) {
        this.value = 0;
        this.value = v;
        this.next = n;
    }
}

class Queue {
    constructor() {
        this.head = null;
        this.tail = null;
        this.size = 0;
    }

    length() {
        return this.size;
    }

    isEmpty() {
        return this.size === 0;
    }
```

```
    peek() {
        if (this.isEmpty())
            throw new Error("StackEmptyError");
        return this.head.value;
    }

    print() {
        let temp = this.head;
        while (temp != null) {
            process.stdout.write(`${temp.value} `)
            temp = temp.next;
        };
    }
}

/* Testing Code */
const que = new Queue();
que.add(1);
que.add(2);
que.add(3);
while (que.isEmpty() === false) {
    console.log(que.remove());
}
```

Output:
```
1
2
3
```

Add

Enqueue into a queue using circular linked list. Nodes are added to the end of the linked list. Below diagram indicates how a new node is added to the list. The tail is modified every time when a new value is added to the queue.

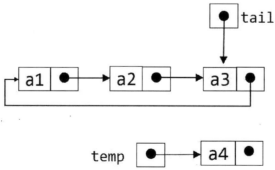

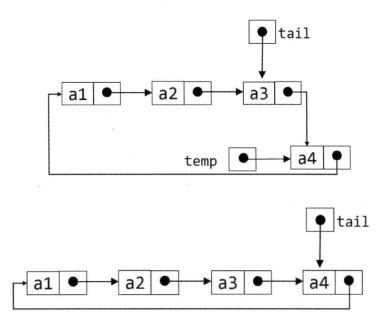

Example 8.3:

```
add(value) {
    const temp = new QueueNode(value, null);
    if (this.head == null)
        this.head = this.tail = temp;
    else {
        this.tail.next = temp;
        this.tail = temp;
    }
    this.size++;
}
```

Analysis: add operation add one element at the end of the Queue (circular linked list).

Remove

Dequeue operation is done by deleting head node. Next node of the tail node is the head node we store head node location in deleteMe temporary pointer. Tail node next will point to the next of the deleteMe node. Finally, head node which is stored in deleteMe pointer is deleted.

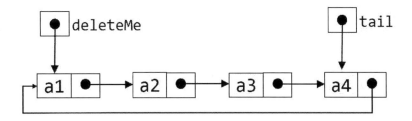

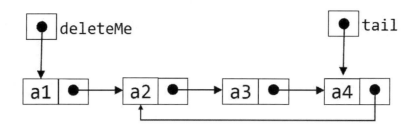

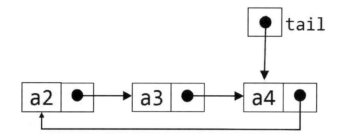

Example 8.4:

```
remove() {
    if (this.isEmpty())
        throw new Error("StackEmptyError");
    const value = this.head.value;
    this.head = this.head.next;
    this.size--;
    return value;
}
```

Analysis: Remove operation removes first node from the start of the queue (circular linked list).

Double-Ended Queue / Dequeue

A Double-Ended Queue or Dequeue is an abstract data type in which elements can be added or removed from either the front or back. Lets look at linked-list implementation of Dequeue. Double linked list is used to implement Dequeue.

Example 8.5:

```
class DeQueueNode {
    constructor(v) {
        this.value = 0;
        this.value = v;
        this.next = null;
        this.prev = null
    }
}

class DeQueue {
    constructor() {
        this.head = null;
        this.tail = null;
```

```
        this.size = 0;
}

length() {
    return this.size;
}

isEmpty() {
    return this.size === 0;
}

peekFirst() {
    if (this.isEmpty())
        throw new Error("DeQueueEmptyError");
    return this.tail.value;
}

peekLast() {
    if (this.isEmpty())
        throw new Error("DeQueueEmptyError");
    return this.head.value;
}

addLast(value) {
    const temp = new DeQueueNode(value);
    if (this.head == null)
        this.head = this.tail = temp;
    else {
        temp.next = this.head;
        this.head.prev = temp
        this.head = temp;
    }
    this.size++;
}

removeLast() {
    if (this.isEmpty())
        throw new Error("DeQueueEmptyError");

    this.size--;
    const value = this.head.value;
    this.head = this.head.next;

    if(this.head !== null){
        this.head.prev = null
    } else {
        this.tail = null
    }

    return value;
```

```
        }

    addFirst(value) {
        const temp = new DeQueueNode(value, null);
        if (this.head == null)
            this.head = this.tail = temp;
        else {
            this.tail.next = temp;
            temp.prev = this.tail
            this.tail = temp;
        }
        this.size++;
    }

    removeFirst() {
        if (this.isEmpty())
            throw new Error("DeQueueEmptyError");

        this.size--;
        const value = this.tail.value;
        this.tail = this.tail.prev

        if(this.tail !== null){
            this.tail.next = null
        } else {
            this.head = null
        }
        return value;
    }

    print() {
        let temp = this.head;
        while (temp != null) {
            process.stdout.write(`${temp.value} `)
            temp = temp.next;
        };
        console.log()
    }
}

/* Testing Code */
const que = new DeQueue();
que.addFirst(1);
que.addFirst(1);
que.addLast(2);
que.addLast(2);
while (que.isEmpty() === false) {
    console.log(que.removeLast());
}
```

Output:
```
2
2
1
1
```

Problems in Queue

Queue using a stack

Problem: How to implement a queue using a stack. You can use multiple one stack.

Solution: We can use two stacks to implement queue.
1. **Enqueue Operation**: new elements are added to the top of first stack.
2. **Dequeue Operation**: elements are popped from the second stack. When second stack is empty then all the elements of first stack are popped one by one and pushed into second stack.

Example 8.6:
```
class Queue {
    constructor() {
        this.stk1 = [];
        this.stk2 = [];
    }

    length() {
        return (this.stk1.length + this.stk2.length);
    }

    isEmpty() {
        return (this.stk1.length + this.stk2.length) === 0;
    }

    add(value) {
        this.stk1.push(value);
    }

    remove() {
        let value;
        if (this.stk2.length > 0) {
            return this.stk2.pop();
        }
        while (this.stk1.length > 0) {
            value = this.stk1.pop();
            this.stk2.push(value);
        };
        return this.stk2.pop();
    }
}
```

```
/* Testing Code */
const que = new Queue();
que.add(1);
que.add(2);
que.add(3);
while (que.isEmpty() === false)
    console.log(que.remove());
```

Output:
```
1
2
3
```

Analysis: All add() happens to stack 1. When remove() is called removal happens from stack 2. When the stack 2 is empty then stack 1 is popped and pushed into stack 2. This popping from stack 1 and pushing into stack 2 revert the order of retrieval there by making queue behaviour out of two stacks.

Time complexity is O(1) on an average, elements are added to first stack only once. They are taken to second stack only once and taken out using pop operation.

Stack using a Queue

Problem: Implement stack using a queue.

First Solution: use two queues
Push: add new elements to queue1.
Pop: while size of queue1 is bigger than 1. Push all items from queue 1 to queue 2 except the last item. Switch the name of queue 1 and queue 2. Then return the last item.
Push operation is **O(1)** and Pop operation is **O(n)**

Second Solution: This same can be done using just one queue.
Push:add the element to queue.
Pop: find the size of queue. If size is zero then return error. Else, if size is positive then remove size- 1 elements from the queue and again add to the same queue. At last, remove the next element and return it.
Push operation is **O(1)** and Pop operation is **O(n)**

Third Solution: In the above solutions, the push is efficient and pop is inefficient can we make pop efficient **O(1)** and push inefficient **O(n)**
Push: add new elements to queue2. Then add all the elements of queue 1 to queue 2. Then switch names of queue1 and queue 2.
Pop: remove from queue1

Reverse a stack

Problem: Reverse a stack using a queue

First Solution:
• Pop all the elements of stack and add them into a queue.

- Then remove all the elements of the queue into stack
- We have the elements of the stack reversed.

Second Solution:
- Since dynamic list or [ ] list is used to implement stack in C, we can iterate from both the directions of the array and swap the elements.

Reverse a queue

Problem: Reverse a queue-using stack

Solution:
- Dequeue all the elements of the queue into stack(append to the C list [ ])
- Then pop all the elements of stack and add them into a queue. (pop the elements from the array)
- We have the elements of the queue reversed.

Breadth-First Search with a Queue

In breadth-first search, we explore all the nearest nodes first by finding all possible successors and add them to a queue.
- Create a queue
- Create a start point
- Enqueue the start points onto the queue
- while (value searching not found and the queue is not empty)
  - Dequeue from the queue
  - Find all possible paths from the dequeued point.
  - Enqueue these paths in the queue

Josephus problem

Problem: There are n people standing in a queue waiting to be executed. The counting begins at the front of the queue. In each step, k number of people are removed and again added one by one from the queue. Then the next person is executed. The execution proceeds around the circle until only the last person remains, who will be freedom. Find that position where you want to stand and gain your freedom.

Solution:
- Just insert integer for 1 to k in a queue. (corresponds to k people)
- Define a Kpop() function such that it will remove and add the queue k-1 times and then remove one more time. (This man is dead.)
- Repeat second step until size of queue is 1.
- Print the value in the last element. This is the solution.

Circular tour

Problem: There are N number of petrol pumps in a circular path. Each petrol pump has some limited amount of petrol. You are given the amount of petrol each petrol pump has and the distance from next petrol pump. Find if there is a circular tour possible to visit all the petrol pumps.

First Solution: For each find all the possible paths starting from different petrol pump.
For each petrol pump we will add (net petrol available − net petrol needed to reach its next petrol pump.). While iterating the pumps if we are able to find a path with petrol value always positive then it is the path which we are searching. Otherwise find another path by selecting other staring point.

Time complexity is $O(n^2)$

Solution: There is inefficiency in the above problem. Net petrol calculations are done repeatedly for same node. If we had started from i^{th} pump and got a negative value of net petrol after visiting k^{th} petrol pump. Then we can find net petrol value starting form i+1th pump and ends to kth pump in constant time by subtracting petrol value of ith pump.

So, when we are traversing the array of pumps, we go on adding index of pumps to the array. When we get a positive value of net petrol then we go on adding next petrol pump and keep track of net petrol. When we get a negative net petrol value then we remove starting pumps id from queue and do needed calculation on the net petrol. Once a value is added to queue, we don't need to do more calculations for it. So, this solution is linear in nature. Time complexity is O(N).

Example 8.7:

```
function CircularTour(arr, n) {
    const que = new Queue();
    let nextPump = 0;
    let prevPump;
    let count = 0;
    let petrol = 0;
    while (que.size() !== n) {
        while (petrol >= 0 && que.size() !== n) {
            que.add(nextPump);
            petrol += (arr[nextPump][0] - arr[nextPump][1]);
            nextPump = (nextPump + 1) % n;
        }
        while (petrol < 0 && que.size() > 0) {
            prevPump = que.remove();
            petrol -= (arr[prevPump][0] - arr[prevPump][1]);
        }
        count += 1;
        if (count === n)
            return -1;
    }
    if (petrol >= 0)
        return que.remove();
    else
        return -1;
}

function test() {
    const tour = [[8, 6], [1, 4], [7, 6]];
    console.info(`Circular Tour : ${CircularTour(tour, 3)}`);
};
```

Output:

```
Circular Tour : 2
```

Convert XY

Problem: Given two values X and Y. You need to convert X to Y by performing various steps. In a step, we can either multiply 2 to the value or subtract 1 from it.

Solution: Breadth first traversal (BFS) of the possible values that can be generated from source value is done. The various values that can be generated are added to the queue for BFS. In addition, the various vales are added to map to keep track of the values already processed. Each value is added to the queue only once so the time complexity of this algorithm is O(n).

Example 8.8:

```
function convertXY(src, dst) {
    const que = new Queue();
    const arr = new Array(100);
    let steps = 0;
    let index = 0;
    let value;
    que.add(src);
    while (que.size() !== 0) {
        value = que.remove();
        arr[index++] = value;
        if (value === dst) {
            for (let i = 0; i < index; i++) {
                process.stdout.write(`${arr[i]} `);
            }
            console.info(`Steps count :: ${steps}`);
            return steps;
        }
        steps++;
        if (value < dst)
            que.add(value * 2);
        else
            que.add(value - 1);
    }
    return -1;
}

function test() {
    convertXY(2, 7);
};
```

Output:

```
2 4 8 7 Steps count :: 3
```

Maximum value in Sliding Windows

Problem: Given an array of integer, find maximum value in all the sliding windows of length k.
Input: 11, 2, 75, 92, 59, 90, 55 and k = 3
Output: 75, 92, 92, 92, 90

First Solution: Brute force approach, run loop for all the index of array. Inside a loop run another loop of length k, find the maximum of this inner loop and display it to the screen. This time complexity is O(nk).

Second Solution:
- We traverse the input array and add the index values to a queue.
- When the index added to the queue is out of range then we remove them from the queue.
- We are searching for maximum value so those values which are in the queue and which are less than the value of current index will be of no use so we will pop them from the queue.
- So the maximum value of the window is always present at the index que[0] so they will be displayed.

Note: Problems that involve sliding windows, are solved efficiently using a doubly ended queue.

Example 8.9:

```
function maxSlidingWindows(arr, size, k) {
    const que = new Deque();
    for (let i = 0; i < size; i++) {
        if (que.size() > 0 && que.peek() <= i - k)
            que.remove();
        while (que.size() > 0 && arr[que.peekLast()] <= arr[i]) {
            que.removeLast();
        };
        que.add(i);
        if (i >= (k - 1))
            process.stdout.write(`${arr[que.peek()]} `);
    }
}

function test() {
    const arr = [11, 2, 75, 92, 59, 90, 55];
    const k = 3;
    process.stdout.write("Max Sliding Windows : ")
    maxSlidingWindows(arr, 7, 3);
    console.log()
};
```

Output:
```
Max Sliding Windows : 75 92 92 92 90
```

Minimum of Maximum Values in Sliding Windows

Problem: Given an array of integer, find minimum of all the maximum values in the sliding windows of length k.
Input: 11, 2, 75, 92, 59, 90, 55 and k = 3

Output: 75

Solution: Same as above problem. You will keep track of the minimum of all the maximum values in sliding windows too.

Example 8.10:
```
function minOfMaxSlidingWindows(arr, size, k) {
    const que = new Queue();
    let minVal = 999999;
    for (let i = 0; i < size; i++) {
        if (que.size() > 0 && que.peek() <= i - k)
            que.remove();
        while (que.size() > 0 && arr[que.peekLast()] <= arr[i]) {
            que.remove();
        };
        que.add(i);
        if (i >= (k - 1) && minVal > arr[que.peek()])
            minVal = arr[que.peek()];
    }
    console.info(`Min of max is :: ${minVal}`);
    return minVal;
}

function test() {
    const arr = [11, 2, 75, 92, 59, 90, 55];
    const k = 3;
    minOfMaxSlidingWindows(arr, 7, 3);
};
```

Output:
```
Min of max is :: 75
```

Maximum of Minimum Values in Sliding Windows

Problem: Given an array of integer, find maximum of all the minimum values in the sliding windows of length k.
Input: 11, 2, 75, 92, 59, 90, 55 and k = 3
Output: 59, as minimum values in sliding windows are [2, 2, 59, 59, 55]

Solution: Same as above problem. You will keep track of the minimum of all the maximum values in sliding windows too.

Example 8.11:
```
function maxOfMinSlidingWindows(arr, size, k) {
    const que = new Queue();
    let maxVal = -999999;
    for (let i = 0; i < size; i++) {
        if (que.size() > 0 && que.peek() <= i - k)
            que.remove();
        while (que.size() > 0 && arr[que.peekLast()] >= arr[i]) {
```

```
            que.remove();
        };
        que.add(i);
        if (i >= (k - 1) && maxVal < arr[que.peek()])
            maxVal = arr[que.peek()];
    }
    console.info(`Max of min is :: ${maxVal}`);
}

function test() {
    const arr = [11, 2, 75, 92, 59, 90, 55];
    const k = 3;
    maxOfMinSlidingWindows(arr, 7, 3);
};
```

Output:
```
Max of min is :: 59
```

First Negative Sliding Windows

Problem: Given an array of integer, find first negative of all the values in the sliding windows of length k.
Input:
Arr = [13, -2, -6, 10, -14, 50, 14, 21]
k = 3

Output: [-2, -2, -6, -14, -14, NAN]

Solution: We will create a queue. Only those indices are added to queue which have negative values. Pop those values which are out of range of window.

Example 8.12:
```
function firstNegSlidingWindows(arr, size, k) {
    const que = new Queue();
    for (let i = 0; i < size; i++) {
        if (que.size() > 0 && que.peek() <= i - k)
            que.remove();
        if (arr[i] < 0)
            que.add(i);
        if (i >= (k - 1)) {
            if (que.size() > 0)
                process.stdout.write(`${arr[que.peek()]} `);
            else
                process.stdout.write("NAN ");
        }
    }
}

function test() {
    const arr = [3, -2, -6, 10, -14, 50, 14, 21, 11, -2, -11, 2, 3];
    const k = 3;
```

256

```
      firstNegSlidingWindows(arr, 13, 3);
}
```

Output:

```
-2 -2 -6 -14 -14 NAN NAN -2 -2 -2 -11
```

Exercise

1. Implement queue using dynamic memory allocation, such that the implementation should follow the following constraints.
    a. The user should use memory allocation from the heap using new operator. In this, you need to take care of the max value in the queue.
    b. Once you are done with the above exercise and you can test your queue. Then you can add some more complexity to your code. In add() function when the queue is full, in place of printing, "Queue is full" you should allocate more space using new operator.
    c. Once you are done with the above exercise. Now in remove function once you are below half of the capacity of the queue, you need to decrease the size of the queue by half. You should add one more variable "min" to queue so that you can track what is the original value capacity passed at initialization() function. Moreover, the capacity of the queue will not go below the value passed in the initialization.

    (If you are not able to solve the above exercise, and then have a look into stack chapter, where we have done similar problems for stack)

2. Implement the below function for the queue:
    a. IsEmpty: This is left as an exercise for the user. Take a variable, which will take care of the size of a queue if the value of that variable is zero, isEmpty should return true. If the queue is not empty, then it should return false.
    b. Size: Use the size variable to be used under size function call. Size() function should return the number of elements in the queue.

3. Implement stack using a queue. Write a program for this problem. You can use just one queue.

4. Write a program to Reverse a stack using queue

5. Write a program to Reverse a queue using stack

6. Write a CompStack() function which takes pointer to two stack as an argument and return true or false depending upon whether all the elements of the stack are equal or not. You are given isEqual(int, int) which will compare and return true if both values are equal and 0 if they are different.

7. Given two values X and Y. You need to convert X to Y by performing various steps. In a step, we can either multiply 2 to the value or subtract 1 from it. You need to display the number of steps and the path. To reach 3 from 1, the path will be [1, 2, 4, 3] and number of steps will be 3.
    Hint: Create an array to keep track of the number of steps and another array to keep track of parent value.

CHAPTER 9: TREE

Introduction

We have already read about various linear data structures like an array, linked list, stack, queue etc. Both array and linked list have a drawback of linear time required for searching an element.

A tree is a non-linear data structure, which is used to represent hierarchical relationships (parent-child relationship). Each node is connected by another node by directed edges.

Example 1: Tree in team of some manager

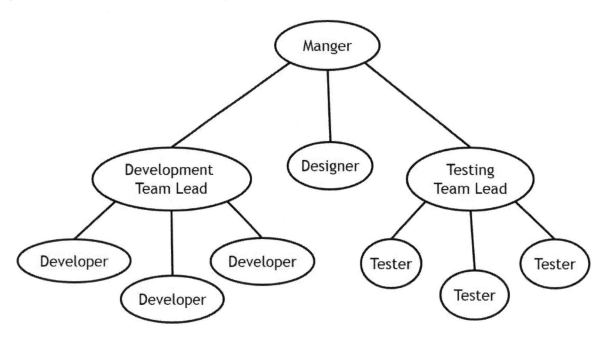

Example 2: Tree in a file system

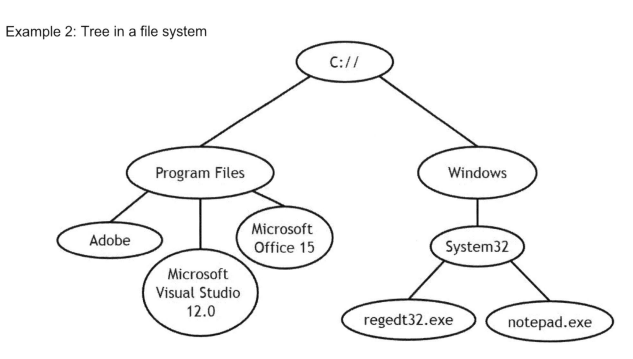

Terminology in tree

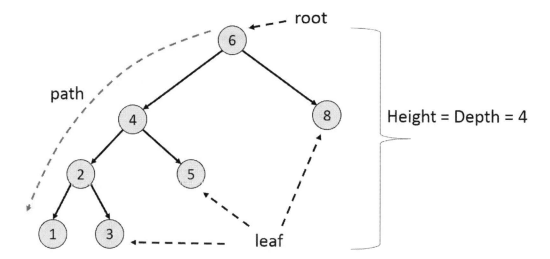

Root: The root of the tree is the only node without incoming edges. It is the top node of a tree.

Node: It is a fundamental element of a tree. Each node has data and two pointers that may point to null or its children

Edge: It is also a fundamental part of a tree, which is used to connect two nodes.

Path: A path is an ordered list of nodes that are connected by edges.

Leaf: A leaf node is a node that has no children.

Height of the tree: The height of a tree is the number of edges on the longest path between the root and a leaf.

The level of node: The level of a node is the number of edges on the path from the root node to that node.

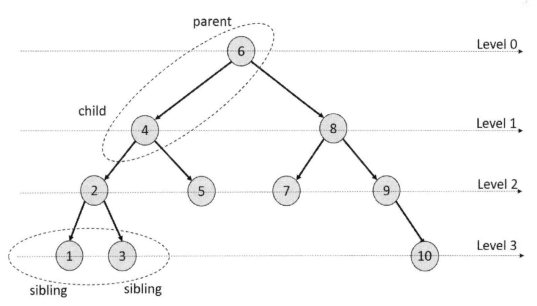

Children: Nodes that have incoming edges from the same node is said to be the children of that node.

Parent: Node is a parent of all the child nodes that are linked by outgoing edges.

Sibling: Nodes in the tree that are children of the same parent are called siblings.

Ancestor: A node reachable through repeated moving from child to parent.

Binary Tree

A binary tree is a type tree in which each node has at most two children (0, 1 or 2), which are referred to as the left child and the right child.

Below is a node of the binary tree with "a" stored as data and whose left child (lChild) and whose right child (rchild) both are pointing towards null.

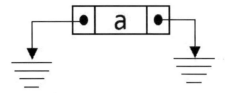

Example 9.1: Binary tree class.

```
class TreeNode {
    constructor(data, left = null, right = null) {
        this.value = data;
        this.lChild = left;
        this.rChild = right;
    }
}

class Tree {
    constructor() {
        this.root = null;
    }

    /* Other Function */
}
```

Below is a binary tree whose nodes contains data from 1 to 10

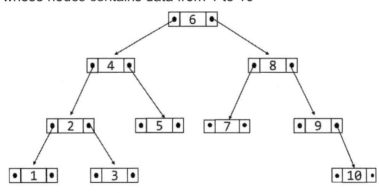

6,4,2,5,1,3,8,7,9,10

In the rest of the book, binary tree will be represented as below:

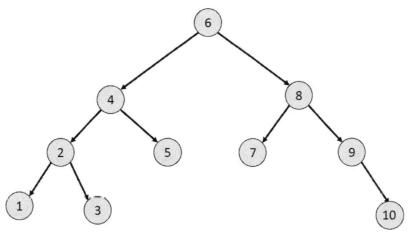

Properties of Binary tree are:
1. The maximum number of nodes on level i of a binary tree is 2^i, where i >= 1
2. The maximum number of nodes in a binary tree of depth k is 2^{k+1}, where k >= 1
3. There is exactly one path from the root to any nodes in a tree.
4. A tree with N nodes has exactly N-1 edges connecting these nodes.
5. The height of a complete binary tree of N nodes is $\log_2 N$.

Types of Binary trees

Complete binary tree

In a complete binary tree, every level except the last one is filled. All nodes in the left are filled first, then the right one. A binary heap is an Example of a complete binary tree.

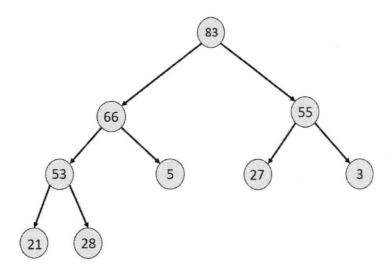

Full/ Strictly binary tree

The full binary tree is a binary tree in which each node has exactly zero or two children.

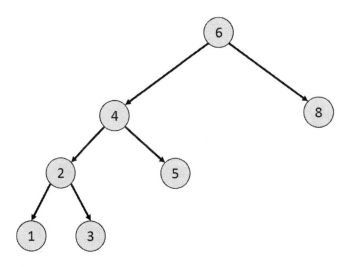

Perfect binary tree

The perfect binary tree is a type of full binary tree in which each non-leaf node has exactly two child nodes. All leaf nodes have identical path length and all possible node slots are occupied

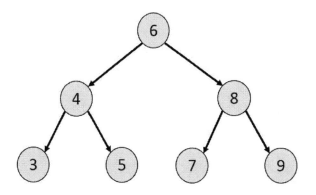

Right skewed binary tree

A binary tree in which either each node is has a right child or no child (leaf) is called as right skewed binary tree

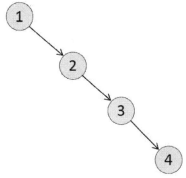

Left skewed binary tree

A binary tree in which either each node is has a left child or no child (leaf) is called as Left skewed binary tree

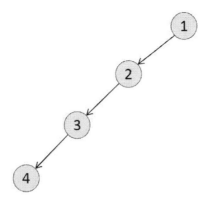

Height-balanced Binary Tree

A height-balanced binary tree is a binary tree such that the left & right subtrees for any given node differs in height by max one. AVL tree and RB tree are an Example of height-balanced tree.

Note: Each complete binary tree is a height-balanced binary tree

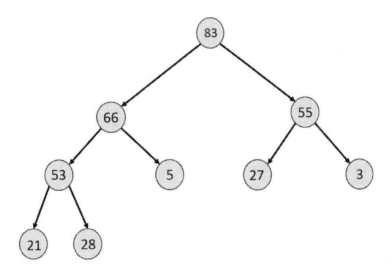

Problems in Binary Tree

Create a Complete binary tree

Problem: Create a complete binary tree from values given as array.

Solution: Since there is no order defined in a binary tree, so nodes can be inserted in any order so it can be a skewed binary tree. But it is inefficient to do anything in a skewed binary tree so we will create a Complete binary tree. At each node, the middle value stored in the array is assigned to node. The left of array is passed to the left child of the node to create left sub-tree and the right portion of array is passed to right child of the node to create right sub-tree.

Example 9.2:
```
levelOrderBinaryTree(arr) {
    this.root = this.levelOrderBinaryTreeUtil(arr, 0);
}
```

263

```
levelOrderBinaryTreeUtil(arr, start) {
    const size = arr.length;
    const curr = new TreeNode(arr[start]);
    const left = 2 * start + 1;
    const right = 2 * start + 2;

    if (left < size)
        curr.lChild = this.levelOrderBinaryTreeUtil(arr, left);
    if (right < size)
        curr.rChild = this.levelOrderBinaryTreeUtil(arr, right);

    return curr;
}

/* Testing Code */
const t = new Tree();
const arr = [1, 2, 3, 4, 5, 6, 7, 8, 9, 10];
t.levelOrderBinaryTree(arr2);
```

Complexity Analysis: This is an efficient algorithm for creating a complete binary tree.
Time Complexity: O(n), Space Complexity: O(n)

Below tree is created using levelOrderBinaryTree() function.

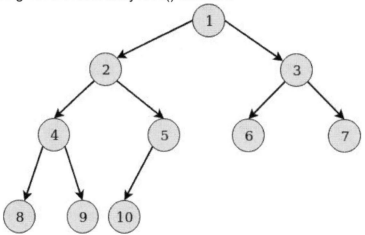

Pre-Order Traversal

Problem: Perform Pre-Order Traversal of binary tree.

Solution: In Pre-Order Traversal, parent is visited / traversed first, then left child subtree and then right child subtree. At each node, the value stored in it is printed and then followed by the values of left child subtree and right child subtree.

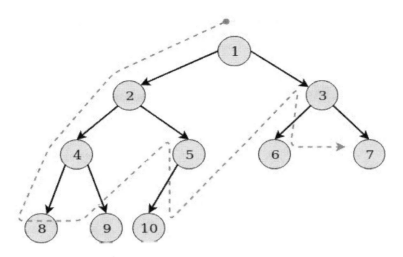

Example 9.3:
```
PrintPreOrder() {
    process.stdout.write("Pre Order Tree: ");
    this.PrintPreOrderUtil(this.root);
    process.stdout.write("\n")
}

PrintPreOrderUtil(node) {
    if (node != null) {
        process.stdout.write(`${node.value} `);
        this.PrintPreOrderUtil(node.lChild);
        this.PrintPreOrderUtil(node.rChild);
    }
}

/* Testing Code */
const t = new Tree();
const arr = [1, 2, 3, 4, 5, 6, 7, 8, 9, 10];
t.levelOrderBinaryTree(arr);
t.PrintPreOrder()
```

Output:
```
Pre Order Tree: 1 2 4 8 9 5 10 3 6 7
```

Complexity Analysis: Time Complexity: O(n), Space Complexity: O(n)

Note: If there is an algorithm, in which all nodes are traversed then complexity cannot be less than O(n). When there is a large portion of the tree, which is not traversed, then complexity reduces.

Post-Order Traversal

Problem: Perform Post-Order Traversal of binary tree.

Solution: In Post-Order Traversal, left child is visited / traversed first, then right child and then parent node. At each node, left child subtree is traversed then right child subtree and, in the end, current node value is printed to the screen.

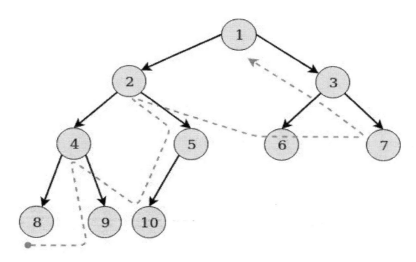

Example 9.4:

```
PrintPostOrder() {
    process.stdout.write("Post Order Tree: ");
    this.PrintPostOrderUtil(this.root);
    process.stdout.write("\n");
}

PrintPostOrderUtil(node) {
    if (node != null) {
        this.PrintPostOrderUtil(node.lChild);
        this.PrintPostOrderUtil(node.rChild);
        process.stdout.write(`${node.value} `);
    }
}

/* Testing Code */
const t = new Tree();
const arr = [1, 2, 3, 4, 5, 6, 7, 8, 9, 10];
t.levelOrderBinaryTree(arr);
t.PrintPostOrder()
```

Output:
```
Post Order Tree: 8 9 4 10 5 2 6 7 3 1
```

Complexity Analysis: Time Complexity: O(n), Space Complexity: O(n)

In-Order Traversal

Problem: Perform In-Order Traversal of binary tree.

Solution: In In-Order traversal, the nodes of left child subtree are traversed, then the value of node is printed to the screen and then the values of right child subtree are traversed.

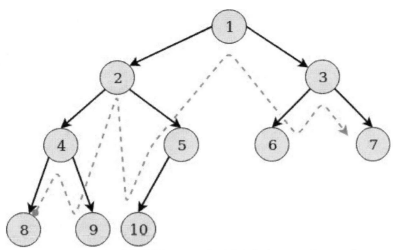

Note: The output of In-Order traversal of BST is a sorted list in increasing order.

Example 9.5:
```
PrintInOrder() {
    process.stdout.write("In Order Tree: ");
    this.PrintInOrderUtil(this.root);
    process.stdout.write("\n")
}

PrintInOrderUtil(node) {
    if (node != null) {
        this.PrintInOrderUtil(node.lChild);
        process.stdout.write(`${node.value} `);
        this.PrintInOrderUtil(node.rChild);
    }
}

/* Testing Code */
const t = new Tree();
const arr = [1, 2, 3, 4, 5, 6, 7, 8, 9, 10];
t.levelOrderBinaryTree(arr);
t.PrintInOrder()
```

Output:
```
In Order Tree: 8 4 9 2 10 5 1 6 3 7
```

Complexity Analysis: Time Complexity: O(n), Space Complexity: O(n)

Note: Pre-Order, Post-Order, and In-Order traversal are meant for all binary trees. They can be used to traverse any kind of a binary tree.

Level order traversal / Breadth First traversal

Problem: Write code to implement level order traversal of a tree. Such that nodes at depth k is printed before nodes at depth k+1.

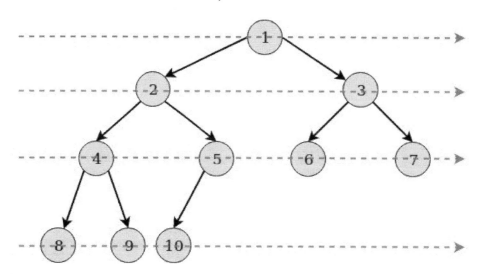

Solution: Level order traversal or Breadth First traversal of a tree is done using a queue. At first, the root node pointer is added to a queue. The traversal of tree is done until the queue is empty. When we traverse the tree, we first remove an element from the queue, print the value stored in that node and then its left child and right child will be added to the queue.

Example 9.6:
```
PrintBredthFirst() {
    const que = new Queue();
    let temp;

    if (this.root != null)
        que.add(this.root);

    process.stdout.write("Breadth First : ");
    while (que.isEmpty() === false) {
        temp = que.remove();
        process.stdout.write(`${temp.value} `);
        if (temp.lChild != null)
            que.add(temp.lChild);
        if (temp.rChild != null)
            que.add(temp.rChild);
    }
    process.stdout.write("\n");
}

/* Testing Code */
const t = new Tree();
const arr = [1, 2, 3, 4, 5, 6, 7, 8, 9, 10];
t.levelOrderBinaryTree(arr);
t.PrintBredthFirst()
```

Output:
```
Breadth First : 1 2 3 4 5 6 7 8 9 10
```

Complexity Analysis: Time Complexity: O(n), Space Complexity: O(n)

268

Print Depth First without using the recursion / system stack.

Problem: Perform depth first search of a binary tree without using recursion.

Solution: Depth first traversal of the tree is done using recursion by using system stack. The same can be done using stack. In the beginning, root node reference is added to the stack. The whole tree is traversed until the stack is empty. In each iteration, an element is popped from the stack, its value is printed to screen. Then right child and then left child of the node is added to stack.

Example 9.7:
```
PrintDepthFirst() {
    const stk = ([]);
    let temp;
    if (this.root != null)
        stk.push(this.root);

    process.stdout.write("Depth First : ");
    while (stk.length > 0) {
        temp = stk.pop();
        process.stdout.write(`${temp.value} `);
        if (temp.rChild != null)
            stk.push(temp.rChild);
        if (temp.lChild != null)
            stk.push(temp.lChild);
    }
    process.stdout.write("\n");
}

/* Testing Code */
const t = new Tree();
const arr = [1, 2, 3, 4, 5, 6, 7, 8, 9, 10];
t.levelOrderBinaryTree(arr);
t.PrintDepthFirst()
```

Output:
```
Depth First : 1 2 4 8 9 5 10 3 6 7
```

Complexity Analysis: Time Complexity: O(n), Space Complexity: O(n)

Print Level Order Line by Line

Problem: Perform level order traversal of binary tree, such that the levels are printed line by line.

First Solution: We will use two queues to preform level order traversal. Alternatively, we will process queues and put the children of elements of queue into another queue so that when each level is processed, we can print the output in different line.

Example 9.8:
```
PrintLevelOrderLineByLine() {
    const que1 = new Queue();
```

```
        const que2 = new Queue();
        let temp = null;
        if (this.root != null)
            que1.add(this.root);
        process.stdout.write("Level Order LineByLine : \n");
        while (que1.length() !== 0 || que2.length() !== 0) {
            while (que1.length() !== 0) {
                temp = que1.remove();
                process.stdout.write(` ${temp.value}`);
                if (temp.lChild != null)
                    que2.add(temp.lChild);
                if (temp.rChild != null)
                    que2.add(temp.rChild);
            }
            process.stdout.write("\n");

            while (que2.length() !== 0) {
                temp = que2.remove();
                process.stdout.write(` ${temp.value}`);
                if (temp.lChild != null)
                    que1.add(temp.lChild);
                if (temp.rChild != null)
                    que1.add(temp.rChild);
            }
            process.stdout.write("\n");
        }
}

/* Testing Code */
const t = new Tree();
const arr = [1, 2, 3, 4, 5, 6, 7, 8, 9, 10];
t.levelOrderBinaryTree(arr);
t.PrintLevelOrderLineByLine()
```

Output:

```
Level Order LineByLine :
 1
 2 3
 4 5 6 7
 8 9 10
```

Second Solution: We can solve this problem using single queue. Let us suppose at any time we have all the nodes of kth level present in a queue. We can find the count of these elements. We can process elements from the queue count number of time and add their children to the queue. Then we can print a new line. At this point we have all the nodes at k+1th level. Start with adding root node as the first level to the queue and follow the steps mentioned above.

Example 9.9:

```
PrintLevelOrderLineByLine2() {
    const que = new Queue();
    let temp = null;
    let count = 0;
    if (this.root != null)
        que.add(this.root);

    process.stdout.write("Level Order LineByLine : \n");
    while (que.length() !== 0) {
        count = que.length();
        while (count > 0) {
            temp = que.remove();
            process.stdout.write(` ${temp.value}`);
            if (temp.lChild != null)
                que.add(temp.lChild);
            if (temp.rChild != null)
                que.add(temp.rChild);
            count -= 1;
        }
        process.stdout.write("\n");
    }
}
```

Print Spiral Tree

Problem: Given a binary tree, print the nodes breadth first in spiral order.

Solution: Stacks are last in first out, so two stacks are used to process each level alternatively. The nodes are added and processed in such an order that nodes are printed in spiral order.

Example 9.10:

```
PrintSpiralTree() {
    const stk1 = ([]);
    const stk2 = ([]);
    let temp;
    if (this.root != null)
        stk1.push(this.root);

    process.stdout.write("Spiral Tree : \n");
    while (stk1.length !== 0 || stk2.length !== 0) {
        while (stk1.length !== 0) {
            temp = stk1.pop();
            process.stdout.write(` ${temp.value}`);
            if (temp.rChild != null)
                stk2.push(temp.rChild);
            if (temp.lChild != null)
                stk2.push(temp.lChild);
        }
        process.stdout.write("\n");
```

```
        while (stk2.length !== 0) {
            temp = stk2.pop();
            process.stdout.write(` ${temp.value}`);
            if (temp.lChild != null)
                stk1.push(temp.lChild);
            if (temp.rChild != null)
                stk1.push(temp.rChild);
        }
        process.stdout.write("\n");
    }
}

/* Testing Code */
const t = new Tree();
const arr = [1, 2, 3, 4, 5, 6, 7, 8, 9, 10];
t.levelOrderBinaryTree(arr);
t.PrintSpiralTree()
```

Output:
```
Spiral Tree :
 1
 2 3
 7 6 5 4
 8 9 10
```

Nth Pre-Order

Problem: Given a binary tree, print the value of nodes that will be at nth index when tree is traversed in pre-order.

Solution: We want to print the node, which will be at the nth index when we print the tree in PreOrder traversal. Therefore, we keep a counter to keep track of the index. When the counter is equal to index, then we print the value and return the Nth preorder index node.

Example 9.11:
```
NthPreOrder(index) {
    const counter = [0];
    this.NthPreOrderUtil(this.root, index, counter);
}

NthPreOrderUtil(node, index, counter) {
    if (node != null) {
        counter[0]++;
        if (counter[0] === index) {
            console.info(`Nth Preorder node is :: ${node.value}`);
        }
        this.NthPreOrderUtil(node.lChild, index, counter);
        this.NthPreOrderUtil(node.rChild, index, counter);
    }
}
```

```
/* Testing Code */
const t = new Tree();
const arr = [1, 2, 3, 4, 5, 6, 7, 8, 9, 10];
t.levelOrderBinaryTree(arr);
t.NthPreOrder(5)
```

Output:
```
Nth Preorder node is :: 9
```

Complexity Analysis: Time Complexity: O(n), Space Complexity: O(n)

Nth Post-Order

Problem: Given a binary tree, print the value of nodes that will be at nth index when tree is traversed in post-order.

Solution: We want to print the node that will be at the nth index when we print the tree in post order traversal. Therefore, we keep a counter to keep track of the index, but at this time, we will increment the counter after left child and right child traversal. When the counter is equal to index, then we print the value and return the nth post-order index node.

Example 9.12:
```
NthPostOrder(index) {
    const counter = [0];
    this.NthPostOrderUtil(this.root, index, counter);
}

NthPostOrderUtil(node, index, counter) {
    if (node != null) {
        this.NthPostOrderUtil(node.lChild, index, counter);
        this.NthPostOrderUtil(node.rChild, index, counter);
        counter[0]++;
        if (counter[0] === index) {
            console.info(`Nth Post order : ${node.value}`);
        }
    }
}

/* Testing Code */
const t = new Tree();
const arr = [1, 2, 3, 4, 5, 6, 7, 8, 9, 10];
t.levelOrderBinaryTree(arr);
t.NthPostOrder(5)
```

Output:
```
Nth Post order : 5
```

Complexity Analysis: Time Complexity: O(n), Space Complexity: O(n)

Nth In Order

Problem: Given a binary tree, print the value of nodes that will be at nth index when tree is traversed in In-order.

Solution: We want to print the node that will be at the nth index when we print the tree in in-order traversal. Therefore, we keep a counter to keep track of the index, but at this time, we will increment the counter after left child traversal but before the right child traversal. When the counter is equal to index, then we print the value and return the nth in-order index node.

Example 9.13:

```
NthInOrder(index) {
    const counter = [0];
    this.NthInOrderUtil(this.root, index, counter);
}

NthInOrderUtil(node, index, counter) {
    if (node != null) {
        this.NthInOrderUtil(node.lChild, index, counter);
        counter[0]++;
        if (counter[0] === index) {
            console.log(`Nth InOrder Node : ${node.value}`);
        }
        this.NthInOrderUtil(node.rChild, index, counter);
    }
}

/* Testing Code */
const t = new Tree();
const arr = [1, 2, 3, 4, 5, 6, 7, 8, 9, 10];
t.levelOrderBinaryTree(arr);
t.NthInOrder(5)
```

Output:

```
Nth InOrder Node : 10
```

Complexity Analysis: Time Complexity: O(n), Space Complexity: O(1)

Print all the paths

Problem: Given a binary tree, print all the paths from the roots to the leaf.

Solution: Whenever we traverse a node, we add that node to the stack. When we reach a leaf, we print the whole list. When we return from a function, then we remove the element that was added to the stack when we entered this function.

Example 9.14:

```
printAllPath() {
    const stk = ([]);
    console.info("Print All Path : ");
```

```
        this.printAllPathUtil(this.root, stk);
}

printAllPathUtil(curr, stk) {
    if (curr == null)
        return;
    stk.push(curr.value);

    if (curr.lChild == null && curr.rChild == null) {
        console.info(stk);
        stk.pop();
        return;
    }

    this.printAllPathUtil(curr.rChild, stk);
    this.printAllPathUtil(curr.lChild, stk);
    stk.pop();
}

/* Testing Code */
const t = new Tree();
const arr = [1, 2, 3, 4, 5, 6, 7, 8, 9, 10];
t.levelOrderBinaryTree(arr);
t.printAllPath()
```

Output:
```
Print All Path :
[ 1, 3, 7 ]
[ 1, 3, 6 ]
[ 1, 2, 5, 10 ]
[ 1, 2, 4, 9 ]
[ 1, 2, 4, 8 ]
```

Complexity Analysis: Time Complexity: O(n), Space Complexity: O(n)

Number of Element

Problem: Find total number of nodes in binary tree.

Solution: Number of nodes at the right child and the number of nodes at the left child is added by one and we get the total number of nodes in any tree / sub-tree.

Example 9.15:
```
numNodes() {
    return this.numNodesUtil(this.root);
}

numNodesUtil(curr) {
    if (curr == null)
        return 0;
```

```
      else
          return (1 + this.numNodesUtil(curr.rChild) +
this.numNodesUtil(curr.lChild));
}

/* Testing Code */
const t = new Tree();
const arr = [1, 2, 3, 4, 5, 6, 7, 8, 9, 10];
t.levelOrderBinaryTree(arr);
console.log(t.numNodes())
```

Output:
```
10
```

Complexity Analysis: Time Complexity: O(n), Space Complexity: O(n)

Sum of All nodes in a BT

Problem: Given a binary tree, find sum of values of all the nodes of it.

Solution: We will find the sum of all the nodes recursively. sumAllBT() will return the sum of all the node of left and right subtree then we will add the value of current node and will return the final sum.

Example 9.16:
```
sumAllBT() {
    return this.sumAllBTUtil(this.root);
}

sumAllBTUtil(curr) {
    if (curr == null)
        return 0;
    return (curr.value + this.sumAllBTUtil(curr.lChild) +
this.sumAllBTUtil(curr.rChild));
}

/* Testing Code */
const t = new Tree();
const arr = [1, 2, 3, 4, 5, 6, 7, 8, 9, 10];
t.levelOrderBinaryTree(arr);
console.log(t.sumAllBT())
```

Output:
```
55
```

Number of Leaf nodes

Problem: Given a binary tree, find the number of leaf nodes in it.

Solution: If we add the number of leaf node in the right child with the number of leaf nodes in the left child, we will get the total number of leaf node in any tree or subtree.

Example 9.17:

```
numLeafNodes() {
    return this.numLeafNodesUtil(this.root);
}


numLeafNodesUtil(curr) {
    if (curr == null)
        return 0;

    if (curr.lChild == null && curr.rChild == null)
        return 1;
    else
        return (this.numLeafNodesUtil(curr.rChild) +
this.numLeafNodesUtil(curr.lChild));
}

/* Testing Code */
const t = new Tree();
const arr = [1, 2, 3, 4, 5, 6, 7, 8, 9, 10];
t.levelOrderBinaryTree(arr);
console.log(t.numLeafNodes())
```

Output:
5

Complexity Analysis: Time Complexity: O(n), Space Complexity: O(n)

Number of Full Nodes in a BT

Problem: Given a binary tree, find count of full nodes in it. A full node is one that have non-null left and right child.

Solution: A full node is a node that has both left and right child. We will recursively traverse the whole tree and will increase the count of full node as we find them.

Example 9.18:

```
numFullNodesBT() {
    return this.numFullNodesBTUtil(this.root);
}


numFullNodesBTUtil(curr) {
    let count;
    if (curr == null)
        return 0;
    count = this.numFullNodesBTUtil(curr.rChild) +
this.numFullNodesBTUtil(curr.lChild);
    if (curr.rChild != null && curr.lChild != null)
```

```
        count++;
    return count;
}

/* Testing Code */
const t = new Tree();
const arr = [1, 2, 3, 4, 5, 6, 7, 8, 9, 10];
t.levelOrderBinaryTree(arr);
console.log(t.numFullNodesBT())
```

Output:
4

Search value in a Binary Tree

Problem: Search a particular value in binary tree.

Solution: To find if some value is there in a binary tree or not it is done using exhaustive search of the binary tree. First, the value of current node is compared with the value, which we are looking for. Then it is compared recursively inside the left child and right child.

Example 9.19:
```
searchBT(value) {
    return this.searchBTUtil(this.root, value);
}

searchBTUtil(curr, value) {
    if (curr == null)
        return false;

    if (curr.value === value)
        return true;

    const left = this.searchBTUtil(curr.lChild, value);

    if (left)
        return true;

    const right = this.searchBTUtil(curr.rChild, value);

    if (right)
        return true;

    return false;
}

/* Testing Code */
const t = new Tree();
const arr = [1, 2, 3, 4, 5, 6, 7, 8, 9, 10];
t.levelOrderBinaryTree(arr);
```

```
console.info(t.searchBT(9))
```

Output:
```
true
```

Find Max in Binary Tree

Problem: Given a binary tree, find maximum value in it.

Solution: We recursively traverse the nodes of a binary tree. We will find the maximum value in the left and right subtree of any node then will compare the value with the value of the current node and finally return the largest of the three values.

Example 9.20:
```
findMaxBT() {
    const ans = this.findMaxBTUtil(this.root);
    return ans;
}

findMaxBTUtil(curr) {
    if (curr == null)

        return MIN_INT;

    let max = curr.value;
    const left = this.findMaxBTUtil(curr.lChild);
    const right = this.findMaxBTUtil(curr.rChild);

    if (left > max)
        max = left;
    if (right > max)
        max = right;
    return max;
}

/* Testing Code */
const t = new Tree();
const arr = [1, 2, 3, 4, 5, 6, 7, 8, 9, 10];
t.levelOrderBinaryTree(arr);
console.log(t.findMaxBT())
```

Output:
```
10
```

Tree Depth

Problem: Given a binary tree, find it depth.

Solution: Depth of tree is calculated recursively by traversing left and right child of the root. At each level of traversal depth of both left & right child is calculated. The greater depth among the left and right child is added by one (which is the depth of the current node) and this value is returned.

Example 9.21:

```
TreeDepth() {
    return this.TreeDepthUtil(this.root);
}

TreeDepthUtil(curr) {
    if (curr == null)
        return 0;
    else {
        const lDepth = this.TreeDepthUtil(curr.lChild);
        const rDepth = this.TreeDepthUtil(curr.rChild);

        if (lDepth > rDepth)
            return lDepth + 1;
        else
            return rDepth + 1;
    }
}

/* Testing Code */
const t = new Tree();
const arr = [1, 2, 3, 4, 5, 6, 7, 8, 9, 10];
t.levelOrderBinaryTree(arr);
console.log(t.TreeDepth())
```

Output:
4

Complexity Analysis: Time Complexity: O(n), Space Complexity: O(n)

Maximum Length Path in a BT/ Diameter of BT

Problem: Given a binary tree, find maximum length path in it.

Solution: To find the diameter of BT we need to find the depth of left child and right child then will add these two values and increment it by one so that we will get the maximum length path (diameter candidate) which contains the current node. Then we will find max length path in the left child sub-tree. We will also find the max length path in the right child sub-tree. Finally, we will compare the three values and return the maximum value among them. This value will be the diameter of the Binary tree.

Example 9.22:

```
maxLengthPathBT() {
    return this.maxLengthPathBTUtil(this.root);
}
```

```
maxLengthPathBTUtil(curr) {
    if (curr == null)
        return 0;

    const leftPath = this.TreeDepthUtil(curr.lChild);
    const rightPath = this.TreeDepthUtil(curr.rChild);
    let max = leftPath + rightPath + 1;

    const leftMax = this.maxLengthPathBTUtil(curr.lChild);
    const rightMax = this.maxLengthPathBTUtil(curr.rChild);

    if (leftMax > max)
        max = leftMax;

    if (rightMax > max)
        max = rightMax;

    return max;
}

/* Testing Code */
const t = new Tree();
const arr = [1, 2, 3, 4, 5, 6, 7, 8, 9, 10];
t.levelOrderBinaryTree(arr);
console.log(t.maxLengthPathBT())
```

Output:
6

Copy Tree

Problem: Given a binary tree, copy its value in another binary tree.

Solution: Copy tree is done by copy nodes of the input tree at each level of the traversal of the tree. At each level of the traversal of nodes of the tree, a new node is created and the value of the input tree node is copied to it. The left child tree is copied recursively and then pointer to new subtree is returned which will be assigned to the left child pointer of the current new node. Similarly, for the right child node too. Finally, the tree is copied.

Example 9.23:
```
CopyTree() {
    const tree2 = new Tree();
    tree2.root = this.CopyTreeUtil(this.root);
    return tree2;
}

CopyTreeUtil(curr) {
    if (curr != null) {
        const temp = new TreeNode(curr.value);
        temp.lChild = this.CopyTreeUtil(curr.lChild);
```
281

```
            temp.rChild = this.CopyTreeUtil(curr.rChild);
            return temp;
        }
        else
            return null;
}
```

```
/* Testing Code */
const t = new Tree();
const arr = [1, 2, 3, 4, 5, 6, 7, 8, 9, 10];
t.levelOrderBinaryTree(arr);
const t2 = t.CopyTree()
t.PrintInOrder()
t2.PrintInOrder()
```

Output:
```
In Order Tree: 8 4 9 2 10 5 1 6 3 7
In Order Tree: 8 4 9 2 10 5 1 6 3 7
```

Complexity Analysis: Time Complexity: O(n), Space Complexity: O(n)

Copy Mirror Tree

Problem: Given a binary tree, copy its value to create another tree, which is mirror image of the original tree.

Solution: Copy mirror image of the tree is done same as copy tree, but in place of left child pointing to the tree that is formed by left child traversal of input tree. This time left child points to the tree formed by right child traversal of the input tree. Similarly, right child points to the tree formed by the traversal of the left child of the input tree.

Example 9.24:
```
const t = new Tree();
const arr = [1, 2, 3, 4, 5, 6, 7, 8, 9, 10];
t.levelOrderBinaryTree(arr);
const t2 = t.CopyMirrorTree()
t.PrintLevelOrderLineByLine()
t2.PrintLevelOrderLineByLine()
```

Output:
```
Level Order LineByLine :
 1
 2 3
 4 5 6 7
 8 9 10
Level Order LineByLine :
 1
 3 2
 7 6 5 4
 10 9 8
```

Complexity Analysis: Time Complexity: O(n), Space Complexity: O(n)

Identical

Problem: Find if two binary trees have identical value.

Solution: Two trees have identical values if at each level the value is equal.

Example 9.25:
```
isEqual({root}) {
    return this.isEqualUtil(this.root, root);
}

isEqualUtil(node1, node2) {
    if (node1 == null && node2 == null)
        return true;
    else if (node1 == null || node2 == null)
        return false;
    else
        return (this.isEqualUtil(node1.lChild, node2.lChild) &&
            this.isEqualUtil(node1.rChild, node2.rChild) &&
            (node1.value === node2.value));
}

/* Testing Code */
const t = new Tree();
const arr = [1, 2, 3, 4, 5, 6, 7, 8, 9, 10];
t.levelOrderBinaryTree(arr);
const t2 = t.CopyTree()
console.log(t.isEqual(t2))
```

Output:
```
true
```

Complexity Analysis: Time Complexity: O(n), Space Complexity: O(n)

Free Tree

Problem: Given a binary tree, free all its nodes.

Solution: Point root of tree to null. The memory of nodes of tree will be freed using garbage collection.

Example 9.26:
```
Free() {
    this.root = null;
}
```

Complexity Analysis: Time Complexity: O(1), Space Complexity: O(1)

Is Complete Tree

Problem: Given a binary tree find if it is a complete tree.

First Solution: We perform breadth first traversal of tree using a queue. If we get a node that does not have left child then it cannot have right child too. In general, if we have any node which does not have both the child then it is not possible for any other node in breadth first traversal to have any child.

Example 9.27:

```
isCompleteTree() {
    const que = new Queue();
    let temp = null;
    let noChild = 0;
    if (this.root != null)
        que.add(this.root);

    while (que.length() !== 0) {
        temp = que.remove();
        if (temp.lChild != null) {
            if (noChild === 1)
                return false;
            que.add(temp.lChild);
        }
        else
            noChild = 1;

        if (temp.rChild != null) {
            if (noChild === 1)
                return false;
            que.add(temp.rChild);
        }
        else
            noChild = 1;
    }
    return true;
}

/* Testing Code */
const t = new Tree();
const arr = [1, 2, 3, 4, 5, 6, 7, 8, 9, 10];
t.levelOrderBinaryTree(arr);
console.info(t.isCompleteTree());
```

Output:
```
true
```

Second Solution: Just like a heap if we number child based on parent. Let parent location is index so left child location will be (2*index +1) and right child location will be (2*index +2).

Example 9.28:

```
isCompleteTreeUtil(curr, index, count) {
    if (curr == null)
        return true;
    if (index > count)
        return false;
    return this.isCompleteTreeUtil(curr.lChild, index * 2 + 1, count) &&
this.isCompleteTreeUtil(curr.rChild, index * 2 + 2, count);
}

isCompleteTree2() {
    const count = this.numNodes();
    return this.isCompleteTreeUtil(this.root, 0, count);
}
```

Is a Heap

Problem: Given a binary tree find if it represents a Min Heap.

To see if tree is a heap, we need to check two conditions:
1) It is a complete tree.
2) Value of a parent node is smaller than or equal to its left and right child.

First Solution: First solution is to test if given tree is complete and second is to check if parent-child property is followed. If tree is a complete tree and all parent nodes in tree have value less than or equal to its children than tree represents a Min Heap.

isComleteTree() function call takes linear time so is the isHeapUtil() function. So, the total time complexity is O(n), the whole tree is traversed three times. First to find total number of elements in tree, second to find if it is complete tree. Then once for testing heap property.

Example 9.29:

```
isHeapUtil(curr, parentValue) {
    if (curr == null)
        return true;
    if (curr.value < parentValue)
        return false;
    return (this.isHeapUtil(curr.lChild, curr.value) &&
        this.isHeapUtil(curr.rChild, curr.value));
}

isHeap() {
    const infi = MIN_INT;
    return (this.isCompleteTree() && this.isHeapUtil(this.root, infi));
}
/* Testing Code */
const t = new Tree();
const arr = [1, 2, 3, 4, 5, 6, 7, 8, 9, 10];
t.levelOrderBinaryTree(arr);
console.info(t.isHeap());
```

Output:
```
true
```

Second Solution: We can combine isCompleteTree and isHeapUtil function inside single function.

Example 9.30:
```
isHeapUtil2(curr, index, count, parentValue) {
    if (curr == null)
        return true;
    if (index > count)
        return false;
    if (curr.value < parentValue)
        return false;
    return this.isHeapUtil2(curr.lChild, index * 2 + 1, count, curr.value)
&& this.isHeapUtil2(curr.rChild, index * 2 + 2, count, curr.value);
}


isHeap2() {
    const count = this.numNodes();
    const parentValue = MIN_INT;
    return this.isHeapUtil2(this.root, 0, count, parentValue);
}
```

Tree to List Recursively

Problem: Given a binary tree, create a doubly linked list from this such that the elements are in the order of in-order traversal of tree.

Solution: Tree to the array is done recursively. At each node, we must assume that the tree to list function will do its job for the left child and right child. Then we will combine the result of the left child and right child traversal. We need a head and tail pointer of the left list and right list to combine them with the current node. In the process of integration, the current node will be added to the tail of the left list and current node will be added to the head to the right list. Head of the left list will become the head of the newly formed list and tail of the right list will become the tail of the newly created list.

Example 9.31:
```
treeToListRec() {
    const head = this.treeToListRecUtil(this.root);
    const temp = head;
    return temp;
}


treeToListRecUtil(curr) {
    let Head = null;
    let Tail = null;
    if (curr == null)
        return null;

    if (curr.lChild == null && curr.rChild == null) {
```

```
        curr.lChild = curr;
        curr.rChild = curr;
        return curr;
    }

    if (curr.lChild != null) {
        Head = this.treeToListRecUtil(curr.lChild);
        Tail = Head.lChild;
        curr.lChild = Tail;
        Tail.rChild = curr;
    }
    else
        Head = curr;

    if (curr.rChild != null) {
        const tempHead = this.treeToListRecUtil(curr.rChild);
        Tail = tempHead.lChild;
        curr.rChild = tempHead;
        tempHead.lChild = curr;
    }
    else
        Tail = curr;

    Head.lChild = Tail;
    Tail.rChild = Head;
    return Head;
}

printDLL() {
    if (this.root == null) {
        return;
    }
    let curr = this.root;
    let tail = curr.lChild;
    process.stdout.write(`DLL nodes are : `);
    while (curr !== tail) {
        process.stdout.write(`${curr.value} `);
        curr = curr.rChild;
    };
    process.stdout.write(`${curr.value}\n`);
}

/* Testing Code */
const t = new Tree();
const arr = [1, 2, 3, 4, 5, 6, 7, 8, 9, 10];
t.levelOrderBinaryTree(arr);
t.PrintInOrder()
t2 = t.treeToListRec();
t2.printDLL()
```

Output:
```
In Order Tree: 8 4 9 2 10 5 1 6 3 7
DLL nodes are : 8 4 9 2 10 5 1 6 3 7
```

Complexity Analysis: Time Complexity: O(n), Space Complexity: O(n)

Binary Search Tree (BST)

A binary search tree (BST) is a binary tree on which nodes are ordered in the following way:
- The key in the left subtree is less than the key in its parent node.
- The key in the right subtree is greater the key in its parent node.
- No duplicate key is allowed.

Below are few diagrams of BST with nodes with values 1 to 10

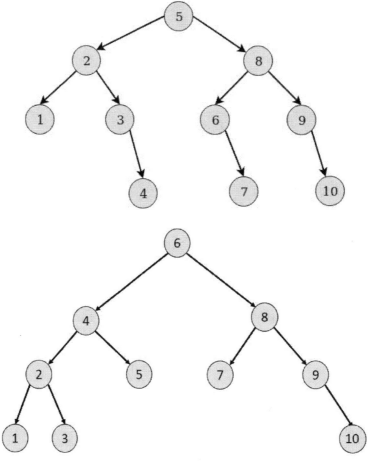

Note: there can be two separate key and value fields in the tree node. But for simplicity, we are considering value as the key. All problems in the binary search tree are solved using this supposition that the value in the node is key for the tree.

Note: Since binary search tree is a binary tree. So all the above algorithm of a binary tree are applicable to a binary search tree.

Problems in Binary Search Tree (BST)

All binary tree algorithms are valid for binary search tree too.

Create a binary search tree from sorted list

Problem: Create a binary tree from list of values in sorted order. Since the elements in the array are in sorted order and we want to create a binary search tree in which left subtree nodes are having values less than the current node and right subtree nodes have value greater than the value of the current node.

Solution: We have to find the middle node to create a current node and send the rest of the array to construct left and right subtree.

Example 9.32:
```
CreateBinarySearchTree(arr) {
    this.root = this.CreateBinarySearchTreeUtil(arr, 0, arr.length - 1);
}

CreateBinarySearchTreeUtil(arr, start, end) {
    if (start > end)
        return null;

    const mid = Math.floor((start + end) / 2);
    const curr = new TreeNode(arr[mid]);
    curr.lChild = this.CreateBinarySearchTreeUtil(arr, start, mid - 1);
    curr.rChild = this.CreateBinarySearchTreeUtil(arr, mid + 1, end);
    return curr;
}

/* Testing Code */
const t = new Tree();
const arr = [1, 2, 3, 4, 5, 6, 7, 8, 9, 10];
t.CreateBinarySearchTree(arr)
t.PrintPreOrder()
```

Output:
```
Pre Order Tree: 5 2 1 3 4 8 6 7 9 10
```

Insertion

Below is a step by step creation of tree after inserting nodes in the order. Nodes with key 6,4,2,5,1,3,8,7,9,10 are inserted in a tree.

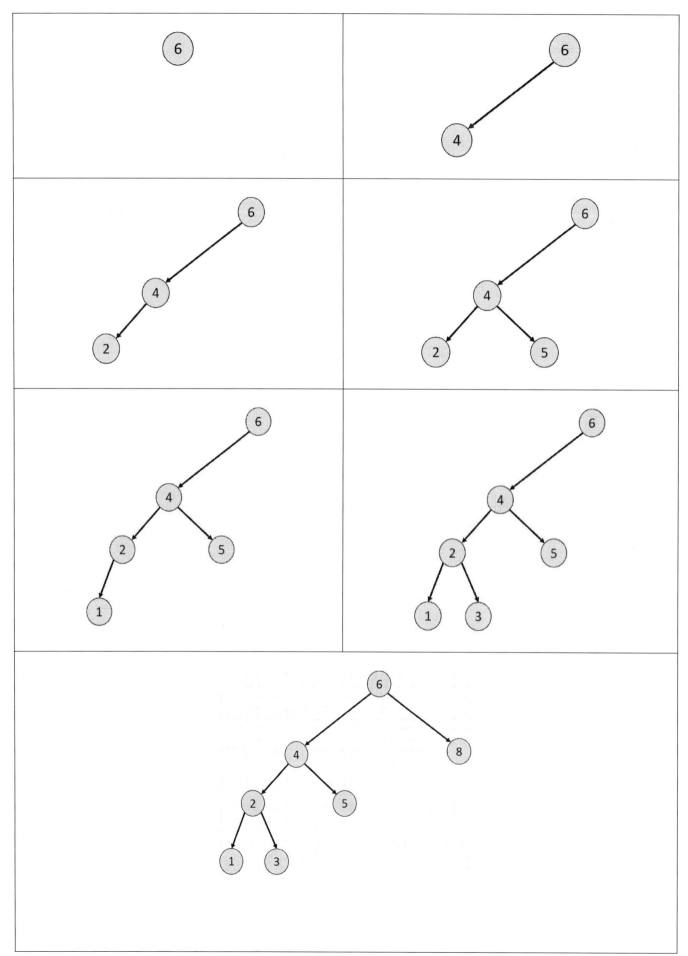

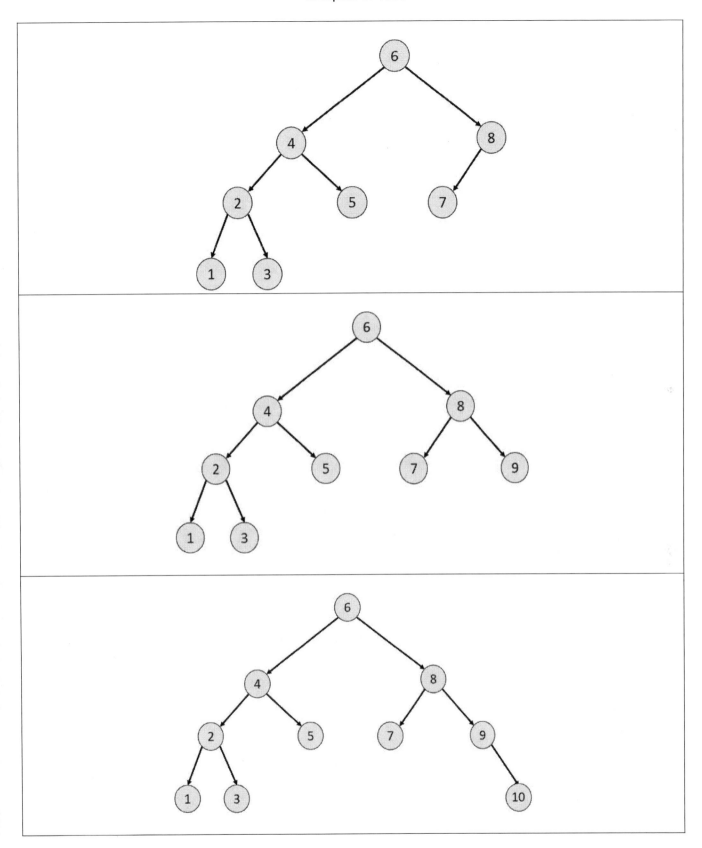

Solution: Smaller values will be added to the left child sub-tree of a node and greater value will be added to the right child sub-tree of the current node.

Example 9.33:

```
InsertNode(value) {
    this.root = this.InsertNodeUtil(this.root, value);
}

InsertNodeUtil(node, value) {
    if (node == null) {
        node = new TreeNode(value, null, null);
    }
    else {
        if (node.value > value) {
            node.lChild = this.InsertNodeUtil(node.lChild, value);
        }
        else {
            node.rChild = this.InsertNodeUtil(node.rChild, value);
        }
    }
    return node;
}

/* Testing Code */
const t = new Tree();
t.InsertNode(6)
t.InsertNode(4)
t.InsertNode(2)
t.InsertNode(5)
t.InsertNode(1)
t.InsertNode(3)
t.InsertNode(8)
t.InsertNode(7)
t.InsertNode(9)
t.InsertNode(10)
t.PrintInOrder()
t.PrintPreOrder()
```

Output:
```
In Order Tree: 1 2 3 4 5 6 7 8 9 10
Pre Order Tree: 6 4 2 1 3 5 8 7 9 10
```

Complexity Analysis: Time Complexity: O(n), Space Complexity: O(n)

Find Node

Problem: Find the node with the value given.

Solution: The value greater than the current node value will be in the right child sub-tree and the value smaller than the current node is there in the left child sub-tree. We can find a value by traversing the left or right subtree iteratively.

Example 9.34:
```
Find(value) {
    let curr = this.root;
    while (curr != null) {
        if (curr.value === value) {
            return true;
        }
        else if (curr.value > value) {
            curr = curr.lChild;
        }
        else {
            curr = curr.rChild;
        }
    }
    return false;
}

/* Testing Code */
/* Above tree is used */
console.log(t.Find(6))
```

Output:
```
true
```

Complexity Analysis: Time Complexity: O(n), Space Complexity: O(1)

Find Min

Find the node with the minimum value.

Solution: left most child of the tree will be the node with the minimum value.

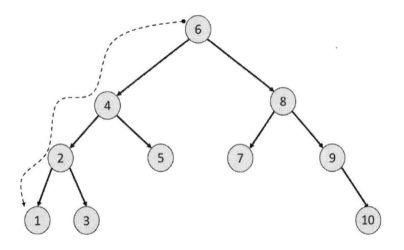

Example 9.35:
```
FindMin() {
    let node = this.root;
    if (node == null) {
        return MAX_INT;
```

293

```
    }
    while (node.lChild != null) {
        node = node.lChild;
    }
    return node.value;
}

/* Testing Code */
/* Above tree is used */
console.log(t.FindMin())
```

Output:
```
1
```

Example 9.36:
```
FindMinNode(curr) {
    let node = curr;
    if (node == null) {
        return null;
    }

    while (node.lChild != null) {
        node = node.lChild;
    }

    return node;
}
```

Complexity Analysis: Time Complexity: O(n), Space Complexity: O(1)

Find Max

Problem: Find the node in the tree with the maximum value.

Solution: Right most node of the tree will be the node with the maximum value.

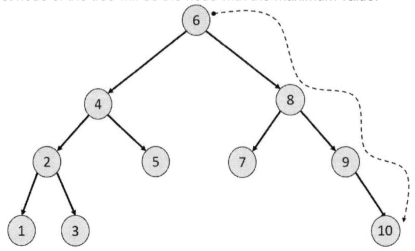

Example 9.37:
```
FindMax() {
    let node = this.root;
    if (node == null) {
        return MIN_INT;
    }
    while (node.rChild != null) {
        node = node.rChild;
    }
    return node.value;
}

/* Testing Code */
/* Above tree is used */
console.log(t.FindMax())
```

Output:
```
10
```

Example 9.38:
```
FindMaxNode(curr) {
    let node = curr;
    if (node == null) {
        return null;
    }

    while (node.rChild != null) {
        node = node.rChild;
    }

    return node;
}
```

Complexity Analysis: Time Complexity: O(n), Space Complexity: O(1)

Is tree a BST

Problem: Find is a given binary tree is a binary search tree.

First Solution: At each node we check whether, max value of left subtree is smaller than the value of current node and min value of right subtree is greater than the current node or not.

Example 9.39:
```
isBST3(root) {
    if (root == null)
        return true;
    if (root.lChild != null && this.FindMaxNode(root.lChild).value >
root.value)
        return false;
```

```
    if (root.rChild != null && this.FindMinNode(root.rChild).value <=
root.value)
        return false;
    return (this.isBST3(root.lChild) && this.isBST3(root.rChild));
}
/* Testing Code */
/* Above tree is used */
console.log(t.isBST3())
```

Output:

```
true
```

Complexity Analysis: Time Complexity: O(n), Space Complexity: O(n)

The above solution is correct but it is not efficient, as same tree nodes are traversed many times.

Second Solution: A better solution will be the one in which we will traverse each node only once. This is done by narrowing the range. We will be use an isBSTUtil() function which takes the max and min range of the values of the nodes. The initial value of min and max should be minimum and maximum value of integer (for simplicity we are taking -999999 and 999999).

Example 9.40:

```
isBST() {
    return this.isBSTUtil(this.root, MIN_INT, MAX_INT);
}

isBSTUtil(curr, min, max) {
    if (curr == null)
        return true;
    if (curr.value < min || curr.value > max)
        return false;
    return this.isBSTUtil(curr.lChild, min, curr.value) &&
this.isBSTUtil(curr.rChild, curr.value, max);
}
```

Complexity Analysis: Time Complexity: O(n), Space Complexity: O(n) for stack.

Third Solution: Above method is correct and efficient but there is an easy method to do the same. We can do in-order traversal of nodes and see if we are getting a strictly increasing sequence

Example 9.41:

```
isBST2() {
    const count = [0];
    return this.isBST2Util(this.root, count);
}

isBST2Util(root, count) {
    let ret;
    if (root != null) {
        ret = this.isBST2Util(root.lChild, count);
```

```
        if (!ret)
            return false;
        if (count[0] > root.value)
            return false;

        count[0] = root.value;
        ret = this.isBST2Util(root.rChild, count);
        if (!ret)
            return false;
    }
    return true;
}
```

Complexity Analysis: Time Complexity: O(n), Space Complexity: O(n) for stack

Delete Node

Problem: Remove the node x from the binary search tree, reorganize nodes of binary search tree to maintain its necessary properties.

There are three cases in delete node, let us call the node that need to be deleted as x.
Case 1: node x has no children. Just delete it (i.e. Change parent node so that it does not point to x)
Case 2: node x has one child. Splice out x by linking x's parent to x's child
Case 3: node x has two children. Splice out the x's successor and replace x with x's successor

When the node to be deleted has no children
This is a trivial case, in which we directly remove the node by returning null.

When the node to be deleted has only one child.
In this case, we return the child of the node.

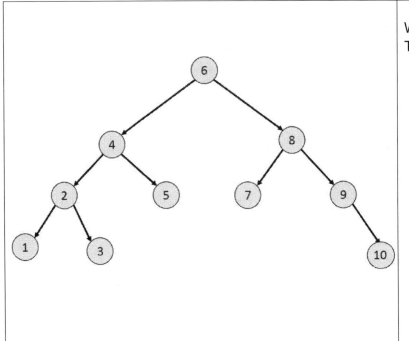

We want to remove node with value 9. The node has only one child.

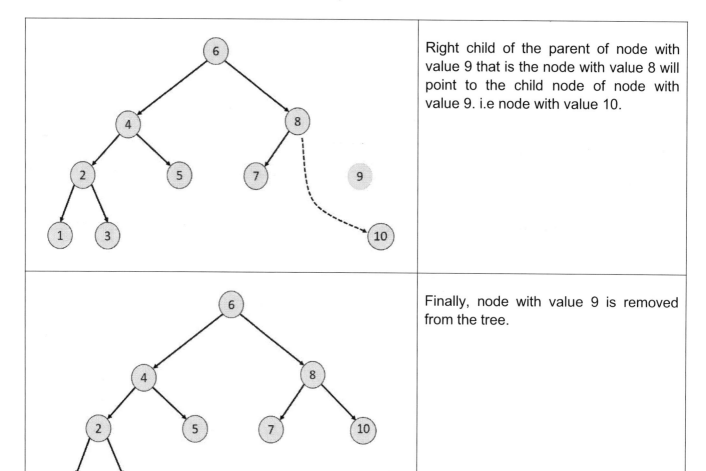

Right child of the parent of node with value 9 that is the node with value 8 will point to the child node of node with value 9. i.e node with value 10.

Finally, node with value 9 is removed from the tree.

When the node to be deleted has two children.

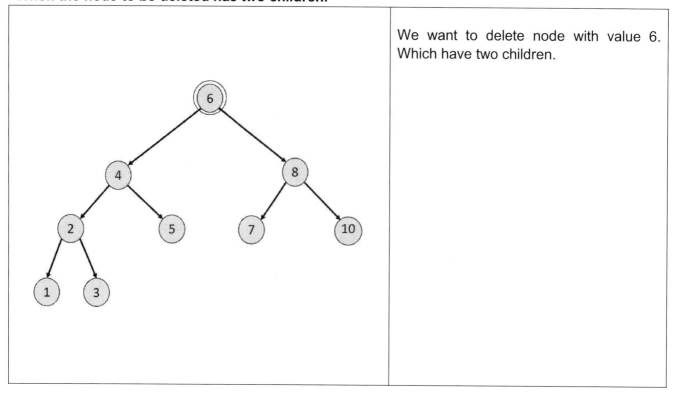

We want to delete node with value 6. Which have two children.

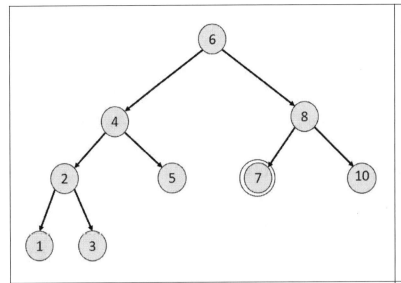	We have found minimum value node of the right subtee of node with value 6.
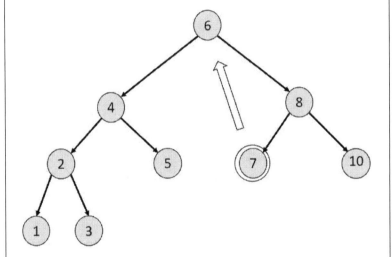	Minimum value is copied to the node with value 6.
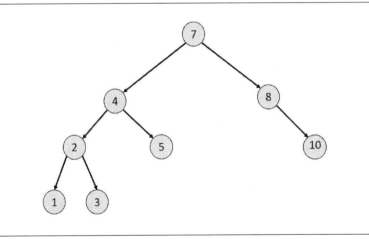	Delete node with minimum value 7 is called over the right subtree of the node. Finally the value 6 removed from the tree.

Example 9.42:

```
DeleteNode(value) {
    this.root = this.DeleteNodeUtil(this.root, value);
}

DeleteNodeUtil(node, value) {
    let temp = null;
```

```
    if (node != null) {
        if (node.value === value) {
            if (node.lChild == null && node.rChild == null) {
                return null;
            }
            else {
                if (node.lChild == null) {
                    temp = node.rChild;
                    return temp;
                }
                if (node.rChild == null) {
                    temp = node.lChild;
                    return temp;
                }
                const minNode = this.FindMinNode(node.rChild);
                const minValue = minNode.value;
                node.value = minValue;
                node.rChild = this.DeleteNodeUtil(node.rChild, minValue);
            }
        }
        else {
            if (node.value > value) {
                node.lChild = this.DeleteNodeUtil(node.lChild, value);
            }
            else {
                node.rChild = this.DeleteNodeUtil(node.rChild, value);
            }
        }
    }
    return node;
}

/* Testing Code */
const t = new Tree();
t.InsertNode(6)
t.InsertNode(4)
t.InsertNode(2)
t.InsertNode(5)
t.InsertNode(1)
t.InsertNode(3)
t.InsertNode(8)
t.InsertNode(7)
t.InsertNode(9)
t.InsertNode(10)
console.log("Before delete operation.")
t.PrintInOrder()
t.DeleteNode(2)
console.log("After delete operation.")
t.PrintInOrder()
```

Output:

```
Before delete operation.
In Order Tree: 1 2 3 4 5 6 7 8 9 10
After delete operation.
In Order Tree: 1 3 4 5 6 7 8 9 10
```

Analysis: Time Complexity: O(n), Space Complexity: O(n)

Least Common Ancestor

Problem: In a tree T. The least common ancestor between two nodes n1 and n2 is defined as the lowest node in T that has both n1 and n2 as descendants.

Example 9.43:

```
func (t *Tree) LcaBST(first int, second int) (int, bool) {
    return LcaBST(t.root, first, second)
}

func LcaBST(curr *Node, first int, second int) (int, bool) {
    if curr == nil {
        fmt.Println("NotFoundException")
        return 0, false
    }

    if curr.value > first && curr.value > second {
        return LcaBST(curr.left, first, second)
    }
    if curr.value < first && curr.value < second {
        return LcaBST(curr.right, first, second)
    }
    return curr.value, true
}

/* Testing Code */
const t = new Tree();
const arr = [1, 2, 3, 4, 5, 6, 7, 8, 9, 10];
t.CreateBinarySearchTree(arr)
console.log(t.LcaBST(3, 4))
console.log(t.LcaBST(1, 4))
console.log(t.LcaBST(10, 4))
```

Output:

```
3
2
5
```

Trim the Tree nodes which are Outside Range

Problem: Given a binary search tree and arrange as min, max. We need to delete all the nodes of the tree that are out of this range.

Solution: Traverse the tree and each node that is having value outside the range will delete itself. All the deletion will happen from inside out so we do not have to care about the children of a node as if they are out of range then they had already had deleted themselves.

Example 9.44:

```
trimOutsideRange(min, max) {
    this.trimOutsideRangeUtil(this.root, min, max);
}

trimOutsideRangeUtil(curr, min, max) {
    if (curr == null)
        return null;

    curr.lChild = this.trimOutsideRangeUtil(curr.lChild, min, max);
    curr.rChild = this.trimOutsideRangeUtil(curr.rChild, min, max);

    if (curr.value < min) {
        return curr.rChild;
    }
    if (curr.value > max) {
        return curr.lChild;
    }
    return curr;
}

/* Testing Code */
const t = new Tree();
const arr = [1, 2, 3, 4, 5, 6, 7, 8, 9, 10];
t.CreateBinarySearchTree(arr)
t.trimOutsideRange(3, 9)
t.PrintInOrder()
```

Output:
```
In Order Tree: 3 4 5 6 7 8 9
```

Print Tree nodes which are in Range

Problem: Print only those nodes of the tree whose value is in the given range.

Solution: Just normal inorder traversal and at the time of printing we will check if the value is inside the given range.

Example 9.45:

```
printInRange(min, max) {
    process.stdout.write("Print In Range : ");
    this.printInRangeUtil(this.root, min, max);
    process.stdout.write("\n");
}

printInRangeUtil(curr, min, max) {
    if (curr == null)
        return;
    this.printInRangeUtil(curr.lChild, min, max);
    if (curr.value >= min && curr.value <= max)
        process.stdout.write(`${curr.value} `);
    this.printInRangeUtil(curr.rChild, min, max);
}

/* Testing Code */
const t = new Tree();
const arr = [1, 2, 3, 4, 5, 6, 7, 8, 9, 10];
t.CreateBinarySearchTree(arr)
t.printInRange(3, 9)
```

Output:
```
Print In Range : 3 4 5 6 7 8 9
```

Find Ceil and Floor value inside BST given key

Problem: In given tree and a value, we need to find the floor value in tree which is smaller than the given value and need to find the ceil value in tree which is bigger. For a given value our aim is to find ceil and floor value as close as possible.

Solution: Just use search in BST to find ceil and floor of a value in a BST. When we are searching for ceil, if we find any value greater than the given input, we save this value as probable value. We narrow down our search for a value much closer to our input value. This algorithm taken O(logn) time if BST is balanced. Similarly, we can find floor too.

Example 9.46:

```
CeilBST(val) {
    let curr = this.root;
    let ceil = MIN_INT;
    while (curr != null) {
        if (curr.value === val) {
            ceil = curr.value;
            break;
        }
        else if (curr.value > val) {
            ceil = curr.value;
            curr = curr.lChild;
        }
        else {
```

```
            curr = curr.rChild;
        }
    }
    return ceil;
}

FloorBST(val) {
    let curr = this.root;
    let floor = MAX_INT;
    while (curr != null) {
        if (curr.value === val) {
            floor = curr.value;
            break;
        }
        else if (curr.value > val) {
            curr = curr.lChild;
        }
        else {
            floor = curr.value;
            curr = curr.rChild;
        }
    }
    return floor;
}

/* Testing Code */
const t = new Tree();
const arr = [1, 2, 4, 5, 6, 9, 10];
t.CreateBinarySearchTree(arr)
console.log(t.CeilBST(8))
console.log(t.FloorBST(8))
```

Output:
9
6

Smaller element in right side

Problem: Given an array. Construct an output array which the number of elements on the right side which are smaller than elements of given array.

First Solution: Brute force, use two loops for each value loop through all the elements in the right side of it and count the values which are smaller than it. Time complexity is $O(n^2)$

Second Solution: Another efficient solution is to use balanced BST. Traverse from right to left put values in tree. The nodes of the tree will keep track the number of elements in its left child or nodes which have value less than it. So, finding nodes which have value less than it is O(logn) this step will be repeated for all the nodes. Time complexity is O(nlogn)

Is a BST Array

Problem: Given an array of integers, you need to find if it represents a PreOrder traversal of binary search tree.

Solution: In PreOrder traversal <Root><Left child><Right child>. Once we have a value greater than root value then we are in Right child subtree. So, all the nodes that will come will have value greater than root value.

Example 9.47:

```
function isBSTArray(preorder, size) {
    const stk = ([]);
    let value;
    let root = MIN_INT;

    for (let i = 0; i < size; i++) {
        value = preorder[i];
        // If value of the right child is less than root.
        if (value < root)
            return false;
        // First left child values will be popped
        // Last popped value will be the root.
        while (stk.length > 0 && stk[stk.length - 1] < value) {
            root = stk.pop();
        };
        // add current value to the stack.
        stk.push(value);
    }
    return true;
}

/* Testing Code */
const t = new Tree();
const arr = [5, 2, 4, 6, 9, 10];
console.log(isBSTArray(arr, arr.length))

const arr2 = [5, 2, 6, 4, 7, 9, 10];
console.log(isBSTArray(arr2, arr2.length))
```

Output:
```
true
false
```

Segment Tree

Segment tree is a binary tree that is used to make multiple range queries and range update in an array.

Examples of problems for which Segment Tree can be used are:
1. Finding the sum of all the elements of an array in given range of index

2. Finding the maximum value of the array in given range of index.
3. Finding the minimum value of the array in given range of index (also known as Range Minimum Query problem)

Properties of Segment Tree:
1. Segment tree is a binary tree.
2. Each node in a segment tree represents an interval in the array.
3. The root of tree represents the whole array.
4. Each leaf node represents a single element.

Note: Segment tree solves problems, which can be solve in linear time by just scanning and updating the elements of array. The only benefit we are getting from segment tree is that it does update and query operation in logarithmic time that is more efficient than the linear solution.

Let us consider a simple problem:
Given an array of N numbers. You need to perform the following operations:
1. Update any element in the array
2. Find the maximum in any given range (i, j)

First Solution:
Updating: Just update the element in the array, a[i] =x. Finding maximum in the range (i, j), by traversing through the elements of the array in that range.
Time Complexity of Update is O(1) and of Finding is O(n)

Second Solution: The above solution is good. However, can we improve performance of Finding?
The answer is yes. In fact, we can do both the operations in O(log n) where n is the size of the array. This we can do using a segment tree.

Let us suppose we are given an input array A = {1, 8, 2, 7, 3, 6, 4, 5}. Moreover, the below diagram will represent the segment tree formed corresponding to the input array A.

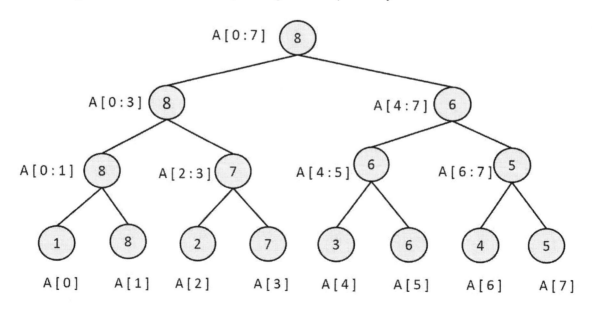

Input Array: A = { 1 , 8 , 2 , 7 , 3 , 6 , 4 , 5 }

AVL Trees

An AVL tree is a binary search tree (BST) with an additional property that the subtrees of every node differ in height by at most one. An AVL tree is a height balanced BST.

AVL tree is a balanced binary search tree. Adding or removing a node form AVL tree may make the AVL tree unbalanced. Such violations of AVL balance property is corrected by one or two simple steps called rotations. Let us assume that insertion of a new node converted a previously balanced AVL tree into an unbalanced tree. Since the tree is previously balanced and a single new node is added to it, the unbalance maximum difference in height will be 2.

Therefore, in the bottom most unbalanced node there are only four cases:
Case 1: The new node is left child of the left child of the current node.
Case 2: The new node is right child of the left child of the current node.
Case 3: The new node is left child of the right child of the current node.
Case 4: The new node is right child of the right child of the current node.

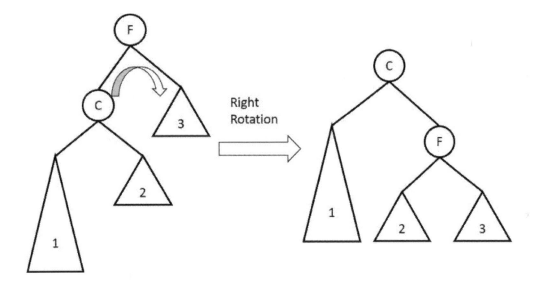

Case 1 can be re-balanced using a single Right Rotation.
Case 4 is symmetrical to Case 1: can be re-balanced using a single Left Rotation

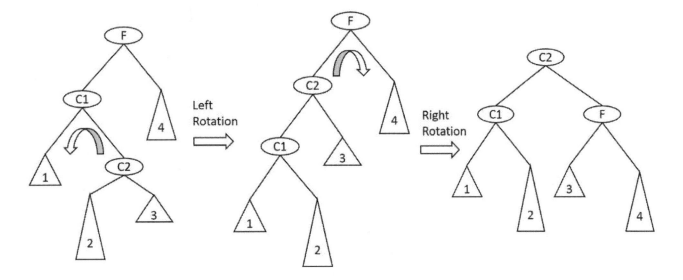

Case 2 can be re-balanced using a double rotation. First, rotate left than rotation right.
Case 3 is symmetrical to Case 2: can be re-balanced using a double rotation. First, rotate right than rotation left.

Time Complexity of Insertion: To search the location where a new node needs to be added is done in O(log(n)). Then on the way back, we look for the AVL balanced property and fixes them with rotation. Since the rotation at each node is done in constant time, the total amount of word is proportional to the length of the path. Therefore, the final time complexity of insertion is O(log(n)).

Red-Black Tree

The red-black tree contains its data, left and right children like any other binary tree. In addition to this its node also contains an extra bit of information which represents colour which can either red or black. Red-Black tree also contains a specialized type of nodes called null nodes. null nodes are pseudo nodes that exists at the leaf of the tree. All internal nodes have their own data associated with them.

Red-Black tree has the following properties:
1. Root of tree is black.
2. Every leaf node (null node) is black.
3. If a node is red then both of its children are black.
4. Every path from a node to a descendant leaf contains the same number of black nodes.

The first three properties are self-explanatory. The forth property states that, from any node in the tree to any leaf (null), the number of black nodes must be the same.

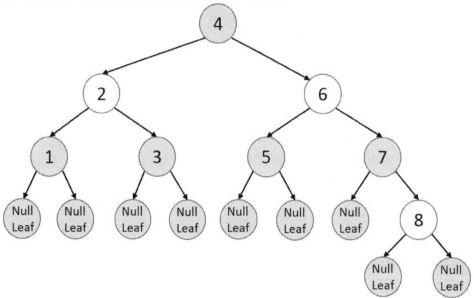

In the above figure, from the root node to the leaf node (null) the number of black node is always three nodes.

Like the AVL tree, red-black trees are also self-balancing binary search tree. Whereas the balance property of an AVL tree has a direct relationship between the heights of left and right subtrees of each node. In red-black trees, the balancing property is governed by the four rules mentioned above. Adding or removing a node form red-black tree may violate the properties of a red-black tree. The red-black properties are restored through recolouring and rotation. Insert, delete, and search operation time complexity is O(log(n))

Splay tree

A **splay tree** is a self-adjusting binary search tree with the additional property that recently accessed elements are quick to access again. It performs basic operations such as insertion, look-up and removal in O(log n) amortized time.

Elements of the tree are rearranged so that the recently accessed element is placed at the top of the tree. When an element is searched then we use standard BST search and then use rotation to bring the element to the top.

	Average Case	Worst Case
Space complexity	O(n)	O(n)
Time complexity search	O(log(n))	Amortized O(log(n))
Time complexity insert	O(log(n))	Amortized O(log(n))
Time complexity delete	O(log(n))	Amortized O(log(n))

Unlike the AVL tree, the splay tree is not guaranteed to be height balanced. What is guaranteed is that the total cost of the entire series of accesses will be cheap.

B-Tree

As we had already seen various types of binary tree for searching, insertion and deletion of data in the main memory. However, these data structures are not appropriate for huge data that cannot fit into main memory, the data that is stored in the disk.

A B-tree is a self-balancing search tree that allows searches, insertions, and deletions in logarithmic time. The B-tree is a tree in which a node can have multiple children. Unlike self-balancing binary search trees, the B-tree is optimized for systems that read and write entire blocks (page) of data. The read - write operation from disk is very slow as compared with the main memory. The main purpose of B-Tree is to reduce the number of disk access. The node in a B-Tree has a huge number of pointers to the children nodes. Thereby reducing the size of the tree. While accessing data from disk, it makes sense to read an entire block of data and store into a node of tree. B-Tree nodes are designed such that entire block of data (page) fits into it. It is commonly used in databases and file systems.

B-Tree of minimum degree d has the following properties:
1. All the leaf nodes must be at same level.
2. All nodes except root must have at least (d-1) keys and maximum of (2d-1) keys. Root may contain minimum 1 key.
3. If the root node is a non-leaf node, then it must have at least 2 children.
4. A non-leaf node with N keys must have (N+1) number of children.
5. All the key values within a node must be in Ascending Order.
6. All keys of a node are sorted in ascending order. The child between two keys, K1 and K2 contains all keys in range from K1 and K2.

B-Tree	Average Case	Worst Case
Space complexity	O(n)	O(n)
Time complexity search	O(log(n))	O(log(n))
Time complexity insert	O(log(n))	O(log(n))
Time complexity delete	O(log(n))	O(log(n))

Below is the steps of creation of B-Tree by adding value from 1 to 7.

1		Insert 1 to the tree.	Stable
2		Insert 2 to the tree.	Stable
3		Insert 3 to the tree.	Intermediate
4		New node is created and data is distributed.	Stable
5		Insert 4 to the tree.	Stable
6		Insert 5 to the tree.	Intermediate
7		New node is created and data is distributed.	Stable

8		Insert 6 to the tree.	Stable
9		Insert 7 to the tree. New node is created and data is distributed.	Intermediate
10		After rearranging the intermediate node, still another intermediate node have more keys than maximum number of allowed keys.	Intermediate
11		New node is created and data is distributed. The height of the tree is increased.	Stable

Note: 2-3 tree is a B-tree of degree three.

B+ Tree

B+ Tree is a variant of B-Tree. The B+ Tree stores records only at the leaf nodes. The internal nodes store keys. These keys are used for insertion, deletion and search. The rules of splitting and merging of nodes are same as B-Tree.

b-order B+ tree	Average Case	Worst Case
Space complexity	$O(n)$	$O(n)$
Time complexity search	$O(\log_b(n))$	$O(\log_b(n))$
Time complexity insert	$O(\log_b(n))$	$O(\log_b(n))$
Time complexity delete	$O(\log_b(n))$	$O(\log_b(n))$

Below is the B+ Tree created by adding value from 1 to 5.

| 1. | ```
1
``` | Value 1 is inserted to leaf node. |
| 2. | ```
1 2
``` | Value 2 is inserted to leaf node. |
| 3. | ```
    2
   / \
  1 → 2 3
``` | Value 3 is inserted to leaf node. Content of the leaf node passed the maximum number of elements. Therefore, node is split and intermediate / key node is created. |
| 4. | ```
      2 3
     / | \
 1 → 2 → 3 4
``` | Value 4 is further inserted to the leaf node. Which further splits the leaf node. |
| 5. | ```
        3
       / \
      2   4
     / \  / \
 1 → 2 → 3 → 4 5
``` | Value 5 is added to the leaf node the number of nodes in the leaf passed the maximum number of nodes limit that it could contain so it is divided into 2. One more key is added to the intermediate node, which also make it passed maximum number of nodes it can contain, and finally divided and a new node is created. |

B* Tree

The B* tree is identical to the B+ tree, except for the rules for splitting and merging of nodes. Instead of splitting a node into two halves when it overflows, the B* tree node tries to give some of its records to its neighbouring sibling. If the sibling is also full, then a new node is created and records are distributed into three.
```

Exercise

1. Construct a tree given its in-order and pre-order traversal strings.
   - inorder: 1 2 3 4 5 6 7 8 9 10
   - pre-order: 6 4 2 1 3 5 8 7 9 10

2. Construct a tree given its in-order and post-order traversal strings.
   - inorder: 1 2 3 4 5 6 7 8 9 10
   - post-order: 1 3 2 5 4 7 10 9 8 6

3. Write a delete node function in Binary tree.

4. Write a function print depth first in a binary tree without using system stack
   Hint: you may want to keep another element to tree node like visited flag.

5. Check whether a given Binary Tree is Complete or not
   - In a complete binary tree, every level except the last one is filled. All nodes in the left are filled first, then the right one.

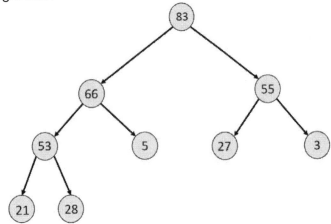

6. Check whether a given Binary Tree is Full/ Strictly binary tree or not. The full binary tree is a binary tree in which each node has zero or two children.

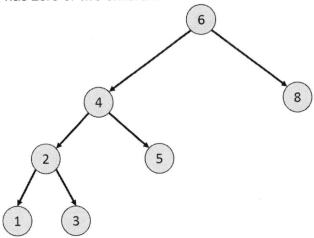

7. Check whether a given Binary Tree is a Perfect binary tree or not. The perfect binary tree-is a type of full binary trees in which each non-leaf node has exactly two child nodes.

8. Check whether a given Binary Tree is Height-balanced Binary Tree or not. A height-balanced binary tree is a binary tree such that the left & right subtrees for any given node differs in height by not more than one

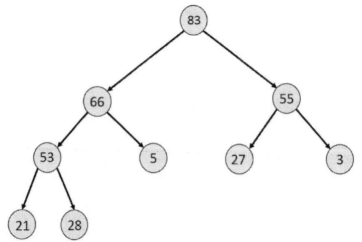

9. Isomorphic: two trees are isomorphic if they have the same shape, it does not matter what the value is. Write a program to find if two given trees are isomorphic or not.

10. The worst-case runtime Complexity of building a BST with n nodes
    o O(n²)
    o O(n * log n)
    o O(n)
    o O(logn)

11. The worst-case runtime Complexity of insertion into a BST with n nodes is
    o O(n2)
    o O(n * log n)
    o O(n)
    o O(logn)

12. The worst-case runtime Complexity of a search of a value in a BST with n nodes is:
    o O(n²)
    o O(n * log n)
    o O(n)
    o O(logn)

13. Which of the following traversals always gives the sorted sequence of the elements in a BST?
    o Preorder
    o Ignored
    o Postorder
    o Undefined

14. The height of a Binary Search Tree with n nodes in the worst case?
    o O(n * log n)
    o O(n)
    o O(logn)
    o O(1)

15. Try to optimize the above solution to give a DFS traversal without using recursion use some stack or queue.

16. This is an open exercise for the readers. Every algorithm that is solved using recursion (system stack) can also be solved using user defined or library defined stack. So, try to figure out what all algorithms that uses recursion and try to figure out how you will do this same using user defined stack.

17. In a binary tree, print the nodes in zigzag order. In the first level, nodes are printed in the left to right order. In the second level, nodes are printed in right to left and in the third level again in the order left to right.

    Hint: Use two stacks. Pop from first stack and push into another stack. Swap the stacks alternatively.

18. Find nth smallest element in a binary search tree.
    Hint: Nth inorder in a binary tree.

19. Find the floor value of key that is inside a BST.

20. Find the Ceil value of key, which is inside a BST.

21. What is Time Complexity of the below pseudo code?

```
Function DFS(head):
    curr = head
    count = 0
    while (curr != None && curr.visited == False):
        count++
        if (curr.lChild != None && curr.lChild.visited == False):
            curr= curr.lChild
        else if (curr.rChild != None && curr.rChild.visited == False):
            curr= curr.rChild
        else
            print curr.value
            curr.visited = 1
            curr = head

    print "count is : ", count
```

CHAPTER 10: PRIORITY QUEUE / HEAPS

Introduction

A Priority-Queue, also known as Heap, is a variant of queue. Items are removed from the beginning of the queue. However, in a Priority-Queue the logical ordering of objects is determined by their priority. The highest priority item is at the front of the Priority-Queue. When you add an item to the Priority-Queue, the new item more to it proper position according to its priority. A Priority-Queue is a very important data structure. Priority-Queue is used in various Graph algorithms like Prim's Algorithm and Dijkstra's algorithm. Priority-Queue is also used in the timer implementation etc.

A Priority-Queue is implemented using Heap. A Heap data structure is an array of elements that can be observed as a complete binary tree.

A heap is a binary tree that satisfy the following properties:
1. The tree is a complete binary tree. A heap is a complete binary tree so the height of tree with N nodes is always **O(logn)**.
2. Heap satisfies the heap ordering property. In max-heap, the parent's value is greater than or equal to its children value. In min-heap, the parent's value is less than or equal to its children value.

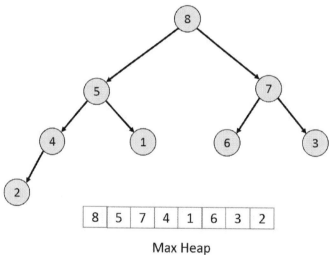

Max Heap

A heap is not a sorted data structure and can be regarded as partially ordered. As you can see in the picture, there is no relationship among nodes at any given level, even among the siblings.

Heap is implemented using an array. Moreover, because heap is a complete binary tree, the left child of a parent (at position x) is the node that is found in position (2x+1) in the array. Similarly, the right child of the parent is at position (2x+2) in the array. To find the parent of any node in the heap, we can simply make division. In given index y of a node, the parent index will by (y-1)/2.

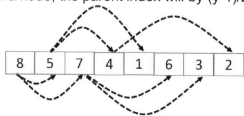

Parent-Child relationship in heap array.

Types of Heap

There are two types of heap and the type depends on the ordering of the elements. The ordering can be done in two ways: Min-Heap and Max-Heap

Max Heap

Max-Heap: the value of each node is less than or equal to the value of its parent, with the largest-value element at the root.

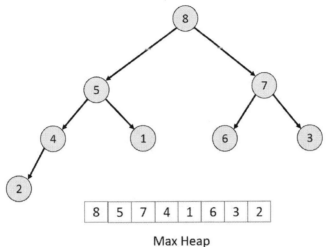

Max Heap

Max Heap Operations

Insert	O(logn)
DeleteMax	O(logn)
Remove	O(logn)
FindMax	O(1)

Min Heap

Min-Heap: the value of each node is greater than or equal to the value of its parent, with the minimum-value element at the root.

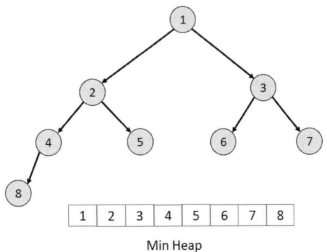

Min Heap

Use it whenever you need quick access to the smallest item, because that item will always be at the root of the tree or the first element in the array. However, the remainder of the array is kept partially sorted. Thus, instant access is only possible for the smallest item.

Min Heap Operations

Insert	O(logn)
DeleteMin	O(logn)
Remove	O(logn)
FindMin	O(1)

Heap ADT Operations

The basic operations of binary heap are as follows:

Binary Heap	Creates a new empty binary heap	O(1)
Insert	Adding a new element to the heap	O(logn)
DeleteMax	Deletes the maximum element form the heap.	O(logn)
FindMax	Finds the maximum element in the heap.	O(1)
isEmpty	Returns true if the heap is empty else return false	O(1)
Size	Returns the number of elements in the heap.	O(1)
BuildHeap	Builds a new heap from the array of elements	O(logn)

Operation on Heap

Before looking in detail of how to initialize heap, add or remove elements into it we need to understand two important operations involved in heap. These operations are used to restore heap order property when single element is out of its position.

There are two cases are:

1. When a node (parent node) is not following heap property with its children. This is resolved by procolateDown() operation in which parent node value is swapped with one of the child value and heap property is restored recursively.
2. When a node (child node) is not following heap property with its parent. This is resolved by proclateUp() or bubbleUp() operation in which child node value is swapped with parent node value and heap property is restored recursively.

Example 10.1: Below is the code of proclateUp and proclateDown operation.

```
proclateDown(parent) {
    const lChild = 2 * parent + 1;
    const rChild = lChild + 1;
    let child = -1;
    let temp;
    if (lChild <= this.size) {
        child = lChild;
    }
    if (rChild <= this.size && this.comp(this.arr[lChild],
this.arr[rChild])) {
```

```
        }
        child = rChild;
    }
    if (child !== -1 && this.comp(this.arr[parent], this.arr[child])) {
        temp = this.arr[parent];
        this.arr[parent] = this.arr[child];
        this.arr[child] = temp;
        this.proclateDown(child);
    }
}
```

```
proclateUp(child) {
    const parent = Math.floor((child - 1) / 2);
    if (parent < 0) {
        return;
    }
    if (this.comp(this.arr[parent], this.arr[child])) {
        const temp = this.arr[child];
        this.arr[child] = this.arr[parent];
        this.arr[parent] = temp;
        this.proclateUp(parent);
    }
}
```

Heap is represented using a class. The following elements of heap class are:
- "array" that is used to store heap.
- "capacity", which is capacity of array
- "size", which is the number of elements in the heap.
- "comp" is the compare function of the heap depending upon which the created heap will be min heap or max heap.

Heap

Example 10.2: Heap Class

```
class Heap {
    constructor(array, cmp) {
        this.comp = (typeof cmp === 'function') ? cmp : less;

        if (array === undefined || array === null) {
            this.size = 0;
            this.arr = [];
        } else if (array != null && array instanceof Array) {
            this.size = array.length;
            this.arr = array;
            for (let i = Math.floor(this.size / 2); i >= 0; i--) {
                this.proclateDown(i);
            }
        } else {
            throw new Error('invalid arguments');
        }
    }
```

```
    /* Other methods */
}
```

Analysis:
- Empty heap is created by creating an empty array. Later values can be added to heap by calling add function.
- When heap is created from an input array. We need to perform heapify operation to create heap from existing array.

Heapify is the process of converting an array into Heap. The various steps are:
1. Values are present in the input array.
2. Starting from middle of the array move downward towards the start of the array. At each step, compare parent value with its left child and right child. In addition, restore the heap property by shifting the parent value with its largest-value child. Such that the parent value will always be greater than or equal to left child and right child.
3. For all elements from middle of the array to the start of the array. We make comparisons and shift, until we reach the leaf nodes of the heap.

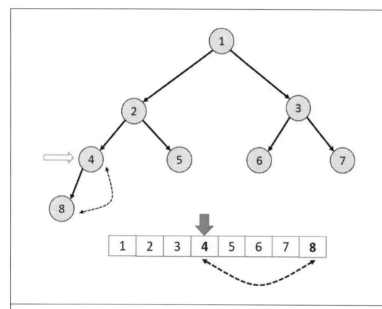

Given an array as input to create heap function. Value of index i is compared with value of its children nodes that is at index (i*2 + 1) and (i*2 + 2). Middle of list N/2, that is index 3, is compared with index 7. If the children node value is greater than parent node then the value will be swapped.

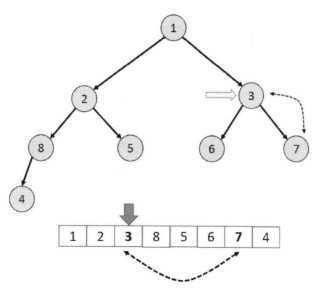

Similarly, value of index 2 is compared with index 5 and 6. The largest of all the values is 7 will be swapped with the value at the index 2.

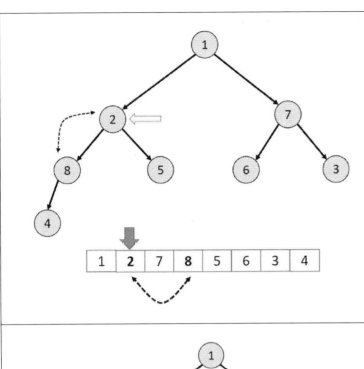

Similarly, value of index 1 is compared with index 3 and 4 The largest of all the values is 8 which will be swapped with the value at the index 1.

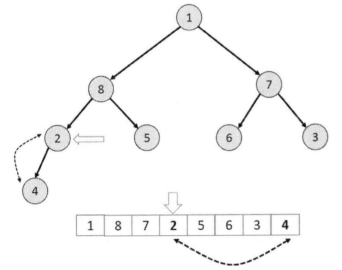

Percolate down function is used to subsequently adjust the value replased in the previous step by comparing it with its children nodes.

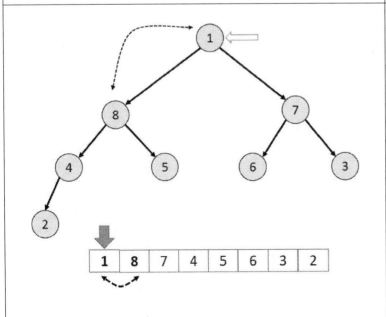

Now value at index 0 is compared with index 1 and 2. 8 is the largest value so it is swapped with the value at index 0.

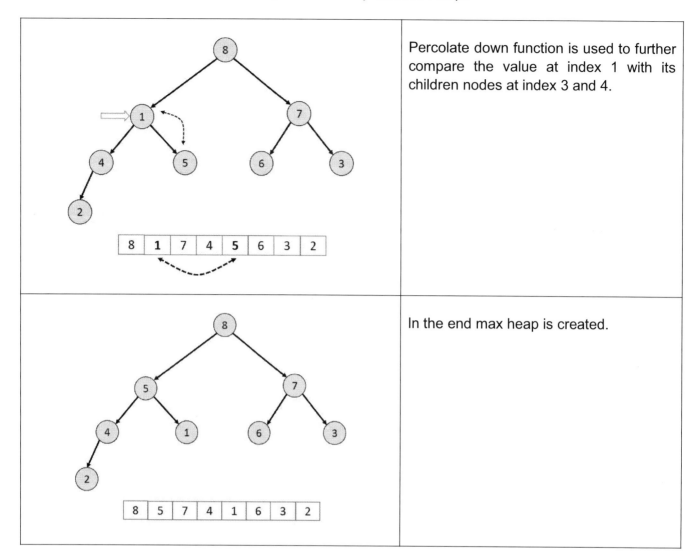

Percolate down function is used to further compare the value at index 1 with its children nodes at index 3 and 4.

In the end max heap is created.

Complexity Analysis:
Time Complexity of build heap from input array is **O(N)**. The number of comparisons is related to the height of the node. Total number of comparison will be represented as: (1*n/4) + (2*n/8)+ (3*n/16)...... ((h-1)*1) == N Where "h" is height of the heap.

Example 10.3: Other useful methods of Heap class.

```
print() {
    console.log(this.arr);
}

isEmpty() {
    return (this.size === 0);
}

length() {
    return this.size;
}

peek() {
    if (this.isEmpty()) {
        throw new Error("IllegalStateException");
```

```
    }
    return this.arr[0]
}
```

Analysis:
- Empty() function return true if heap is empty else return false.
- Size() function return the number of elements in the heap.
- Peek() function will return highest priority element form the heap without deleting it.

Enqueue / add

1. Add the new element at the end of the array. This keeps the values as a complete binary tree, but it might no longer be a heap since the new element might have a value greater than its parent's value.
2. Swap the new element with its parent until it has value greater than its parent's value.
3. Step 2 will be terminated when the new element reaches the root or when the new element's parent has a value greater than or equal to the new element's value.

Let us take an Example of the Max heap created in the above Example .

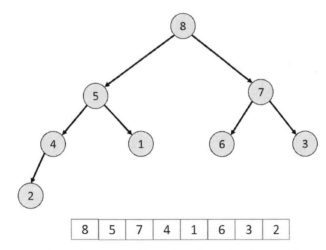

Let us take an Example by inserting element with value 9 to the heap. The element is added to the end of the Heap array. Now the value will be percolated up by comparing it with the parent. The value is added to index 8 and its parent will be (N-1)/2 = index 3.

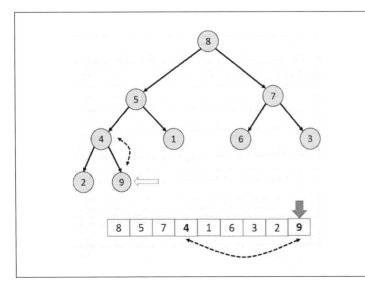

New bvalue 9 added to the end of array. Since the value 9 is greater than 4 it will be swapped with it.

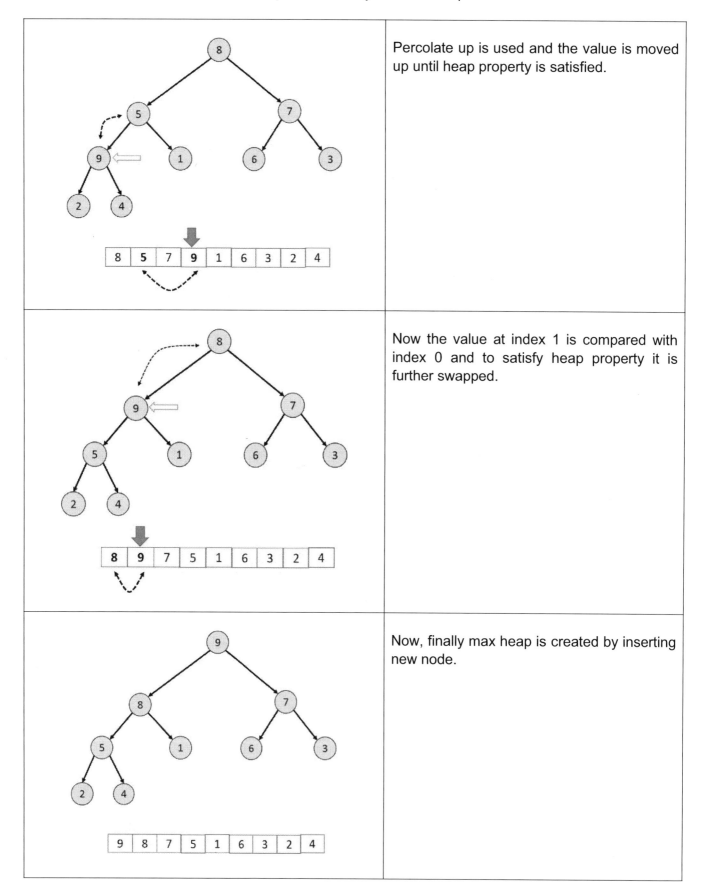

	Percolate up is used and the value is moved up until heap property is satisfied.
	Now the value at index 1 is compared with index 0 and to satisfy heap property it is further swapped.
	Now, finally max heap is created by inserting new node.

Example 10.4:
```
add(value) {
    this.arr[this.size] = value;
```

324

```
    this.size++;
    this.proclateUp(this.size - 1);
}
```

Analysis: We check if the heap is full. In case when heap is already full then we create another array of twice capacity. Copy the content of heap into it. Then add the new element to the heap and then use proclateUp() operation to restore heap property.
Time complexity of insertion in heap is O(logn)

Dequeue / remove

1. Copy the value at the root of the heap to the variable that will be used to return that value.
2. Copy the last element of the heap to the root, and then reduce the size of heap by 1. This element is called the "out-of-place" element.
3. Restore heap property by swapping the out-of-place element with its greatest-value child. Repeat this process until the out-of-place element reaches a leaf or it has a value that is greater or equal to all its children.
4. Return the answer that was saved in Step 1.

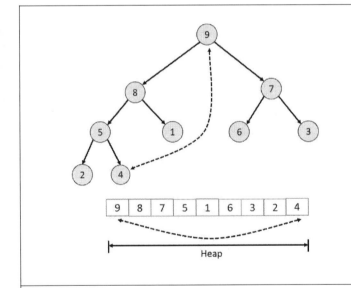

Value at start and end of the heap are swapped. Heap size is reduced by one. Heap property is disturbed so we need to percolate down by comparing node with its children nodes and restore heap property.

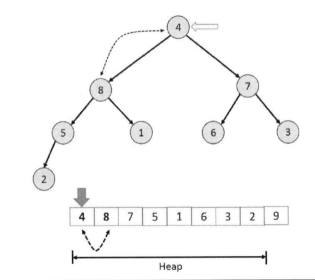

Percolate down is continued by comparing with its children nodes.

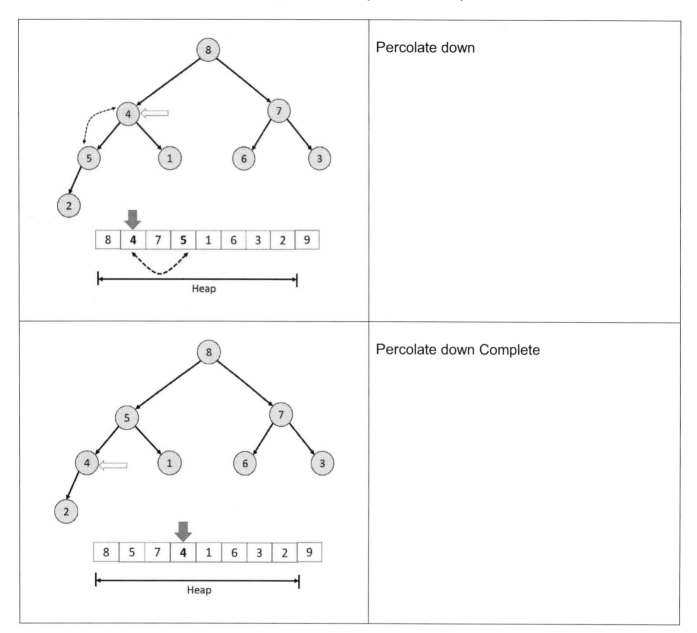

	Percolate down

| | Percolate down Complete |

Example 10.5:

```
remove() {
    if (this.isEmpty()) {
        throw new Error("IllegalStateException");
    }
    const value = this.arr[0];
    this.arr[0] = this.arr[this.size - 1];
    this.size--;
    this.proclateDown(0);
    return value;
}
```

Analysis: Value at the top of heap is swapped with the value at the end of the heap array. Size of heap is reduced by one and proclateDown is called to restore heap property.

Time complexity of remove element of heap is O(logn)

Example 10.6: Creating Empty min heap and adding values to it.

```
function test() {
    const hp = new Heap()
    hp.print();
    hp.add(1)
    hp.add(9)
    hp.add(6)
    hp.add(7)
    hp.print()
    while (hp.isEmpty() == false) {
        console.log(hp.remove())
    }
}
```

Output:

```
[]
[ 1, 7, 6, 9 ]
1
6
7
9
```

Example 10.7: Creating min heap and using input arrya.

```
function test() {
    const a = [1, 0, 2, 4, 5, 3];
    const hp = new Heap(a); // Min Heap
    hp.print();
    while (hp.isEmpty() == false) {
        console.log(hp.remove())
    }
}
```

Output:

```
[ 0, 1, 2, 4, 5, 3 ]
0
1
2
3
4
5
```

Example 10.8: Creating max heap and using input arrya.

```
function test() {
    const a = [1, 0, 2, 4, 5, 3];
    const hp = new Heap(a, more); // Max Heap
    hp.print();
    while (hp.isEmpty() == false) {
        console.log(hp.remove())
    }
}
```

Output:
```
[ 5, 4, 3, 1, 0, 2 ]
5
4
3
2
1
0
```

Heap-Sort

1. Use create heap function to build a max heap from the given list of elements. This operation will take **O(N)** time.
2. Dequeue the max value from the heap and store this value to the end of the array at location arr[size-1]
   a) Copy the value at the root of the heap to end of the array.
   b) Copy the last element of the heap to the root, and then reduce the size of heap by 1. This element is called the "out-of-place" element.
   c) Restore heap property by swapping the out-of-place element with its greatest-value child. Repeat this process until the out-of-place element reaches a leaf or it has a value that is greater or equal to all its children
3. Repeat this operation until there is just one element in the heap.

Let us take an Example of the heap that we had already created at the start of the chapter. Heap sort is algorithm starts by creating a heap of the given list, which is done in linear time. Then at each step head of the heap is swapped with the end of the heap and the heap size is reduced by 1. Then percolate down is used to restore the heap property. Moreover, the same is done multiple times until the heap contain just one element.

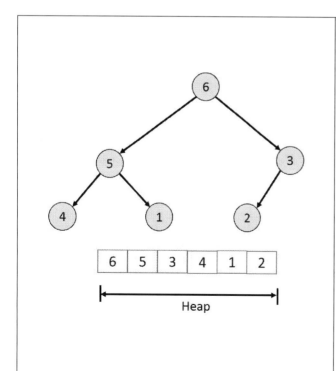

Max heap is created form the input array.

328

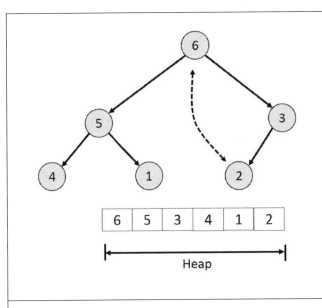

The maximum value, which is the first element of the Heap array, is swapped with the last element of the array. Now the largest value is at the end of the array. Then we will reduce the size of the heap by one.

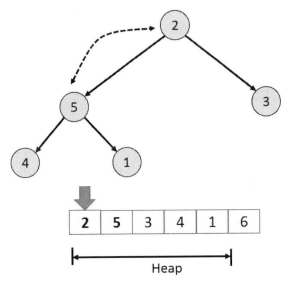

Since 2 is at the top of the heap. Its, heap property is lost. We will use Percolate down method to regain the heap property.

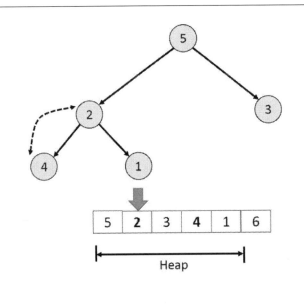

Percolate down continued.

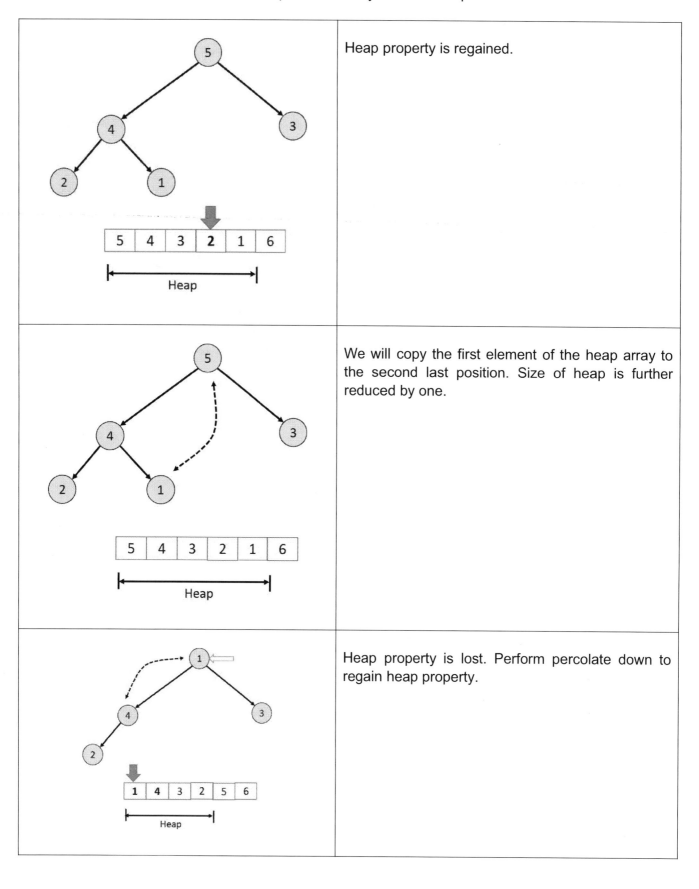

Heap property is regained.

We will copy the first element of the heap array to the second last position. Size of heap is further reduced by one.

Heap property is lost. Perform percolate down to regain heap property.

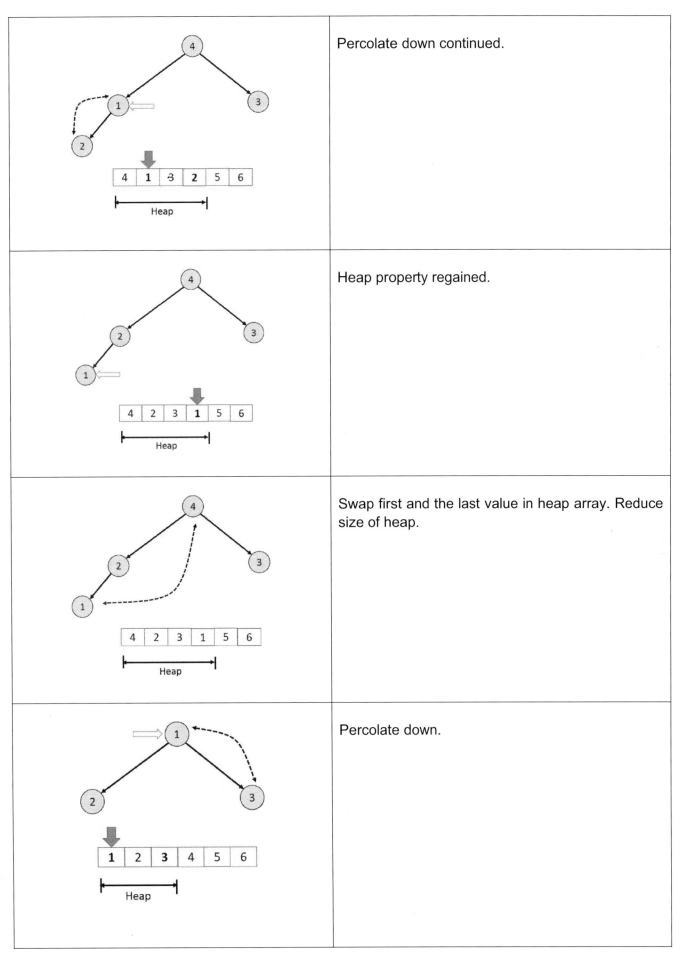

Percolate down continued.

Heap property regained.

Swap first and the last value in heap array. Reduce size of heap.

Percolate down.

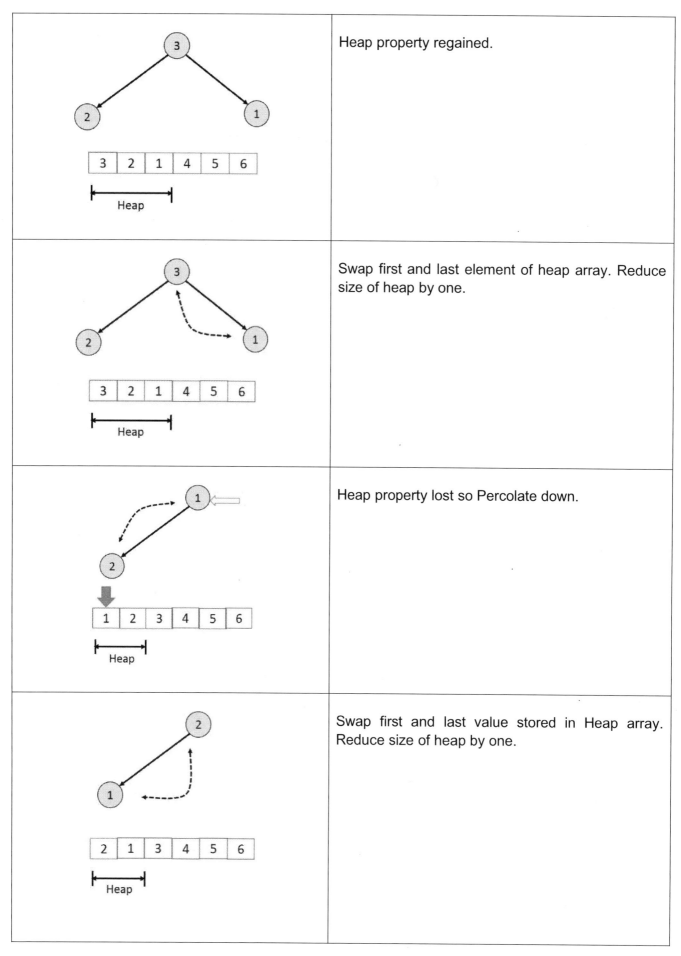

	Heap property regained.
	Swap first and last element of heap array. Reduce size of heap by one.
	Heap property lost so Percolate down.
	Swap first and last value stored in Heap array. Reduce size of heap by one.

	End
1 2 3 4 5 6	

Example 10.9:

```
function HeapSort(array, cmp) {
    const hp = new Heap(array, cmp);
    for (let i = 0; i < array.length; i++) {
        array[array.length - i - 1] = hp.remove();
    }
};

function test() {
    const b = [6, 5, 3, 4, 1, 2];
    HeapSort(b, more); // Increasing Order
    console.log(b);
}
```

Output:
```
[ 1, 2, 3, 4, 5, 6]
```

Data structure	List
Worst Case time complexity	O(nlogn)
Best Case time complexity	O(nlogn)
Average case time complexity	O(nlogn)
Space Complexity	O(1)

Time complexity analysis: Build heap of the input array takes O(n) time and each element removal and adding to the end of heap take O(logn). So, the total time complexity will be O(n) + O(nlogn). Final time complexity of this sorting is O(n.logn)

Note: Heap-Sort is not a Stable sort and does not require any extra space for sorting an array.

Uses of Heap

1. **Heapsort**: One of the best sorting methods being in-place and log(N) time complexity in all scenarios.

2. **Selection algorithms**: Finding the min, max, both the min and max, median, or even the kth largest element can be done in linear time (often constant time) using heaps.

3. **Priority Queues**: Heap Implemented priority queues are used in Graph algorithms like Prim's Algorithm and Dijkstra's algorithm. A heap is a useful data structure when you need to remove the object with the highest (or lowest) priority. Schedulers, timers

4. **Graph algorithms**: By using heaps as internal traversal data structures, run time will be reduced by polynomial order. Examples of such problems are Prim's minimal

5. Because of the lack of pointers, the operations are faster than a binary tree. In addition, some more complicated heaps (such as binomial) can be merged efficiently, which is not easy to do for a binary tree.

Problems in Heap

Kth Smallest using Min Heap

Problem: Given an unsorted array, find kth smallest value.

First Solution: Sort the given array and then give the value at index K-1. Time complexity is O(NlogN).

Example 10.10:
```
function KthSmallest(arr, size, k) {
    arr = arr.sort();
    return arr[k - 1];
};

function test() {
    const arr = [8, 7, 6, 5, 7, 5, 2, 1];
    console.info(`Kth Smallest :: ${KthSmallest(arr, arr.length, 3)}`);
};
```

Output:
```
Kth Smallest :: 5
```

Second Solution: Create a min heap from the array, call DeleteMin() operation K times and the last operation will give Kth smallest value. Time Complexity O(KlogN)

Example 10.11:
```
function KthSmallest2(arr, size, k) {
    let value = 0;
    const pq = new Heap(arr);
    let i = 0;
    while (i < size && i < k) {
        value = pq.remove();
        i += 1;
    }
    return value;
};
```

Kth Largest using Max Heap

Problem: Given an unsorted array, find kth largest element.

Solution: Same as above problem we will create a Max Heap from the input array. Then we call DeleteMax() operation K times and the last operation will give Kth largest value. Time Complexity O(KlogN)

Kth largest/ smallest in an infinite stream of number

Problem: Find kth largest value in an infinite stream of number.

First Solution: Keep a sorted array, which will contain k largest elements. For each element of the stream, compare it with the smallest value in the array. If it is smaller than ignore it. If it is greater than the smallest value in the array, then remove the smallest value and insert the new value in its proper position in the array to keep it sorted. This solution will take O(K) time for each compare and insert operation.

Second Solution: We can keep the elements in Balanced Binary Search tree. First k elements are added to the tree. After this for each new element of the stream we first find the smallest element in the binary tree this operation will take O(logk) time then we compare the smallest value with the new value. If the new value is smaller than the smallest value then we ignore it. If the new value is greater than the smallest value ten, we delete the smallest value and insert the new value these operations also take O(logn) time. This solution will take O(logk) time for each compare and insert operation.

100 Largest in a Stream

Problem: There are billions of integers coming out of a stream some getInt() function is providing integers one by one. How would you determine the largest 100 numbers?

Solution: Large hundred (or smallest hundred etc.), such problems are solved very easily using a Heap. In this case, we will create a min heap.
1. First, from 100 integers build a min heap.
2. Then for each coming integer compare if it is greater than the top of the min heap.
3. If not, then look for next integer. If yes, then remove the top min value from the min heap, insert the new value at the top of the heap, use procolateDown, and move it to its proper position, down the heap.
4. Every time you have largest 100 values stored in your head

Merge two Heap

Problem: Given two heaps, you need to merge them to create a single heap.

Solution: There is no single solution for this. Let us suppose the size of the bigger heap is N and the size of the smaller heap is M.
1. If both heaps are comparable in size, then put both Heap arrays in same bigger Lists. Alternatively, in one of the arrays if they are big enough, then apply CreateHeap() function which will take theta(N+M) time.
2. If M is much smaller than N then add() each element of M list one by one to N heap. This will take O(MlogN) the worst case or O(M) the best case.

Is Min Heap

Problem: In given list, find if it represents a binary Min Heap

Solution: Min Heap property we are going to check is that value at parent index is always less than or equal to its children index.

Example 10.12:

```
function isMinHeap(arr) {
    const size = arr.length;
    const mid = Math.floor((size - 2) / 2);

    for (i = 0; i <= mid; i++) {
        if (2 * i + 1 < size) {
            if (arr[i] > arr[2 * i + 1])
                return false;
        }
        if (2 * i + 2 < size) {
            if (arr[i] > arr[2 * i + 2])
                return false;
        }
    }
    return true;
}

function test() {
    const arr4 = [1, 2, 3, 4, 5, 6, 7, 8];
    console.info(`isMinHeap :: ${isMinHeap(arr4, arr4.length)}`);
};
```

Output:
```
isMinHeap :: true
```

Is Max Heap

Problem: In given list, find if it represents a binary Max Heap

Solution: Max Heap property we are going to check is that the value at parent index is always greater than or equal to its children index.

Example 10.13:

```
function isMaxHeap(arr) {
    const size = arr.length;
    const mid = Math.floor((size - 2) / 2);

    for (i = 0; i <= mid; i++) {
        if (2 * i + 1 < size && arr[i] < arr[2 * i + 1])
            return false;

        if (2 * i + 2 < size && arr[i] < arr[2 * i + 2])
            return false;
    }
    return true;
}
```

```
function test() {
    const arr3 = [8, 7, 6, 5, 7, 5, 2, 1];
    console.info(`isMaxHeap :: ${isMaxHeap(arr3, arr3.length)}`);
};
```

Output:
```
isMaxHeap :: true
```

Analysis: If each parent value is greater than its children value then heap property is true. We will traverse from start to half of the array and compare the value of index node with its left child and right child node.

Traversal in Heap

Heaps are not designed to traverse, to find some element. They are made to get min or max element quickly. Still if you want to traverse a heap just traverse the array sequentially. This traversal will be level order traversal. This traversal will have linear Time Complexity.

Deleting Arbiter element from Min Heap

Again, heap is not designed to delete an arbitrary element, still if you want to do so. Find the element by linear search in the Heap array. Replace it with the value stored at the end of the Heap value. Reduce the size of the heap by one. Compare the new inserted value with its parent. If its value is smaller than the parent value, then percolate up. Else if its value is greater than its left and right child then percolate down. Time Complexity is **O(logn)**

Deleting Kth element from Min Heap

Again, heap is not designed to delete an arbitrary element, still if you want to do so. Replace the kth value with the value stored at the end of the Heap value. Reduce the size of the heap by one. Compare the new inserted value with its parent. If its value is smaller than the parent value, then percolate up. Else if its value is greater than its left and right child then percolate down. Time Complexity is **O(logn)**

Print value in Range in Min Heap

Linearly traverse through the heap and print the value that are in the given range.

Product of K minimum elements

Problem: Given an array of positive elements. Find product of k minimum elements in array.

First Solution: Sorting, Sort the array and find product of first K elements. Sorting will take O(n.logn) time. And then finding product will take O(n) time so total time complexity is O(n.logn).

Example 10.14:
```
function KSmallestProduct(arr, size, k) {
    arr = arr.sort();
```

```
    let product = 1;
    for (let i = 0; i < k; i++) {
        product *= arr[i];
    }
    return product;
};

function test() {
    const arr = [8, 7, 6, 5, 7, 5, 2, 1];
    console.info(`Kth Smallest product:: ${KSmallestProduct(arr, 8, 3)}`);
};
```

Output:
```
Kth Smallest product:: 10
```

Second Solution: Min Heap, Create min heap from the array. Then pop K elements from heap and find their product. Heapify will take O(n) time. Pop elements from heap take O(logn) time. K elements are popped from heap. So total time complexity is O(k.logn)

Example 10.15:
```
function KSmallestProduct2(arr, size, k) {
    const pq = new Heap(arr);
    let i = 0;
    let product = 1;
    while (i < size && i < k) {
        product *= pq.remove();
        i += 1;
    }
    return product;
};
```

Third Solution: Max heap, Max heap of size K can be created from first K elements. Then traverse the rest of array if the value at top of array is greater than the current value traversed. Then pop from the heap and then add the current value to the heap. Repeat this process till all the elements of array are traversed. In the end the heap contains the K minimum values then find their product.

Fourth Solution: Quick select method, this method is the bi-product of quick select method to find the kth element of an array. Run quick select method to find kth element of an array. The values at the left of kth index is less than the value at kth index. Find product of first k element. Average case time complexity of this solution is O(n).

Example 10.16:
```
function KSmallestProduct3(arr, size, k) {
    QuickSelectUtil(arr, 0, size - 1, k);
    let product = 1;
    for (let i = 0; i < k; i++) {
        product *= arr[i];
    }
    return product;
};
```

Print larger half of array

Problem: Given an array, print the larger half of the array when it will be sorted.

First Solution: Sorting, Sort the array and then print the larger half of the array. Sorting will take O(n.logn) time. And then print the larger half will take O(n) time so total time complexity is O(n.logn).

Example 10.17:
```
function PrintLargerHalf(arr, size) {
    arr = arr.sort();
    for (let i = Math.floor(size / 2); i < size; i++) {
        process.stdout.write(`${arr[i]} `);
    }
    console.info();
};

function test() {
    const arr = [8, 7, 6, 4, 7, 5, 2, 1];
    PrintLargerHalf(arr, 8);
};
```

Output:
6 7 7 8

Second Solution: Min Heap, Create min heap from the array. Then pop first half n/2 elements from heap and find print the rest part. Heapify will take O(n) time. Pop elements from heap take O(logn) time. n/2-time elements are popped from heap. So total time complexity is O(n.logn).

Example 10.18:
```
function PrintLargerHalf2(arr, size) {
    const pq = new Heap(arr);
    for (let i = 0; i < (size / 2); i++) {
        pq.remove();
    }
    while (pq.isEmpty() === false){
        process.stdout.write(`${pq.remove()} `);
    }
    console.info();
};
```

Third Solution: Quick select method, run quick select method to find the middle element of the array. The values at the right half of the array will be greater than the middle element's value. Finally print the value at the middle and right of it. Average case time complexity of this solution is O(n).

Example 10.19:
```
function PrintLargerHalf3(arr, size) {
    QuickSelectUtil(arr, 0, size - 1, (size / 2));
    for (let i = (size / 2); i < size; i++) {
        process.stdout.write(`${arr[i]} `);
```
339

```
    }
    console.info();
};
```

Nearly sorted array

Problem: Given a nearly sorted array, in which an element is at max k units away from its sorted position.

First Solution: If you use sorting then it will take O(NlogN) time

Second Solution: There is one algorithm by which it can be done in O(NlogK) time.
1. You can create a min Heap of size K+1 from first K+1 elements of input array.
2. Create an empty output array.
3. Pop an element from heap and store it into output array.
4. Push next element from array to heap.
5. Repeat this process 3 and 4 till all the elements of array are consumed and heap is empty.
6. In the end you have sorted array.

Example 10.20:
```
function sortK(arr, size, k) {
    const pq = new Heap();
    let i = 0;
    for (i = 0; i < k; i++) {
        pq.add(arr[i]);
    };
    const output = new Array(size);
    let index = 0;
    for (i = k; i < size; i++) {
        output[index++] = pq.remove();
        pq.add(arr[i]);
    }

    while (pq.isEmpty() === false) {
        output[index++] = pq.remove();
    };
    for (i = 0; i < size; i++) {
        arr[i] = output[i];
    }
    console.info(arr);
};

function test() {
    const k = 3;
    const arr = [1, 5, 4, 10, 50, 9];
    const size = arr.length;
    sortK(arr, size, k);
};
```

Output:
```
[ 1, 4, 5, 9, 10, 50 ]
```

Chota Bhim

Problem: A boy named Chota Bhim had visited his grandfather Takshak. Takshak had offered Bhim to drink elixir of power. He had offered number of cups filled with different quantity of elixir. Bhim is instructed to drink maximum quantity of elixir from the cups one by one. The cups are magical when Bhim empties a cup, it refills itself with half the previous quantity it uses ceil [previous amount // 2] function to fill itself. Bhim is given 1 minute's time. He is efficient, in each second, he drinks from one cup and puts it back. Bhim had consumed lot of elixir by always picking the cup with maximum elixir. Now Takshak had called you to find how much he had consumed.

Example :
5 Cups
Step 1 Cups: 2, 1, 7, 4, 2
>> 7 is selected
Step 2 Cups: 2, 1, 4, 4, 2
>> 4 is selected two times
Step 3 Cups: 2, 1, 2, 2, 2
>> 2 is selected four times
Step 4 and rest of days Cups: 1, 1, 1, 1, 1
>> rest all 1

Total: 7+4+4+2+2+2+2+(60 - 7) = 76 units of elixir

First Solution: Sorted list method, First sort the ropes list. The minimum two will be at the start of the array. We remove the first two and then join them and add them to the sorted list in such a way that it remains sorted. Now repeat this process till all the arrays are added.

Each insertion into proper position such that the array remains sorted takes linear time so the total time complexity is $O(n^2)$

Example 10.21:
```
function ChotaBhim(cups, size){
    let time = 60;
    let total = 0;
    let index;
    let temp;
    cups.sort();

    while (time > 0) {
        total += cups[0];
        cups[0] = Math.ceil(cups[0] / 2.0);
        index = 0;
        temp = cups[0];
        while (index < size - 1 && temp < cups[index + 1]) {
            cups[index] = cups[index + 1];
            index += 1;
        }
```

```
        cups[index] = temp;
        time -= 1;
    }
    console.info(`Total : ${total}`);
    return total;
};

function test(){
    const cups = [2, 1, 7, 4, 2];
    ChotaBhim(cups, cups.length);
};
```

Output:

Total : 76

Second Solution: Performance can be improved by using a heap to store values. Create a min heap of all the ropes. Then remove the lowest two values from the heap. Add these two values and then insert them into the heap. Deletion and Insertion will take O(LogN) time, so the total time complexity of this algorithm will be O(NlogN)

Example 10.22:
```
function ChotaBhim3(cups, size){
    let time = 60;
    let total = 0;
    let value;
    const pq = new Heap(cups, more);

    while (time > 0) {
        value = pq.remove();
        total += value;
        value = (Math.ceil(value / 2.0));
        pq.add(value);
        time -= 1;
    }
    console.info(`Total : ${total}`);
    return total;
};
```

Join Rope

Problem: Given N number of ropes of various length. You need to join these ropes to make a single rope. The cost of joining two ropes of length X and Y is (X+Y) which is their combined length. You need to find the minimum cost of joining all the ropes. Minimum cost of joining rope is obtained when we always join two smallest ropes.

First Solution: Sorted list method, First sort the ropes list. The minimum two will be at the start of the array. We remove the first two and then join them and add them to the sorted list in such a way that it remains sorted. Now repeat this process till all the arrays are added.

Each insertion into proper position such that the array remains sorted takes linear time so the total time complexity is O(n²)

Example 10.23:
```
function JoinRopes(ropes, size) {
    ropes.sort().reverse();
    let total = 0;
    let value = 0;
    let temp;
    let index;
    let length = size;

    while (length >= 2) {
        value = ropes[length - 1] + ropes[length - 2];
        total += value;
        index = length - 2;
        while (index > 0 && ropes[index - 1] < value) {
            ropes[index] = ropes[index - 1];
            index -= 1;
        }
        ropes[index] = value;
        length--;
    }
    console.info(`Total : ${total}`);
    return total;
}

function test(){
    const ropes = [2, 1, 7, 4, 2];
    JoinRopes(ropes, ropes.length);
    const rope2 = [2, 1, 7, 4, 2];
    JoinRopes2(rope2, rope2.length);
};
```

Output:
```
Total : 33
```

Second Solution: Performance can be improved by using a heap to store values. Create a min heap of all the ropes. Then remove the lowest two values from the heap. Add these two values and then insert them into the heap. Deletion and Insertion will take O(LogN) time, so the total time complexity of this algorithm will be O(NlogN)

Example 10.24:
```
function JoinRopes2(ropes, size) {
    const pq = new Heap(ropes);
    let total = 0;
    let value = 0;

    while (pq.length() > 1) {
        value = pq.remove();
```

```
        value += pq.remove();
        pq.add(value);
        total += value;
    }
    console.info(`Total : ${total}`);
    return total;
};
```

Get Median function

Problem: Give a data structure that will provide median of given values in constant time.

Solution: We will use two heaps, one min heap and another max heap. Max heap will contain the first half of data and min heap will contain the second half of the data. Max heap will contain the smaller half of the data and its max value that is at the top of the heap will be the median contender. Similarly, the Min heap will contain the larger values of the data and its min value that is at its top will contain the median contender. We will keep track of the size of heaps. Whenever we insert a value to heap, we will make sure that the size of two heaps differs by max one element, otherwise we will pop one element from one and insert into another to keep them balanced.

Example 10.25:

```
class MedianHeap {
    constructor() {
        this.minHeap = new Heap([], less);
        this.maxHeap = new Heap([], more);
    }

    insert(value) {
        if (this.maxHeap.isEmpty() === true || this.maxHeap.peek() >= value)
{
            this.maxHeap.add(value);
        }
        else {
            this.minHeap.add(value);
        }
        if (this.maxHeap.length() > this.minHeap.length() + 1) {
            value = this.maxHeap.remove();
            this.minHeap.add(value);
        }
        if (this.minHeap.length() > this.maxHeap.length() + 1) {
            value = this.minHeap.remove();
            this.maxHeap.add(value);
        }
    }

    getMedian() {
        if (this.maxHeap.isEmpty() === true && this.minHeap.isEmpty() ===
true)
            return MAX_VALUE;
        if (this.maxHeap.length() === this.minHeap.length())
```

```
            return ((this.maxHeap.peek() + this.minHeap.peek()) / 2 | 0);
        else if (this.maxHeap.length() > this.minHeap.length())
            return this.maxHeap.peek();
        else
            return this.minHeap.peek();
    }
}

function test(){
    const arr = [1, 9, 2, 8, 3, 7, 4, 6, 5, 1, 9];
    const hp = new MedianHeap();
    for (let i = 0; i < 10; i++) {
        hp.insert(arr[i]);
        console.log(`Median after insertion of ${arr[i]} is  $
{hp.getMedian()}`);
    }
};
```

Output:
```
Median after insertion of 1 is  1
Median after insertion of 9 is  5
Median after insertion of 2 is  2
Median after insertion of 8 is  5
Median after insertion of 3 is  3
Median after insertion of 7 is  5
Median after insertion of 4 is  4
Median after insertion of 6 is  5
Median after insertion of 5 is  5
Median after insertion of 1 is  4
```

Exercise

1. What is the worst-case runtime Complexity of finding the smallest item in a min-heap?

2. Find max in a min heap.
   Hint: normal search in the complete list. There is one more optimization you can search from the mid of the array at index N/2

3. What is the worst-case time complexity of finding the largest item in a min-heap?

4. What is the worst-case time complexity of deleteMin in a min-heap?

5. What is the worst-case time complexity of building a heap by insertion?

6. Is a heap full or complete binary tree?

7. What is the worst time runtime Complexity of sorting an array of N elements using heapsort?

8. In given sequence of numbers: 1, 2, 3, 4, 5, 6, 7, 8, 9
   a. Draw a binary Min-heap by inserting the above numbers one by one

    b.   Also draw the tree that will be formed after calling Dequeue() on this heap

9. In given sequence of numbers: 1, 2, 3, 4, 5, 6, 7, 8, 9
    a.   Draw a binary Max-heap by inserting the above numbers one by one
    b.   Also draw the tree that will be formed after calling Dequeue() on this heap

10. In given sequence of numbers: 3, 9, 5, 4, 8, 1, 5, 2, 7, 6. Construct a Min-heap by calling CreateHeap function.

11. Show an array that would be the result after the call to deleteMin() on this heap

12. In given list: [3, 9, 5, 4, 8, 1, 5, 2, 7, 6]. Apply heapify over this to make a min heap and sort the elements in decreasing order?

13. In Heap-Sort once a root element has been put in its final position, how much time, does it take to reheapify the array so that the next removal can take place? In other words, what is the Time Complexity of a single element removal from the heap of size N?

14. What do you think the overall Time Complexity for heapsort is? Why do you feel this way?

CHAPTER 11: HASH-TABLE

Introduction

In the searching chapter, we have gone through into various searching techniques. Consider a problem of searching a value in an array. If the array is not sorted then we have no other option, but to investigate each element one by one so the searching time complexity will be **O(n)**. If the array is sorted then we can search the value in **O(logn)** logarithmic time using binary search.

What if it is possible to get location / index of value we are looking in the array by a magic function that return index in constant time? We can directly go into that location and see whether the value we are searching for is present or not in **O(1)** constant time. Hash function works just like that of course, there is no magic involved.

Hash-Table

A Hash-Table is a data structure that maps keys to values. Each position of the Hash-Table is called a slot. The Hash-Table uses a hash function to calculate an index of an array. We use the Hash-Table when the number of keys is small relatively to the number of possible keys.

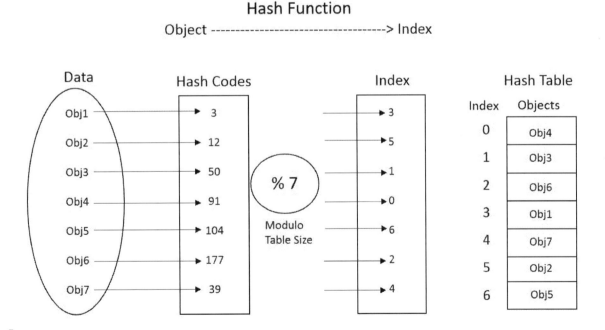

The process of storing data using a hash table is as follows:
1. Create an array of size M to store data; this array is called Hash-Table.
2. Find a hash code of a data by passing it through the hash function.
3. Take module of hash code by the size of Hashtable to get the index of the table where data will be stored.
4. Finally store this data in the designated index.

347

The process of searching value in Hash-Table using a hash function is as follows:
1. Find a hash code of the key we are searching for by passing it through the hash function.
2. Take module of hash code by the size of Hashtable to get the index of the table where value is stored.
3. Finally, retrieve the value from the designated index.

Hash-Table Abstract Data Type (ADT)

ADT of Hash-Table contains the following functions:
1. Insert(x), add x to the data set.
2. Delete(x), delete x from the data set.
3. Search(x), search x in data set.

Hash Function

A hash function is a function that generates an index in a table for a given key. An ideal hash function that generate a unique index for every key is called the perfect hash function.

Example 11.1: Most simple hash function

```
ComputeHash(key) {
    return this.HashFun(key) % this.tableSize;
}
```

There are many hash functions. The above function is a very simple hash function. Various hash generation logics will be added to this function to generate a better hash.

Collisions

When a hash function generates the same index for the two or more different keys, the problem is known as the collision. Ideally, hash function should return a unique address for each key, but practically it is not possible.

Properties of good hash function:

1. It should provide a uniform distribution of hash values. A non-uniform distribution increases the number of collisions and the cost of resolving them.
2. Choose a hash function, which can be computed quickly and returns values within the range of the Hash-Table.
3. Chose a hash function with a good collision resolution algorithm which can be used to compute alternative index if the collision occurs.
4. Choose a hash function, which uses the necessary information provided in the key.
5. It should have high load factor for a given set of keys.

Load Factor

Load factor = (Maximum Allowed Number of elements in Hash-Table) / Hash-Table size

Based on the above definition, Load factor is a measure of how many elements hash table can contain before its capacity is increased. When the number of elements exceeds the product of load factor and current capacity, the hash table is rehashed. Normally the hash table size is doubled in this case.

For Example , if load factor is 0.8 and hash table capacity is 1000 then we can add 800 elements to Hashtable without rehashing it.

Collision Resolution Techniques

Hash collisions are practically unavoidable when hashing large number of keys. Techniques that are used to find the alternate location in the Hash-Table is called collision resolution. There are several collision resolution techniques to handle the collision in hashing.

Most common and widely used techniques are:
- Open addressing
- Separate chaining

Hashing with Open Addressing

When using linear open addressing, the Hash-Table is represented by a one-dimensional array with indices that range from 0 to the table size-1.

One method of resolving collision is to investigate a Hash-Table and find another free slot to hold the value that have caused the collision. A simple way is to move from one slot to another in some sequential order until we find a free space. This collision resolution process is called Open Addressing.

Linear Probing

In Linear Probing, we try to resolve the collision of an index of a Hash-Table by sequentially searching the Hash-Table free location. Let us assume, if k is the index retrieved from the hash function. If the kth index is already filled then we will look for (k+1) %M, then (k+2) %M and so on. When we get a free slot, we will insert the data into that free slot.

Example 11.2: The resolver function of linear probing
```
resolverFun(index) {
    return index;
}
```

Quadratic Probing

In Quadratic Probing, we try to resolve the collision of the index of a Hash-Table by quadratic increasing the search index of free location. Let us assume, if k is the index retrieved from the hash function. If the kth index is already filled then we will look for (k+1^2) %M, then (k+2^2) %M and so on. When we get a free slot, we will insert the data into that free slot.

Example 11.3: The resolver function of quadratic probing
```
resolverFun(index) {
    return index * index;
}
```

Note: Table size should be a prime number to prevent early looping it should not be too close to 2powN

Linear Probing implementation

Hash table class consist of an array which is used to store data, and another array flags which is used to track if some slot is occupied or not. It also contains size of the array.

Example 11.4: Below is Hash-Table class.

```
EMPTY_VALUE = -1;
DELETED_VALUE = -2;
FILLED_VALUE = 0;

class HashTable {
    constructor(tSize, cmp, hashFun) {
        if (cmp === undefined || cmp === null)
            cmp = this.DefaultCompare;

        this.comp = cmp;

        if (hashFun === undefined || hashFun === null)
            hashFun = this.DefaultHashFun;

        this.HashFun = hashFun;
        this.tableSize = tSize;
        this.KeyArr = new Array(tSize + 1);
        this.DataArr = new Array(tSize + 1);
        this.FlagArr = new Array(tSize + 1).fill(EMPTY_VALUE);
    }
    /* Other methods */
}
```

Example 11.5: Below is hash code generation and collision resolution function.

```
ComputeHash(key) {
    return this.HashFun(key) % this.tableSize;
}
```

When the hash index is already occupied, the resolver function is used to get new index.

Example 11.6:

```
add(key, value) {
    if (key === undefined || key === null)
        return false;

    if (value === undefined || value === null)
        value = key;

    let hashValue = this.ComputeHash(key);
    for (let i = 0; i < this.tableSize; i++) {
        if ((this.FlagArr[hashValue] === EMPTY_VALUE) ||
            (this.FlagArr[hashValue] === DELETED_VALUE))
```

```
        {
            this.DataArr[hashValue] = value;
            this.KeyArr[hashValue] = key;
            this.FlagArr[hashValue] = FILLED_VALUE;
            return true;
        }
        else if (this.FlagArr[hashValue] === FILLED_VALUE &&
            this.KeyArr[hashValue] === key)
        {
            this.DataArr[hashValue] = value;
            return true;
        }

        hashValue += this.resolverFun(i);
        hashValue %= this.tableSize;
    }
    return false;
}
```

add() function is used to add values to the hash table. First hash is calculated. Then we try to place that value in the Hash-Table. We look for empty node or lazy deleted node to insert value. In case insert did not success, we try new location using a resolver function.

Example 11.7:

```
find(key) {
    if (key === undefined || key === null)
        return false;

    let hashValue = this.ComputeHash(key);
    for (let i = 0; i < this.tableSize; i++) {
        if (this.FlagArr[hashValue] === EMPTY_VALUE) {
            return false;
        }
        if (this.FlagArr[hashValue] === FILLED_VALUE
            && this.KeyArr[hashValue] === key) {
            return true;
        }
        hashValue += this.resolverFun(i);
        hashValue %= this.tableSize;
    }
    return false;
}
```

find() function is used to search particular key in hash table. First hash is calculated. Then we try to find that key in the Hash-Table. We look for over desired key or empty node. In case we find the key that we are looking for, then we return true or in case it is not found we return false. We use a resolver function to find the next probable index to search.

Example 11.8:

```
get(key) {
    if (key === undefined || key === null)
        return false;

    let hashValue = this.ComputeHash(key);
    for (let i = 0; i < this.tableSize; i++) {
        if (this.FlagArr[hashValue] === EMPTY_VALUE) {
            return 0;
        }
        if (this.FlagArr[hashValue] === FILLED_VALUE
            && this.KeyArr[hashValue] === key) {
            return this.DataArr[hashValue];
        }
        hashValue += this.resolverFun(i);
        hashValue %= this.tableSize;
    }
    return 0;
}
```

get() function is used to search values corresponding to key in hashtable. First hash is calculated. Then we try to find that key in the Hash-Table. We look for over desired value or empty node. In case we find the key that we are looking for, then we return its corresponding value or in case it is not found we return 0. We use a resolver function to find the next probable index to search.

Example 11.9:

```
delete(key) {
    if (key === undefined || key === null)
        return false;

    let hashValue = this.ComputeHash(key);
    for (let i = 0; i < this.tableSize; i++) {
        if (this.FlagArr[hashValue] === EMPTY_VALUE) {
            return false;
        }
        if (this.FlagArr[hashValue] === FILLED_VALUE
            && this.KeyArr[hashValue] === key) {
            this.FlagArr[hashValue] = DELETED_VALUE;
            return true;
        }
        hashValue += this.resolverFun(i);
        hashValue %= this.tableSize;
    }
    return false;
}
```

delete() function is used to delete values from a Hashtable. We do not actually delete the value we just mark that value as DELETED_NODE. Same as the insert and search we use resolverFun to find the next probable location of the key.

Example 11.10:
```
print() {
    for (let i = 0; i < this.tableSize; i++) {
        if (this.FlagArr[i] === FILLED_VALUE) {
            console.log(`Node at index [${i} ] :: ${this.DataArr[i]}`);
        }
    }
}
```

Print method print the content of hash table. Main function demonstrating how to use hash table.

Example 11.11:
```
const ht = new HashTable(1000);
ht.add(1, 10);
ht.add(2, 20);
ht.add(3, 30);
ht.print();

console.log("Find key 2 : ", ht.find(2));
console.log("Value at key 2 : ",ht.get(2))
ht.delete(1)
ht.print()
```

Output:
```
Node at index [1 ] :: 10
Node at index [2 ] :: 20
Node at index [3 ] :: 30
Find key 2 :   true
Value at key 2 :   20
Node at index [2 ] :: 20
Node at index [3 ] :: 30
```

Quadratic Probing implementation.

Everything will be same as linear probing implementation only resolver function will be changed.
```
resolverFun(index) {
    return index*index;
}
```

Hashing with separate chaining

Another method for collision resolution is based on an idea of putting the keys that collide in a linked list. This method is called separate chaining. To speed up search we use Insertion-Sort or keeping the linked list sorted.

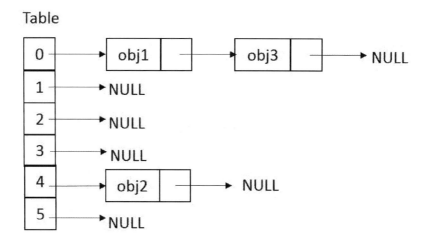

Separate Chaining implementation

Example 11.12: Below is separate chaining implementation of hash tables.

```
class HashTableNode {
    constructor(k, v, n) {
        this.key = k;
        this.value = v;
        this.next = n;
    }
}

class HashTable {
    constructor(cmp, hashFun) {
        if (cmp === undefined || cmp === null)
            cmp = this.DefaultCompare;

        this.comp = cmp;

        if (hashFun === undefined || hashFun === null)
            hashFun = this.DefaultHashFun;

        this.HashFun = hashFun;

        this.tableSize = 512;
        this.listArray = new Array(this.tableSize).fill(null);
    }

    ComputeHash(key) {
        return this.HashFun(key) % this.tableSize;
    }

    DefaultCompare(first, second) {
        return first - second;
    }
```

```
DefaultHashFun(key) {
    return key;
}

add(key, value) {
    if (key === undefined || key === null)
        return false;

    if (value === undefined || value === null)
        value = key;

    const index = this.ComputeHash(key);
    this.listArray[index] = new HashTableNode(key, value,
        this.listArray[index]);
}

delete(key) {
    const index = this.ComputeHash(key);
    let nextNode;
    let head = this.listArray[index];
    if (head != null && head.key === key) {
        this.listArray[index] = head.next;
        return true;
    }

    while (head != null) {
        nextNode = head.next;
        if (nextNode != null && nextNode.key === key) {
            head.next = nextNode.next;
            return true;
        }
        else {
            head = nextNode;
        }
    };
    return false;
}

print() {
    for (let i = 0; i < this.tableSize; i++) {
        let head = this.listArray[i];
        let data = "";

        while (head != null) {
            data += (`${head.value} `)
            head = head.next;
        }

        if (data != "") {
            console.log(`Index value :: ${i} Data :: ${data}`);
```

```
                }
            }
        }

    find(key) {
        const index = this.ComputeHash(key);
        let head = this.listArray[index];
        while (head != null) {
            if (head.key === key) {
                return true;
            }
            head = head.next;
        };
        return false;
    }

    get(key) {
        const index = this.ComputeHash(key);
        let head = this.listArray[index];
        while (head != null) {
            if (head.key === key) {
                return head.value;
            }
            head = head.next;
        };
        return 0;
    }
}

const ht = new HashTable();
ht.add(1, 10);
ht.add(2, 20);
ht.add(3, 30);
ht.print();

console.log("Find key 2 : ", ht.find(2));
console.log("Value at key 2 : ",ht.get(2))
ht.delete(1)
ht.print()
```

Output:
```
Index value :: 1 Data :: 10
Index value :: 2 Data :: 20
Index value :: 3 Data :: 30
Find key 2 :  true
Value at key 2 :  20
Index value :: 2 Data :: 20
Index value :: 3 Data :: 30
```

Note: It is important to note that the size of the table should be such that all the slots in the table will eventually be occupied. Otherwise, part of the table will be unused. It is suggested that the table size should be a prime number for better distribution of keys.

Problems in Hashing

Anagram solver

Problem: Find if two strings are anagrams, an anagram is a word or phrase formed by reordering the letters of another word or phrase.

Example 11.13: Two words are anagram If they are of same size and their characters are same.

```
function isAnagram(str1, str2){
    const size1 = str1.length;
    const size2 = str2.length;
    if (size1 !== size2)
        return false;

    const cm = new CountMap();
    for (var index = 0; index < str1.length; index++) {
        var ch = str1[index];
        cm.insert(ch);
    }
    for (var index = 0; index < str2.length; index++) {
        var ch = str2[index];
        cm.remove(ch);
    }
    return (cm.size() === 0);
}

function test(){
    const first = "hello";
    const second = "elloh";
    const third = "world";
    console.info(`isAnagram : ${isAnagram(first, second)}`);
    console.info(`isAnagram : ${isAnagram(first, third)}`);
}
```

Output:
```
isAnagram : true
isAnagram : false
```

Remove Duplicate

Problem: Remove duplicates in an array of numbers.

Solution: We can use a second array or the same array, as the output array. In the following Example , Hash-Table is used to solve this problem.

Example 11.14:
```
function removeDuplicate(str){
    let str2 = "";
    const hs = new Set();
    for (let ind = 0; ind < str.length; ind++) {
        const ch = str[ind];
        if (hs.has(ch.charCodeAt(0)) === false) {
            str2 += ch;
            hs.add(ch.charCodeAt(0));
        }
    }
    return str2;
};

function test(){
    const first = "hello";
    console.info(removeDuplicate(first));
}
```

Output:
```
helo
```

Find Missing

Problem: Given an array of integers, you need to find the missing number in the array.

Example 11.15:
```
function findMissing(arr, start, end){
    const hs = new Set();
    for (let index = 0; index < arr.length; index++) {
        hs.add(arr[index]);
    }
    for (let curr = start; curr <= end; curr++) {
        if (hs.has(curr) === false)
            return curr;
    }
    return -1;
};

function test(){
    const arr = [1, 2, 3, 5, 6, 7, 8, 9, 10];
    console.info("Missing element is : ", findMissing(arr, 1, 10));
}
```

Output:
```
Missing element is :  4
```

Analysis: All the elements in the array is added to a HashTable. The missing element is found by searching into HashTable and final missing value is returned.

Print Repeating

Problem: Given an array of integers, print the repeating integers in the array.

Example 11.16:
```
function printRepeating(arr) {
    const hs = new Set();
    console.log("Repeating elements are:");
    for (let insert = 0; insert < arr.length; insert++) {
        const val = arr[insert];

        if (hs.has(val))
            console.log(val);
        else
            hs.add(val);
    }
}

function test(){
    const arr1 = [1, 2, 3, 4, 4, 5, 6, 7, 8, 9, 1];
    printRepeating(arr1);
}
```

Output:
```
Repeating elements are:
4
1
```

Analysis: All the values are added to the hash table, when some value came which is already in the hash table then that is the repeated value.

Print First Repeating

Problem: It is same as the above problem in this we need to print the first repeating number. Care should be taken to find the first repeating number. It should be the one number that is repeating. For Example , 1, 2, 3, 2, 1. The answer should be 1 as it is the first number, which is repeating.

Example 11.17:
```
function printFirstRepeating(arr){
    const size = arr.length;
    const hs = new CountMap();
    for (var i = 0; i < size; i++) {
        hs.insert(arr[i]);
    }
 for (var i = 0; i < size; i++) {
        hs.remove(arr[i]);
        if (hs.find(arr[i])) {
            console.log(`First Repeating number is : ${arr[i]}`);
            return;
```

```
            }
        }
}

function test(){
    const arr1 = [1, 2, 3, 4, 4, 5, 6, 7, 8, 9, 1];
    printFirstRepeating(arr1);
}
```

Output:

```
First Repeating number is : 1
```

Analysis: Add values to the count map the one that is repeating will have multiple count. Now traverse the array again and see if the count is more than one. Therefore, that is the first repeating.

Exercise

1. Design a number (ID) generator system that generates numbers between 0-99999999 (8-digits).
    The system should support two functions:
    a. int getNumber();
    b. boolean requestNumber();
    getNumber() function should find out a number that is not assigned, then mark it as assigned and return that number.requestNumber() function checks the number if it is assigned or not. If it is assigned returns false, else marks it as assigned and return true.

2. In given large string, find the most occurring words in the string. What is the Time Complexity of the above solution?

    Hint:-
    a. Create a Hashtable which will keep track of <word, frequency>
    b. Iterate through the string and keep track of word frequency by inserting into Hash-Table.
    c. When we have a new word, we will insert it into the Hashtable with frequency 1. For all repetition of the word, we will increase the frequency.
    d. We can keep track of the most occurring words whenever we are increasing the frequency we can see if this is the most occurring word or not.
    e. Time Complexity is O(**n**) where n is the number of words in the string and Space Complexity is the O(m) where m is the unique words in the string.

3. In the above question, what if you are given whole work of OSCAR WILDE, most popular playwrights in the early 1890s.

    Hint:-
    a. Who knows how many books are there, let us assume there is a lot and we cannot put everything in memory. First, we need a Streaming Library so that we can read section by section in each document. Then we need a tokenizer that will give words to our program. In addition, we need some sort of dictionary let us say we will use HashTable.
    b. What you need is - 1. A streaming library tokenizer, 2. A tokenizer 3. A hashmap
        Method:
        1. Use streamers to find a stream of the given words
        2. Tokenize the input text

3. If the stemmed word is in hash map, increment its frequency count else add a word to hash map with frequency 1

c. We can improve the performance by looking into parallel computing. We can use the map-reduce to solve this problem. Multiple nodes will read and process multiple documents. Once they are done with their processing, then we can do the reduce operation by merging them.

4. In the above question, what if we want to find the most common PHRASE in his writings.

Hint:- We can keep <phrase, frequency>Hash-Table and do the same process of the 2nd and 3rd problems.

5. Write a hashing algorithm for strings.

Hint: Use Horner's method

```
function hornerHash(key, tableSize){
    const size = key.length;
    let h = 0;
    for (let i = 0;  i < size; i++) {
        h = (32 * h + key[i]) % tableSize;
    }
    return h;
}
```

6. Pick two data structures to use in implementing a Map. Describe lookup, insert, & delete operations. Give time &Space Complexity for each. Give pros & cons for each.

Hint:-
a) Linked List
    I.   Insert is **O(1)**
    II.   Delete is **O(1)**
    III.   Lookup is **O(1)** auxiliary and **O(N)** worst case.
    IV.   Pros: Fast inserts and deletes, can use for any data type.
    V.   Cons: Slow lookups.

b) Balanced Search Tree (RB Tree)
    I.   Insert is **O(logn)**
    II.   Delete is **O(logn)**
    III.   Lookup is **O(logn)**
    IV.   Pros: Reasonably fast inserts/deletes and lookups.
    V.   Cons: Data needs to have order defined on it.

CHAPTER 12: GRAPHS

Introduction

In this chapter, we will study about Graph Data Structure.

Graph data structure consists of following two components:
1. A finite set of nodes called **vertices**.
2. A finite set of pair of vertices called **edges**. Edges are connection between two vertices.

Some of the real-world Examples of graphs are:
1. Google Maps: Various locations can be represented as Vertices of Graph and path between them are represented by Edges of Graph. Graph theory, algorithms are used to suggest a shortest and quickest path between two locations.
2. Facebook Friend Suggestion: Each user profile is represented as vertices of graphs and their friend relationship is represented by the edges of Graph. Graph theory, algorithms are used for friend suggestion.
3. Topology Sorting: Topology sorting is a method to find sequence in which some event need be performed to complete some task by looking into the dependency of various events on each other. For Example , a sequence of classes that we take to become a graduate in computer science. Or a sequence of steps that we take to become ready for jobs daily
4. Transportation Network: Map of airlines is represented as Graph. Various airports are represented as nodes of the graph and if there is a non-stop flight from airport u and airport v then then in the graph there is an edge from node u to node v. You may want to go from one location to another, through graph theory algorithms we can compute shortest, quickest or cheapest path from source to destination.

The flight connection between major cities of India can also be represented by the graph given below. Each city is represented as vertices and flight between cities is represented as edges.

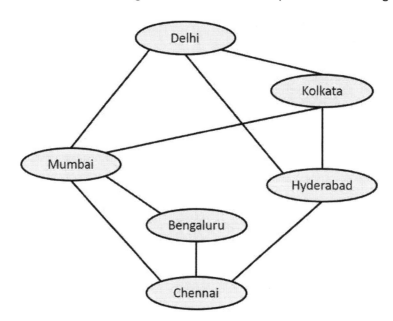

Graph Definition: A Graph is represented by ordered pair G where G = (V, E), where V is a finite set of points called **Vertices** and E is a finite set of **Edges**. Each **edge** is a pair (u, v) where u, v ∈ V.

Graph Terminology

Undirected Graph: An Undirected Graph is a graph in which edges have no directions. Hear the edges of the graph are two ways. An edge (x, y) is identical to edge (y, x).

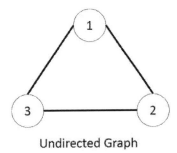

Undirected Graph

Directed Graph or Digraph: A Directed Graph is a graph in which edges have a direction. Hear the edges of graph are one way. An edge (x, y) is not identical to edge (y, x).

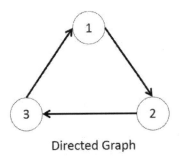

Directed Graph

Weighted Graph: A Graph is weighted if its edges have some value or weight associated with them.

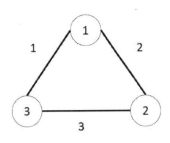

Weighted Graph

Unweighted Graph: A Graph in which edges do not have any weight associated with them.

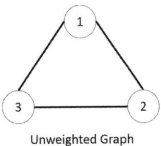

Unweighted Graph

Path: A Path is a sequence of edges between two vertices. The length of a path is defined as the sum of the weight of all the edges in the path.

Simple Path: A path with distinct vertices is called simple path.

Adjacent Vertex: Two vertices u and v are **adjacent** if there is an edge whose endpoints are u and v.

In the below graph: V = {V1, V2, V3, V4, V5, V6, V7, V8, V9}

$$E = \begin{Bmatrix} (V1,\ V0,\ 1),\ (V2,\ V1,\ 2),\ (V3,\ V2,\ 3),\ (V3,\ V4,\ 4),\ (V5,\ V4,\ 5), \\ (V1,\ V5,\ 6),\ (V2,\ V5,\ 7),\ (V3,\ V5,\ 8),\ (V4,\ V5,\ 9) \end{Bmatrix}$$

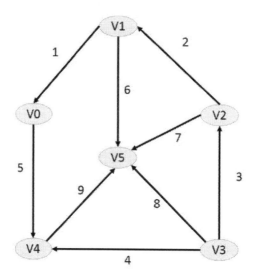

The **in-degree** of a vertex v, denoted by indeg(v) is the number of incoming edges to the vertex v.

The **out-degree** of a vertex v, denoted by outdeg(v) is the number of outgoing edges of a vertex v.

The **degree** of a vertex v, denoted by deg(v) is the total number of edges whose one endpoint is v. deg(v) = Indeg (v) + outdeg (v)

In the above graph: deg(V4) =3, indeg(V4) =2 and outdeg(V4) =1

A **Cycle** is a path that starts and ends at the same vertex and includes at least one vertex.

An edge is a **Self-Loop** if two if its two endpoints coincide. This is a form of a cycle.

Cyclic Graph: A Graph that has one or more cycles in called a Cyclic Graph.

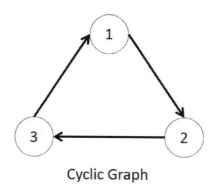

Cyclic Graph

Acyclic Graph: A Graph that has no cycle in called an Acyclic Graph.

Directed Acyclic Graph / DAG: A directed graph that does not have any cycle is called Directed Acyclic Graph.

Reachable: A vertex v is **Reachable** from vertex u or u reaches v, if there is a path from u to v. In an undirected graph if v is reachable from u then u is reachable from v. However, in a directed graph it is possible that u reaches v but there is no path from v to u.

Connected Graph: A graph is **a Connected** if for any two vertices there is a path between them.

Strongly Connected Graph: A directed graph is strongly connected if for each pair of vertices u and v, there is a path from u to v and a path from v to u.

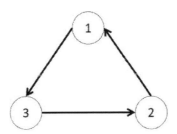

Strongly Connected Graph

Strongly Connected Components: A directed graph may have different sub-graphs that are strongly connected. These sub-graphs are called strongly connected components.

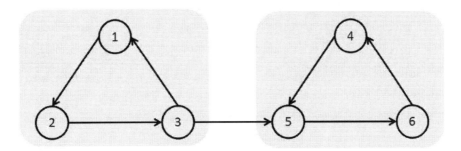

Strongly Connected Component

Weakly Connected Graph: A directed graph is weakly connected if for each pair of vertices u and v, there is a path from u to v or a path from v to u.

Complete Graph: A graph is complete if any vertex is connected by an edge to all the other vertices of the graph. A complete graph has maximum number of edges. For an undirected graph of n vertices, the total number of edges will be n(n-1)/2 and for a directed graph the total number of edges will be n(n-1).

A **Sub-Graph** of a graph G is a graph whose vertices and edges are a subset of the vertices and edges of G.

A **Spanning Sub-Graph** of G is a graph that connects all the vertices of G.

A **Forest** is a graph without cycles.

A **Tree** is a connected graph with no cycles. There is only one simple path between any two vertices u and v. If we remove any edge of a tree, it becomes a forest.

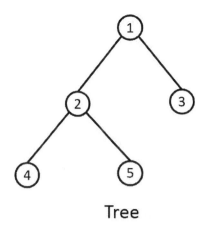

Tree

A **Spanning tree** of a graph is a tree that connects all the vertices of the graph. Since a Spanning-Tree is a tree, so it should not have any cycle.

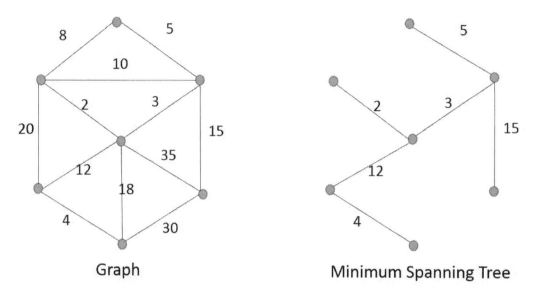

Graph   Minimum Spanning Tree

Hamiltonian path is a path in which every vertex is visited exactly once with no repeats, it does not have to start and end at the same vertex.

Hamiltonian circuit is a Hamiltonian Path such that there is an edge from its last vertex to its first vertex. A **Hamiltonian circuit** is a circuit that visits every vertex exactly once and it must start and end at the same vertex.

Eulerian Path is a path in the graph that visits every edge exactly once.

Eulerian Circuit is a Eulerian Path, which starts and ends on the same vertex. Or **EulerianCircuit** is a path in the graph that visits every edge exactly one and it starts and ends on the same vertex.

Travelling salesman problem (TSP) a salesperson needs to visit various cities. He looks up the distance between each city, and puts the distance in a graph. In what order should he travel to visit each city and in the end return home city with the least distance travelled. This problem can be rephrased as find the lowest cost Hamiltonian circuit

Graph Representation

The two are the most common way of representing a graph are:
1. Adjacency Matrix
2. Adjacency List

Adjacency Matrix

Adjacency Matrix is a two-dimensional matrix of size V rows and V columns where V is the number of vertices in a graph. Adjacency matrix is represented using V x V size two-dimensional array.

Let us suppose the array is "adj", so the node adj[i][j] corresponds to the edge from vertex i to vertex j. If adj[i][j] is not zero, then it means that there is a path from vertex i to vertex j. For an unweighted graph, the values in the array are either 0 for no path or 1 for a path exist. But in case of weighted graph the value in the matrix indicates the cost / weight of a path from vertex i to j.

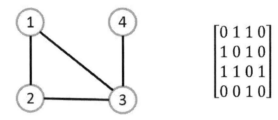

$$\begin{bmatrix} 0 & 1 & 1 & 0 \\ 1 & 0 & 1 & 0 \\ 1 & 1 & 0 & 1 \\ 0 & 0 & 1 & 0 \end{bmatrix}$$

In the above graph, each node has weight 1 so the adjacency matrix has just 1s or 0s. If the edges are of different weights, then that weight will be filled in the matrix.

Example 12.1: adjacency matrix representation of a graph

```
class GraphEdge {
    constructor(dst, cst) {
        if (cst === undefined)
            cst = 1
        this.dest = dst
        this.cost = cst
    }
}

class Graph {
    constructor(cnt) {
        if (cnt === undefined)
            throw new Error('Invalid argument')

        this.count = cnt;
        this.adj = new Array(cnt)
        for (let i = 0; i < cnt; i++) {
            this.adj[i] = new Array(cnt).fill(0);
        }
    }
```

```
    addDirectedEdge(src, dst, cost) {
        this.adj[src][dst] = cost;
    }

    addUndirectedEdge(src, dst, cost) {
        this.addDirectedEdge(src, dst, cost);
        this.addDirectedEdge(dst, src, cost);
    }

    print() {
        console.info(this.adj);
    }

    print2() {
        for (let i = 0; i < this.count; i++) {
            let t = `Node index [ ${i} ] is connected with : `;
            for (let j = 0; j < this.count; j++) {
                if (this.adj[i][j] !== 0)
                    t += j +"(" + this.adj[i][j] +") "
            }
            console.info(t)
        }
    }
}

function test(){
    const graph = new Graph(4);
    graph.addUndirectedEdge(0, 1, 1);
    graph.addUndirectedEdge(0, 2, 1);
    graph.addUndirectedEdge(1, 2, 1);
    graph.addUndirectedEdge(2, 3, 1);
    graph.print2();
};
```

Output:
```
Node index [ 0 ] is connected with : 1(1) 2(1)
Node index [ 1 ] is connected with : 0(1) 2(1)
Node index [ 2 ] is connected with : 0(1) 1(1) 3(1)
Node index [ 3 ] is connected with : 2(1)
```

Analysis:
- In the constructor of graph of N vertices, an NxN size of two-dimensional array adj is created.
- AddDirectedEdge function is used to add a directed edge from source to destination by setting adj[source][destination] field of adj array as one.
- AddUndirectedEdge function is used to add an undirected edge. It call's AddDirectedEdge function twice to join source and destination both ways.

Complexity Analysis:
- Space complexity of Adjacency Matrix representation is $O(n^2)$ because two-dimensional array is created.

- Time complexity of search is O(1). To find if there is an edge from vertex u to vertex v can be done in constant time.

Pros and cons of adjacency matrix

Pros of adjacency matrix:
1. Queries if there is an edge from vertex 'u' to vertex 'v' is takes O(1) time.
2. Removing an edge takes O(1) time.

Cons of adjacency matrix:
1. Space complexity is $O(n^2)$.
2. Even if the graph is sparse (with few edges), space complexity remains same.
3. Adding a new vertex takes $O(n^2)$ time.

Sparse Matrix: In a huge graph, each node is connected to few nodes. So most of the places in the adjacency matrix remain empty. Such matrix is called sparse matrix. In most of the real-worldproblem's adjacency matrix is not a good choice for sore graph data.

Adjacency List

A more space efficient way of storing graph is adjacency list. **An adjacency list is an array of linked list. Each list element corresponds an edge of Graph.** Size of the array is equal to the number of vertices in the graph. Let the array be Arr[]. An entry Arr[k] corresponds to Kth vertex and is a list of vertices directly connected to kth vertex. The weights of edges can be stored in nodes of linked lists.

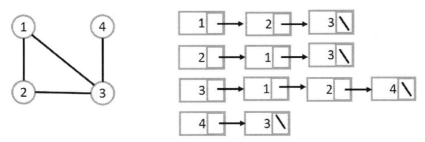

The adjacency list helps us to represent a sparse graph. An adjacency list representation also allows us to find all the vertices that are directly connected to any vertices by just one link list scan. In all our programs, we are going to use the adjacency list to store the graph.

Example 12.2: adjacency list representation of a graph

```
class GraphEdge {
    constructor(dst, cst) {
        if (cst === undefined)
            cst = 1
        this.dest = dst
        this.cost = cst
    }
}

GraphEdgeComparator = (x, y) => x - y;
```

```
class Graph {
    constructor(cnt) {
        if (cnt === undefined)
            throw new Error('Invalid argument')

        this.count = cnt
        this.Adj = new Array()

        for (let i = 0; i < cnt; i++) {
            this.Adj[i] = new Array()
        }
    }

    addDirectedEdge(source, dest, cost) {
        if ((typeof source === 'number') && (typeof dest === 'number') &&
            (typeof cost === 'number')) {
            var edge = new GraphEdge(dest, cost)
            this.Adj[source].push(edge)
        }
        else if ((typeof source === 'number') && (typeof dest === 'number')
&&
            cost === undefined) {
            var edge = new GraphEdge(dest, 1)
            this.Adj[source].push(edge)
        }
        else
            throw new Error('Invalid argument')
    }

    addUndirectedEdge(source, dest, cost) {
        this.addDirectedEdge(source, dest, cost)
        this.addDirectedEdge(dest, source, cost)
    }

    print() {
        for (let i = 0; i < this.count; i++) {
            const ad = this.Adj[i];
            let output = ""
            output += `Vertex ${i} is connected to : `
            for (let j = 0; j < ad.length; j++) {
                const adn = ad[j];
                output += `${adn.dest}(${adn.cost}) `
            }
            console.log(output)
        }
    }
    /* Other Methods */
}
```

```
function test(){
    const graph = new Graph(4);
    graph.addUndirectedEdge(0, 1, 1);
    graph.addUndirectedEdge(0, 2, 1);
    graph.addUndirectedEdge(1, 2, 1);
    graph.addUndirectedEdge(2, 3, 1);
    graph.print();
};
```

Output:
```
Vertex 0 is connected to : 1(1) 2(1)
Vertex 1 is connected to : 0(1) 2(1)
Vertex 2 is connected to : 0(1) 1(1) 3(1)
Vertex 3 is connected to : 2(1)
```

Analysis:
- In the constructor of graph of N vertices, an array of lists of size N is created.
- addDirectedEdge() function is used to add a directed edge from source to destination by adding a touple (destination, cost) to the corresponding vertex list.
- addUndirectedEdge() function is used to add an undirected edge. It call's addDirectedEdge() function twice to join source and destination both ways.

Complexity Analysis:
Space Complexity of Adjacency list is O(E+V), to create vertices array and to store edges from each vertex.
Time complexity of search if there is an edge from vertex u to vertex v is done in outdegree(u). We need to traverse the neighbours list of vertex u. In worst case, it can be O(E)

Graph traversals

Traversal is the process of exploring a graph by examining all its edges and vertices.
A list of some of the problems that are solved using graph traversal are:
1. Determining a path from vertex u to vertex v, or report an error if there is no such path.
2. Given a starting vertex s, finding the minimum number of edges from vertex s to all the other vertices of the graph.
3. Testing if a graph G is connected.
4. Finding a spanning tree of a Graph.
5. Finding if there is some cycle in the graph.

The **Depth first search (DFS)** and **Breadth first search (BFS)** are the two algorithms used to traverse a graph. These same algorithms can also be used to find some node in the graph, find if a node is reachable etc.

Depth First Traversal

We start the DFS algorithm from starting point and go into depth of graph until we reach a dead end and then move up to parent node (Backtrack). In DFS, we use stack to get the next vertex to start a search. Alternatively, we can use recursion (system stack) to do the same. Depth First Traversal of a graph is like Depth First Traversal of a tree. The only difference is that graphs may contain cycles (trees do not have cycles). So, while traversing we may come back to the same node again. To avoid processing same node again, we use a Boolean visited array.

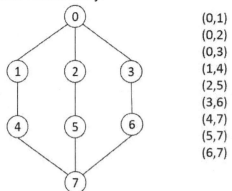

(0,1)
(0,2)
(0,3)
(1,4)
(2,5)
(3,6)
(4,7)
(5,7)
(6,7)

Below diagram, demonstrate DFS traversal.

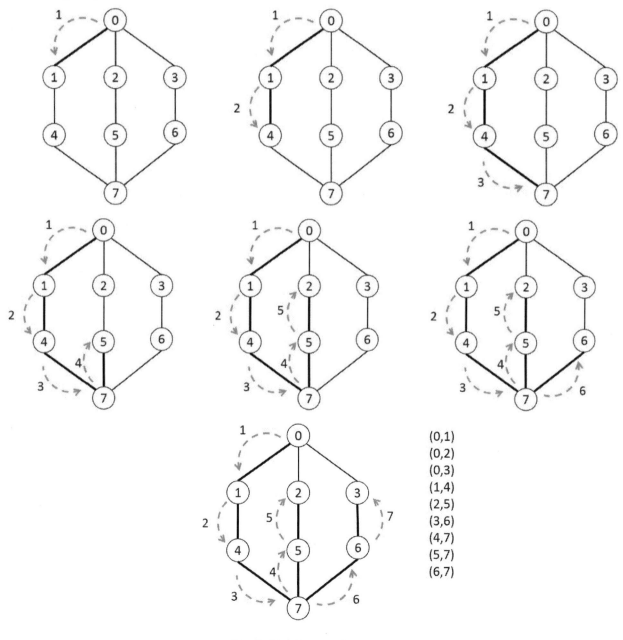

(0,1)
(0,2)
(0,3)
(1,4)
(2,5)
(3,6)
(4,7)
(5,7)
(6,7)

Depth First Traversal
0, 1, 4, 7 , 5, 2, 6, 3

Stack based implementation of DFS

Algorithm steps for DFS
1. Push the starting node in the stack.
2. Loop until the stack is empty.
3. Pop node from the stack call this node current.
4. Process the current node. //Print, etc.
5. Traverse all the child nodes of the current node and push them into stack.
6. Repeat steps 3 to 5 until the stack is empty.

Example 12.3: Stack based implementation of DFS.

```
dfsStack(source, target) {
    const count = this.count;
    const visited = new Array(count).fill(false);
    const stk = ([]);
    const path = [];
    stk.push(source)
    visited[source] = true
    while (stk.length != 0) {
        const curr = stk.pop();
        path.push(curr);
        const adl = this.Adj[curr];
        for (let index = adl.length - 1; index >=  0; index--) {
            const adn = adl[index];
            if (visited[adn.dest] === false) {
                visited[adn.dest] = true
                stk.push(adn.dest)
            }
        }
    }
    console.log("DFS Path is : ", path)
    return visited[target]
}
function test(){
    const gph = new Graph(8);
    gph.addUndirectedEdge(0, 1)
    gph.addUndirectedEdge(0, 2)
    gph.addUndirectedEdge(0, 3)
    gph.addUndirectedEdge(1, 4)
    gph.addUndirectedEdge(2, 5)
    gph.addUndirectedEdge(3, 6)
    gph.addUndirectedEdge(4, 7)
    gph.addUndirectedEdge(5, 7)
    gph.addUndirectedEdge(6, 7)
    console.log("Path between 0 & 6 : ", gph.dfsStack(0, 6))
}
```

Output:
```
DFS Path is :  [ 0, 1, 4, 7, 5, 2, 6, 3 ]
Path between 0 & 6 :  true
```

Complexity Analysis:
- Time complexity of DFS algorithm when the graph is represented as adjacency list is O(V+E) where V is the total number of vertices and E are the total number of edges in the graph.
- When the graph is represented as adjacency matrix the time complexity of algorithms is $O(V^2)$. We need to traverse adjacent vertices of a vertex, which is efficient in the graph when it is represented by adjacency list.

Recursion based implementation of DFS

Algorithm steps for DFS
1. In DFS() function, create a visited array to keep track of visited nodes.
2. In DFS() function, source node is passed as current node to DFSRec() recursion function.
3. All the nodes which are visited from index node are further passed to DFSRec() function as recursion.
4. This recursion will return to DFS() function when all the nodes which are visited from source are visited. Finally, we can find if target is visited or not by looking into visited array.

Example 12.4:

```
dfs(source, target) {
    const count = this.count;
    const visited = new Array(count).fill(false);
    const path = []
    this.dfsUtil(source, visited, path)
    console.log("DFS Path is : ", path)
        return visited[target]
}

dfsUtil(index, visited, path) {
    visited[index] = true
    const adl = this.Adj[index];
    path.push(index)
    for (var index = 0; index < adl.length; index++) {
        const adn = adl[index];
        if (visited[adn.dest] === false)
            this.dfsUtil(adn.dest, visited, path)
    }
}
function test(){
    const gph = new Graph(8);
    gph.addUndirectedEdge(0, 1)
    gph.addUndirectedEdge(0, 2)
    gph.addUndirectedEdge(0, 3)
    gph.addUndirectedEdge(1, 4)
    gph.addUndirectedEdge(2, 5)
    gph.addUndirectedEdge(3, 6)
    gph.addUndirectedEdge(4, 7)
    gph.addUndirectedEdge(5, 7)
    gph.addUndirectedEdge(6, 7)
    console.log("Path between 0 & 6 : ", gph.dfs(0, 6))
}
```

Output:
```
DFS Path is :   [ 0, 1, 4, 7, 5, 2, 6, 3 ]
Path between 0 & 6 :   true
```

Complexity Analysis:
- Time complexity of DFS algorithm when the graph is represented as adjacency list is O(V+E) where V is the total number of vertices and E are the total number of edges in the graph.
- When the graph is represented as adjacency matrix the time complexity of algorithms become O(V²).

Breadth First Traversal

In BFS algorithm, a graph is traversed in layer-by-layer fashion. The graph is traversed, closer to the starting point. The queue is used to implement BFS. Breadth First Traversal of a graph is like Breadth First Traversal of a tree. The only difference is that graphs may contain cycles (trees do not have cycles). So, while traversing we may come back to the same node again. To avoid processing same node again, we use a Boolean visited array.

Algorithm steps for BFS
1. Push the starting node into the Queue.
2. Loop until the Queue is empty.
3. Remove a node from the Queue inside loop, and call this node current.
4. Process the current node. //print etc.
5. Traverse all the child nodes of the current node and push them into the Queue.
6. Repeat steps 3 to 5 until Queue is empty.

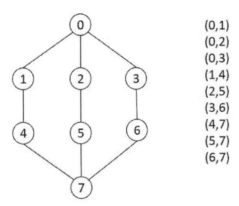

Below diagram, demonstrate Graph Breadth First Traversal.

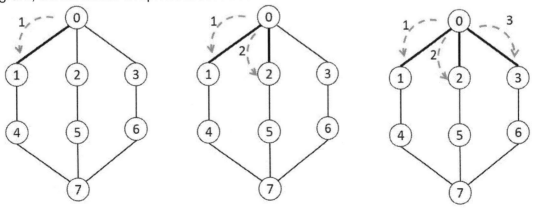

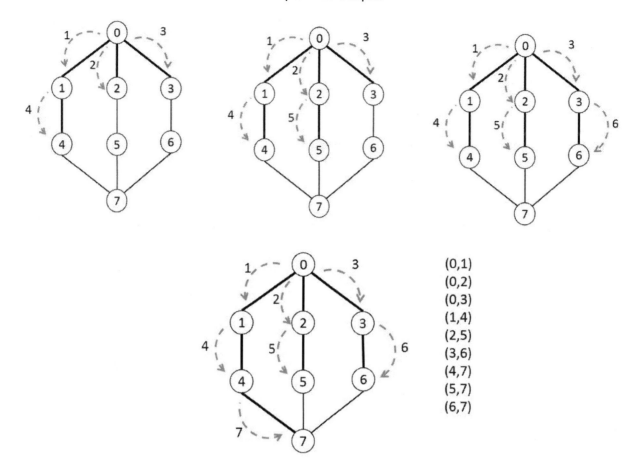

Breadth First Traversal
0, 1, 2, 3, 4, 5, 6, 7

(0,1)
(0,2)
(0,3)
(1,4)
(2,5)
(3,6)
(4,7)
(5,7)
(6,7)

Example 12.5:

```
bfs(source, target) {
    const count = this.count;
    const visited = new Array(count).fill(false);
    const que = new Queue();
    const path = []
    que.add(source)
    visited[source] = true
    while (que.isEmpty() === false) {
        const curr = que.remove();
        path.push(curr)
        const adl = this.Adj[curr];
        for (let index = 0; index < adl.length; index++) {
            const adn = adl[index];
            if (visited[adn.dest] === false) {
                visited[adn.dest] = true
                que.add(adn.dest)
            }
        }
    }
    console.log("BFS Path is : ", path)
    return visited[target]
}
```

```
function test(){
    const gph = new Graph(8);
    gph.addUndirectedEdge(0, 1)
    gph.addUndirectedEdge(0, 2)
    gph.addUndirectedEdge(0, 3)
    gph.addUndirectedEdge(1, 4)
    gph.addUndirectedEdge(2, 5)
    gph.addUndirectedEdge(3, 6)
    gph.addUndirectedEdge(4, 7)
    gph.addUndirectedEdge(5, 7)
    gph.addUndirectedEdge(6, 7)
    console.log("Path between 0 & 6 : ", gph.bfs(0, 6))
}
```

Output:
```
BFS Path is :  [ 0, 1, 2, 3, 4, 5, 6, 7 ]
Path between 0 & 6 :  true
```

Complexity Analysis: A runtime analysis of DFS and BFS traversal is O(V+E) time, where V is the number of edges reachable from source node and E is the number of edges in the graph.

Uses of BFS and DFS

The following problems are solved using DFS:
1. Find if path exists between two vertices can be done using BFS or DFS.
2. Given a starting vertex u, finding the minimum number of edges from vertex s to all the other vertices of the graph is done using BFS.
3. Testing of a graph G is connected can be done using BFS or DFS.
4. Finding if there is a cycle in the graph or check if given graph is a tree is done using DFS.
5. Topological Sorting is done using DFS.
6. Strongly connected components or graph in directed graph is done using DFS.

DFS & BFS based problems

Directed Acyclic Graph and Topological Sort

A Directed Acyclic Graph (DAG) is a directed graph with no cycle. A DAG represents a relationship, which is more general than a tree. Below is an Example of DAG, this is how someone becomes ready for work. There are N other real-life Examples of DAG such as coerces selection to be a graduate from college

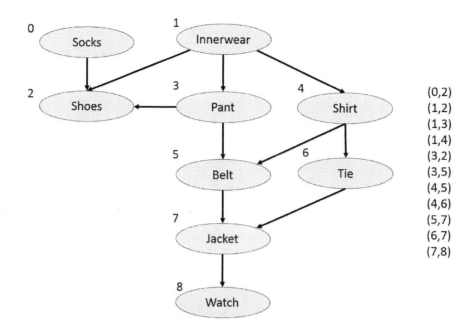

A topological sort is a method of ordering the nodes of a directed graph in which nodes represent activities and the edges represent dependency among those tasks. For topological sorting to work it is required that the graph should be a DAG which means it should not have any cycle. Just use DFS to get topological sorting.

Example 12.6:

```
topologicalSort() {
    const stk = ([]);
    const count = this.count;
    const visited = new Array(count).fill(false);
    const output = []
    for (let i = 0; i < count; i++) {
        if (visited[i] === false) {
            this.dfsUtil2(i, visited, stk)
        }
    }

    while (stk.length != 0) {
        output.push(stk.pop())
    }
    console.log(output)
}

dfsUtil2(src, visited, stk) {
    visited[src] = true
    const adl = this.Adj[src];
    for (let index = 0; index < adl.length; index++) {
        const adn = adl[index];
        if (visited[adn.dest] === false) {
            this.dfsUtil2(adn.dest, visited, stk)
        }
    }
```

```
        stk.push(src)
}

function test(){
    const gph = new Graph(6);
    gph.addDirectedEdge(5, 2, 1)
    gph.addDirectedEdge(5, 0, 1)
    gph.addDirectedEdge(4, 0, 1)
    gph.addDirectedEdge(4, 1, 1)
    gph.addDirectedEdge(2, 3, 1)
    gph.addDirectedEdge(3, 1, 1)
    gph.topologicalSort()
}
```

Output:
```
[ 5, 4, 2, 3, 1, 0 ]
```

Topology sort is a DFS traversal of topology graph. First, all the children of a node are added to the stack, then only the current node is added. So, the sorting order is maintained. Reader is requested to run some Examples to understand this algorithm.

Determining a path from vertex u to vertex v

Problem: Find if there is a path from vertex u to vertex v.

Solution: If there is a path from vertex u to vertex v then when we perform DFS from vertex u we will visit vertex v.

Example 12.7:
```
pathExist(source, dest) {
    const count = this.count;
    const visited = new Array(count).fill(false);
    this.dfsUtil3(source, visited)
    return visited[dest]
}

dfsUtil3(index, visited) {
    visited[index] = true
    const adl = this.Adj[index];
    for (var index = 0; index < adl.length; index++) {
        const adn = adl[index];
        if (visited[adn.dest] === false)
            this.dfsUtil3(adn.dest, visited)
    }
}

function test(){
    const gph = new Graph(5);
    gph.addDirectedEdge(0, 1, 1)
    gph.addDirectedEdge(0, 2, 1)
```

```
    gph.addDirectedEdge(2, 3, 1)
    gph.addDirectedEdge(1, 3, 1)
    gph.addDirectedEdge(3, 4, 1)
    gph.addDirectedEdge(1, 4, 1)
    console.log(`PathExist :: ${gph.pathExist(0, 4)}`)
}
```

Output:
```
PathExist :: true
```

Complexity Analysis: Time Complexity same as DFS for adjacency list implementation of the graph it is O(V+E) and for adjacency matrix implementation it is $O(V^2)$

Count All Path DFS

Problem: Given a source vertex and a destination vertex, find all the possible paths from source to destination.

Example 12.8:
```
countAllPathDFS(visited, source, dest) {
    if (source === dest) {
        return 1
    }
    let count = 0;
    visited[source] = true
    const adl = this.Adj[source];

    for (let index = 0; index < adl.length; index++) {
        const adn = adl[index];
        if (visited[adn.dest] === false) {
            count += this.countAllPathDFS(visited, adn.dest, dest)
        }
    }
    visited[source] = false
    return count
}

countAllPath(src, dest) {
    const count = this.count;
    const visited = new Array(count).fill(false);
    return this.countAllPathDFS(visited, src, dest)
}

function test(){
    const gph = new Graph(5);
    gph.addDirectedEdge(0, 1, 1)
    gph.addDirectedEdge(0, 2, 1)
    gph.addDirectedEdge(2, 3, 1)
    gph.addDirectedEdge(1, 3, 1)
    gph.addDirectedEdge(3, 4, 1)
```

```
    gph.addDirectedEdge(1, 4, 1)
    console.log("Path Count :: " , gph.countAllPath(0, 4))
}
```

Output:
```
Path Count ::   3
```

Analysis: DFS traversal of a graph and count from various paths is added.

Print All Path

Problem: Print all the paths from source vertex to the destination vertex.

Example 12.9:
```
printAllPathDFS(visited, source, dest, path) {
    path.push(source)
    if (source === dest) {
        console.log(path)
        path.pop()
        return
    }

    visited[source] = true
    const adl = this.Adj[source];

    for (let index = 0; index < adl.length; index++) {
        const adn = adl[index];
        if (visited[adn.dest] === false) {
            this.printAllPathDFS(visited, adn.dest, dest, path)
        }
    }
    visited[source] = false
    path.pop()
}

printAllPath(src, dest) {
    const count = this.count;
    const visited = new Array(count).fill(false);
    const path = ([]);
    this.printAllPathDFS(visited, src, dest, path)
}

function test(){
    const gph = new Graph(5);
    gph.addDirectedEdge(0, 1, 1)
    gph.addDirectedEdge(0, 2, 1)
    gph.addDirectedEdge(2, 3, 1)
    gph.addDirectedEdge(1, 3, 1)
    gph.addDirectedEdge(3, 4, 1)
    gph.addDirectedEdge(1, 4, 1)
```

```
    gph.printAllPath(0, 4)
}
```

Output:
```
[ 0, 1, 3, 4 ]
[ 0, 1, 4 ]
[ 0, 2, 3, 4 ]
```

Analysis: DFS traversal of a graph is performed by keeping track of the visited vertices. When the destination is found, then the path is printed.

Root Vertex

Problem: Find Root vertex in a graph. The root vertex is the vertex, which have path of all other vertices in a graph. If there are multiple root vertex, then return any one of them.

Hint: You need to return the top node of stack in topology sort.

Example 12.10:
```
rootVertex() {
    const count = this.count;
    const visited = new Array(count).fill(false);
    let retVal = -1;
    for (let i = 0; i < count; i++) {
        if (visited[i] === false) {
            this.dfsUtil3(i, visited)
            retVal = i
        }
    }
    console.log(`Root vertex is :: ${retVal}`)
    return retVal
}

function test(){
    const gph = new Graph(7);
    gph.addDirectedEdge(0, 1, 1)
    gph.addDirectedEdge(0, 2, 1)
    gph.addDirectedEdge(1, 3, 1)
    gph.addDirectedEdge(4, 1, 1)
    gph.addDirectedEdge(6, 4, 1)
    gph.addDirectedEdge(5, 6, 1)
    gph.addDirectedEdge(5, 2, 1)
    gph.addDirectedEdge(6, 0, 1)
    gph.rootVertex()
}
```

Output:
```
Root vertex is :: 5
```

Transitive Closure

Problem: Given a directed graph, construct a transitive closure matrix or reachability matrix. Vertex v is reachable from vertex u if there is a path from u to v.

Transitive closure of a graph G is a graph G', which contains the same set of vertices as G and whenever there is a path from vertex u to vertex v in G there is an edge from u to v in G'.

Example 12.11:

```
transitiveClosureUtil(source, dest, tc) {
    tc[source][dest] = 1;
    const adl = this.Adj[dest];
    for (let index = 0; index < adl.length; index++) {
        const adn = adl[index];
        if (tc[source][adn.dest] === 0)
            this.transitiveClosureUtil(source, adn.dest, tc)
    }
}


transitiveClosure() {
    const count = this.count;
    const tc = new Array(count);
    for (var i = 0; i < count; i++) {
        tc[i] = new Array(count).fill(0);
    }

    for (var i = 0; i < count; i++) {
        this.transitiveClosureUtil(i, i, tc)
    }
    return tc
}

function test(){
    const gph = new Graph(4);
    gph.addDirectedEdge(0, 1, 1)
    gph.addDirectedEdge(0, 2, 1)
    gph.addDirectedEdge(1, 2, 1)
    gph.addDirectedEdge(2, 0, 1)
    gph.addDirectedEdge(2, 3, 1)
    gph.addDirectedEdge(3, 3, 1)
    const tc = gph.transitiveClosure();
    for (let i = 0; i < 4; i++) {
        console.log(tc[i])
    }
}
```

Output:
```
[ 1, 1, 1, 1 ]
[ 1, 1, 1, 1 ]
[ 1, 1, 1, 1 ]
[ 0, 0, 0, 1 ]
```

Analysis: We create a two-dimensional array tc and assign all it to zero. Traverse the graph by keeping track of source vertex u and when we are able to traverse to a vertex v we will mark tc[u][v] as reachable.

BFS Level Node

Problem: Perform BFS traversal of the graph. Along with the nodes, also print their distance from the starting source vertex.

Example 12.12:

```
bfsLevelNode(source) {
    const count = this.count;
    const visited = new Array(count).fill(false);
    const level = new Array(count).fill(0);

    visited[source] = true
    level[source] = 0
    const que = new Queue();
    que.add(source)

    console.log('Node  - Level')
    while (que.isEmpty() === false) {
        let curr = que.remove()
        const depth = level[curr];
        const adl = this.Adj[curr];
        console.log(`${curr} - ${depth}`)
        for (let index = 0; index < adl.length; index++) {
            const adn = adl[index];
            if (visited[adn.dest] === false) {
                visited[adn.dest] = true
                que.add(adn.dest)
                level[adn.dest] = depth + 1
            }
        }
    }
}

function test(){
    const gph = new Graph(7);
    gph.addUndirectedEdge(0, 1, 1)
    gph.addUndirectedEdge(0, 2, 1)
    gph.addUndirectedEdge(0, 4, 1)
    gph.addUndirectedEdge(1, 2, 1)
    gph.addUndirectedEdge(2, 5, 1)
    gph.addUndirectedEdge(3, 4, 1)
    gph.addUndirectedEdge(4, 5, 1)
    gph.addUndirectedEdge(4, 6, 1)
    gph.bfsLevelNode(1)
}
```

Output:
```
Node   - Level
1 - 0
0 - 1
2 - 1
4 - 2
5 - 2
3 - 3
6 - 3
```

Analysis: Along with the adjacent nodes, their distance from source is also added to the queue.

BFS Distance

Problem: Find the distance between source and destination vertex in a Graph.

Example 12.13:
```
bfsDistance(source, dest) {
    const count = this.count;
    const visited = new Array(count).fill(false);
    const level = new Array(count).fill(0);

    visited[source] = true
    level[source] = 0
    const que = new Queue();
    que.add(source)

    while (que.isEmpty() === false) {
        const curr = que.remove();
        const depth = level[curr];
        const adl = this.Adj[curr];
        for (let index = 0; index < adl.length; index++) {
            const adn = adl[index];
            if (adn.dest === dest) {
                return depth + 1
            }
            if (visited[adn.dest] === false) {
                visited[adn.dest] = true
                que.add(adn.dest)
                level[adn.dest] = depth + 1
            }
        }
    }
    return -1
}

function test(){
    const gph = new Graph(7);
    gph.addUndirectedEdge(0, 1, 1)
```
385

```
    gph.addUndirectedEdge(0, 2, 1)
    gph.addUndirectedEdge(0, 4, 1)
    gph.addUndirectedEdge(1, 2, 1)
    gph.addUndirectedEdge(2, 5, 1)
    gph.addUndirectedEdge(3, 4, 1)
    gph.addUndirectedEdge(4, 5, 1)
    gph.addUndirectedEdge(4, 6, 1)
    console.log("BfsDistance :: " , gph.bfsDistance(1, 6))
}
```

Output:
```
BfsDistance ::  3
```

Analysis: Perform BFS traversal of the graph starting from source vertex and keep track of distance of adjacent nodes before adding them to the queue.
If we find the destination vertex, then return its distance from the source vertex. And if the destination vertex is not reachable then return -1.

Find cycle in an Undirected Graph.

Problem: Find if there is a cycle in an undirected graph.

Solution: Complete connected component is traversed in a single DFS traversal. So, keeping track of visited vertices is enough to find cycles in undirected graph.

Example 12.14:
```
isCyclePresentUndirectedDFS(src, parentIndex, visited) {
    visited[src] = true
    let dest;
    const adl = this.Adj[src];

    for (let index = 0; index < adl.length; index++) {
        const adn = adl[index];
        dest = adn.dest
        if (visited[dest] === false) {
            if (this.isCyclePresentUndirectedDFS(dest, src, visited))
                return true
        }
        else if (parentIndex !== dest)
            return true
    }
    return false
}

isCyclePresentUndirected() {
    const count = this.count;
    const visited = new Array(count).fill(false);

    for (let i = 0; i < count; i++) {
        if (visited[i] === false)
```

```
            if (this.isCyclePresentUndirectedDFS(i, -1, visited))
                return true
    }
    return false
}

function test(){
    const gph = new Graph(6);
    gph.addUndirectedEdge(0, 1, 1)
    gph.addUndirectedEdge(1, 2, 1)
    gph.addUndirectedEdge(3, 4, 1)
    gph.addUndirectedEdge(4, 2, 1)
    gph.addUndirectedEdge(2, 5, 1)
    gph.addUndirectedEdge(3, 5, 1)
    console.log(gph.isCyclePresentUndirected())
}
```

Output:
```
true
```

Complexity Analysis: Time Complexity same as DFS for adjacency list implementation of the graph it is O(V+E) and for adjacency matrix implementation it is $O(V^2)$

Find cycle in a Directed Graph.

Problem: Given a directed graph, find if there is a cycle in Graph. In a single traversal, if some node is traversed twice then there is a cycle.

Solution 1: We will be using DFS traversal for a single traversal; we will use a marked array to keep track of the number of nodes visited in a single traversal.

Example 12.15: Finding if there is a cycle in a graph using marked array.
```
isCyclePresentDFS(index, visited, marked) {
    visited[index] = true
    marked[index] = 1
    const adl = this.Adj[index];
    for (var index = 0; index < adl.length; index++) {
        const adn = adl[index];
        const dest = adn.dest;
        if (marked[dest] === 1)
            return true
        if (visited[dest] === false)
            if (this.isCyclePresentDFS(dest, visited, marked))
                return true
    }
    marked[index] = 0
    return false
}
```

```
isCyclePresent() {
    const count = this.count;
    const visited = new Array(count).fill(false);
    const marked = new Array(count).fill(0);

    for (let index = 0; index < count; index++) {
        if (visited[index] === false)
            if (this.isCyclePresentDFS(index, visited, marked))
                return true
    }
    return false
}

function test(){
    const gph = new Graph(5);
    gph.addDirectedEdge(0, 1, 1)
    gph.addDirectedEdge(0, 2, 1)
    gph.addDirectedEdge(2, 3, 1)
    gph.addDirectedEdge(1, 3, 1)
    gph.addDirectedEdge(3, 4, 1)
    gph.addDirectedEdge(4, 1, 1)
    console.log(gph.isCyclePresent())
}
```

Output:
```
true
```

Complexity Analysis: Time Complexity same as DFS for adjacency list implementation of the graph it is O(V+E) and for adjacency matrix implementation it is $O(V^2)$

Solution 2: Find if there is a cycle in a graph using colour method.

In colour method, initially visited array is assigned the value "white" which means that nodes are not visited. When we visit a node, we mark its colour as "Grey". Nodes that are currently in visited path remain "Grey" and when all the connected nodes are traversed, and then the colour is changed to "Black". If a node that is marked "Grey" is visited again, then there is a cycle in that path.

Example 12.16: Cycle detection using colouring method.
```
isCyclePresentDFSColor(index, visited) {
    visited[index] = 1
    let dest;
    const adl = this.Adj[index];
    for (var index = 0; index < adl.length; index++) {
        const adn = adl[index];
        dest = adn.dest
        if (visited[dest] === 1)
            return true
        if (visited[dest] === 0)
            if (this.isCyclePresentDFSColor(dest, visited))
                return true
```

```
        }
        visited[index] = 2
        return false
}

isCyclePresentColor() {
    const count = this.count;
    const visited = new Array(count).fill(0); // fill with 0

    for (let i = 0; i < count; i++) {
        if (visited[i] === 0)
            if (this.isCyclePresentDFSColor(i, visited))
                return true
    }
    return false
}
```

Complexity Analysis: Time Complexity same as DFS for adjacency list implementation of the graph it is O(V+E) and for adjacency matrix implementation it is O(V²)

Transpose Graph

Problem: Transpose of a Graph G is a graph G' that has the same set of vertices, but the direction of edges is reversed.

Example 12.17:
```
transposeGraph() {
    const count = this.count;
    const g = new Graph(count);
    for (let i = 0; i < count; i++) {
        const adl = this.Adj[i];
        for (let index = 0; index < adl.length; index++) {
            const adn = adl[index];
            const dest = adn.dest;
            g.addDirectedEdge(dest, i)
        }
    }
    return g
}

function test(){
    const graph = new Graph(4);
    graph.addDirectedEdge(0, 1);
    graph.addDirectedEdge(0, 2);
    graph.addDirectedEdge(1, 2);
    graph.addDirectedEdge(2, 3);
    const g = graph.transposeGraph()
    g.print();
};
```

Output:
```
Vertex 0 is connected to :
Vertex 1 is connected to : 0(1)
Vertex 2 is connected to : 0(1) 1(1)
Vertex 3 is connected to : 2(1)
```

Complexity Analysis: Time Complexity for adjacency list implementation of the graph it is O(V+E) and for adjacency matrix implementation it is $O(V^2)$

Test if an undirected graph is connected.

Problem: Given an undirected graph. Start from any vertex if we can visit all the other vertices using DFS or BFS then the graph is connected.

Example 12.18:
```
isConnectedUndirected() {
    const count = this.count;
    const visited = new Array(count).fill(false);

    this.dfsUtil3(0, visited)
    for (let i = 0; i < count; i++) {
        if (visited[i] === false) {
            return false
        }
    }
    return true
}

function test(){
    const gph = new Graph(6);
    gph.addUndirectedEdge(0, 1, 1)
    gph.addUndirectedEdge(1, 2, 1)
    gph.addUndirectedEdge(3, 4, 1)
    gph.addUndirectedEdge(4, 2, 1)
    gph.addUndirectedEdge(2, 5, 1)
    gph.addUndirectedEdge(3, 5, 1)
    console.log("IsConnectedUndirected : ", gph.isConnectedUndirected())
}
```

Output:
```
IsConnectedUndirected :  true
```

Complexity Analysis: Time Complexity same as DFS for adjacency list implementation of the graph it is O(V+E) and for adjacency matrix implementation it is $O(V^2)$

Strongly Connected Graph

A directed graph is strongly connected if for each pair of vertices u and v, there is a path from u to v and a path from v to u.

To prove that the graph is connected graph we need to prove two conditions as true for any one vertex:
1) First condition, that every vertex can be visited from some vertex u. Or every vertex is reachable from vertex u.
2) Second condition, that vertex u is reachable from every other vertex.

First conditions can be verified by doing a DFS from some vertex u. We need to check that all the vertices of the graph are visited. Second condition can be verified by first creating transpose graph G'. Then perform DFS over G' from vertex u. If all other vertices are visited from vertex u in graph G'. It means that vertex u is reachable from all the vertices of the original graph G.

Kosaraju's Algorithm to find if the graph is connected based on DFS:
1) Create a visited array of size V, and Initialize all vertices in the visited array as False.
2) Choose any vertex and perform a DFS traversal of the graph. For all visited vertices, mark them visited by setting their values as True in visited array.
3) If DFS traversal does not mark all vertices as True, then return false.
4) Find transpose or reverse of the graph
5) Repeat step 1, 2 and 3 for the reversed graph.
6) If DFS traversal mark all the vertices as True, then return true.

Example 12.19:
```
isStronglyConnected() {
    const count = this.count;
    const visited = new Array(count).fill(false);

    this.dfsUtil3(0, visited)
    for (var i = 0; i < count; i++) {
        if (visited[i] === false) {
            return false
        }
    }
    const gReversed = this.transposeGraph();
    visited.fill(false)

    gReversed.dfsUtil3(0, visited)
    for (var i = 0; i < count; i++) {
        if (visited[i] === false) {
            return false
        }
    }
    return true
}

function test(){
    const gph = new Graph(5);
    gph.addDirectedEdge(0, 1, 1)
    gph.addDirectedEdge(1, 2, 1)
    gph.addDirectedEdge(2, 3, 1)
    gph.addDirectedEdge(3, 0, 1)
    gph.addDirectedEdge(2, 4, 1)
```

```
    gph.addDirectedEdge(4, 2, 1)
    console.log(`IsStronglyConnected:: ${gph.isStronglyConnected()}`)
}
```

Output:

```
IsStronglyConnected:: true
```

Strongly Connected Components

Strongly Connected Components: A directed graph may have different sub-graphs that are strongly connected. These sub-graphs are called strongly connected components. In the below graph the whole graph is not strongly connected but its two sub-graphs are strongly connected components.

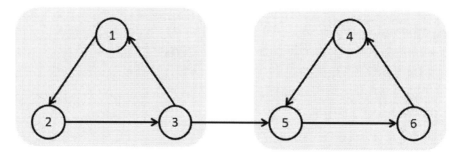

Strongly Connected Component

Algorithm to find Strongly Connected Component
1) Create an empty stack, do DFS traversal on the graph G. Call DFS for adjacent vertices, and push them into the stack.
2) Reverse the graph G to get new graph G'
3) Perform the DFS traversal on the graph G' by picking vertices from the top of the stack.
4) Each strongly connected component is traversed in one single iteration.

Example 12.20:

```
stronglyConnectedComponent() {
    const count = this.count;
    const visited = new Array(count).fill(false);
    const stk = ([]);

    for (let i = 0; i < count; i++) {
        if (visited[i] === false) {
            this.dfsUtil2(i, visited, stk)
        }
    }
    const gReversed = this.transposeGraph();
    visited.fill(false)

    const stk2 = ([]);
    while (stk.length != 0) {
        const curr = stk.pop();
        if (visited[curr] === false) {
            stk2.length = 0
```

```
            gReversed.dfsUtil2(curr, visited, stk2)
            console.log(stk2)
        }
    }
}

function test(){
    const gph = new Graph(7);
    gph.addDirectedEdge(0, 1, 1)
    gph.addDirectedEdge(1, 2, 1)
    gph.addDirectedEdge(2, 0, 1)
    gph.addDirectedEdge(2, 3, 1)
    gph.addDirectedEdge(3, 4, 1)
    gph.addDirectedEdge(4, 5, 1)
    gph.addDirectedEdge(5, 3, 1)
    gph.addDirectedEdge(5, 6, 1)
    gph.stronglyConnectedComponent()
}
```

Output:
```
[ 1, 2, 0 ]
[ 4, 5, 3 ]
[ 6 ]
```

Minimum Spanning Trees (MST)

A **Spanning Tree** of a graph G is a tree that contains all the vertices of the Graph.
A **Minimum Spanning Tree** is a spanning-tree whose sum of length / weight of edges is minimum as possible.

For Example , if you want to setup communication between a set of cities, then you may want to use the least amount of wire as possible. MST can be used to find the network path and wire cost estimate.

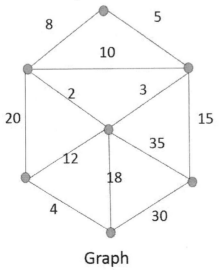

Graph

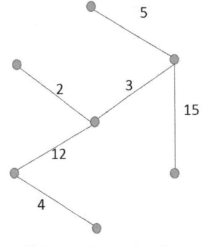

Minimum Spanning Tree

393

Prim's Algorithm for MST

Prim's algorithm grows a single tree T, one edge at a time, until it becomes a spanning tree.
We initialize T with zero edges and U with a single node. Where T is spanning tree, edges set and U is spanning tree vertex set.

At each step, Prim's algorithm adds the smallest value edge with one endpoint in U and other not in us. Since each edge adds one new vertex to U, after n − 1 additions, U contains all the vertices of the spanning tree and T becomes a spanning tree.

Example 12.21:

```
// Returns the MST by Prim's Algorithm
// Input: A weighted connected graph G = (V, E)
// Output: Set of edges comprising a MST

Algorithm Prim(G)
    T = {}
    Let r be any vertex in G
    U = {r}
    for i = 1 to |V| - 1 do
        e = minimum-weight edge (u, v)
            With u in U and v in V-U
        U = U + {v}
        T = T + {e}
    return T
```

Prim's Algorithm using a priority queue to get the closest next vertex
Time complexity is O(E log V) where V vertices and E edges of the MST.

Example 12.22: Prim's algorithm implementation for adjacency list representation of graph.

```
prims() {
    const count = this.count;
    const previous = new Array(count).fill(-1);
    const infi = 2147483647;
    const dist = new Array(count).fill(infi);
    const visited = new Array(count).fill(false);
    let source = 0;
    dist[source] = 0

    const queue = new PriorityQueue(null, GraphEdgeComparator);
    let node = new GraphEdge(source, 0);
    queue.add(node)

    while (queue.isEmpty() === false) {
        node = queue.remove()
        source = node.dest

        if (visited[source] == true) {
            continue
        }
```

```
        visited[source] = true

        const adl = this.Adj[source];
        for (let index = 0; index < adl.length; index++) {
            const adn = adl[index];
            const dest = adn.dest;
            const alt = adn.cost;
            if (dist[dest] > alt && visited[dest] === false) {
                dist[dest] = alt
                previous[dest] = source
                node = new GraphEdge(dest, alt)
                queue.add(node)
            }
        }
    }
    for (let i = 0; i < count; i++) {
        if (dist[i] === infi) {
            console.log(`Node id ${i} is Unreachable`)
        } else {
            console.log(`Node id ${i}, prev : ${previous[i]}, cost : $
{dist[i]}`)
        }
    }
}

function test(){
    const gph = new Graph(9);
    gph.addUndirectedEdge(0, 1, 4)
    gph.addUndirectedEdge(0, 7, 8)
    gph.addUndirectedEdge(1, 2, 8)
    gph.addUndirectedEdge(1, 7, 11)
    gph.addUndirectedEdge(2, 3, 7)
    gph.addUndirectedEdge(2, 8, 2)
    gph.addUndirectedEdge(2, 5, 4)
    gph.addUndirectedEdge(3, 4, 9)
    gph.addUndirectedEdge(3, 5, 14)
    gph.addUndirectedEdge(4, 5, 10)
    gph.addUndirectedEdge(5, 6, 2)
    gph.addUndirectedEdge(6, 7, 1)
    gph.addUndirectedEdge(6, 8, 6)
    gph.addUndirectedEdge(7, 8, 7)
    gph.prims()
}
```

Output:
```
Node id 0, prev : -1, cost : 0
Node id 1, prev : 0, cost : 4
Node id 2, prev : 5, cost : 4
Node id 3, prev : 2, cost : 7
Node id 4, prev : 3, cost : 9
```

```
Node id 5, prev : 6, cost : 2
Node id 6, prev : 7, cost : 1
Node id 7, prev : 0, cost : 8
Node id 8, prev : 2, cost : 2
```

Example 12.23: Prim's algorithm implementation for adjacency matrix representation of graph.

```
prims(gph) {
    const count = this.count;
    const previous = new Array(count).fill(-1);
    const dist = new Array(count).fill(Infinity);
    const visited = new Array(count).fill(false);

    let source = 0;
    dist[source] = 0
    previous[source] = -1

    const queue = new PriorityQueue(null, GraphEdgeComparator);
    let node = new GraphEdge(source, 0);
    queue.add(node)

    while (queue.isEmpty() === false) {
        node = queue.remove();
        source = node.dest;
        visited[source] = true;

        for (let dest = 0; dest < count; dest++) {
            const cost = this.adj[source][dest];
            if (cost !== 0) {
                const alt = cost;
                if (dist[dest] > alt && visited[dest] === false) {
                    dist[dest] = alt;
                    previous[dest] = source;
                    node = new GraphEdge(dest, alt);
                    queue.add(node);
                }
            }
        }
    }

    for (let i = 0; i < count; i++) {
        if (dist[i] === Infinity) {
            console.info(`Node id ${i},  prev : ${previous[i]}, cost :
Unreachable`);
        }
        else {
            console.info(`Node id ${i},  prev : ${previous[i]}, cost : $
{dist[i]}`);
        }
    }
}
```

```
function test(){
    const gph = new Graph(9);
    gph.addUndirectedEdge(0, 1, 4)
    gph.addUndirectedEdge(0, 7, 8)
    gph.addUndirectedEdge(1, 2, 8)
    gph.addUndirectedEdge(1, 7, 11)
    gph.addUndirectedEdge(2, 3, 7)
    gph.addUndirectedEdge(2, 8, 2)
    gph.addUndirectedEdge(2, 5, 4)
    gph.addUndirectedEdge(3, 4, 9)
    gph.addUndirectedEdge(3, 5, 14)
    gph.addUndirectedEdge(4, 5, 10)
    gph.addUndirectedEdge(5, 6, 2)
    gph.addUndirectedEdge(6, 7, 1)
    gph.addUndirectedEdge(6, 8, 6)
    gph.addUndirectedEdge(7, 8, 7)
    gph.prims()
};
```

Output:
```
Node id 0,  prev : -1, cost : 0
Node id 1,  prev : 0, cost : 4
Node id 2,  prev : 5, cost : 4
Node id 3,  prev : 2, cost : 7
Node id 4,  prev : 3, cost : 9
Node id 5,  prev : 6, cost : 2
Node id 6,  prev : 7, cost : 1
Node id 7,  prev : 0, cost : 8
Node id 8,  prev : 2, cost : 2
```

Kruskal's Algorithm

Kruskal's Algorithm repeatedly chooses the smallest-weight edge that does not form a cycle.
Sort the edges in non-decreasing order of cost: $c(e1) \leq c(e2) \leq \cdots \leq c(em)$.
Set T to be the empty tree. Add edges to tree one by one, if it does not create a cycle.

```
// Returns the MST by Kruskal's Algorithm
// Input: A weighted connected graph G = (V, E)
// Output: Set of edges comprising a MST

Algorithm Kruskal(G)
    Sort the edges E by their weights
    T = { }
    while |T| + 1 < |V| do
        e = next edge in E
        if T + {e} does not have a cycle then
            T = T + {e}
    return T
```

Kruskal's Algorithm is O(E log V) using efficient cycle detection.

Shortest Path Algorithms in Graph

Single Source Shortest Path

For a graph G= (V, E), the single source shortest path problem is to find the shortest path from a given source vertex s to all the vertices of V.

Single Source Shortest Path for unweighted Graph.

Find single source shortest path for unweighted graph or a graph with all the vertices of same weight.

Or

Given a starting vertex s, finding the minimum number of edges from vertex s to all the other vertices of the graph.

Example 12.24:

```
shortestPath(source) {
    let curr;
    const count = this.count;
    const infi = 2147483647;
    const distance = new Array(count).fill(infi);
    const path = new Array(count).fill(0);

    const que = new Queue();
    que.add(source)
    distance[source] = 0

    while (que.isEmpty() === false) {
        curr = que.remove()
        const adl = this.Adj[curr];
        for (let index = 0; index < adl.length; index++) {
            const adn = adl[index];
            if (distance[adn.dest] === infi) {
                distance[adn.dest] = distance[curr] + 1
                path[adn.dest] = curr
                que.add(adn.dest)
            }
        }
    }

    for (let i = 0; i < count; i++) {
        console.log(`${path[i]} to ${i} weight ${distance[i]}`)
    }
}

function test(){
    const gph = new Graph(9);
    gph.addDirectedEdge(0, 1)
    gph.addDirectedEdge(0, 7)
```

```
    gph.addDirectedEdge(1, 2)
    gph.addDirectedEdge(1, 7)
    gph.addDirectedEdge(2, 3)
    gph.addDirectedEdge(2, 8)
    gph.addDirectedEdge(2, 5)
    gph.addDirectedEdge(3, 4)
    gph.addDirectedEdge(3, 5)
    gph.addDirectedEdge(4, 5)
    gph.addDirectedEdge(5, 6)
    gph.addDirectedEdge(6, 7)
    gph.addDirectedEdge(6, 8)
    gph.addDirectedEdge(7, 8)
    gph.shortestPath(0)
}
```

Output:

```
0 to 0 weight 0
0 to 1 weight 1
1 to 2 weight 2
2 to 3 weight 3
3 to 4 weight 4
2 to 5 weight 3
5 to 6 weight 4
0 to 7 weight 1
7 to 8 weight 2
```

Analysis:
- First, the starting point source is added to a queue.
- Breadth first traversal is performed
- Nodes that are closer to the source are traversed first and processed.

Dijkstra's algorithm

Dijkstra's algorithm is used for single-source shortest path problem for weighted edges with no negative weight. Given a weighted connected graph G, find shortest paths from the source vertex s to each of the other vertices. Dijkstra's algorithm is like prims algorithm. It maintains a set of nodes for which shortest path is known.

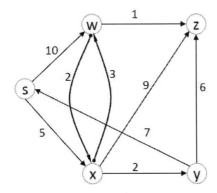 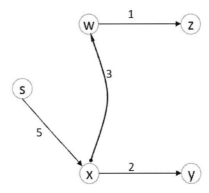

Single-Source shortest path

The algorithm starts by keeping track of the distance of each node and its parents. All the distance is set to infinite in the beginning as we do not know the actual path to the nodes and parents of all the vertices are set to null. All the vertices are added to a priority queue (min heap implementation)

At each step algorithm takes one vertex from the priority queue (which will be the source vertex in the beginning). Then update the distance list corresponding to all the adjacent vertices. When the queue is empty, then we will have the distance and a parent list fully populated.

```
// Solves SSSP by Dijkstra's Algorithm
// Input: A weighted connected graph G = (V, E)
// with no negative weights, and source vertex v
// Output: The length and path from s to every v
Algorithm Dijkstra(G, s)
for each v in V do
    D[v] = infinite     // Unknown distance
    P[v] = null     //unknown previous node
    add v to PQ     //adding all nodes to priority queue

D[source] = 0 // Distance from source to source

while (PQ is not empty)
    u = vertex from PQ with smallest D[u]
    remove u from PQ
    for each v adjacent from u do
        alt = D[u] + length ( u , v )
        if alt < D[v] then
            D[v] = alt
            P[v] = u
Return D[] , P[]
```

Time complexity is O(|E|log|V|) Where V is the number of vertices and E is the number of edges in the given graph.

Note: Dijkstra's algorithm does not work for graphs with negative edge weight.
Note: Dijkstra's algorithm is applicable to both undirected and directed graphs.

Example 12.25: Dijkstra's algorithm for adjacency list implementation of graph.
```
dijkstra(source) {
    const count = this.count;
    const previous = new Array(count).fill(-1);
    const Infinity = 2147483647;
    const dist = new Array(count).fill(Infinity);
    const visited = new Array(count).fill(false);

    dist[source] = 0
    previous[source] = -1

    const queue = new PriorityQueue(null, GraphEdgeComparator);
    let node = new GraphEdge(source, 0);
    queue.add(node)
```

```
    while (queue.isEmpty() === false) {
        node = queue.remove()
        source = node.dest

        if (visited[source] == true) {
            continue
        }
        visited[source] = true

        const adl = this.Adj[source];
        for (let index = 0; index < adl.length; index++) {
            const adn = adl[index];
            const dest = adn.dest;
            const alt = adn.cost + dist[source];
            if (dist[dest] > alt && visited[dest] === false) {
                dist[dest] = alt
                previous[dest] = source
                node = new GraphEdge(dest, alt)
                queue.add(node)
            }
        }
    }
    for (let i = 0; i < count; i++) {
        if (dist[i] === Infinity) {
            console.log(`Node id ${i} is Unreachable`)
        } else {
            console.log(`Node id ${i}, prev : ${previous[i]}, cost : $
{dist[i]}`)
        }
    }
}

function test(){
    const gph = new Graph(9);
    gph.addUndirectedEdge(0, 1, 4)
    gph.addUndirectedEdge(0, 7, 8)
    gph.addUndirectedEdge(1, 2, 8)
    gph.addUndirectedEdge(1, 7, 11)
    gph.addUndirectedEdge(2, 3, 7)
    gph.addUndirectedEdge(2, 8, 2)
    gph.addUndirectedEdge(2, 5, 4)
    gph.addUndirectedEdge(3, 4, 9)
    gph.addUndirectedEdge(3, 5, 14)
    gph.addUndirectedEdge(4, 5, 10)
    gph.addUndirectedEdge(5, 6, 2)
    gph.addUndirectedEdge(6, 7, 1)
    gph.addUndirectedEdge(6, 8, 6)
    gph.addUndirectedEdge(7, 8, 7)
    gph.dijkstra(1)
}
```

Output:
```
Node id 0, prev : 1, cost : 4
Node id 1, prev : -1, cost : 0
Node id 2, prev : 1, cost : 8
Node id 3, prev : 2, cost : 15
Node id 4, prev : 5, cost : 22
Node id 5, prev : 2, cost : 12
Node id 6, prev : 7, cost : 12
Node id 7, prev : 1, cost : 11
Node id 8, prev : 2, cost : 10
```

Example 12.26: Dijkstra's algorithm for adjacency matrix implementation of graph.

```
dijkstra(source) {
    const count = this.count
    const previous = new Array(count).fill(-1);
    const dist = new Array(count).fill(Infinity);
    const visited = new Array(count).fill(false);

    dist[source] = 0
    previous[source] = -1

    const queue = new PriorityQueue(null, GraphEdgeComparator);
    let node = new GraphEdge(source, 0);
    queue.add(node)

    while (queue.isEmpty() === false) {
        node = queue.remove();
        source = node.dest;
        visited[source] = true;
        for (let dest = 0; dest < count; dest++) {
            const cost = this.adj[source][dest];
            if (cost !== 0) {
                const alt = cost + dist[source];
                if (dist[dest] > alt && visited[dest] === false) {
                    dist[dest] = alt;
                    previous[dest] = source;
                    node = new GraphEdge(dest, alt);
                    queue.add(node);
                }
            }
        }
    }
    for (let i = 0; i < count; i++) {
        if (dist[i] === Infinity) {
            console.log(`Node id ${i} is Unreachable`)
        } else {
            console.log(`Node id ${i}, prev : ${previous[i]}, cost : $
{dist[i]}`)
        }
    }
}
```

```
}

function test(){
    const gph = new Graph(9);
    gph.addUndirectedEdge(0, 1, 4)
    gph.addUndirectedEdge(0, 7, 8)
    gph.addUndirectedEdge(1, 2, 8)
    gph.addUndirectedEdge(1, 7, 11)
    gph.addUndirectedEdge(2, 3, 7)
    gph.addUndirectedEdge(2, 8, 2)
    gph.addUndirectedEdge(2, 5, 4)
    gph.addUndirectedEdge(3, 4, 9)
    gph.addUndirectedEdge(3, 5, 14)
    gph.addUndirectedEdge(4, 5, 10)
    gph.addUndirectedEdge(5, 6, 2)
    gph.addUndirectedEdge(6, 7, 1)
    gph.addUndirectedEdge(6, 8, 6)
    gph.addUndirectedEdge(7, 8, 7)
    gph.dijkstra(1);
};
```

Output:
```
Node id 0, prev : 1, cost : 4
Node id 1, prev : -1, cost : 0
Node id 2, prev : 1, cost : 8
Node id 3, prev : 2, cost : 15
Node id 4, prev : 5, cost : 22
Node id 5, prev : 2, cost : 12
Node id 6, prev : 7, cost : 12
Node id 7, prev : 1, cost : 11
Node id 8, prev : 2, cost : 10
```

Bellman Ford Shortest Path

Single source shortest path from a source vertex s to all other vertices in a graph containing negative weight edges but no negative cycle is done using Bellman Ford algorithm. It does not work if there is some cycle in the graph whose total weight is negative. In this algorithm, distance of all the vertices is assigned to ∞ and the source vertex distance is assigned as 0. Then V-1 passes (V is total no of vertices) over all the edges is performed and the distance to destination is updated for each vertices.

We can check over all the edges again and if there is change in the weights in the distance then it detect a negative weight cycle. If distance is changed after V-1 relaxation then we have a negative cycle. We can stop the algorithm if an iteration does not modify distance estimates. This is beneficial if shortest paths are likely to be less than V-1.

Time complexity is O(V.E), where V is number of vertices and E is the total number of edges.

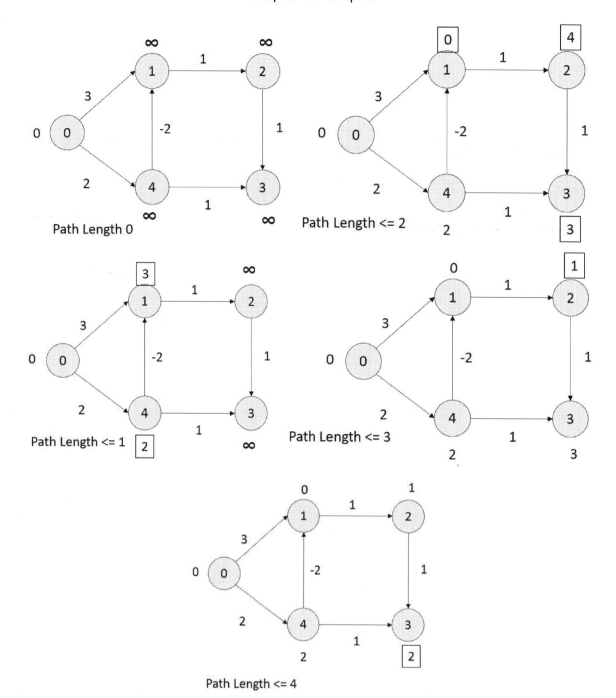

Path Length 0

Path Length <= 2

Path Length <= 1

Path Length <= 3

Path Length <= 4

Example 12.27:

```
bellmanFordshortestPath(source) {
    const count = this.count;
    const path = new Array(count).fill(-1);
    const infi = 2147483647;
    const distance = new Array(count).fill(infi);

    distance[source] = 0
    for (var i = 0; i < count - 1; i++) {
        for (let j = 0; j < count; j++) {
            const adl = this.Adj[j];
            for (let index = 0; index < adl.length; index++) {
```

```
            const adn = adl[index];
            const newDistance = distance[j] + adn.cost;
            if (distance[adn.dest] > newDistance) {
                distance[adn.dest] = newDistance
                path[adn.dest] = j
            }
        }
    }
}
for (var i = 0; i < count; i++) {
    console.log(`${path[i]} to ${i} weight ${distance[i]}`)
}
}

function test(){
    const gph = new Graph(5);
    gph.addDirectedEdge(0, 1, 3)
    gph.addDirectedEdge(0, 4, 2)
    gph.addDirectedEdge(1, 2, 1)
    gph.addDirectedEdge(2, 3, 1)
    gph.addDirectedEdge(4, 1, -2)
    gph.addDirectedEdge(4, 3, 1)
    gph.bellmanFordshortestPath(0)
}
```

Output:
```
-1 to 0 weight 0
4 to 1 weight 0
1 to 2 weight 1
2 to 3 weight 2
0 to 4 weight 2
```

All Pairs Shortest Paths

Given a weighted graph G(V, E), the all pair shortest path problem is used to find the shortest path between all pairs of vertices u, v ∈ V. Execute V instances of single source shortest path algorithm for each vertex of the graph.

The complexity of this algorithm will be $O(V^3)$

Hamiltonian Path and Hamiltonian Circuit

Hamiltonian path is a path in which every vertex is visited exactly once with no repeats, it does not have to start and end at the same vertex.

Hamiltonian path is a Np-Complete problem, so the only solution is possible using backtracking, which starts from a vertex s and try all adjacent vertices recursively. If we do not find the path, then we backtrack and try other vertices.

Example 12.28:

```javascript
hamiltonianPathUtil(path, pSize, added) {
    if (pSize === this.count)
        return true;

    for (let vertex = 0; vertex < this.count; vertex++) {
        if (pSize === 0 || (this.adj[path[pSize - 1]][vertex] === 1 &&
added[vertex] === 0)) {
            path[pSize++] = vertex;
            added[vertex] = 1;

            if (this.hamiltonianPathUtil(path, pSize, added))
                return true;

            pSize--;
            added[vertex] = 0;
        }
    }
    return false;
}

hamiltonianPath() {
    const count = this.count;
    const path = new Array(count).fill(0);
    const added = new Array(count).fill(0);

    if (this.hamiltonianPathUtil(path, 0, added)) {
        console.info("Hamiltonian Path found :: " , path);
        return true;
    }
    console.info("Hamiltonian Path not found");
    return false;
}

function test(){
    const count = 5;
    const graph = new Graph(count);
    const adj =
        [[0, 1, 0, 1, 0],
         [1, 0, 1, 1, 0],
         [0, 1, 0, 0, 1],
         [1, 1, 0, 0, 1],
         [0, 1, 1, 1, 0]];

    for (var i = 0; i < count; i++) {
        for (var j = 0; j < count; j++) {
            if (adj[i][j] === 1)
                graph.addDirectedEdge(i, j, 1);
        }
    }
```

```
console.info(`hamiltonianPath : ${graph.hamiltonianPath()}`);

const graph2 = new Graph(count);
const adj2 =
    [[0, 1, 0, 1, 0],
     [1, 0, 1, 1, 0],
     [0, 1, 0, 0, 1],
     [1, 1, 0, 0, 0],
     [0, 1, 1, 0, 0]];

for (var i = 0; i < count; i++) {
    for (var j = 0; j < count; j++) {
        if (adj2[i][j] === 1)
            graph2.addDirectedEdge(i, j, 1);
    }
}
console.info(`hamiltonianPath :  ${graph2.hamiltonianPath()}`);
};
```

Output:
```
Hamiltonian Path found ::  [ 0, 1, 2, 4, 3 ]
hamiltonianPath : true
Hamiltonian Path found ::  [ 0, 3, 1, 2, 4 ]
hamiltonianPath :  true
```

Hamiltonian circuit is a Hamiltonian Path such that there is an edge from its last vertex to its first vertex. A **Hamiltonian circuit** is a circuit that visits every vertex exactly once and it must start and end at the same vertex.

Solution of Hamiltonian circuit is also NP-compete problem. The only difference is the base condition in which there should be a path from last node of the Hamiltonian path to the first element.

Example 12.29:
```
hamiltonianCycleUtil(path, pSize, added) {
    const count = this.count;
    if (pSize === count) {
        if (this.adj[path[pSize - 1]][path[0]] === 1) {
            path[pSize] = path[0];
            return true;
        }
        else
            return false;
    }

    for (let vertex = 0; vertex < count; vertex++) {
        if (pSize === 0 || (this.adj[path[pSize - 1]][vertex] === 1 &&
added[vertex] === 0)) {
            path[pSize++] = vertex;
            added[vertex] = 1;
```

```
            if (this.hamiltonianCycleUtil(path, pSize, added))
                return true;
            pSize--;
            added[vertex] = 0;
        }
    }
    return false;
}

hamiltonianCycle() {
    const count = this.count;
    const path = new Array(count + 1).fill(0);
    const added = new Array(count).fill(0);

    if (this.hamiltonianCycleUtil(path, 0, added)) {
        console.info("Hamiltonian Cycle found :: ", path);
        return true;
    }
    console.info("Hamiltonian Cycle not found");
    return false;
}

function test(){
    const count = 5;
    const graph = new Graph(count);
    const adj =
        [[0, 1, 0, 1, 0],
         [1, 0, 1, 1, 0],
         [0, 1, 0, 0, 1],
         [1, 1, 0, 0, 1],
         [0, 1, 1, 1, 0]];

    for (var i = 0; i < count; i++) {
        for (var j = 0; j < count; j++) {
            if (adj[i][j] === 1)
                graph.addDirectedEdge(i, j, 1);
        }
    }

    console.info(`hamiltonianCycle : ${graph.hamiltonianCycle()}`);

    const graph2 = new Graph(count);
    const adj2 =
        [[0, 1, 0, 1, 0],
         [1, 0, 1, 1, 0],
         [0, 1, 0, 0, 1],
         [1, 1, 0, 0, 0],
         [0, 1, 1, 0, 0]];
```

```
    for (var i = 0; i < count; i++) {
        for (var j = 0; j < count; j++) {
            if (adj2[i][j] === 1)
                graph2.addDirectedEdge(i, j, 1);
        }
    }
    console.info(`hamiltonianCycle :  ${graph2.hamiltonianCycle()}`);
};
```

Output:
```
Hamiltonian Cycle found ::  [ 0, 1, 2, 4, 3, 0 ]
hamiltonianCycle : true
Hamiltonian Cycle not found
hamiltonianCycle :  false
```

Euler path and Euler Circuit

Eulerian Path is a path in the graph that visits every edge exactly once.

Eulerian Circuit is an Eulerian Path, which starts and ends on the same vertex. Or **Eulerian Circuit** is a path in the graph that visits every edge exactly one and it starts and ends on the same vertex.

A graph is called Eulerian if there is an Euler circuit in it. A graph is called Semi-Eulerian if there is an Euler Path in the graph. If there is no Euler path possible in the graph, then it is called non-Eulerian.

A graph is Eulerian if all the edges have even number of number of edges in it. A graph is Semi-Eulerian if it has exactly two vertices with odd number of edges or odd degree. In all other cases, the graph is Non-Eulerian.

Example 12.30: Check if the graph is Eulerian.
```
isEulerian() {
    const count = this.count;

    if (this.isConnected() === false) {
        console.log('graph is not Eulerian')
        return 0
    }
    let odd = 0;
    const inDegree = new Array(count).fill(0);
    const outDegree = new Array(count).fill(0);

    for (var i = 0; i < count; i++) {
        let adl = this.Adj[i]
        for (let index = 0; index < adl.length; index++) {
            const adn = adl[index];
            outDegree[i] += 1
            inDegree[adn.dest] += 1
        }
    }
```

```
    for (var i = 0; i < count; i++) {
        if ((inDegree[i] + outDegree[i]) % 2 !== 0) {
            odd += 1
        }
    }

    if (odd === 0) {
        console.log('graph is Eulerian')
        return 2
    } else if (odd === 2) {
        console.log('graph is Semi-Eulerian')
        return 1
    } else {
        console.log('graph is not Eulerian')
        return 0
    }
}

function test(){
    const gph = new Graph(5);
    gph.addDirectedEdge(1, 0, 1)
    gph.addDirectedEdge(0, 2, 1)
    gph.addDirectedEdge(2, 1, 1)
    gph.addDirectedEdge(0, 3, 1)
    gph.addDirectedEdge(3, 4, 1)
    gph.isEulerian()
}
```

Output:
```
graph is Semi-Eulerian
```

Travelling Salesman Problem (TSP)

Problem: The travelling salesperson problem tries to find the shortest tour through a given set of n cities that visits each city exactly once before returning to the city where it started.

Alternatively, find the shortest Hamiltonian circuit in a weighted connected graph. A cycle that passes through all the vertices of the graph exactly once.

```
Algorithm TSP
Select a city
MinTourCost = infinite
For ( All permutations of cities ) do
    If( LengthOfPathSinglePermutation < MinTourCost )
        MinTourCost = LengthOfPath
```

Total number of possible combinations = (n-1)!
Cost for calculating the path: $\Theta(n)$
So, the total cost of finding the shortest path: $\Theta(n!)$

It is an NP-Hard problem there is no efficient algorithm to find its solution. Even if some solution is given, it is equally hard to verify that this is a correct solution or not. However, some approximate algorithms can be used to find a good solution. We will not always get the best solution, but will get a good solution.

Our approximate algorithm is based on the minimum spanning tree problem. In which we have to construct a tree from a graph such that every node is connected by edges of the graph and the total sum of the cost of all the edges is minimum.

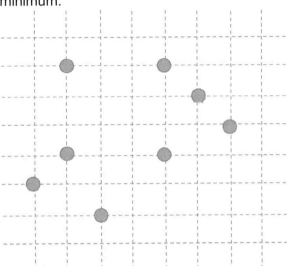

In the above diagram, we have a group of cities (each city is represented by a circle.) Which are located in the grid and the distance between the cities is same as per the actual distance. And there is a path from each city to another city which is a straight path from one to another.

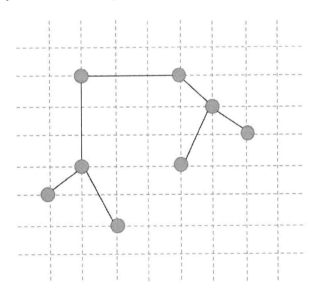

We have made a minimum spanning tree for the above city graph.

What we want to prove that the shortest path in a TSP will always be greater than the length of MST. Since in MST all nodes are connected to the next node, which is also the minimum distance from the group of node. Therefore, to make it a path without repeating the nodes we need to go directly from one node to other without following MST. At that point, when we are not following MST we are choosing an edge, which is greater, then the edges provided by MST. So TSP path will always be greater than or equal to MST path.

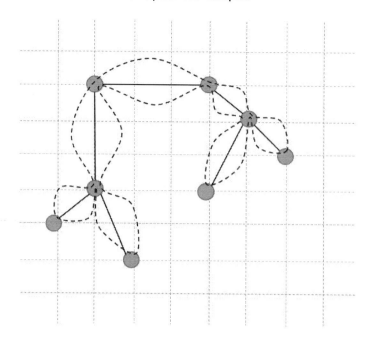

Now let us take a path from starting node and traverse each node on the way given above and then come back to the starting node. The total cost of the path is 2MST. The only difference is that we are visiting many nodes multiple times.

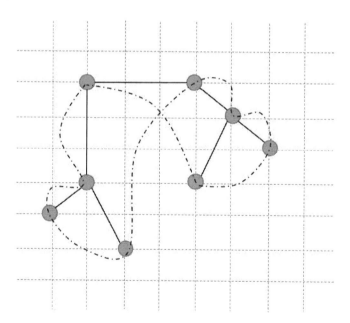

Now let us change our traversal algorithm so that it will become TSP in our traversal, we do not visit an already visited node we will skip them and will visit the next unvisited node. In this algorithm, we will reach the next node by as shorter path. (The sum of the length of all the edges of a polygon is always greater than a single edge.) Ultimately, we will get the TSP and its path length is not more than twice the optimal solution. Therefore, the proposed algorithm gives a good result.

Exercise

1. In the various path-finding algorithms, we have created a path array that just stores immediate parent of a node, print the complete path for it.

2. All the functions are implemented considering as if the graph is represented by adjacency list. Write all those functions for graph representation as adjacency matrix.

3. In a given start string, end string and a set of strings, find if there exists a path between the start string and end string via the set of strings.

   A path exists if we can get from start string to end the string by changing (no addition/removal) only one character at a time. The restriction is that the new string generated after changing one character has to be in the set.

   Start: "cog"
   End: "bad"
   Set: ["bag", "cag", "cat", "fag", "con", "rat", "sat", "fog"]
   One of the paths: "cog" -> "fog" -> "fag" -> "bag" -> "bad"

CHAPTER 13: STRING ALGORITHMS

Introduction

String in Javascript language is an array of character. We use string algorithm in so many tasks, when we are using some copy-paste, some string replacement, and some string search. When we are using some dictionary program, we are using string algorithms. When we are searching something in google, we are passing some information that is also a string and that will further convert and processed by google.

Note: This chapter is very important for the interview point of view as many interview problems are from this chapter.

String Matching

Every word processing program has a search function in which you can search all occurrences of any word in a long text file. For this, we need string-matching algorithms.

Problem: Search a pattern in given text. The pattern is of length m and the text is of length n. Where m < n.

Approach 1: Brute Force Search
The brute force search algorithm will check the pattern at all possible value of "i" in the text where the value of "i" ranges from 0 to n-m. The pattern is compared with the text, character by character from left to right. When a mismatch is detected, then pattern is compared by shifting the compare window by one character.

Example 13.1:
```
function BruteForceSearch(text, pattern) {
    if ((typeof text === 'string') && (typeof pattern === 'string')) {
        let i = 0;
        let j = 0;
        const n = text.length;
        const m = pattern.length;
        while (i <= n - m) {
            j = 0;
            while (j < m && pattern[j] === text[i + j]) {
                j++;
            };
            if (j === m) {
                return (i);
            }
            i++;
        };
        return -1;
    }
    else
```

```
            throw new Error('invalid arguments');
};

/* Testing Code */
const st1 = "hello, world!";
const st2 = "world";
console.log(`Using BruteForceSearch pattern found at index : $
{BruteForceSearch(st1, st2)}`);
```

Output:
```
Using BruteForceSearch pattern found at index : 7
```

Worst case time complexity of the algorithm is O(m*n), we get the pattern at the end of the text or we do not get the pattern at all.

Approach 2: Robin-Karp algorithm

Robin-Karp algorithm is somewhat like the brute force algorithm in which the pattern is compared to each portion of the text of length m. Instead of comparing pattern, character by character its hash code is compared. The hash code of the pattern is compared with the hash code of the text window. We try to keep the hash code as unique as possible. So that when hash code matches then the text should also match.

The two features of good hash code are:
- The collision should be excluded as much as possible. A collision occurs when hash code matches, but the pattern does not.
- The hash code of text must be calculated in constant time.

In this algorithm, hash code of some window is calculated from hash code of previous window in constant time. In the start, hash value of text of length m is calculated. We compare its hash code with the hash code of pattern string. To get hash code of next window we exclude one character and include next character. The portion of text that need to be compared moves as a window of characters. For each window calculation of hash is done in constant time, one member leaves the window and a new number enters the window.

Multiplication by 2 is same as left shift operation. Multiplication by 2^{m-1} is same as left shift m-1 times. If the pattern is "m" character long. Then when we want to remove the left most character from hash, we will subtract its ASCII value multiplied by 2^{m-1}. We shift the whole hash calculation by multiplying it by 2. Finally, the hash value of the new window is calculated by adding the ASCII value of right most element of this window.

We do not want to do large multiplication operations so modular operation with a prime number is used.

Example 13.2:
```
function RobinKarp(text, pattern) {
    if ((typeof text === 'string') && (typeof pattern === 'string')) {
        return RobinKarpUtil(text, pattern);
    } else
        throw new Error('invalid overload');
};
```

```
function RobinKarpUtil(text, pattern) {
    const n = text.length;
    const m = pattern.length;
    let i;
    let j;
    const prime = 101;
    let powm = 1;
    let TextHash = 0;
    let PatternHash = 0;
    if (m === 0 || m > n) {
        return -1;
    }
    for (i = 0; i < m - 1; i++) {
        powm = (powm << 1) % prime;
    }
    for (i = 0; i < m; i++) {
        PatternHash = ((PatternHash << 1) + (pattern[i]).charCodeAt(0)) %
prime;
        TextHash = ((TextHash << 1) + (text[i]).charCodeAt(0)) % prime;
    }
    for (i = 0; i <= (n - m); i++) {
        if (TextHash === PatternHash) {
            for (j = 0; j < m; j++) {
                if (text[i + j] !== pattern[j]) {
                    break;
                }
            }
            if (j === m)
                return i;
        }
        TextHash = (((TextHash - (text[i]).charCodeAt(0) * powm) << 1) +
(text[i + m]).charCodeAt(0))
            % prime;
        if (TextHash < 0) {
            TextHash = (TextHash + prime);
        }
    }
    return -1;
};

/* Testing code */
const st1 = "hello, world!";
const st2 = "world";
console.log(`Using RobinKarp pattern found at index : ${RobinKarp(st1,
st2)}`);
```

Output:
```
Using RobinKarp pattern found at index : 7
```

Worst case time complexity of the algorithm is O(n).

Approach 3: Knuth-Morris-Pratt algorithm

There is an inefficiency in the brute force method of string matching. After a shift of the pattern, the brute force algorithm forgotten all the information about the previous matched symbols. This is because of which its worst-case time complexity is O(mn).

The Knuth-Morris-Pratt algorithm makes use of this information that is computed in the previous comparison. It never re compares the whole text. It uses preprocessing of the pattern. The preprocessing takes O(m) time and whole algorithm is O(n) In Preprocessing step, we try to find the border of the pattern at a different prefix of the pattern.

A **prefix** is a string that comes at the beginning of a string.
A **proper prefix** is a prefix that is not the complete string. Its length is less than the length of the string.
A **suffix** is a string that comes at the end of a string.
A **proper suffix** is a suffix that is not a complete string. Its length is less than the length of the string.
A **border** is a string that is both proper prefix and a proper suffix.

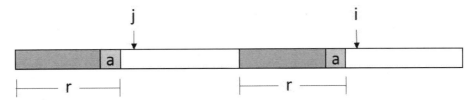

Example 13.3:

```
function KMPPreprocess(pattern, ShiftArr) {
    const m = pattern.length;
    let i = 0;
    let j = -1;
    ShiftArr[i] = -1;
    while (i < m) {
        while (j >= 0 && pattern[i] !== pattern[j]) {
            j = ShiftArr[j];
        };
        i++;
        j++;
        ShiftArr[i] = j;
    };
};
```

We must loop outer loop for the text and inner loop for the pattern when we have matched the text and pattern mismatch, we shift the text such that the widest border is considered and then the rest of the pattern matching is resumed after this shift. If again a mismatch happens then the next mismatch is taken.

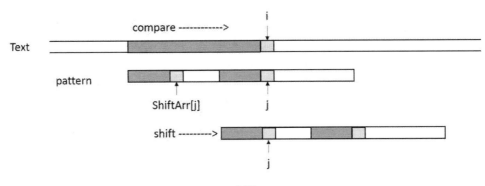

Example 13.4:

```
function KMP(text, pattern) {
    if ((typeof text === 'string') && (typeof pattern === 'string')) {
        return KMPUtil(text, pattern);
    } else
        throw new Error('invalid overload');
};

function KMPUtil(text, pattern) {
    let i = 0;
    let j = 0;
    const n = text.length;
    const m = pattern.length;
    const ShiftArr = new Array(m + 1);
    KMPPreprocess(pattern, ShiftArr);
    while (i < n) {
        while (j >= 0 && text[i] !== pattern[j])
            j = ShiftArr[j];
        i++;
        j++;
        if (j === m) {
            return (i - m);
        }
    };
    return -1;
}

/* Testing code */
const st1 = "hello, world!";
const st2 = "world";
console.log(`Using KMP pattern found at index : ${KMP(st1, st2)}`);
```

Output:

```
Using KMP pattern found at index : 7
```

Problem: Use the same KMP algorithm to find the number of occurrences of the pattern in a text.

Example 13.5:

```
function KMPFindCount(text, pattern) {
    let i = 0;
    let j = 0;
    let count = 0;
    const n = text.length;
    const m = pattern.length;
    const ShiftArr = new Array(m + 1);
    KMPPreprocess(pattern, ShiftArr);
    while (i < n) {
        while (j >= 0 && text[i] !== pattern[j]) {
            j = ShiftArr[j];
        };
```

```
            i++;
            j++;
            if (j === m) {
                count++;
                j = ShiftArr[j];
            }
        };
        return count;
};


/* Testing Code */
const str3 - "Only time will tell if we stand the test of time"
console.log('Frequency of "time" is', KMPFindCount(str3, "time"))
```

Output:
```
Frequency of "time" is 2
```

Dictionary / Symbol Table

A symbol table is a mapping between a string(key) and a value that can be of any type. A value can be an integer such as occurrence count, dictionary meaning of a word and so on. Dictionary can be implemented in various ways. We will be studying Binary Search Tree of strings, Hash-Table, Tries and Ternary Search Tree.

Binary Search Tree (BST) for Strings

Binary Search Tree (BST) is the simplest way to implement symbol table. Simple strcmp() function can be used to compare two strings. If all the keys are random and the tree is balanced, then on an average key lookup can be done in O(logn) time.

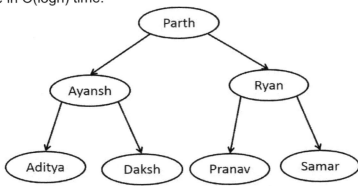

Binary Search Tree as Dictionary

Below is an implementation of binary search tree to store string as key. This will keep track of the occurrence count of words in a text.

Example 13.6:
```
class StringTreeNode {
    constructor() {
        this.count = 0;
```

```
            this.lChild = null;
            this.rChild = null;
        }
}

class StringTree {
    constructor() {
        this.root = null;
    }

    print() {
        this.printUtil(this.root);
    }

    printUtil(curr) {
        if (curr != null) {
            console.log(` value is ::${curr.value}`);
            console.log(` count is :: ${curr.count}`);
            this.printUtil(curr.lChild);
            this.printUtil(curr.rChild);
        }
    }

    insert(value) {
        this.root = this.insertUtil(value, this.root);
    }

    insertUtil(value, curr) {
        let compare;
        if (curr == null) {
            curr = new StringTreeNode(this);
            curr.value = value;
            curr.lChild = curr.rChild = null;
            curr.count = 1;
        }
        else {
            compare = curr.value.localeCompare(value);
            if (compare === 0)
                curr.count++;
            else if (compare === 1)
                curr.lChild = this.insertUtil(value, curr.lChild);
            else
                curr.rChild = this.insertUtil(value, curr.rChild);
        }
        return curr;
    }

    freeTree() {
        this.root = null;
    }
```

```
    find(value) {
        const ret = this.findUtil(this.root, value);
        return ret;
    }

    findUtil(curr, value) {
        let compare;
        if (curr == null)
            return false;

        compare = curr.value.localeCompare(value);
        if (compare === 0)
            return true;
        else {
            if (compare === 1)
                return this.findUtil(curr.lChild, value);
            else
                return this.findUtil(curr.rChild, value);
        }
    }

    frequency(value) {
        return this.frequencyUtil(this.root, value);
    }

    frequencyUtil(curr, value) {
        let compare;
        if (curr == null)
            return 0;

        compare = curr.value.localeCompare(value);
        if (compare === 0)
            return curr.count;
        else {
            if (compare > 0)
                return this.frequencyUtil(curr.lChild, value);
            else
                return this.frequencyUtil(curr.rChild, value);
        }
    }
}

/* Testing Code */
const tt = new StringTree();
tt.insert("banana");
tt.insert("apple");
tt.insert("mango");
console.log("Apple Found :", tt.find("apple"));
console.log("Grapes Found :", tt.find("grapes"));
console.log("Banana Found :", tt.find("banana"));
```

Output:
```
Apple Found : true
Grapes Found : false
Banana Found : true
```

Hash-Table

The Hash-Table is another data structure that can be used for symbol table implementation. Below Hash-Table diagram, we can see the name of that person is taken as key, and their meaning is the value of the search. The first key is converted into a hash code by passing it to appropriate hash function. Inside hash function the size of Hash-Table is also passed, which is used to find the actual index where values will be stored. Finally, the value, which is the meaning of name, is stored in the Hash-Table, or you can store a reference to the string which stores meaning is stored into the Hash-Table.

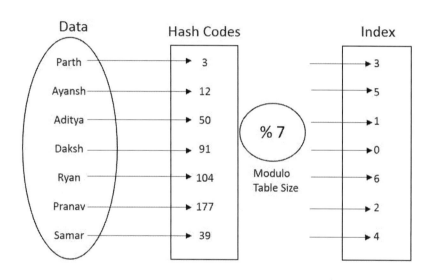

Hash-Table has an excellent lookup of O(1).

Let us suppose we want to implement autocomplete the box feature of Google search. When you type some string to search in google search, it proposes some complete string even before you have done typing. BST cannot solve this problem as related strings can be in both right and left subtree.

The Hash-Table is also not suited for this job. One cannot perform a partial match or range query on a Hash-Table. Hash function transforms string to a number. Moreover, a good hash function will give a distributed hash code even for partial string and there is no way to relate two strings in a Hash-Table. Trie and Ternary Search tree are a special kind of tree that solves partial match and range query problem efficiently.

Trie

Trie is a tree, in which we store only one character at each node. The final key value pair is stored in the leaves. Each node has R children, one for each possible character. For simplicity purpose, let us consider that the character set is 26, corresponds to different characters of English alphabets.

Trie is an efficient data structure. Using Trie, we can search the key in O(M) time. Where M is the maximum string length. Trie is also suitable for solving partial match and range query problems.

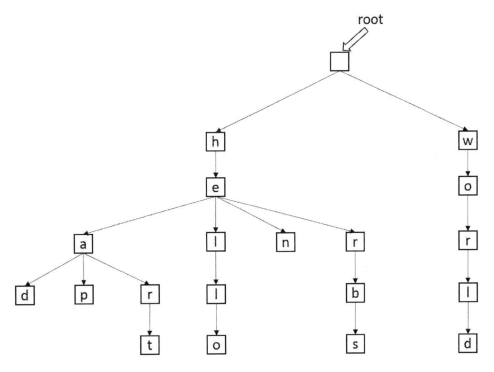

TRIE DICTIONARY

Example 13.7:

```
class TrieNode {
    constructor(c) {
        this.child = new Array(Trie.CharCount).fill(null);
        this.isLastChar = false;
        this.ch = c;
    }
}

class Trie {
    constructor() {
        Trie.CharCount = 26;
        this.root = new TrieNode(' ');
    }

    Insert(str) {
        if (str == null) {
            return this.root;
        }
        const temp = str.toString().toLowerCase();
        return this.InsertUtil(this.root, temp, 0);
    }
```

```
    InsertUtil(curr, str, index) {
        if (curr == null) {
            curr = new TrieNode(this, str[index - 1]);
        }
        if (str.length === index) {
            curr.isLastChar = true;
        }
        else {
            curr.child[str[index].charCodeAt(0) - 'a'.charCodeAt(0)] =
this.InsertUtil(curr.child[str[index].charCodeAt(0) - 'a'.charCodeAt(0)],
str, index + 1);
        }
        return curr;
    }

    Remove(str) {
        if (str == null) {
            return;
        }
        str = str.toLowerCase();
        this.RemoveUtil(this.root, str, 0);
    }

    RemoveUtil(curr, str, index) {
        if (curr == null) {
            return;
        }
        if (str.length === index) {
            if (curr.isLastChar) {
                curr.isLastChar = false;
            }
            return;
        }
        this.RemoveUtil(curr.child[str[index].charCodeAt(0) -
'a'.charCodeAt(0)], str, index + 1);
    }

    Find(str) {
        if (str == null) {
            return false;
        }
        str = str.toLowerCase();
        return this.FindUtil(this.root, str, 0);
    }

    FindUtil(curr, str, index) {
        if (curr == null) {
            return false;
        }
        if (str.length === index) {
```

```
            return curr.isLastChar;
        }
        return this.FindUtil(curr.child[str[index].charCodeAt(0) -
'a'.charCodeAt(0)], str, index + 1);
    }
}

/* Testing Code */
const t = new Trie();
t.Insert("apple")
t.Insert("tree")

console.log(t.Find("apple"));
console.log(t.Find("appletree"));
console.log(t.Find("app"));
console.log(t.Find("tree"));
```

Output:
```
true
false
false
true
```

Ternary Search Trie/ Ternary Search Tree

Tries have a very good search performance of O(M) where M is the maximum size of the search string. However, tries have a very high space requirement. In every node, Trie contains pointers to multiple nodes which are pointer corresponds to possible characters of the key. To avoid this high space requirement Ternary Search Trie (TST) is used.

A TST avoids heavy space requirement of traditional Trie, keeping many of its advantages. In a TST, each node contains a character, an end of key indicator and three pointers. The three pointers are corresponding to current char hold by the node(equal), characters less than and character greater than.

Time Complexity of ternary search tree operation is proportional to the height of the ternary search tree. In the worst case, we need to traverse up to 3 times the length of largest string. However, this case is rare. Therefore, TST is a very good solution for implementing Symbol Table, Partial match and range query.

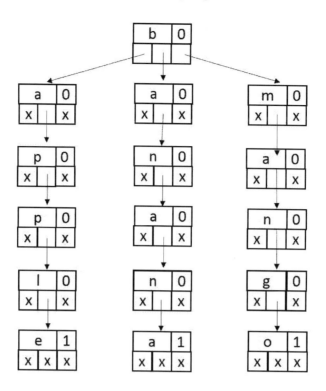

Ternary Search Tree

Example 13.8:

```
class TSTNode {
    constructor(d) {
        this.data = d;
        this.isLastChar = false;
        this.left = this.equal = this.right = null;
    }
}

class TST {
    constructor() {
        this.root = null;
    }

    insert(word) {
        this.root = this.insertUtil(this.root, word, 0);
    }

    insertUtil(curr, word, wordIndex) {
        if (curr == null)
            curr = new TSTNode(word.charAt(wordIndex));

        if ((word.charAt(wordIndex)).charCodeAt(0) <
(curr.data).toString().charCodeAt(0))
            curr.left = this.insertUtil(curr.left, word, wordIndex);
        else if ((word.charAt(wordIndex)).charCodeAt(0) >
(curr.data).toString().charCodeAt(0))
            curr.right = this.insertUtil(curr.right, word, wordIndex);
```

```
        else {
            if (wordIndex < word.length - 1)
                curr.equal = this.insertUtil(curr.equal, word, wordIndex +
1);
            else
                curr.isLastChar = true;
        }
        return curr;
    }

    findUtil(curr, word, wordIndex) {
        if (curr == null)
            return false;
        if ((word.charAt(wordIndex)).charCodeAt(0) <
(curr.data).toString().charCodeAt(0))
            return this.findUtil(curr.left, word, wordIndex);
        else if ((word.charAt(wordIndex)).charCodeAt(0) >
(curr.data).toString().charCodeAt(0))
            return this.findUtil(curr.right, word, wordIndex);
        else {
            if (wordIndex === word.length - 1)
                return curr.isLastChar;
            return this.findUtil(curr.equal, word, wordIndex + 1);
        }
    }

    find(word) {
        const ret = this.findUtil(this.root, word, 0);
        return ret;
    }
}

/* Testing Code */
const tt = new TST();
tt.insert("banana");
tt.insert("apple");
tt.insert("mango");

console.log("Apple Found :", tt.find("apple"));
console.log("Banana Found :", tt.find("banana"));
console.log("Mango Found :", tt.find("mango"));
console.log("Grapes Found :", tt.find("grapes"));
```

Output:

```
Apple Found : true
Banana Found : true
Mango Found : true
Grapes Found : false
```

Problems in String

Regular Expression Matching

Problem: Implement regular expression matching with the support of '?' and '*' special character.
'?' Matches any single character.
'*' Matches zero or more of the preceding elements.

Example 13.9:

```
unction matchExpUtil(exp, str, i, j) {
    if (i === exp.length && j === str.length) {
        return true;
    }
    if ((i === exp.length && j !== str.length) ||
        (i !== exp.length && j === str.length)) {
        return false;
    }
    if (exp[i] === '?' || exp[i] === str[j]) {
        return matchExpUtil(exp, str, i + 1, j + 1);
    }
    if (exp[i] === '*') {
        return matchExpUtil(exp, str, i + 1, j)
            || matchExpUtil(exp, str, i, j + 1)
            || matchExpUtil(exp, str, i + 1, j + 1);
    }
    return false;
};

function matchExp(exp, str) {
    return matchExpUtil(exp, str, 0, 0);
};

function test() {
    console.log(matchExp("hello*", "helloworld"));
    console.log(matchExp("hello?d", "hellowd"));
    console.log(matchExp("hello*hemant", "helloworldfsdfsdfdsfhemant"));
    console.log(matchExp("*hemantj", "helloworldfsdfsdfdsfhemant"));
};
```

Output:

```
true
true
true
false
```

Time complexity: O(n), where n is length of text string.

Order Matching

Problem: In given long text string and a pattern string, find if the characters of pattern string are in the same order in text string. E.g.Text String: ABCDEFGHIJKLMNOPQRSTUVWXYZ Patternstring: JOST

Example 13.10:

```
function match(source, pattern) {
    let iSource = 0;
    let iPattern = 0;
    const sourceLen = source.length;
    const patternLen = pattern.length;
    for (iSource = 0; iSource < sourceLen; iSource++) {
        if (source[iSource] === pattern[iPattern]) {
            iPattern++;
        }
        if (iPattern === patternLen) {
            return true;
        }
    }
    return false;
};

function test() {
    console.log(match("hellofskdlfjsdlfjsldjflksdworld", "helloworld"));
    console.log(match("hellod", "hellowd"));
    console.log(match("hello*xxxxxxxxxhemantxxxxxxxxxxxx", "hellnt"));
    console.log()
};
```

Output:

```
true
false
true
```

Time complexity: O(n), where n is length of text string.

Unique Characters

Problem: Write a function that will take a string as input and return true if it contains all unique characters, else return false.

Example 13.11:

```
function isUniqueChar(str) {
    const bitarr = new Array(26).fill(0);
    let index;
    var size = str.length;
    const small = "a".charCodeAt(0);
    const big = "A".charCodeAt(0);
```

```
    var size = str.length;
    for (let i = 0; i < size; i++) {
        let c = str.charCodeAt(i);
        if ((big <= c) && (big + 26 >= c)) {
            c = (c - big);
        } else if ((small <= c) && (small + 26 >= c)) {
            c = (c - small);
        } else {
            console.log("Unknown Char.");
            return false;
        }
        if (bitarr[c] !== 0) {
            console.log("Duplicate detected.");
            return false;
        }
        bitarr[c] = 1;
    }
    console.log("No duplicate detected.");
    return true;
};

function test() {
    isUniqueChar("aple");
    isUniqueChar("apple");
};
```

Output:
```
No duplicate detected.
Duplicate detected.
```

Time complexity: O(n), where n is number of characters in input text.

Permutation Check

Problem: Write a function to check if two strings are permutation of each other.

Example 13.12:
```
function isPermutation(s1, s2) {
    const count = new Array(256).fill(0);
    const length = s1.length;
    if (s2.length !== length) {
        return false;
    }

    for (var i = 0; i < length; i++) {
        count[s1.charCodeAt(i)]++;
        count[s2.charCodeAt(i)]--;
    }

    for (var i = 0; i < length; i++) {
```

```
            if (count[s1.charCodeAt(i)] !== 0) {
                return false;
            }
        }

        return true;
};

function test() {
    console.info("isPermutation :", isPermutation("apple", "plepa"));
    console.info("isPermutation :", isPermutation("appleb", "plepaa"));
};
```

Output:
```
isPermutation : true
isPermutation : false
```

Time complexity: O(n), where n is number of characters in text.

Palindrome Check

Problem: Find if the string is a palindrome or not

Example 13.13:
```
function isPalindrome(str) {
    let i = 0;
    let j = str.length - 1;
    while ((i < j) && (str[i] == str[j])) {
        i++;
        j--;
    }

    if (i < j) {
        console.info(str, "is not a Palindrome");
        return false;
    }
    else {
        console.info(str, "is a Palindrome");
        return true;
    }
};

function test() {
    isPalindrome("hello");
    isPalindrome("eoloe");
};
```

Output:
```
hello is not a Palindrome
eoloe is a Palindrome
```

Time Complexity is **O(n)** and Space Complexity is **O(1)**

Power function

Problem: Write a function which will calculate x^n, Taking x and n as argument.

Example 13.14:
```
function pow(x, n) {
    let value;
    if (n === 0) {
        return (1);
    }
    else if (n % 2 === 0) {
        value = pow(x, Math.floor(n / 2));
        return (value * value);
    }
    else {
        value = pow(x, Math.floor(n / 2));
        return (x * value * value);
    }
};

function test() {
    console.info(pow(5, 2));
};
```

Output:
25

Time complexity: O(logN), where N is exponent in the desired value.

String Compare function

Problem: Write a function strcmp() to compare two strings. The function return values should be:
   a) The return value is 0 indicates that both first and second strings are equal.
   b) The return value is negative it indicates that the first string is less than the second string.
   c) The return value is positive it indicates that the first string is greater than the second string.

Example 13.15:
```
function myStrcmp(a, b) {
    let index = 0;
    const len1 = a.length;
    const len2 = b.length;
    let minlen = len1;

    if (len1 > len2) {
        minlen = len2;
    }
```

```
    while ((index < minlen) && (a[index] === b[index])) {
        index++;
    }
    if (index === len1 && index === len2) {
        return 0;
    }
    else if (len1 === index) {
        return -1;
    }
    else if (len2 === index) {
        return 1;
    }
    else {
        return (a.charCodeAt(index) - b.charCodeAt(index));
    }
};

function test() {
    console.info("StrCmp returns :", myStrcmp("aba", "aas"));
};
```

Output:
```
StrCmp returns : 1
```

Time complexity: O(n), where n is length of smaller string.

Reverse String

Problem: Reverse all the characters of a string.

Example 13.16:
```
function reverseString(str) {
    const a = (str).split('');
    reverseStringUtil(a);
    const expn = a.join('');
    return expn;
};

function reverseStringUtil(a) {
    let lower = 0;
    let upper = a.length - 1;
    let tempChar;

    while (lower < upper) {
        tempChar = a[lower];
        a[lower] = a[upper];
        a[upper] = tempChar;
        lower++;
        upper--;
    }
```

```
};

function test() {
    console.info(reverseString("apple"));
};
```

Output:
```
elppa
```

Time complexity: O(n), where n is number of characters in input string.

Reverse Words

Problem: Reverse order of words in a sentence.

Example 13.17:
```
function reverseStringUtil2(a, lower, upper) {
    let tempChar;

    while (lower < upper) {
        tempChar = a[lower];
        a[lower] = a[upper];
        a[upper] = tempChar;
        lower++;
        upper--;
    }
};

function reverseWords(str) {
    const a = str.split("");
    const length = a.length;
    let lower;
    let upper = -1;
    lower = 0;
    for (let i = 0; i <= length; i++) {
        if (a[i] === ' ') {
            reverseStringUtil2(a, lower, upper);
            lower = i + 1;
            upper = i;
        } else {
            upper++;
        }
    }
    reverseStringUtil2(a, lower, upper - 1);
    reverseStringUtil2(a, 0, length - 1);
    return a.join("");
};

function test() {
    console.info(reverseWords("hello world"));
```

```
};
```

Output:
```
world hello
```

Time complexity: O(n), where n is number of characters in input string.

Print Anagram

Problem: Given a string as character list, print all the anagram of the string.

Example 13.18:
```
function printAnagramUtil(a, max, n) {
    if (max === 1) {
        console.info(a.join(""));
    }
    let temp;
    for (let i = -1; i < max - 1; i++) {
        if (i !== -1) {
            temp = a[i];
            a[i] = a[max - 1];
            a[max - 1] = temp;
        }
        printAnagramUtil(a, max - 1, n);
        if (i !== -1) {
            temp = a[i];
            a[i] = a[max - 1];
            a[max - 1] = temp;
        }
    }
};

function test() {
    printAnagram("123");
};
```

Output:
```
123
213
321
231
132
312
```

Time complexity: O(n!), where n is number of characters in input string.

Shuffle String

Problem: Write a program to convert list ABCDE12345 to A1B2C3D4E5.

Example 13.19:

```javascript
function shuffle(str) {
    const ar = str.split('');
    const n = Math.floor(ar.length / 2);
    let count = 0;
    let k = 1;
    let temp;
    let temp2;
    for (let i = 1; i < n; i = i + 2) {
        temp = ar[i];
        k = i;
        do {
            k = (2 * k) % (2 * n - 1);
            temp2 = temp;
            temp = ar[k];
            ar[k] = temp2;
            count++;
        } while (i !== k);

        if (count === (2 * n - 2)) {
            break;
        }
    }
    return ar.join("")
};

function test() {
    console.log(shuffle("ABCDE12345"));
};
```

Output:

A1B2C3D4E5

Time complexity: $O(n^2)$, where n is number of characters in input string.

Exercise

1. In given string, find the longest substring without reputed characters.

2. The function memset() copies ch into the first 'n' characters of the string

3. Serialize a collection of string into a single string and de serializes the string into that collection of strings.

4. Write a smart input function, which takes 20 characters as input from the user. Without cutting some word.
   User input: "Harry Potter must not go"
   First 20 chars: "Harry Potter must no"
   Smart input: "Harry Potter must"

5. Write a code that find if a string is palindrome and it should return true for below inputs too.
   Stella won no wallets.
   No, it is open on one position.
   Rise to vote, Sir.
   Won't lovers revolt now?

6. Write an ASCII to integer function, which ignore the non-integral character and give the integer. For Example , if the input is "12AS5" it should return 125.

7. Write code that would parse a Bash brace expansion.
   Example : the expression "(a, b, c) d, e" and would give output all the possible strings: ad, bd, cd, e

8. In given string write a function to return the length of the longest substring with only unique characters

9. Replace all occurrences of "a" with "the"

10. Replace all occurrences of %20 with ' '.
    E.g. Input: www.Hello%20World.com
    Output: www.Hello World.com

11. Write an expansion function that will take an input string like "1..5,8,11..14,18,20,26..30" and will print "1,2,3,4,5,8,11,12,13,14,18,20,26,27,28,29,30"

12. Suppose you have a string like "Thisisasentence". Write a function that would separate these words. Moreover, will print whole sentence with spaces.

13. In given three string str1, str2 and str3. Write a complement function to find the smallest sub-sequence in str1 which contains all the characters in str2 and but not those in str3.

14. In given two strings A and B, find whether any anagram of string A is a sub string of string B.
    For eg: IfA = xyz and B = afdgzyxksldfm then the program should return true.

15. In given string, find whether it contains any permutation of another string. For Example , given "abcdefgh" and "ba", the function should return true, because "abcdefgh" has substring "ab", which is a permutation of the given string "ba".

16. In give algorithm which removes the occurrence of "a" by "bc" from a string? The algorithm must be in-place.

17. In given string "1010101010" in base2 convert it into string with base4. Do not use an extra space.

18. In Binary Search tree to store strings, delete() function is not implemented, implement it.

19. If you implement delete() function, then you need to make changes in find() function. Do the needful.

CHAPTER 14: ALGORITHM DESIGN TECHNIQUES

Introduction

In real life, when we are asked to do some work, we try to correlate it with our experience and then try to solve it. Similarly, when we get a new problem to solve. We first try to find the similarity of the current problem with some problems for which we already know the solution. Then solve the current problem and get our desired result.

This method provides following benefits:
1) It provides a template for solving a wide range of problems.
2) It provides us an idea of the suitable data structure for the problem.
3) It helps us in analysing space and Time Complexity of algorithms.

In the previous chapters, we have used various algorithms to solve different kind of problems. In this chapter, we will read about various techniques of solving algorithmic problems.

Various Algorithm design techniques are:
1) Brute Force
2) Greedy Algorithms
3) Divide-and-Conquer, Decrease-and-Conquer
4) Dynamic Programming
5) Reduction / Transform-and-Conquer
6) Backtracking and Branch-and-Bound

Brute Force Algorithm

Brute Force is a straightforward approach of solving a problem based on the problem statement. It is one of the easiest approaches to solve a problem. It is useful for solving small size dataset problem.

Some Examples of brute force algorithms are:
- Bubble-Sort
- Selection-Sort
- Sequential search in an array
- Computing pow(a, n) by multiplying a, n times.
- Convex hull problem
- String matching
- Exhaustive search: Travelling salesman, Knapsack, and Assignment problems

Greedy Algorithm

Greedy algorithms are generally used to solve optimization problems. In greedy algorithm, solution is constructed through a sequence of steps. At each step, choice is made which is locally optimal.

Note: Greedy algorithms does not always give optimum solution.

Some Examples of greedy algorithms are:
- Minimal spanning tree: Prim's algorithm, Kruskal's algorithm
- Dijkstra's algorithm for single-source shortest path problem
- Greedy algorithm for the Knapsack problem
- The coin exchange problem
- Huffman trees for optimal encoding

Divide-and-Conquer, Decrease-and-Conquer

Divide-and-Conquer algorithms involve basic three steps. First, split the problem into several smaller sub-probloms. Second, solve each sub-problem. Finally, combine the sub-problems results to produce the desired result.

In divide-and-conquer the size of the problem is reduced by a factor (half, one-third, etc.), While in decrease-and-conquer the size of the problem is reduced by a constant.

Examples of divide-and-conquer algorithms:
- Merge-Sort algorithm (using recursion)
- Quicksort algorithm (using recursion)
- Computing the length of the longest path in a binary tree (using recursion)
- Computing Fibonacci numbers (using recursion)
- Quick-hull

Examples of decrease-and-conquer algorithms:
- Computing pow(a, n) by calculating pow(a, n/2) using recursion.
- Binary search in a sorted list (using recursion)
- Searching in BST
- Insertion-Sort
- Graph traversal algorithms (DFS and BFS)
- Topological sort
- Warshall's algorithm (using recursion)
- Permutations (Minimal change approach, Johnson-Trotter algorithm)
- Computing a median, Topological sorting, Fake-coin problem (Ternary search)

Consider the problem of exponentiation Compute x^n

Brute Force:	n-1 multiplications
Divide and conquer:	$T(n) = 2*T(n/2) + 1 = n-1$
Decrease by one:	$T(n) = T(n-1) + 1 = n-1$
Decrease by constant factor:	$T(n) = T(n/a) + a-1$ $= (a-1) n$ $= n$ when $a = 2$

Dynamic Programming

While solving problems using Divide-and-Conquer method, there may be a case when recursively sub-problems can result in the same computation being performed multiple times. This problem arises when there are identical sub-problems arise repeatedly in a recursion.

Dynamic programming is used to avoid the requirement of repeated calculation of same sub-problem. In this method, we usually store the result of sub - problems in a table and refer that table to find if we have already calculated the solution of sub - problems before calculating it again.

Dynamic programming is a bottom up technique in which the smaller sub-problems are solved first and the result of these are sued to find the solution of the larger sub-problems.

Examples:
- Fibonacci numbers computed by iteration.
- Warshall's algorithm for transitive closure implemented by iterations
- Floyd's algorithms for all-pairs shortest paths

```
function fibonacci2 (n) {
  let first = 0;
  let second = 1;
  let temp = 0;

  if (n === 0)
    return first
  else if (n === 1)
    return second

  let i = 2;
  while (i <= n) {
    temp = first + second
    first = second
    second = temp
    i += 1
  }
  return temp
}

function test () {
  console.log(fibonacci2(5))
}
```

Output

5

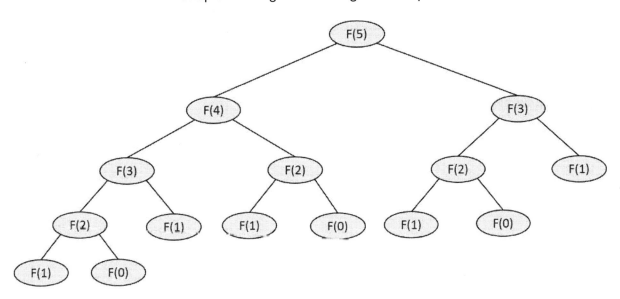

Using divide and conquer the same sub problem is solved again and again, which reduce the performance of the algorithm. This algorithm has an exponential Time Complexity and linear Space Complexity.

```
function fibonacci (n) {
  if (n <= 1) {
    return n
  }
  return fibonacci(n - 1) + fibonacci(n - 2)
}
```

Using this algorithm, we will get Fibonacci in linear Time Complexity and constant Space Complexity.

Reduction / Transform-and-Conquer

These methods work as a two-stage procedure. First, the problem is transformed into a known problem for which we know optimal solution. In the second stage, the problem is solved.

The most common type of transformation is sorting of an array. For Example , in given list of numbers finds the two closest number.

Brute-force solution, we will find distance between each element in the array and will keep the minimum distance pair. In this approach, total time complexity is **O(n²)**

Transform and conquer solution, we will first sort the array in **O(nlogn)** time and then find the closest number by scanning the array in another single pass with time complexity **O(n)**. Thus, the total time complexity is **O(nlogn)**.

Examples:
- Gaussian elimination
- Heaps and Heapsort

Backtracking

In real life, let us suppose someone has given you a lock with a number (three-digit lock, number range from 1 to 9). Moreover, you do not have the exact password key for the lock. You need to test every combination until you got the right one. Obviously, you need to test starting from something like "111", then "112" and so on. You will get your key before you reach "999". Therefore, what you are doing is backtracking.

Suppose the lock produces some sound "click" if correct digit is selected for any level. If we can listen to this sound such intelligence/ heuristics will help you to reach your goal much faster. These functions are called Pruning function or bounding functions.

Backtracking is a method by which solution is found by exhaustively searching through large but finite number of states, with some pruning or bounding function, we can narrow down our search.

For all the problems (like NP hard problems) for which there does not exist any other efficient algorithm we use backtracking algorithm.

Backtracking problems have the following components:
1. Initial state
2. Target / Goal state
3. Intermediate states
4. Path from the initial state to the target / goal state
5. Operators to get from one state to another
6. Pruning function (optional)

The solving process of backtracking algorithm starts with the construction of state's tree, whose nodes represents the states. The root node is the initial state and one or more leaf node will be our target state. Each edge of the tree represents some operation. The solution is obtained by searching the tree until a Target state is found.

Backtracking uses depth-first search:
1) Store the initial state in a stack
2) While the stack is not empty, repeat:
3) Read a node from the stack.
4) While there are available operators, do:
   a. Apply an operator to generate a child
   b. If the child is a goal state, return solution
   c. If it is a new state and pruning function does not discard it, then push the child into the stack.

There are three monks and three demons at one side of a river. We want to move all of them to the other side using a small boat. The boat can carry only two persons at a time. Given if on any shore the number of demons will be more than monks then they will eat the monks. How can we move all these people to the other side of the river safely?

Same as the above problem there is a farmer who has a goat, a cabbage and a wolf. If the farmer leaves, goat with cabbage, goat will eat the cabbage. If the farmer leaves wolf alone with goat, wolf will kill the goat. How can the farmer move all his belongings to the other side of the river?

You are given two jugs, a 4-gallon one and a 3-gallon one. There are no measuring markers on jugs. A tap can be used to fill the jugs with water. How can you get 2 gallons of water in the 4-gallon jug?

Branch-and-bound

Branch and bound method is used when we can evaluate cost of visiting each node by a utility function. At each step, we choose the node with the lowest cost to proceed further. Branch-and bound algorithms are implemented using a priority queue. In branch and bound, we traverse the nodes in breadth-first manner.

A* Algorithm

A* is a sort of an elaboration on branch-and-bound. In branch-and-bound, at each iteration we expand the shortest path that we have found so far. In A*, instead of just picking the path with the shortest length so far, we pick the path with the shortest estimated total length from start to goal, where the total length is estimated as length traversed so far plus a heuristic estimate of the remaining distance from the goal.

Branch-and-bound will always find an optimal solution, which is the shortest path. A* will always find an optimal solution if the heuristic is correct. Choosing a good heuristic is the most important part of A* algorithm.

Conclusion

Usually a given problem can be solved using several methods; however, it is not wise to settle for the first method that comes to our mind. Some methods result in a much more efficient solution than others do.

For Example , the Fibonacci numbers calculated recursively (decrease-and-conquer approach), and computed by iterations (dynamic programming). In the first case, the complexity is **O(2^n),** and in the other case, the complexity is **O(n)**.

Another Example , consider sorting based on the Insertion-Sort and basic bubble sort. For almost sorted files, Insertion-Sort will give almost linear complexity, while bubble sort sorting algorithms have quadratic complexity.

So, the most important question is how to choose the best method?
First, you should understand the problem statement.
Second by knowing various problems and their solutions.

CHAPTER 15: BRUTE FORCE ALGORITHM

Introduction

Brute Force is a straightforward approach of solving a problem based on the problem statement. It is one of the easiest approaches to solve a problem. It is useful for solving small size dataset problem.

Most of the cases there are other algorithm techniques can be used to get a better solution of the same problem.

Some Examples of brute force algorithms are:
- Bubble-Sort
- Selection-Sort
- Sequential search in an array
- Computing pow (a, n) by multiplying a, n times.
- Convex hull problem
- String matching
- Exhaustive search
- Travelling salesman
- Knapsack
- Assignment problems

Problems in Brute Force Algorithm

Bubble-Sort

In Bubble-Sort, adjacent elements of the array are compared and are exchanged if they are out of order.

```
// Sorts a given list by Bubble Sort
// Input: An array A of order able elements
// Output: List A[0..n - 1] sorted in ascending order

Algorithm BubbleSort(A[0..n - 1])
    sorted = false
    while !sorted do
        sorted = true
        for j = 0 to n - 2 do
            if A[j] > A[j + 1] then
                swap A[j] and A[j + 1]
                sorted = false
```

Time Complexity is $\Theta(n^2)$

Selection-Sort

The entire given list of N elements is traversed to find its smallest element and exchange it with the first element. Then, the array is traversed again to find the second element and exchange it with the second element. After N-1 passes, the array will be completely sorted.

```
//Sorts a given list by selection sort
//Input: An array A[0..n-1] of order able elements
//Output: List A[0..n-1] sorted in ascending order

Algorithm SelectionSort (A[0..n-1])
    for i = 0 to n - 2 do
        min = i
        for j = i + 1 to n - 1 do
            if A[j] < A[min]
                min = j
        swap A[i] and A[min]
```

Time Complexity is $\Theta(n^2)$

Sequential Search

The algorithm compares consecutive elements of a given list with a given search keyword until either a match is found or the array is exhausted.

```
Algorithm SequentialSearch (A[0..n], K)
    i = 0
    While A [i] ≠ K do
        i = i + 1
    if i < n
        return i
    else
        return -1
```

Worst case time complexity is $\Theta(n)$.

Computing pow (a, n)

Computing a^n (a > 0, and n is a non-negative integer) based on the definition of exponentiation. N-1 multiplications are required in brute force method.

```
// Input: A real number a and an integer n = 0
// Output: a power n

Algorithm Power(a, n)
    result = 1
    for i = 1 to n do
        result = result * a
    return result
```

The algorithm requires $\Theta(n)$

String matching

A brute force string matching algorithm takes two inputs, first text consists of n characters and a pattern consist of m character (m<=n). The algorithm starts by comparing the pattern with the beginning of the text. Each character of the pattern is compared to the corresponding character of the text. Comparison starts from left to right until all the characters are matched or a mismatch is found. The same process is repeated until a match is found. Each time the comparison starts from one position to the right.

```
//Input: An array T[0..n - 1] of n characters representing a text
// an array P[0..m - 1] of m characters representing a pattern
//Output: The position of the first character in the text that starts the
first
// matching substring if the search is successful and -1 otherwise.

Algorithm BruteForceStringMatch (T[0..n - 1], P[0..m - 1])
    for i = 0 to n - m do
    j = 0
    while j < m and P[j] = T[i + j] do
    j = j + 1
    if j = m then
        return i
    return -1
```

In the worst case, the algorithm is O(mn).

Closest-Pair Brute-Force Algorithm

The closest-pair problem is to find the two closest points in a set of n points in a 2-dimensional space. A brute force implementation of this problem computes the distance between each pair of distinct points and find the smallest distance pair.

```
// Finds two closest points by brute force
// Input: An array P of n >= 2 points
// Output: The closest pair

Algorithm BruteForceClosestPair(P)
    dmin = infinite
    for i = 1 to n - 1 do
        for j = i + 1 to n do
            d = (xi - xj)² + (yi - yj)²
            if d < dmin then
                dmin = d
                imin = i
                jmin = j
    return imin, jmin
```

Time Complexity is $\Theta(n^2)$

Convex-Hull Problem

Convex-hull of a set of points is the smallest convex polygon that contains all the points. All the points of the set will lie on the convex hull or inside the convex hull. The convex-hull of a set of points is a subset of points in the given sets.

How to find this subset?
Answer: Subset points are the boundary of the Convex Hull. We take any two consecutive points of the boundary, and the rest of the points of the set will lie on its one side.

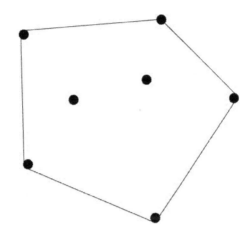

Two points (x1, y1), (x2, y2) make the line ax + by = c
Where a = y2-y1, b = x1-x2, and c = x1y2 - y1x2

And divides the plane by ax + by - c < 0 and ax + by - c > 0
So, we need to check ax + by - c for the rest of the points

If we find all the points in the set lies one side of the line with either all have ax + by - c < 0 or all the points have ax + by - c > 0 then we will add these points to the desired convex hull point set.

For each of n (n -1) /2 pairs of distinct points, one needs to find the sign of ax + by - c in each of the other n - 2 points.

The worst-case performance of the algorithm: $O(n^3)$

```
Algorithm ConvexHull
for i=0 to n-1
    for j=0 to n-1
    if (xi,yi) !=(xj,yj)
        draw a line from (xi,yi) to (xj,yj)
        for k=0 to n-1
        if(i!=k and j!=k)
            if ( all other points lie on the same side of the
                        line (xi,yi) and (xj,yj))
            then add (xi,yi) to (xj,yj) to the convex hull set
```

Exhaustive Search

Exhaustive search is a brute force approach applies to combinatorial problems.
In exhaustive search, we generate all the possible combinations. At each step, we try to find if the combinations satisfy the problem constraints. Either, we get a desired solution, which satisfy the problem constraint or there is no solution.

Examples of exhaustive search are:
- Travelling salesman problem
- Knapsack problem
- Assignment problem

Travelling Salesman Problem (TSP)

In the travelling salesman problem, we need to find the shortest tour through a given set of N cities that salesperson visits each city exactly once before returning to the city where he has started.

Alternatively, finding the shortest Hamiltonian circuit in a weighted connected graph. A cycle that passes through all the vertices of the graph exactly once.

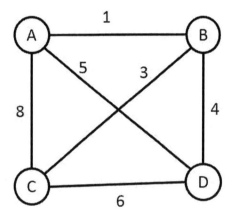

Tours where A is starting city:

Tour	Cost
A→B→C→D→A	1+3+6+5 = 15
A→B→D→C→A	1+4+6+8 = 19
A→C→B→D→A	8+3+4+5 = 20
A→C→D→B→A	8+6+4+1 = 19
A→D→B→C→A	5+4+3+8 = 20
A→D→C→B→A	5+6+3+1 = 15

```
Algorithm TSP
    Select a city
    MinTourCost = infinite
    For ( All permutations of cities ) do
        If( LengthOfPathSinglePermutation < MinTourCost )
            MinTourCost = LengthOfPath
```

Total number of possible combinations = (n-1)!
Cost for calculating the path: $\Theta(n)$
So, the total cost for finding the shortest path: $\Theta(n!)$

Knapsack Problem

Given an item with cost C1, C2,..., Cn, and volume V1, V2,..., Vn and knapsack of capacity Vmax, find the most valuable (max $\sum Cj$) that fits in the knapsack ($\sum Vj \leq$ Vmax).

The solution is one of the subsets of the set of objects taking 1 to n objects at a time, so the Time complexity is $O(2^n)$

```
Algorithm KnapsackBruteForce
    MaxProfit = 0
    For ( All permutations of objects ) do
        CurrProfit = sum of objects selected
        If( MaxProfit < CurrProfit )
            MaxProfit = CurrProfit
            Store the current set of objects selected
```

Conclusion

Brute force is the first algorithm that comes into mind when we see some problem. They are the simplest algorithms that are very easy to understand. However, these algorithms rarely provide an optimum solution. In many cases, we will find other effective algorithm that is more efficient than the brute force method.

CHAPTER 16: GREEDY ALGORITHM

Introduction

Greedy algorithms are generally used to solve optimization problems. To find the solution that minimizes or maximizes some value (cost/profit/count etc.).

In greedy algorithm, solution is constructed through a sequence of steps. At each step, choice is made which is locally optimal. We always take the next data to be processed depending upon the dataset which we have already processed and then choose the next optimum data to be processed.

Greedy algorithms do not always give optimum solution. For some problems, greedy algorithm gives an optimal solution. They are useful for fast approximations.

Greedy is a strategy that works well on optimization problems with the following characteristics:
1. Greedy choice: A global optimum can be arrived at by selecting a local optimum.
2. Optimal substructure: An optimal solution to the problem is made from optimal solutions of sub-problems.

Some Examples of brute force algorithms are:
Optimal solutions:
- Minimal spanning tree:
    - Prim's algorithm,
    - Kruskal's algorithm
- Dijkstra's algorithm for single-source shortest path
- Huffman trees for optimal encoding
- Scheduling problems

Approximate solutions:
- Greedy algorithm for the Knapsack problem
- Coin exchange problem

Problems on Greedy Algorithm

Coin exchange problem

How can a given amount of money N be made with the least number of coins of given denominations D= {d1… dn}?

The Indian coin system {5, 10, 20, 25, 50,100}

Suppose we want to give change of a certain amount of 40 paisa.

We can make a solution by repeatedly choosing a coin ≤ to the current amount, resulting in a new amount. In the greedy algorithm, we always choose the largest coin value possible without exceeding the total amount.
For 40 paisa: {25, 10, and 5}

The optimal solution will be {20, 20}
The greedy algorithm did not give us optimal solution, but it gave us a fair approximation.

```
Algorithm MAKE-CHANGE (N)
    C = {5, 20, 25, 50, 100}    // constant denominations.
    S = {}                 // set that will hold the solution set.
    Value = N
    WHILE Value != 0
        x = largest item in set C such that x < Value
        IF no such item THEN
            RETURN "No Solution"
        S = S + x
        Value = Value - x
    RETURN S
```

Minimum Spanning Tree

A spanning tree of a connected graph is a tree containing all the vertices.
A minimum spanning tree of a weighted graph is a spanning tree with the smallest sum of the edge weights.

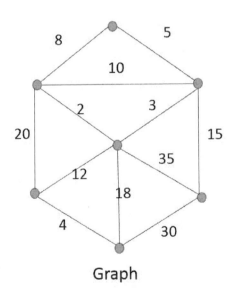

Graph

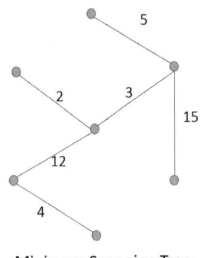

Minimum Spanning Tree

Prim's Algorithm

Prim's algorithm grows a single tree T, one edge at a time, until it becomes a spanning tree.
We initialize T with zero edges and U with single node. Where T is spanning tree, edges set and U is spanning tree vertex set.

At each step, Prim's algorithm adds the smallest value edge with one endpoint in U and other not in us. Since each edge adds one new vertex to U, after n − 1 additions, U contains all the vertices of the spanning tree and T becomes a spanning tree.

```
// Returns the MST by Prim's Algorithm
// Input: A weighted connected graph G = (V, E)
// Output: Set of edges comprising a MST

Algorithm Prim(G)
    T = {}
    Let r be any vertex in G
    U = {r}
    for i = 1 to |V| - 1 do
        e = minimum-weight edge (u, v)
            With u in U and v in V-U
        U = U + {v}
        T = T + {e}
    return T
```

Prim's Algorithm using a priority queue (min heap) to get the closest fringe vertex
Time complexity is O(m log n) where n vertices and m edges of the MST.

Kruskal's Algorithm

Kruskal's Algorithm is used to create minimum spanning tree. Spanning tree is created by choosing smallest weight edge that does not form a cycle. And repeat this process until all the edges from the original set is exhausted.

Sort the edges in non-decreasing order of cost: c (e1) ≤ c (e2) ≤ · · · ≤ c (em).
Set T to be the empty tree. Add edges to tree one by one, if it does not create a cycle. (If the new edge form cycle then ignores that edge.)

```
// Returns the MST by Kruskal's Algorithm
// Input: A weighted connected graph G = (V, E)
// Output: Set of edges comprising a MST

Algorithm Kruskal(G)
    Sort the edges E by their weights
    T = {}
    while |T | + 1 < |V | do
        e = next edge in E
        if T + {e} does not have a cycle then
            T = T + {e}
    return T
```

Kruskal's Algorithm is O(E log V) using efficient cycle detection.

Dijkstra's algorithm

Dijkstra's algorithm is used for single-source shortest path problem for weighted edges with no negative weight. It determines the length of the shortest path from the source to each of the other nodes of the graph. In a given weighted graph G, we need to find shortest paths from the source vertex s to each of the other vertices.

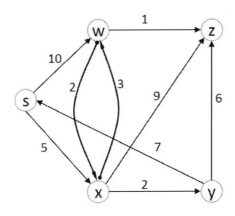 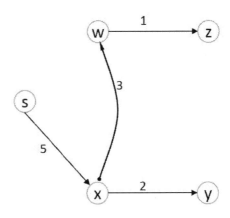

Single-Source shortest path

The algorithm starts by keeping track of the distance of each node and its parents. All the distance is set to infinite in the beginning, as we do not know the actual path to the nodes and parent of all the vertices are set to null. All the vertices are added to a priority queue (min heap implementation)

At each step algorithm takes one vertex from the priority queue (which will be the source vertex in the beginning). Then, update the distance list corresponding to all the adjacent vertices. When the queue is empty, then we will have the distance and parent list fully populated.

```
// Solves SSSP by Dijkstra's Algorithm
// Input: A weighted connected graph G = (V, E)
// with no negative weights, and source vertex v
// Output: The length and path from s to every v

Algorithm Dijkstra(G, s)
    for each v in V do
        D[v] = infinite    // Unknown distance
        P[v] = null        // Unknown previous node
        add v to PQ        // Adding all nodes to priority queue
    D[source] = 0          // Distance from source to source
    while (PQ is not empty)
        u = vertex from PQ with smallest D[u]
        remove u from PQ
        for each v adjacent from u do
            alt = D[u] + length ( u , v)
            if alt < D[v] then
                D[v] = alt
                P[v] = u
    Return D[] , P[]
```

Time complexity is O(|E|log|V|).

Note: Dijkstra's algorithm does not work for graphs with negative edges weight.

Note: Dijkstra's algorithm is applicable to both undirected and directed graphs.

Huffman trees for optimal encoding

Encoding is an assignment of bit strings of alphabet characters.

There are two types of encoding:
- Fixed-length encoding (e.g., ASCII)
- Variable-length encoding (e.g., Huffman code)

Variable length encoding can only work on prefix free encoding. Which means that no code word is a prefix of another code word.

Huffman codes are the best prefix free code.Any binary tree with edges labeled as 0 and 1 will produce a prefix free code of characters assigned to its leaf nodes.

Huffman's algorithm is used to construct a binary tree whose leaf value is assigned a code, which is optimal for the compression of the whole text need to be processed. For Example , the most frequently occurring words will get the smallest code so that the final encoded text is compressed.

Initialize n one-node trees with words and the tree weights with their frequencies. Join the two-binary tree with smallest weight into one and the weight of the new formed tree as the sum of weight of the two small trees. Repeat the above process N-1 times and when there is just one big tree left you are done.

Mark edges leading to left and right subtrees with 0's and 1's, respectively.

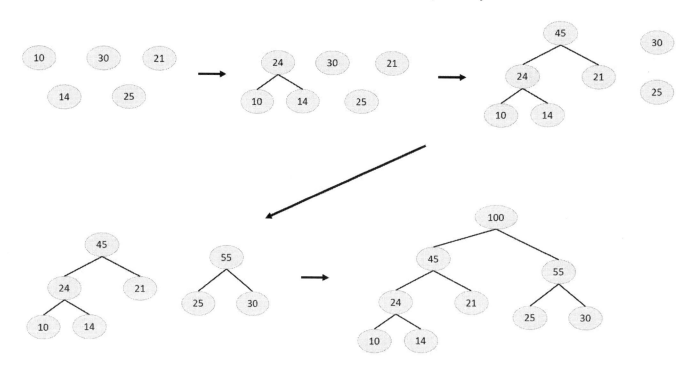

Word	Frequency
Apple	30
Banana	25
Mango	21
Orange	14
Pineapple	10

Word	Value	Code
Apple	30	11
Banana	25	10
Mango	21	01
Orange	14	001
Pineapple	10	000

Higher frequency words get smaller Huffman's code.

```
// Computes optimal prefix code.
// Input: List W of character probabilities
// Output: The Huffman tree.

Algorithm Huffman(C[0..n - 1], W[0..n - 1])
    PQ = {} // priority queue
    for i = 0 to n - 1 do
        T.char = C[i]
        T.weight = W[i]
        add T to priority queue PQ


    for i = 0 to n - 2 do
        L = remove min from PQ
        R = remove min from PQ
        T = node with children L and R
        T.weight = L.weight + R.weight
        add T to priority queue PQ
    return T
```

Time Complexity is O(**nlogn**).

Activity Selection Problem

Suppose that activities require exclusive use of common resources, and you want to schedule as many activities as possible.
Let $S = \{a_1,..., a_n\}$ be a set of n activities.

Each activity a_i needs the resource during a time period starting at s_i and finishing before f_i, i.e., during $[s_i, f_i)$.

The optimization problem is to select the non-overlapping largest set of activities from S. We assume that activities $S = \{a_1,..., a_n\}$ are sorted in finish time $f_1 \le f_2 \le ... f_{n-1} \le f_n$ (this can be done in $\Theta(n \lg n)$).

Example : Consider these activities:

I	1	2	3	4	5	6	7	8	9	10	11
S[i]	1	3	0	5	3	5	6	8	8	2	11
F[i]	4	5	6	7	8	9	10	11	12	13	14

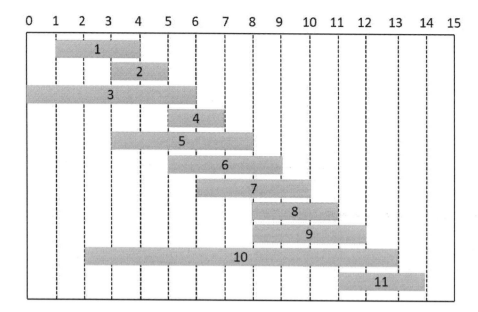

We chose an activity that starts first, and then look for the next activity that starts after it is finished. This could result in {a4, a7, a8}, but this solution is not optimal.

An optimal solution is {a1, a3, a6, a8}. (It maximizes the objective of largest number of activities scheduled.)

Another one is {a2, a5, a7, a9}. (Optimal solutions are not necessarily unique.)
How do we find (one of) these optimal solutions? Let us consider it as a dynamic programming problem.

We are trying to optimize the number of activities. Let us be greedy!
- The time left after running an activity can be used to run subsequent activities.
- If we choose the first activity to finish, the more time will be left.
- Since activities are sorted by finish time, we will always start with a_1.
- Then we can solve the single sub problem of activity scheduling in this remaining time.

```
Algorithm ActivitySelection(S[], F[], N)
    Sort S[] and F [] in increasing order of finishing time
    A = {a1}
    K = 1
    For m = 2 to N do
        If S[m] >= F[k]
            A = A + {am}
            K = m
    Return A
```

Knapsack Problem

A thief enters a store and sees several items with their mentioned cost and weight. His Knapsack can hold a max weight. What should he steal to maximize profit?

Fractional Knapsack problem

A thief can take a fraction of an item (they are divisible substances, like gold powder).

The fractional knapsack problem has a greedy solution one should first sort the items in term of cost density against weight. Then fill up as much of the most valuable substance by weight as one can hold, then as much of the next most valuable substance.

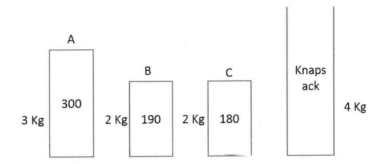

Item	A	B	C
Cost	300	190	180
Weight	3	2	2
Cost/weight	100	95	90

For a knapsack of capacity of 4 kg.
The optimum solution of the above will take 3kg of A and 1 kg of B.

```
Algorithm FractionalKnapsack(W[], C[], Wk)
    For i = 1 to n do
        X[i] = 0
    Weight = 0
    //Use Max heap
    H = BuildMaxHeap(C/W)
    While Weight < Wk do
        i = H.GetMax()
        If(Weight + W[i] <= Wk) do
            X[i] = 1
            Weight = Weight + W[i]
        Else
            X[i] = (Wk – Weight)/W[i]
            Weight = Wk
    Return X
```

0/1 Knapsack Problem

A thief can only take or leave the item. He cannot take a fraction.
A greedy strategy same as above could result in empty space, reducing the overall cost density of the knapsack.

In the above Example, after choosing object A there is no place for B or C. Therefore, there leaves empty space of 1kg. Moreover, the result of the greedy solution is not optimal.

The optimal solution will be when we take object B and C. This problem can be solved by dynamic programming that we will see in the coming chapter.

CHAPTER 17: DIVIDE-AND-CONQUER, DECREASE-AND-CONQUER

Introduction

Divide-and-Conquer algorithms works by recursively breaking down a problem into two or more sub-problems (divide step), until these sub-problems become simple enough so that they can be solved directly (conquer step). The solution of these sub-problems is then combined to give a solution of the original problem.

Divide-and-Conquer algorithms involve basic three steps
1. Divide the problem into smaller problems.
2. Conquer by solving these problems.
3. Combine these results together.

In divide-and-conquer the size of the problem is reduced by a factor (half, one-third etc.), While in decrease-and-conquer the size of the problem is reduced by a constant.

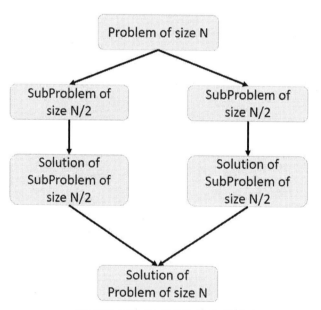

Divide-and-Conquer algorithms

Examples of divide-and-conquer algorithms:
- Merge-Sort algorithm (recursion)
- Quicksort algorithm (recursion)
- Computing the length of the longest path in a binary tree (recursion)
- Computing Fibonacci numbers (recursion)
- Convex Hull

Examples of decrease-and-conquer algorithms:
- Computing POW (a, n) by calculating POW (a, n/2) using recursion
- Binary search in a sorted list (recursion)
- Searching in BST

458

- Insertion-Sort
- Graph traversal algorithms (DFS and BFS)
- Topological sort
- Warshall's algorithm (recursion)
- Permutations (Minimal change approach, Johnson-Trotter algorithm)
- Fake-coin problem (Ternary search)
- Computing a median

General Divide-and-Conquer Recurrence

$T(n) = a \, T(n/b) + f(n)$
- Where $a \geq 1$ and $b > 1$.
- "n" is the size of a problem.
- "a" is the number of sub-problems in the recursion.
- "n/b" is the size of each sub-problem.
- "f(n)" is the cost of the division of the problem into sub problem or merge of the results of sub-problem to get the result.

Problems on Divide-and-Conquer Algorithm

Merge-Sort algorithm

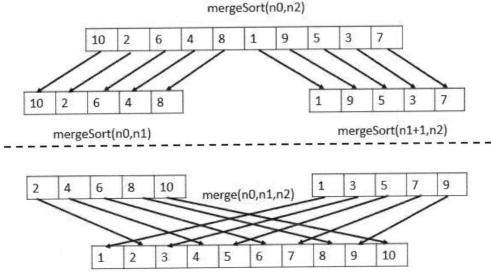

```
// Sorts a given list by Mergesort
// Input: An array A of orderable elements
// Output: List A[0..n - 1] in ascending order

Algorithm Mergesort(A[0..n - 1])
    if n ≤ 1 then
        return;
    copy A[0..⌊n/2⌋- 1] to B[0..⌊n/2⌋- 1]
    copy A[⌊n/2⌋..n - 1] to C[0..⌈n/2⌉- 1]
    Mergesort(B)
    Mergesort(C)
```

```
    Merge(B, C, A)
```

```
// Merges two sorted arrays into one list
// Input: Sorted arrays B and C
// Output: Sorted list A

Algorithm Merge(B[0..p - 1], C[0..q - 1], A[0..p + q - 1])
    i = 0
    j = 0
    for k = 0 to p + q - 1 do
        if i < p and (j = q or B[i] ≤ C[j]) then
            A[k] = B[i]
            i = i + 1
        else
            A[k] = C[j]
            j = j + 1
```

Time Complexity: O(nlogn) & Space Complexity: O(n)
Time Complexity of Merge-Sort is O(nlogn) in all 3 cases (worst, average and best) as Merge-Sort always divides the array into two halves and take linear time to merge two halves.

It requires equal amount of additional space as the unsorted list. Hence, it is not at all recommended for searching large unsorted lists.

Quick-Sort

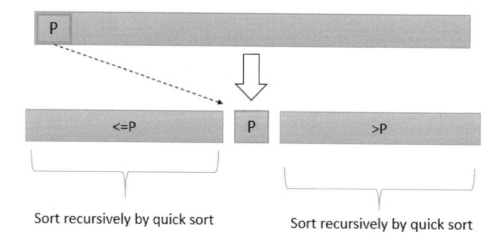

Sort recursively by quick sort   Sort recursively by quick sort

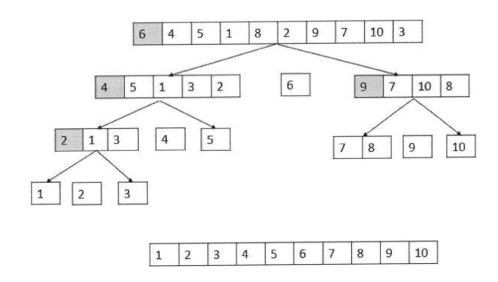

```
// Sorts a subarray by quicksort
// Input: An subarray of A
// Output: List A[l..r] in ascending order

Algorithm Quicksort(A[l..r])
    if l < r then
        p ← Partition(A[l..r]) // p is index of pivot
        Quicksort(A[l..p - 1])
        Quicksort(A[p + 1..r])
```

```
// Partitions a subarray using A[..] as pivot
// Input: Subarray of A
// Output: Final position of pivot

Algorithm Partition(A[], left, right)
    pivot = A[left]
    lower = left
    upper= right
    while lower < upper
        while A[lower] <= pivot
            lower = lower + 1
        while A[upper] > pivot
            upper = upper - 1
        if lower < upper then
            swap A[lower] and A[upper]
    swap A[lower] and A[upper] //upper is the pivot position
    return upper
```

Worst Case time Complexity: O(**n²**),
Average case time Complexity: O(**nlogn),**
Space Complexity: **O(nlogn),** The space required by Quick-Sort is very less, only **O(nlogn)** additional space is required.
Quicksort is not a stable sorting technique, so it might change the occurrence of two similar elements in the array while sorting.

External Sorting

External sorting is also done using divide and conquer algorithm.

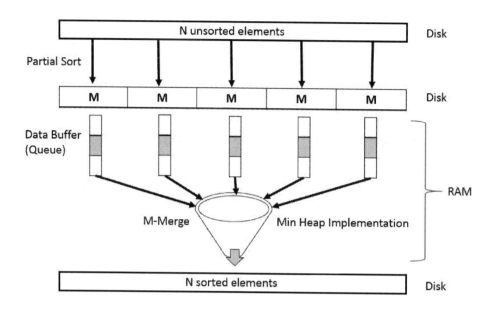

Binary Search

We get the middle point from the sorted list and start comparing with the desired value.

Note: Binary search requires the array to be sorted otherwise binary search cannot be applied.

```
// Searches a value in a sorted list using binary search
// Input: A sorted list A and a key K
// Output: The index of K or -1

Algorithm BinarySearch(A[0..N - 1], N, K) // iterative solution
    low = 0
    high = N-1
    while low <= high do
        mid = ⌊ (low + high)/2⌋
        if K = A[mid] then
            return mid
        else if A[mid] < K
            low = mid + 1
        else
            high = mid - 1
    return -1
```

```
// Searches a value in a sorted list using binary search
// Input: A sorted list A and a key K
// Output: The index of K or -1

Algorithm BinarySearch(A[], low, high, K) //Recursive solution
    If low > high
```

```
        return -1
mid = ⌊ (low + high)/2⌋
if K = A[mid] then
        return mid
else if A[mid] < K
        return BinarySearch(A[],mid + 1, high, K)
else
        return BinarySearch(A[],low, mid - 1, K)
```

Time Complexity: O(**logn**). If you notice the above programs, you should keep in mind that we always take half input and throwing out the other half. So, the recurrence relation for binary search is T (n) = T (n/2) + c. Using a divide and conquer master theorem, we get T (n) =**O(logn)**.
Space Complexity: O(**1**)

Power function

```
// Compute Nth power of X using divide and conquer using recursion
// Input: Value X and power N
// Output: Power( X, N)

Algorithm Power( X, N)
    If N = 0
        Return 1
    Else if N % 2 == 0
        Value = Power(X, N/2)
        Return Value * Value
    Else
        Value = Power(X, N/2)
        Return Value * Value * X
```

Convex Hull

Sort points by X-coordinates. Divide points into equal halves A and B. Recursively compute HA and HB. Merge HA and HB to obtain convex hull

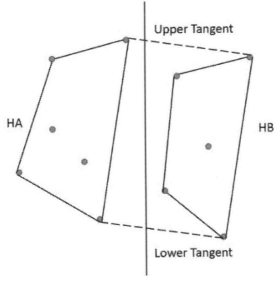

463

```
LowerTangent(HA, HB)
    A = rightmost point of HA
    B = leftmost point of HB
    While ab is not a lower tangent for HA and HB do
        While ab is not a lower tangent to HA do
            a = a - 1 (move a clockwise)
        While ab is not a lower tangent to HB do
            b = b + 1 (move b counterclockwise)
    Return ab
```

Similarly find upper tangent and combine the two hulls.

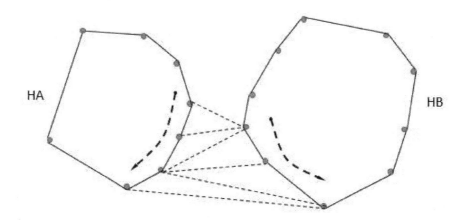

Initial sorting takes **O(nlogn)** time

Recurrence relation T (N) = 2T (N/2) +**O(N)**

Where, **O(N)** time is for tangent computation inside the merge step.

Final Time complexity is T (N) =**O(nlogn)**.

Closest Pair

Given N points in 2-dimensional plane, find two points whose mutual distance is smallest.

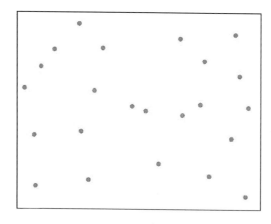

A brute force algorithm takes every point and find its distance with all the other points in the plane. In addition, keep track of the minimum distance points and minimum distance. The closest pair will be found in $O(n^2)$ time.

Let us suppose that there is a vertical line, which divides the graph into two separate parts (let us call it left and right part). In the brute force algorithm, we will notice that we are comparing all the points in the left half with the points in the right half. This is the point where we are doing some extra work.

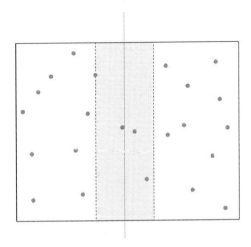

To find the minimum we need to consider only three cases:
1) Closest pair in the right half
2) Closest pair in the left half.
3) Closest pair in the boundary region of the two halves. (Gray)

Every time we will divide the space S into two parts S1 and S2 by a vertical line. Recursively we will compute the closest pair in both S1 and S2. Let us call minimum distance in space S1 as δ1 and minimum distance in space S2 as δ2.
We will find δ = min (δ1, δ2)

Now we will find the closest pair in the boundary region. By taking one point each from S1 and S2 in the boundary range of δ width on both sides.

The candidate pair of point (p, q) where p ∈ S1 and q ∈ S2.

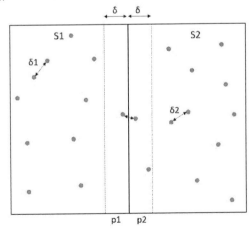

We can find the points that lie in this region in linear time O(N) by just scanning through all the points and finding that all points lie in this region.

Now we can sort them in increasing order in Y-axis in just **O(nlogn)** time. Then scan through them and get the minimum in just one linear pass. Closest pair cannot be far apart from each other.

Let us investigate the next figure.

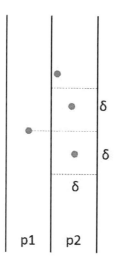

Then the question is how many points we need to compare. We need to compare the points sorted in Y-axis only in the range of δ. Therefore, the number of points will come down to only 6 points.

By doing this, we are getting equation.
$T(N) = 2T(N/2) + N + NlogN + 6N = O(n(logn)^2)$

Can we optimize this further?
Yes

Initially, when we are sorting the points in X coordinate, we are sorting them in Y coordinate too.
When we divide the problem, then we traverse through the Y coordinate list too, and construct the corresponding Y coordinate list for both S1 and S2. And pass that list to them.

Since we have the Y coordinate list passed to a function the δ region points can be found sorted in the Y coordinates in just one single pass in just **O(N)** time.

$T(N) = 2T(N/2) + N + N + 6N = $ **O(nlogn)**

```
// Finds closest pair of points
// Input: A set of n points sorted by coordinates
// Output: Distance between closest pair

Algorithm ClosestPair(P)
    if n <2 then
        return ∞
    else if n = 2 then
        return distance between pair
    else
        m = median value for x coordinate
        δ1 = ClosestPair(points with x < m)
        δ2 = ClosestPair(points with x > m)
```

```
δ= min(δ1, δ2)
δ3 = process points with m−δ< x < m + δ
return min(δ, δ3)
```

First pre-process the points by sorting them in X and Y coordinates. Use two separate lists to keep these sorted points.

Before recursively solving sub-problem pass the sorted list for that sub-problem.

CHAPTER 18: DYNAMIC PROGRAMMING

Introduction

While solving problems using Divide-and-Conquer method, there may be a case when recursively sub-problems can result in the same computation being performed multiple times. This problem arises when there are identical sub-problems arise repeatedly in a recursion.

Dynamic programming is used to avoid the requirement of repeated calculation of same sub-problem. In this method, we usually store the result of sub - problems in some data structure (like a table) and refer it to find if we have already calculated the solution of sub - problems before calculating it again.

Dynamic programming is applied to solve problems with the following properties:
1. Optimal Substructure: An optimal solution constructed from the optimal solutions of its sub-problems.
2. Overlapping Sub-problems: While calculating the optimal solution of sub-problems same computation is repeated repeatedly.

Examples:
- Fibonacci numbers computed by iteration.
- Assembly-line Scheduling
- Matrix-chain Multiplication
- 0/1 Knapsack Problem
- Longest Common Subsequence
- Optimal Binary Tree
- Warshall's algorithm for transitive closure implemented by iterations
- Floyd's algorithms for all-pairs shortest paths
- Optimal Polygon Triangulation
- Floyd-Warshall's Algorithm

Steps for solving / recognizing if DP applies.
1) Optimal Substructure: Try to find if there is a recursive relation between problem and sub-problem.
2) Write recursive relation of the problem. (Observe Overlapping Sub-problems at this step.)
3) Compute the value of sub-problems in a bottom up fashion and store this value in some table.
4) Construct the optimal solution from the value stored in step 3.
5) Repeat step 3 and 4 until you get your solution.

Problems on Dynamic programming Algorithm

Fibonacci numbers

```
function fibonacci (n) {
  if (n <= 1) {
    return n
  }
  return fibonacci(n - 1) + fibonacci(n - 2)
}
```

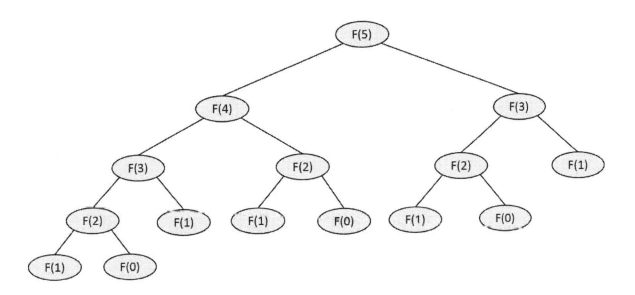

Using divide and conquer same sub-problem is solved again and again, which reduce the performance of the algorithm. This algorithm has an exponential Time Complexity.

Same problem of Fibonacci can be solved in linear time if we sort the results of sub-problems.

```
function fibonacci2 (n) {
  let first = 0;
  let second = 1;
  let temp = 0;

  if (n === 0)
    return first
  else if (n === 1)
    return second

  let i = 2;
  while (i <= n) {
    temp = first + second
    first = second
    second = temp
    i += 1
  }
  return temp
}
```

Using this algorithm, we will get Fibonacci in linear Time Complexity and constant Space Complexity.

Assembly-line Scheduling

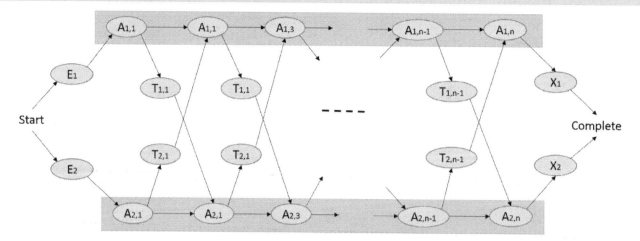

We consider the problem of calculating the least amount of time necessary to build a car when using a manufacturing chain with two assembly lines, as shown in the figure

The problem variables:
- e[i]: entry time in assembly line i
- x[i]: exit time from assembly line i
- a[i, j]: Time required at station S[i, j] (assembly line i, stage j)
- t[i, j]: Time required to transit from station S[i, j] to the other assembly line

Your program must calculate:
- The least amount of time needed to build a car
- The array of stations to traverse to assemble a car as fast as possible.

The manufacturing chain will have no more than 50 stations.

If we want to solve this problem in the brute force approach, there will be in total 2^N Different combinations so the Time complexity is $O(2^N)$

Step 1: Characterizing the class of the optimal solution
To calculate the fastest assembly time, we only need to know the fastest time to $S1_n$ and the fastest time to $S2_n$, including the assembly time for the nth part. Then we choose between the two exit points by taking into consideration the extra time required, x1 and x2. To compute the fastest time to $S1_n$ we only need to know the fastest time to $S1_{n-1}$ and to $S2_{n-1}$. Then there are only two choices.

Step 2: A recursive definition of the values to be computed

$$f1[j] = \begin{cases} e1 + a1,\ 1\ if\ j = 1 \\ min(f1[j-1] + a1,\ j,\ f2[j-1]+t2,\ j-1+a1,\ j) \end{cases}$$

$$f2[j] = \begin{cases} e2 + a2,\ 1\ if\ j = 1 \\ min(f2[j-1] + a2,\ j,\ f1[j-1]+t1,\ j-1+a2,\ j) \end{cases}$$

Step 3: Computing the fastest time finally, compute f* as
Step 4: Computing the fastest path compute as li[j] as the choice made for fi[j] (whether the first or the second term gives the minimum). Also, compute the choice for f* as l*.

```
FASTEST-WAY(a, t, e, x, n)
    f1[1] ← e1 + a1,1
    f2[1] ←e2 + a2,1
    for j ← 2 to n do
        if f1[j - 1] + a1,j ≤ f2[j - 1] + t2,j-1 + a1,j
            then f1[j] ← f1[j - 1] + a1, j
            l1[j] ← 1
        else f1[j] ← f2[j - 1] + t2,j-1 + a1,j
            l1[j] ← 2
        if f2[j - 1] + a2,j ≤ f1[j - 1] + t1,j-1 + a2,j
            then f2[j] ← f2[j - 1] + a2,j
            l2[j] ← 2
        else f2[j] ← f1[j - 1] + t1,j-1 + a2,j
            l2[j] ← 1
    if f1[n] + x1 ≤ f2[n] + x2
        then f* = f1[n] + x1
        l* = 1
    else f* = f2[n] + x2
        l* = 2
```

Largest Increasing subsequence

Given an array of integers, you need to find largest subsequence in increasing order. You need to find largest increasing sequence by selecting the elements from the given array such that their relative order does not change.

Input = [10, 12, 9, 23, 25, 55, 49, 70]
Output will be 6 corresponds to [10, 12, 23, 25, 49, 70]

Let V be the input array.
The optimal substructure in this problem for ith is defined as:
$LIS(k) = \max (LIS(j)) + 1$ such that $j < k$ and $v[j] < v[k]$

```
function LIS(v[], n)
    for i ← 1 to n do
        length[i] ← 1
        for j ← 0 to i do
            if v[i]< v[j]and length[i] < length[j]+1 then
            length[ i] ← length[i] +1

    return max (length[i] where 1≤i≤n)
```

```
function LIS(arr):
    maxValue = 0
    size = len(arr)
    lis = [1]*size
    for i in range(size):
        for j in range(i):
            if arr[j] < arr[i] and lis[i] < lis[j] + 1:
```
471

```
            lis[i] = lis[j] + 1

        if maxValue < lis[i]:
            maxValue = lis[i]

    return maxValue

arr = [10, 12, 9, 23, 25, 55, 49, 70]
print(LIS(arr))
```

Time Complexity: $O(n^2)$, Space Complexity: $O(n)$.

Longest Bitonic Subsequence

Given an array, you need to find longest bitonic subsequence.

```
Function LBS(arr ):
    maxValue = 0
    size = len(arr)
    lis = [1]*size
    lds = [1]*size
    for i in range(size):
        for j in range(i):
            if arr[j] < arr[i] and lis[i] < lis[j] + 1:
                lis[i] = lis[j] + 1

    for i in reversed(range(size)):
        for j in reversed(range(i, size)):
            if arr[j] < arr[i] and lds[i] < lds[j] + 1:
                lds[i] = lds[j] + 1

    for i in range(size):
        maxValue = max((lis[i] + lds[i] - 1), maxValue)
    return maxValue

arr = [1 , 6 , 3, 11, 1, 9 , 5 , 12 , 3 , 14 , 6 , 17, 3, 19 , 2 , 19]
print(LBS(arr))
```

Matrix chain multiplication

Same problem is also known as Matrix Chain Ordering Problem or Optimal-parenthesization of matrix problem.

Given a sequence of matrices, M = M1,..., Mn. The goal of this problem is to find the most efficient way to multiply these matrices. The guild is not to perform the actual multiplication, but to decide the sequence of the matrix multiplications, so that the result will be calculated in minimal operations.

To compute the product of two matrices of dimensions pXq and qXr, pqr number of operations will be required. Matrix multiplication operations are associative in nature. Therefore, matrix multiplication can be done in many ways.

For Example , M1, M2, M3 and M4, can be fully parenthesized as:
(M1· (M2· (M3·M4)))
(M1· ((M2·M3)· M4))
((M1·M2)· (M3·M4))
(((M1·M2)· M3)· M4)
((M1· (M2·M3))· M4)

For Example ,
Let M1 dimensions are 10 × 100, M2 dimensions are 100 × 10, and M3 dimensions are 10 × 50.
((M1·M2)· M3) = (10*100*10) + (10*10^50) = 15000
(M1· (M2·M3) = (100*10*50) + (10*100*50) = 100000
Therefore, in this problem we need to parenthesize the matrix chain so that total multiplication cost is minimized.
Given a sequence of n matrices M1, M2,… Mn. And their dimensions are p0, p1, p2,…, pn.
Where matrix Ai has dimension pi − 1 × pi for 1 ≤ i ≤ n. Determine the order of multiplication that minimizes the total number of multiplications.

If you try to solve this problem using the brute-force method, then you will find all possible parenthesization. Then you will compute the cost of multiplications. Thereafter you will pick the best solution. This approach will be exponential in nature.

There is an insufficiency in the brute force approach. Take an Example of M1, M2,…, Mn. When you have calculated that ((M1·M2) · M3) is better than (M1· (M2·M3) so there is no point of calculating then combinations of (M1· (M2·M3) with (M4, M5…. Mn).

Optimal substructure:
Assume that M (1, N) is the optimum cost of production of the M1,…, Mn.

An array p [] to record the dimensions of the matrices.
P [0] = row of the M1
p[i] = col of Mi 1<=i<=N

For some k,
M(1,N) = M(1,K) + M(K+1,N) + p0*pk*pn

If M (1, N) is minimal then both M (1, K) & M (K+1, N) are minimal.

Otherwise, if there is some M'(1, K) is there whose cost is less than M (1.. K), then M (1.. N) can't be minimal and there is a more optimal solution possible.

For some general i and j.
M(i,j) = M(i,K) + M(K+1,j) + pi-1*pk*pj

Recurrence relation:

$$M(i,j) = \begin{cases} 0 \; if \; i = j \\ min \left[M(i,k) + M(k,j) + pi - 1 * pk * pj \right] \; i \le k < j \end{cases}$$

Overlapping Sub-problems:

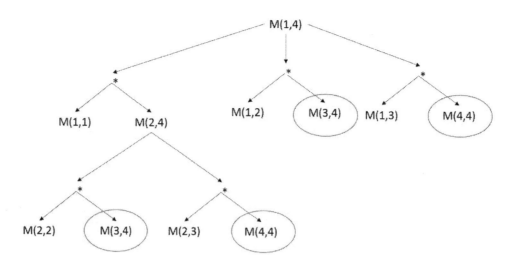

Directly calling recursive function will lead to calculation of same sub-problem multiple times. This will lead to exponential solution.

```
Algorithm MatrixChainMultiplication(p[])
    for i := 1 to n
        M[i, i] := 0;
        for l = 2 to n // l is the moving line
            for i = 1 to n - l +1
                j = i + l - 1;
                M[i, j] = min{M(i,k) + M(k,j)+pi-1*pk*pj}    i≤k<j
```

Time Complexity will O(n^3)
Constructing optimal parenthesis Solution

Use another table s[1..n, 1..n]. Each entry s[i, j] records the value of k such that the optimal parenthesization of Mi Mi+1...Mj splits the product between Mk and Mk+1.

```
Algorithm MatrixChainMultiplication(p[])
    for i := 1 to n
        M[i, i] := 0;
    for l = 2 to n // l is the moving line
        for i = 1 to n - l +1
            j = i + l - 1;
            M[i, j] = min{M(i,k) + M(k,j)+pi-1*pk*pj}    i≤k<j
            S[i, j] = k for min{M(i,k) + M(k,j)+pi-1*pk*pj}    i≤k<j

Algorithm MatrixChainMultiplication(p[])
    for i := 1 to n
    M[i, i] := 0;
        for l = 2 to n // l is the moving line
            for i = 1 to n - l +1
                j = i + l - 1;
                for k = i to j
                    if( (M(i,k) + M(k,j)+pi-1*pk*pj < M[i, j])
                        M[i, j] = (M(i,k) + M(k,j)+pi-1*pk*pj)
                        S[i, j] = k
```

```
Algorithm PrintOptimalParenthesis(s[], i, j)
    If i = j
        Print Ai
    Else
        Print "("
        PrintOptimalParenthesis(s[], i,s[i, j])
        PrintOptimalParenthesis(s[], s[i, j],j)
        Print ")"
```

Longest Common Subsequence

Let X = {x1, x2,...., xm} is a sequence of characters and Y = {y1, y2,..., yn} is another sequence. Z is a subsequence of X if it can be driven by deleting some elements of X. Z is a subsequence of Y if it can be driven by deleting some elements form Y. Z is LCS of it is subsequence to both X and Y, and length of all the subsequence is less than Z.

Optimal Substructure:

Let X = < x1, x2, ..., xm > and Y = < y1, y2, ..., yn > be two sequences, and let Z = < z1, z2, ..., zk > be a LCS of X and Y.

- If xm = yn, then zk = xm = yn $\Rightarrow$ Zk-1 is a LCS of Xm-1 and Yn-1
- If xm != yn, then:
    - zk != xm $\Rightarrow$ Z is an LCS of Xm-1 and Y.
    - zk != yn $\Rightarrow$ Z is an LCS of X and Yn-1.

Recurrence relation
Let c[i, j] be the length of the longest common subsequence between X = {x1, x2,...., xi} and Y = {y1, y2, ..., yj}.
Then c[n, m] contains the length of an LCS of X and Y

$$c[i, j] = \begin{cases} 0 & if \ i=0 \ or \ j=0 \\ c[i-1, \ j-1] + 1 & if \ i,j > 0 \ and \ xi = yi \\ max(c[i-1], \ c[i, \ j-1]) & otherwise \end{cases}$$

```
Algorithm LCS(X[], m, Y[], n)
    for i = 1 to m
        c[i,0] = 0
    for j = 1 to n
        c[0,j] = 0;
    for i = 1 to m
        for j = 1 to n
            if X[i] == Y[j]
                c[i,j] = c[i-1,j-1] + 1
                b[i,j] = ↖
            else
                if c[i-1,j] ≥ c[i,j-1]
```

```
                        c[i,j] = c[i-1,j]
                        b[i,j] = ↑
                else
                        c[i,j] = c[i,j-1]
                        b[i,j] = ←

Algorithm PrintLCS(b[],X[], i, j)
    if i = 0
        return
    if j = 0
        return
    if b[i, j] = ↖
        PrintLCS (b[],X[], i - 1, j - 1)
        print X[i]
    else if b[i, j] = ↑
        PrintLCS (b[],X[], i - 1, j)
    else
        PrintLCS (b[],X[], i, j - 1)
```

Coin Exchanging problem

How can a given amount of money N be made with the least number of coins of given denominations D= {d1... dn}?

For Example , Indian coin system {5, 10, 20, 25, 50,100}. Suppose we want to give change of a certain amount of 40 paisa.

We can make a solution by repeatedly choosing a coin ≤ to the current amount, resulting in a new amount. The greedy solution always chooses the largest coin value possible.
For 40 paisa: {25, 10, and 5}

This is how billions of people around the globe make change every day. That is an approximate solution of the problem. But this is not the optimal way, the optimal solution for the above problem is {20, 20}

Step (I): Characterize the class of a coin-change solution.
Define C [j] to be the minimum number of coins we need to make a change for j cents.

If we knew that an optimal solution for the problem of making change for j cents used a coin of denomination di, we would have:
C[j] = 1+C[j – di]

Strep (II): Recursively defines the value of an optimal solution.

$$c[j] = \begin{cases} infinite \ \ if \ \ j<0 \\ \ \ \ \ 0 \ \ if \ \ i=0 \\ 1+min\big(c[i-di]\big) \ \ 1\leq i \leq k \ \ if \ j \geq 1 \end{cases}$$

Step (III): Compute values in a bottom-up fashion.

```
Algorithm CoinExchange(n, d[], k)
```

```
C[0] = 0
for j = 1 to n do
    C[j] = infinite
    for i = 1 to k do
        if j < di and 1+C[j - di] < C[j] then
            C[j] = 1+C[j - di]
return C
```

Complexity: O(nk)

Stop (iv): Construct an optimal solution
We use an additional list Deno[1.. n], where Deno[j] is the denomination of a coin used in an optimal solution.

```
Algorithm CoinExchange(n, d[], k)
    C[0] = 0
    for j = 1 to n do
        C[j] = infinite
        for i = 1 to k do
            if j < di and 1+C[j - di] < C[j] then
                C[j] = 1+C[j - di]
                Deno[j] = di
    return C
```

```
Algorithm PrintCoins( Deno[], j)
    if j > 0
        PrintCoins (Deno, j -Deno[j])
    print Deno[j]
```

CHAPTER 19: BACKTRACKING

Introduction

Suppose there is a lock, which produce some "click" sound when correct digit is selected for any level. To open it you just need to find the first digit, then find the second digit, then find the third digit and done. This will be a greedy algorithm and you will find the solution very quickly.

However, let us suppose the lock is some old one and it creates same sound not only at the correct digit, but also at some other digits. Therefore, when you are trying to find the digit of the first ring, then it may product sound at multiple instances. So, at this point you are not directly going straight to the solution, but you need to test various states and in case those states are not the solution you are looking for, then you need to backtrack one step at a time and find the next solution. Sure, this intelligence/ heuristics of click sound will help you to reach your goal much faster. These functions are called Pruning function or bounding functions.

Problems on Backtracking Algorithm

N Queens Problem

There are N queens given, you need to arrange them in a chessboard on NxN such that no queen should attach each other.

```
function Feasible (Q, k) {
  for (let i = 0; i < k; i++) {
    if (Q[k] === Q[i] || Math.abs(Q[i] - Q[k]) === Math.abs(i - k)) {
      return false
    }
  }
  return true
}

function NQueens (Q, k, n) {
  if (k === n) {
    console.log(Q)
    return
  }

  for (let i = 0; i < n; i++) {
    Q[k] = i
    if (Feasible(Q, k)) {
      NQueens(Q, k + 1, n)
    }
  }
}

function test () {
```

```
  const Q = [0, 0, 0, 0, 0, 0, 0, 0];
  NQueens(Q, 0, 8)
}
```

Output:
```
[ 0, 4, 7, 5, 2, 6, 1, 3 ]
[ 0, 5, 7, 2, 6, 3, 1, 4 ]
.

.

.
[ 7, 3, 0, 2, 5, 1, 6, 4 ]
```

Tower of Hanoi

The Tower of Hanoi puzzle, disks need to be moved from one pillar to another such that any large disk cannot rest above any small disk.

This is a famous puzzle in the programming world; its origins can be tracked back to India."There is a story about an Indian temple in Kashi Viswanath which contains a large room with three time worn posts in it surrounded by 64 golden disks. Brahmin priests, acting out the command of an ancient Hindu prophecy, have been moving these disks, in accordance with the immutable rules of the Brahma the creator of the universe, since the beginning of time. The puzzle is therefore also known as the Tower of Brahma puzzle. According to the prophecy, when the last move of the puzzle will be completed, the world will end." ;) ;) ;)

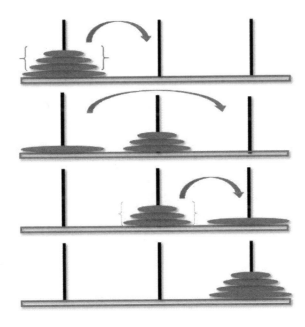

```
function TOHUtil (num, from, to, temp) {
  if (num < 1) {
    return
  }
  TOHUtil(num - 1, from, temp, to)
  console.log(`Move disk ${num} from peg ${from} to peg ${to}`)
  TOHUtil(num - 1, temp, to, from)
}
```

```
function TowersOfHanoi (num) {
  console.log('The sequence of moves involved in the Tower of Hanoi are :')
  TOHUtil(num, 'A', 'C', 'B')
}

function test () {
  TowersOfHanoi(3)
}
```

Output:
```
The sequence of moves involved in the Tower of Hanoi are :
Move disk 1 from peg A to peg C
Move disk 2 from peg A to peg B
Move disk 1 from peg C to peg B
Move disk 3 from peg A to peg C
Move disk 1 from peg B to peg A
Move disk 2 from peg B to peg C
Move disk 1 from peg A to peg C
```

CHAPTER 20: COMPLEXITY THEORY

Introduction

Computational complexity is the measurement of how much resources are required to solve some problem.

There are two types of resources:
1. Time: Number of steps required to solve a problem
2. Space: Amount of memory required to solve a problem

Decision problems

Much of Complexity theory deals with decision problems. A decision problem always has a yes or no answer.

Many problems can be converted to a decision problem that have answer as yes or no. For Example :
1. Searching: The problem of searching element can be a decision problem if we ask, "Find if a particular number is there in the array?".

2. Sorting of list and find if the array is sorted, can be a decision problem, "Is the array is sorted in increasing order?".

3. Graph colouring algorithms: this is can also be converted to a decision problem. Can we do the graph colouring by using X number of colours?

4. Hamiltonian cycle: Is there is a path from all the nodes, each node is visited exactly once and comes back to the starting node without breaking?

Complexity Classes

Problems are divided into many classes based on their difficulty. Or how difficult it is to find if the given solution is correct or not.

Class P problems

The class P consists of a set of problems that can be solved in polynomial time. The complexity of a P problem is $O(n^k)$ where n is input size and k is some constant (it cannot depend on n).

Class P Definition: The class P contains all decision problems for which a Turing machine algorithm leads to the "yes/no" answer in a definite number of steps bounded by a polynomial function.

For Example :
Given a sequence a1, a2, a3…. an. Find if a number X is there in this list.
We can search, the number X in this list in linear time (polynomial time)

Another Example :
Given a sequence a1, a2, a3.... an. If we are asked to sort the sequence.
We can sort and array in polynomial time using Bubble-Sort, this is also linear time.
Note: **O(logn)** is also polynomial. Any algorithm, which has complexity less than some O (nk),is also polynomial.

Some problem of P class is:
1. Shortest path
2. Minimum spanning tree
3. Maximum problem.
4. Max flow graph problem.
5. Convex hull

Class NP problems

Set of problems for which there is a polynomial time checking algorithm. Given a solution if we can check in a polynomial time if that solution is correct or not then, the problem is NP problem.

Class NP Definition: The class NP contains all decision problems for which, given a solution, there exists a polynomial time "proof" or "certificate" that can verify if the solution is the right "yes/no" answer

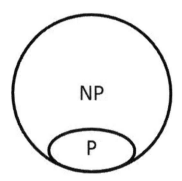

Note: There is no guarantee that you will be able to solve this problem in polynomial time. However, if a problem is an NP problem, then you can verify an answer in polynomial time.

NP does not mean "non-polynomial". It is "Non-Deterministic Polynomial" type of problem. They are the kind of problems that can be solved in polynomial time by a Non-Deterministic Turing machine. At each point, all the possibilities are executed in parallel. If there are n possible choices, then all n cases will be executed in parallel. We do not have non-deterministic computers. Do not be confused with parallel computing because the number of CPU is limited in parallel computing it may be 16 core or 32 cores, but it cannot be N-Core.

In short NP problems are those problems for which, if a solution is given, we can verify that solution (if it is correct or not) in polynomial time.

Boolean Satisfiability problem

A Boolean formula is satisfied if there exist some assignment of the values 0 and 1 to its variables that causes it to evaluate to 1.

(A1 ∨ A2) ∧ (A2 ∨ A4) .... ∧(.... ∨ AN)

There are in total N Different Boolean Variables A1, A2... AN. There are an M number of brackets. Each bracket has K variables.

There is N variable so the number of solutions will be 2^n
And to verify if the solutions really evaluate the equation to 1 will take total ($2^n * km$) steps
In given solution of this problem you can find if the formula satisfies or not in KM steps.

Hamiltonian cycle

Hamiltonian cycle is a path from all the nodes of a graph, each node is visited exactly once and come back to the starting node without breaking.

This is an NP problem, if you have a solution to it, then you just need to see if all the nodes are there in the path and you came back to where you have started and you are done? The checking is done in linear time and you are done.

Determining whether a directed graph has a Hamiltonian cycle or notdoes nothave a polynomial time algorithm. O(n!)

However, if someone has given you a sequence of vertices, determining whether that sequence forms a Hamiltonian cycle can be done in polynomial time (Linear time).
Hamiltonian cycles are in NP

Clique Problem

In given graph find if there is a clique of size K or more. A clique is a subset of nodes, which are completely connected to each other.

This problem is NP problem. Given a set of nodes, you can very easily find out whether it is a clique or not.

For Example :

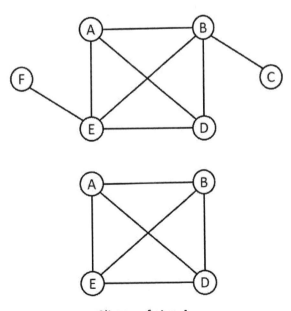

Clique of size 4

Prime Number

Finding Prime number is NP. Given a solution, it is easy to find if it is a Prime or not in polynomial time. Finding prime numbers is important which is heavily used in cryptography.

```
function isPrime (n) {
  let answer = (n > 1) ? true : false;

  for (let i = 2; i * i <= n; ++i) {
    if (n % i === 0) {
      answer = false
      break
    }
  }
  return answer
}

function test () {
  console.log(isPrime(101))
  console.log(isPrime(103))
  console.log(isPrime(105))
}
```

Output:
```
true
true
false
```

Checking will happen until the square root of number so the Time complexity is $O(\sqrt{n})$. Hence, prime number finding is an NP problem as we can verify the solution in polynomial time.

Graph theory have wonderful set of problems
- Shortest path algorithms?
- Longest path is NP complete.
- Eulerian tours are a polynomial time problem.
- Hamiltonian tours are a NP complete

Class co-NP

Set of problems for which there is a polynomial time checking algorithm. Given a solution, if we can check in a polynomial time if that solution is incorrect the problem is co-NP problem.

Class co-NP Definition: The class co-NP contains all decision problems such that there exists a polynomial time proof that can verify if the problem does not have the right "yes/no" answer.

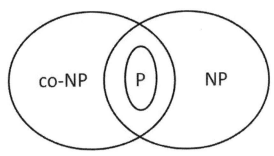

Relationship between P, NP and co-NP

Class P is Subset of Class NP

All problems that are P also are NP (P $\subseteq$ NP). Problem set P is a subset of problem set NP.

Searching
If we have some number sequence a1, a2, a3.... an. We already know that searching a number X inside this list is of type P.
If it is given that number X is inside this sequence, then we can verify by looking into every entry again and find if the answer is correct in polynomial time (linear time.)

Sorting
Another Example of sorting a number sequence, if it is given that the array b1, b2, b3.. bn is a sorted then we can loop through this given list and find if the array is really sorted in polynomial time (linear time again.)

NP–Hard:

A problem is NP-Hard if all the problems in NP can be reduced to it in polynomial time.

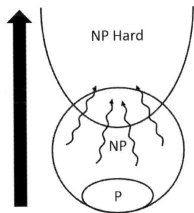

NP–Complete Problems

Set of problem is NP-Complete if it is an NP problem and an NP-Hard problem.

It should follow both the properties:
1) Its solutions can be verified in a polynomial time.
2) All problems of NP are reduced to NP complete problems in polynomial time.

You can always reduce any NP problem into NP-Complete in polynomial time. In addition, when you get the answer to the problem, then you can verify this solution in polynomial time.

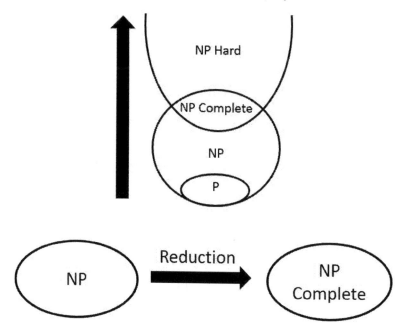

Any NP problem is polynomial reduced to NP-Complete problem, if we can find a solution to a single NP-Complete problem in polynomial time, then we can solve all the NP problems in polynomial time. However, so far no one had found any solution of NP-Complete problem in polynomial time.
$P \neq NP$

Reduction

It is a process of transformation of one problem into another problem. The transformation time should be polynomial. If a problem A is transformed into B and we know the solution of B in polynomial time, then A can also be solved in polynomial time.

For Example , Quadratic Equation Solver: We have a Quadratic Equation Solver, which solves equation of the form $ax^2 + bx + c = 0$. It takes Input a, b, c and generates output r1, r2.
Now try to solve a linear equation $2x+4=0$. Using reduction second equation can be transformed to the first equation.

$2x+4 = 0$, $x^2 + 2x+4 = 0$

ATLAS: We have an atlas and we need to colour maps so that no two countries have the same colour. Let us suppose below is the various countries. Moreover, different patterns represent different colour.

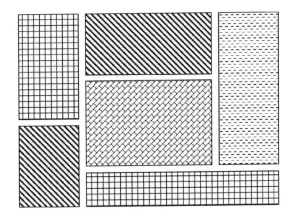

We can see that same problem of atlas colouring can be reduced to graph colouring and if we know the solution of graph colouring then same solution can work for atlas colouring too. Where each node of the graph represents one country and the adjacent country relation is represented by the edges between nodes.

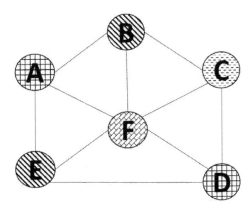

The sorting problem reduces ($\leq$) to Convex Hull problem.

SAT reduces ($\leq$) to 3SAT

End Note

Nobody has come up with such a polynomial-time algorithm to solve a NP-Complete problem. Many important algorithms depend upon it. However, at the same time nobody has proven that no polynomial time algorithm is possible. There is a million US dollars for anyone who can solve any NP Complete problem in polynomial time. The whole economy of the world will fall as most of the banks depend on public key encryption which will be easy to break if P=NP solution is found.

APPENDIX

Appendix A

Algorithms	Time Complexity
Binary Search in a sorted array of N elements	O(logN)
Reversing a string of N elements	O(N)
Linear search in an unsorted array of N elements	O(N)
Compare two strings with lengths L1 and L2	O(min(L1, L2))
Computing the Nth Fibonacci number using dynamic programming	O(N)
Checking if a string of N characters is a palindrome	O(N)
Finding a string in another string using the Aho-Corasick algorithm	O(N)
Sorting an array of N elements using Merge-Sort/Quick-Sort/Heap-Sort	O(N * LogN)
Sorting an array of N elements using Bubble-Sort	O(N!)
Two nested loops from 1 to N	O(N!)
The Knapsack problem of N elements with capacity M	O(N * M)
Finding a string in another string – the naive approach	O(L1 * L2)
Three nested loops from 1 to N	O(N3)
Twenty-eight nested loops … you get the idea	O(N28)
Stack	
Adding a value to the top of a stack	O(1)
Removing the value at the top of a stack	O(1)
Reversing a stack	O(N)
Queue	
Adding a value to end of the queue	O(1)
Removing the value at the front of the queue	O(1)
Reversing a queue	O(N)
Heap	
Adding a value to the heap	O(logN)
Removing the value at the top of the heap	O(logN)
Hash	
Adding a value to a hash	O(1)
Checking if a value is in a hash	O(1)